A CULTURAL HISTORY OF GARDENS

VOLUME 2

A Cultural History of Gardens
General Editors: Michael Leslie and John Dixon Hunt

Volume 1
A Cultural History of Gardens in Antiquity
Edited by Kathryn Gleason

Volume 2
A Cultural History of Gardens in the Medieval Age
Edited by Michael Leslie

Volume 3
A Cultural History of Gardens in the Renaissance
Edited by Elizabeth Hyde

Volume 4
A Cultural History of Gardens in the Age of Enlightenment
Edited by Stephen Bending

Volume 5
A Cultural History of Gardens in the Age of Empire
Edited by Sonja Dümpelmann

Volume 6
A Cultural History of Gardens in the Modern Age
Edited by John Dixon Hunt

A CULTURAL HISTORY

OF GARDENS

IN THE
MEDIEVAL
AGE

Edited by Michael Leslie

Bloomsbury Academic
An imprint of Bloomsbury Publishing Plc

B L O O M S B U R Y
LONDON · OXFORD · NEW YORK · NEW DELHI · SYDNEY

Bloomsbury Academic
An imprint of Bloomsbury Publishing Plc

50 Bedford Square
London
WC1B 3DP
UK

1385 Broadway
New York
NY 10018
USA

www.bloomsbury.com

BLOOMSBURY and the Diana logo are trademarks of Bloomsbury Publishing Plc

Hardback edition first published in 2013 by Bloomsbury Academic
Paperback edition first published in 2016 by Bloomsbury Academic

British Library Cataloguing-in-Publication Data
A catalogue record for this book is available from the British Library.

ISBN: 978-0-8578-5030-0 (HB)
978-1-8478-8265-3 (HB set)
978-1-3500-0990-5 (PB)
978-1-3500-0995-0 (PB set)

Library of Congress Cataloging-in-Publication Data
A catalog record for this book is available from the Library of Congress.

Series: The Cultural Histories Series

Typeset by Apex CoVantage, LLC, Madison, WI, USA
Printed and bound in Great Britain

CONTENTS

LIST OF ILLUSTRATIONS

GENERAL EDITORS' PREFACE

The volumes of this series explore the cultural world of the garden from antiquity to the present day in six particular periods. Each volume addresses the same eight topics, determined by the general editors for their relevance to garden history across different times and cultures. Thus a reader interested more, say, in planting or in types of gardens could read through the chapters devoted to those issues in successive volumes. Contrariwise, either of those interests might be contextualized by a volume's discussion of other aspects of the garden in a given period. There is therefore both a horizontal and a vertical way of using these volumes. Further, each volume includes both its editor's introduction, which rather than abstracting or summarizing the other contributions, surveys the period from a fresh vantage point, and a bibliography, which encompasses references from all the eight chapters augmented with that editor's additional readings.

HISTORY

These volumes are a historical enquiry and not an encyclopedia. They do not pretend to be comprehensive, either geographically or chronologically. The authors of the individual chapters have been encouraged to foreground what seem to be the most significant episodes and examples of their particular topic, leaving it to the reader to envisage how other sites that he or she knows better might further illustrate, challenge, or qualify the given analyses. But in every instance, we intend there to be some narrative of one particular theme as it exists, unfolds, or develops during a particular historical period. The definitions of these historical eras must be taken with some caution and elasticity, since a chronology of garden making does not always fit the divisions of time devised for and endorsed by other histories: André Le Notre did his work after 1650 but is arguably more usefully considered in a volume focused on the Renaissance than on the Enlightenment; similarly, Gertrude Jekyll and William Robinson were designing before 1920, but we understand their work better within the cultural content of the modern age.

CULTURAL HISTORY

There are of course many modes of history that have developed over the centuries. A relatively new one addresses the cultural context of human activity. "Culture" derives from the Latin *colere,* which has as some of its meanings "to inhabit," "to respect," "to pay attention to"; it emerges also in our words "colony" and "cultivation." Gardens, then, must be considered as driven by and evidence of a whole congeries of human concerns; they are not, above all, to be examined in terms of their merely visual appearance, materials, or stylistic histories. The diversity and density of human involvements with those sites we call gardens mean that the discipline of garden history draws upon adjacent disciplines such as anthropology, sociology, economic, and political history, along with histories of the arts with which the garden has been involved. So three large questions are posed: why were gardens created? How were they used or visited (there being no handy term for the "consumption" of gardens)? And how does their representation in different arts express the position and value of the garden within its culture in diverse periods? Regretfully, we were unable to extend the range of these volumes to include the garden making of China and Japan among other Eastern cultures, although inevitably the rich examples of such gardens have been invoked on occasion.

GARDENS

The range of places that can be envisaged within this category is enormous and various, and it changes from place to place, and from time to time. Yet this diversity does not wholly inhibit us from knowing what it is we what to discuss when we speak of the garden. Yet the garden is typically a place of paradox, being the work of men and women, yet created from the elements of nature; just as it is often acknowledged to be a "total environment," a place may be physically separated from other zones but answering and displaying connections with larger environments and concerns. Gardens, too, are often created, and subsequently experienced, as commentary and response: a focus of speculations, propositions, and negotiations concerning what it is to live in the world. Both the physical gardens and the ideas that drive them are cultural constructions, and their history is the topic of these six volumes.

John Dixon Hunt, University of Pennsylvania

Michael Leslie, Rhodes College

Introduction

A Cultural History of the Medieval Garden?
The Social Life of a Subjective Form

MICHAEL LESLIE

A "cultural history of gardens" can encompass many things, as the varied contributions to this series will attest. But the medieval volume perhaps poses at its most pronounced one of the principal ambiguities inherent in a "cultural history" of gardens. What do we mean by "cultural"? In popular usage, culture involves judgments concerning aesthetic quality and taste. But in historical writing and analysis, the word is often employed in a markedly different way.

Cultural history and cultural studies rose to prominence in the twentieth century particularly in response to the sense that traditional forms of history writing enabled political and social systems that marginalized and excluded large sectors of the population. The fact that traditional history often did this unself-consciously and unthinkingly was no defense; that itself was part of the problem. Cultural studies, and then cultural history, were often rooted in Marxist analysis and theories and had as explicit objectives the radical revaluation of what was important and significant in the past and the present. Traditional historical writing had concerned itself with elites of wealth and power; the lives and experience of the mass of the population tended to be ignored in narratives of high political and high cultural activities: monarchs, nobles, and aristocrats, dynasties and wars. Its attention sometimes extended to the affluent middle and merchant classes but no further. Cultural studies has sought to change that, with active political intent, just as John Milton, a radical centuries before, sought to change the subject of epic from "wars, hitherto the only argument / heroic deemed,"[1] replacing narratives of long and tedious havoc with subjects that pertained to all: "not less but more heroic."

In keeping with this activist political goal, cultural studies has, as a discipline, often concerned itself with the contemporary or near contemporary, seeking to discover and preserve evidence and knowledge of the lives of the vast majority, recognizing that the archive of the past is itself a political artifact, the result of selection driven by implicit systems of value. Recovery of a different kind of archive often depends on precariously surviving ephemera and oral history; such materials are hard to gather beyond a few decades into the past.

A history of gardens is inevitably open to challenge from this view of history writing: the garden as normally understood, especially that of earlier periods, is a work of high culture, privileging the aesthetic and being the product and, at times, flamboyant display of surpluses of wealth and leisure. Somewhere behind the bushes and fountains is the labor that produced that surplus wealth and that went into the production and maintenance of the garden—but with rare exceptions that labor is hidden. The ability to conceal labor is itself a statement of exceptional wealth and meant to be read as an affirmation of status. Some cultural study of gardens as pertaining to those beyond the elites of wealth and privilege has been possible when dealing with popular forms of gardening such as the allotment or considering the work and workers involved in making the gardens enjoyed by the elite, where records survive. But the British allotment movement can only be dated from the middle of the nineteenth century, and it is really a twentieth-century story. Extensive knowledge of the lives of actual gardeners is also rare before 1850. Before the nineteenth century, it is hard to write "garden history from below" or "a people's history of gardens."[2]

How then can one write and justify a cultural history of gardens, particularly of the medieval period? Virtually all our knowledge of medieval gardens concerns the very few who lived anything other than a life of labor and subsistence. A small proportion of the population in Christendom before 1500 enjoyed any surpluses of wealth or time; the number grew from the twelfth century onward, but it remained tiny. There were few who could afford leisure and the setting aside of fertile spaces for activities other than the production of necessary food and medical supplies. Gardens associated with clerical institutions such as monasteries are an exception. In these (often ensembles of buildings and spaces akin to small towns), men and women without great personal wealth—though the institutions were often wealthy, particularly after the year 1000—created gardens and other garden-like spaces in orchards, meadows, and woodlands that provided considerable pleasure and solace, as we shall see. But we should bear in mind that the pleasures associated with such spaces were probably, in the main, different from those we normally expect to derive from the pleasure garden: both our word for and our sense of the aesthetic are foreign to medieval culture. Monastic garden spaces were prized and enjoyed because they contributed to a sense of purposefulness and productivity, working with and fulfilling God's creation: the physic garden, the herb garden, the orchard, the cemetery garden. Such purposefulness and productivity added spiritual fulfillment to its pleasures. But the monastic garden is a special case: in the main, medieval gardens are associated with the lay elite. Cultural studies has had as its objective a turning away from the lives of such people; medieval garden history necessarily must concentrate on them.

Yet one might begin by drawing attention to institutional similarities of garden history and cultural studies. Both have a tenuous hold in the academy. There are few departments devoted to either of these fields of study and, in straitened times, those few seem anything but secure. Both are characterized by what the traditional academy perceives as a certain discipline-less-ness, a suspicious eclecticism, a lack of boundaries; both draw seemingly promiscuously from a range of methodologies and bodies of knowledge otherwise the possession of established disciplines such as history, sociology, anthropology, art and architectural history, and literary studies. Both garden history and cultural studies are habitually transdisciplinary, cross-disciplinary, interdisciplinary—the very absence of a settled terminology expresses both newness and instability. In practical terms, existence outside the boundaries of the single disciplinary home has a tendency to be uncomfortable, but intellectually, such a multiplicity of roots offers immense vitality.

More significantly, cultural studies has participated in and been influenced by what has been called "the cultural turn" (in imitation of the "linguistic turn" taken by philosophy, history, and other disciplines in the twentieth century[3]). This "culturality"[4] grows out of the uneasy recognition that ignoring elites and their cultures itself distorts in order to privilege the lives and experiences of those traditionally unregarded. In the last thirty years, a new version of "cultural history" has emerged from cultural studies, sometimes from surprising quarters, and this new form of historical writing aims to find room for the experience of all members of a society. As Peter Burke has recently written, the singular "*imaginaire social*" needs to be replaced by "collective imaginations in the plural that vary with place, time, gender and social class."[5]

One leader in this move to culturality was the Marxist historian of British working-class life, Raphael Samuel, a pioneer and practitioner of "history from below." But, as Luisa Passerini explained shortly after Samuel's death, his later practice of history broadened, involving a "transition from . . . social history to cultural history":

> The whole process from an approach which tried to reflect experience of the under-privileged classes, to an approach which takes into consideration that every experience is culture really, that every experience brings culture, and therefore also to the possibility of not looking for an "authentic" culture, not looking for "the" subjects of the revolutions, but of finding the signs of the historical movement everywhere. It could be in the elites or in the masses, in imagination as well as in a strike. But always with an eye in the end to what connects the legendary, the imaginary, whatever, to agency and subjectivity and experience in fact. So in a way the book [*Theatres of Memory: Volume 1: Past and Present in Contemporary Culture* (1996); *Theatres of Memory: Volume 2: Island Stories: Unravelling Britain* (1997)] seems to me to be the sign of this huge change which is under process and which is not . . . enough reflected upon.[6]

Many of the objectives of cultural history so understood are essential to analysis and interpretation of the Middle Ages in general and the lives of elites in particular. Those who had the opportunity to create and enjoy gardens were themselves members of society; in their representations of gardens, they often express fears and aspirations common to their entire culture, and their imperatives, desires, and imagination of what might constitute the blessed and perfect life cannot be ignored or marginalized if we are to understand that culture.

In addition, their creations and expressions of the ideal are the foundation for "medievalism," or rather the many different versions of medievalism that have influenced later cultures down to the present day, including the later cultures of the garden.[7] The conception of the Middle Ages experienced in later periods and the present, still vital and influencing our own sense of identity and our choices, depends on the evidence that survives from elite medieval culture, though we may not recognize that this evidence often represents fantasies of an ideal rather than actuality.

Failure to incorporate study of such matters into cultural history is itself a distortion: the past, actual and imagined, exists in the consciousness of the present. While we have to acknowledge the methodological challenge of study-ing elite forms, we cannot ignore them. In a 1987 article that remains valuable for its temperate inclusiveness, Richard Johnson, one of the leading writers on cultural studies in the 1980s and 1990s and formerly director of the now closed Centre for Contemporary Cultural Studies at the University of Birming-ham in the United Kingdom, wrote thus:

> The ultimate object of cultural studies is . . . the social life of subjective forms at each moment of their circulation, including their textual em-bodiments.[8]

Both the garden and its visual and verbal representation are "subjective forms" to be thus studied. Both actual and imagined gardens constitute "stories" told by their creators to address the deepest of beliefs, aspirations, and fears.

One frequent "embodiment" in visual and verbal "texts" in the Middle Ages is the Fountain of Youth, derived from the late classical *Romance of Alexander* and known throughout the Islamic world and Christendom dur-ing the Middle Ages.[9] Elderly men and women are bathed in the fountain, emerging at the age of thirty or thirty-three, clearly understood as a perfect age (whether or not associated with the age of Christ at the beginning and end of his ministry in the gospels). We can no doubt look at the illustrations of the Fountain of Youth and speculate as the accuracy of, say, the wheelbarrows represented;[10] but in a cultural history, the larger significance of such illustra-tions lies in the "connect[ion between] the legendary, the imaginary, . . . [and] subjectivity and experience in fact." Those wheeled through the ideal garden to the Fountain of Youth carry with them the experiences, fears, fantasies, and hopes of all members of a society in which short lives were only too common and debilitation commonplace among rich and poor. Though the manuscripts illustrating the fountain are produced for the elite, we should nonetheless study this subjective form's "social life."

Richard Johnson's primary concern is with the near-contemporary in Brit-ain, and his work is in no way separate from a political engagement. Nonethe-less, he delineates a series of stances from which we can productively view the past, including the Middle Ages, and including elite as well as popular culture. Johnson encourages us to avoid codification, instead urging us to develop habits of investigation and critique. In ways that are obviously compatible with, and indeed draw upon, the anthropological and ethnological work of Clifford

Geertz,[11] he urges a focus on particularity, complexity, context, movement, and transition—and the development of skills of dense description, complex explanation, and attention to the subjective and even the romantic evocation of things imagined. Johnson stresses the need for cultural history to be concerned with consciousness and subjectivity and the ways in which these are part of the lived culture and its products. He stresses that both cultural products and cultural processes are inevitably connected with social relations, including but not limited to those beloved of some cultural historians, social relations that involve power. Such matters are central to the consideration of medieval gardens, as the chapters in this volume attest.

WHAT ARE "THE MIDDLE AGES"?

A cultural history that pays due attention to "the social life of subjective forms at each moment of their circulation, including their textual embodiments" is a tall order, more an aspiration than something that we can expect to achieve. And such a cultural history of the garden over a 1,000-year period is all the more daunting. Such is the scale and the selectiveness of surviving evidence that anything we say of the culture of medieval Europe is bound to be of limited sophistication and open to challenge. For this reason, it is worth trying to sketch out some of the principal questions relating to the society and the gardens of the period, not least because the challenges posed are so fascinating.

In his early seventeenth-century essay "Of Gardens," Francis Bacon writes, "When Ages grow to Civility and Elegancie, Men come to *Build Stately*, sooner then to *Garden Finely*: As if *Gardening* were the Greater Perfection."[12] Bacon's is an elegant compliment to the fine art of gardening, and we are perhaps inclined to discount it as little more than a well-turned phrase. But, inevitably with the product of such a rigorous mind, each element of this dramatic rhetorical gambit requires careful attention: the contrast between "stately" and "finely"? The concept of "greater perfection"? But in this context we must ask, when is it that societies and cultures reach the point at which gardening occurs or becomes appropriate? When do ages "grow to Civility and Elegancie," characteristics appropriate to a culture of fine gardening?

Defining the Period; Justifying and Questioning the Definition

In history, cultural, or otherwise, there are few *durées* as long as the period we denote as "medieval." Even more so than most "periods," its boundaries are indistinct and subject to continued debate. Does it begin with Alaric's sack of Rome in 410 or the overthrow of the last Roman emperor in the west, Romulus Augustus, elbowed aside by the Germanic warlord Odoacer, in 476? Does it end in 1500 or with the defeat of Richard III of England in 1485? Or with the extinction of the Roman empire in the East in 1453? Or the commissioning of the doors of the Florence Baptistry in 1401? Does it extend from the beginning of "the calamitous fifth century"—so labeled by the near-contemporary chronicler Gildas (fifth century? sixth century?) in *De excidio et conquestu Britanniae* and used by the Venerable Bede (673/4–735) in *Historia ecclesiastica gentis Anglorum* (completed 731)—to the end of the "calamitous fourteenth century" described by Barbara Tuchman in her influential study *A Distant Mirror* (1978)? Giorgio Vasari's praise of Giotto as an artistic innovator decisively breaking free of earlier styles, "[bringing] back to life the true art of painting," could be a recognition of striking change, at least in visual culture; perhaps we should see the new culture of northern Italy in the overlapping times of Giotto (c. 1266–1337), Dante (c. 1265–1321), Petrarch (1304–1374), or Boccaccio (1313–1375) as marking a distinct break.[13] But this great change applies to the very particular culture of the advanced northern Italian city-states, raising the question of whether such instances can be applied to the whole territory of "Europe." There is wide scholarly consciousness of the temporal mismatch between the term for the next age, the Renaissance, as applied to Italian visual art and also to northern European, and particularly English, literature: the early Renaissance artist Lorenzo Ghiberti was born in 1378; Shakespeare, in 1564. Here, the mismatches pile one on top of another: not only temporal—centuries apart— but geographic (south and north of the Alps, in different language areas, the romance and the Germanic, with markedly different political histories and systems and social structures), and in terms of artistic media, the visual and the verbal. In what sense can a term such as "Renaissance," or even the more tentative "early modern," really help us here?

Two questions are immediately evident. The first has to do with the criteria we are applying. Do we define such a period through political or cultural events? A political event such as the fall of the imperial capital is likely to have a substantial impact on cultural production, including that of gardens and their representations. But what of something like the end of the Wars of the Roses in England, even if it closely coincides with the decisive European voyages to North America in 1492 and key moments in the territorial and political consolidation of Spain, France, and Russia? With hindsight, we see these events as marking a significant point of transition, and we can identify long-term changes to societies and cultures that are either a result of such events or that result from some of the same causes as these events. But in terms of cultural history, are these trustworthy markers?

Any periodization is to a greater or lesser degree arbitrary, as much as anything the product of a retrospective scholarly need. As Peter S. Wells has recently written,

> Too often, modern researchers lose sight of the fact that these fixed points are intended to provide a framework for understanding peoples of the past, not real breaks in the social or cultural development of early Europeans.[14]

A substantial challenge to the very idea of "the Middle Ages" is underway, with revealing arguments—drawn especially from interlocking cultural, social, and religious histories—being made for "late antiquity" extending to 750 in Peter Brown's influential *The World of Late Antiquity: AD 150–750*;[15] to 800 in the essay collection Brown edited with G. W. Bowersock and Oleg Grabar, *Interpreting Late Antiquity: Essays on the Postclassical World*;[16] but now throughout the first millennium, in such works as Garth Fowden's essay "Contextualizing Late Antiquity: The First Millennium," in *The Roman Empire in Context: Historical and Comparative Perspectives*,[17] and Fowden's forthcoming *Before and After Muhammad: The First Millennium Refocused*.

The End of the First Millennium: "Untidy States," Urbanization, Trade, and Agricultural Innovation

Even if we retain the concept of "the Middle Ages" running from roughly 500 to 1500, the development of the concept of "late antiquity" directs our attention to the major change that appears to occur on either side of the year 1000, when the post-Roman world achieves a phase of widespread maturity that the historical sociologist Björn Wittrock calls "classical crystallization"; it might also be called "cultural crystalization."[18] As Peter Heather writes in *Empires and Barbarians: The Fall of Rome and the Birth of Europe*:[19]

> By the tenth century, networks of economic, political and cultural contact were stretching right across the territory between the Atlantic and the Volga, and from the Baltic to the Mediterranean. This turned what had previously been a highly fragmented landscape, marked by massive

disparities of development and widespread non-connection at the birth of Christ into a zone united by significant levels of interaction. Europe is a unit not of physical but of human geography, and by the year 1000 interaction between human populations all the way from the Atlantic to the Volga was for the first time sufficiently intense to give the term some meaning. Trade networks, religious culture, modes of government, even patterns of arable exploitation: all were generating noticeable commonalities right across the European landscape by the end of the millennium.

This is not to say that the pre-1000 world we know as Europe was really Bede's tenebrous age of gloom and shadows; Peter Wells argues,

> Far from being a period of cultural bleakness and unmitigated violence, the centuries known popularly as the Dark Ages were a time of dynamic development, cultural creativity, and long-distance networking.[20]

No one who looks at visual representations of the gardens of the Bible will doubt this "cultural creativity." Even as we write of the collapse of the Roman empire in the West, we have to remind ourselves not to adopt too Gibbonian a tone: the collapse of Rome was a disaster for Rome, but was it equally bad for people far from the imperial centre? How dramatic did this collapse seem to those not closely identified with imperial structures and administration, including the church? Was the scale of change the same at the periphery and in remote regions as it was at the centre and in the provincial power centers? The old narrative of savage obliteration by invading hordes of Huns and Vandals, giving rise to epithets that are still used to describe uncivilized conduct, has given way to a recognition of interaction and the production of hybrid cultures, if not outright assimilation.

But change cannot be denied around 1000. Though there were still frightening challenges from the east, the great age of migrations was ending. Elite groups might still displace each other (as William the Conqueror's Norman French did to the English ruling class in 1066 and as their Norman cousins did in Apulia and Sicily just a few years later), but movements of large bodies of peoples ceased to dominate.

Even before 1000, food production seems to have increased and with it both population and wealth, agriculture transformed by a series of crucial inventions or improvements. From the tenth century onward, land is deliberately cleared in order to be devoted to increased agricultural production, and the evidence suggests that town dwellers and their regional lords both supported such economic change. The moldboard plough is found in seventh century England and deep plowing extensively in northern Europe in the following two centuries. Peter Heather makes the point baldly, directing attention to parts of Europe less studied by Anglo-American scholars in the twentieth century:

> Much more food was being produced in central and eastern Europe by the year 1000 than had been the case five hundred years earlier.[21]

State and cultural formation are limited in conditions of subsistence agriculture. More food enables specialization: one can feed military personnel, administrators, and key cultural communities, in this period not least the monastics, and one can support increasingly stable centers of authority, power, culture, and education—money-based trade and credit extend. The most important towns were increasingly associated with transcontinental trading and communication routes, either close to sea coasts or to the principal rivers of Europe. Such routes communicated not only physical property and the money systems of trade and credit but also cultural awareness of developments elsewhere in Christendom. A slightly later example makes the point: the Moeskroen family of Bruges merchants were actually the Moscheroni, migrants from the banking and trading cities of northern Italy to the principal commercial city of Flanders; Jan—Giovanni—and his brother Alessandro acquired the only Michelangelo statue to leave Italy in the artist's lifetime, giving the Madonna and Child to Onze-Lieve-Vrouwekerk, the Church of Our Lady. Such interchange of necessity had its impact on garden culture.

Even though well beyond 1000, a definably single Christendom is composed of myriad separate and distinct political and cultural entities; throughout the period we see "untidy states" cleaning up their acts as the millennium approaches. The collapse of the Latin empire had resulted in the eclipse of towns, even in the southern European territories more thoroughly "Roman" than the more peripheral provinces; unsurprisingly, urbanization reappears earlier in the south, especially in parts of Italy because of the persistence of Roman cultural and social structures. The populations that migrated into territories further from the heartland of the Western Roman Empire were characterized by a suspicion of towns and by habitual migratory practices. But around and after 1000, the development of urban centers gathers pace throughout Christendom, not least in the shadow of castles and regional nodes of authority. One sign is the movement of markets into towns. Even the staggering shock of the Black Death, which may have reduced Europe's population by between one-third and one-half in the mid-fourteenth century, did not derail this development; indeed, it may have enhanced it. Resulting changes in land tenure and the structure of feudal obligations meant that labor was a scarce and increasingly monetized commodity, with laborers free to move and sell their services to the highest bidder. That often meant a migration from country to town.

The ecclesiastical hierarchy also begins to migrate from isolated monastic estates to the newly vibrant and powerful urban centers; for example, the English bishopric of Bath and Wells, the title of which embodies the tension between the increasingly rich and dynamic town of Bath and the more isolated monastic community of Wells, not to mention the preeminent and powerful Glastonbury Abbey, supposedly site of Joseph of Arimathea's exile and burial place of that chronically peripatetic monarch King Arthur, and actually the site of the *vetusta ecclesia*, one of the earliest Christian establishments in England. It would only be in the reign of Henry VIII in England that the central secular authority would take decisive action to complete this move of bishoprics to the real centers of power in sixteenth-century England, the towns. But the translation had been going on for centuries throughout Europe by that time.

Garden making is much more likely as such centers and their characteristic communities and cultures develop. Garden history of this period is the indubitable concentration of evidence from the thirteenth to fifteenth centuries, and this is certainly in part because of the poor survival of the kind of evidence we use. But it is also because, in a real sense, only in the centuries after 1000 did the age grow to "Civility and Elegancie," or at least to a condition that enabled the growth of a culture that would garden finely.

The tidying-up of states also contributed to the growth of a garden culture in another way. Like King Arthur, lords throughout Europe, but especially north of the Alps, were mobile and itinerant in the earlier part of the period, always on the move to impose and shore up their authority. In England, for instance, one of the principal legal institutions, the Court of King's Bench, which, as its name implies, gained its authority by sedulously accompanying the monarch wherever he went, only settled to a reasonably permanent location, in the royal centre of Westminster, in the early fourteenth century; it last toured with the king in 1421. Such mobility meant that there was limited emphasis on the production of great permanent displays, such as gardens, even in notional capital cities. Borders, as understood in the modern world, were also somewhat illusory. Norman, Angevin, and Plantagenet lords ruled over territories scattered throughout Europe, from the Holy Land, Cyprus, southern Italy, and Sicily to the Atlantic archipelago. They could not rest on or plant laurels in one place for long. The very name of the Normans—the Northmen—conveys

their status as migrants. The list of titles of the Plantagenets gives a sense of
the bewildering diversity of territories over which they periodically ruled or
to which they claimed the right of rulership, including counts and dukes of
much of northern and western France, king of England, king of France, king
of Jerusalem, Lord of Cyprus, king of Sicily, king of Germany, and king of the
Romans. Talk of states and rulers tends to mask the truth of a bewildering
set of social relations and structures of loyalty, fealty, feudal dependency, and
alliance; of land tenure and ownership; and of patterns of settlement. Reading
medieval literature, one is struck by the remarkable itinerant quality of medieval fictions, heroes forever on the move in the "Matter of Britain" and other
romance traditions. Such ceaseless journeying is part of the "imaginary" of the
medieval European, taken for granted as what the elite does. Such journeying
is also often gendered: wives travelled less and this perhaps accounts in part
for the garden being associated with women, becoming often a predominantly
female realm both actually and in the imagination.

Before secular lords and their structures of authority and power became less
peripatetic, the great centers of the church were the most notable examples of
permanent establishments and communities, and it is no surprise that much of
our knowledge of gardens before 1100 comes from monastic institutions. This
is even true of the great and well-known "Carolingian" (later eighth and ninth
centuries) and "Ottonian Renaissances" (tenth and eleventh centuries). Charlemagne and his associates clearly sought to emulate aspects of classical Roman
civilization as they understood it, and the Ottonian rulers emulated Charlemagne's culture and sought to derive inspiration from the continuing Roman
empire of Byzantium. But it is striking that both "renaissances" concentrate
architecturally on ecclesiastical, and particularly monastic, structures. There
is little evidence that these cultures understood or sought to emulate Roman
urban culture, including the political and civic use of gardens, private and
public.

Perhaps the greatest cultural difference is that to do with the division between the clerical and lay worlds in this period. In England, the ultimate dis-
solution of the monasteries and scaling back of the worldly wealth of the
cathedrals in the sixteenth century is a final, sardonic commentary on the
earlier period. There were certainly pleasurable garden spaces associated with
the residences of great ecclesiastics and the monastic houses. Powerful lay
figures sought access to these pleasurable spaces, as in the bridges built from
princely residences over walls into the gardens of senior clerical figures. But
these are isolated instances, even if not best described as exceptions to the
rule. The majority of gardens associated with clerical establishments were

productive, or at least dominated by utility. These included orchards, herb gardens, physic gardens, cemetery gardens, and even managed woodland. There are plenty of records of such spaces being experienced as possessing a value beyond their productiveness and immediate utility: these are often places recorded as having the capacity to provide spiritual solace, a sense of quietness, a space in which to contemplate, a place in which one could read and write and experience a closeness to God. The importance of agricultural and horticultural work to a major monastic order such as the Benedictines would inevitably lead to an appreciation of the natural world, not least as a site in which the devout human could labor with God, to God's glorification and the fulfillment of his purposes.

Medieval gardens appear always in dialogue with other, often more powerful and indeed threatening phenomena of the physical world and landscape. The idea of both the religious and nonreligious garden in this period is closely related to urban space and the idea of the town: the ever-present walls of the garden create a private, contained, controlled, exclusive world in the middle of or in contradistinction to spaces characterized by the reverse of all those attributes. At the same time, this idea of the garden looks beyond the town and the increasingly farmed landscape to the "wilderness" beyond, the "desert" into which monks would exile themselves, there to seek to tame and redeem a disorderly nature.

Diverse Diversities and the Definition of "the Middle Ages"

The definition of "the Middle Ages" remains in exciting flux. One benefit of questioning the definition is that we necessarily confront issues that must be addressed when we consider the period's cultural history. For this volume and most of this series, the centre of attention must be the area once occupied by the Western Roman empire: Latin Christendom.[22] The countries that we now think of as central and western Europe all fell within its boundaries and to that degree formed a single culture. But these territories themselves changed radically over time; for instance, the successive transformations of what we now think of as France, Poland (whose boundaries have shifted violently even to the present), and Spain (whose territorial and cultural definition remains contested and may shift again in the near future), as a result of waves of conquest, immigration, and unification. We have to ask how similar society and culture could be in a geographical area that stretched from the Mediterranean to Scandinavia and the Atlantic archipelago, from the Iberian Peninsula to the North European Plain. Climate varied as radically then as it does now, resulting in profound differences in agriculture, and as a result, it may be argued, in social organization and the cultures those different societies produced. The diversities of both climate and cultures obviously concern garden history.

Nonetheless, despite this diversity and the disintegration of a single political structure, the old Roman empire in the West becomes Christendom, unified by shared descent of language from Latin (to different degrees and with various admixtures), some continuance of Roman culture (not least through the medium of education), and commonalities of political and societal organization through the Church. This organization meant that—again to different degrees at various times and in various places—there was contact throughout Christendom. Roman law may have disappeared from much of northern Europe, but the legal systems developed in its place are inflected by knowledge of what had come before and that persisted in parts of the south. The inhabitants of this western peninsula of the Eurasian landmass recognized their differences from those who lived in the Byzantium that evolved from the Eastern Roman empire based in Constantinople, and from the Muslim peoples mainly in the Middle East and North Africa. As Heather writes, "Europe" is best understood as

> a network of not entirely dissimilar and culturally interconnected political societies clustering at the western end of the great Eurasian landmass.[23]

Such a sense of distinctiveness becomes more powerful in the centuries after 1000: the Crusades in general created a general antagonism with the Islamic world from the eleventh century onward, and peaceful coexistence with the Byzantine Empire became impossible after the sack of Constantinople by the Fourth Crusade in 1204.

The Middle Ages as we understand it in this volume is emphatically European, but we should be conscious that modern scholarship, not least as a result of developments in geopolitics in the past decade, is challenging the notion of the impermeability of boundaries between West and East and between both Christian territories and the world of Islam. This is particularly driven by scholars who emphasize the commonalities of religious development in the three great monotheistic cultures of the period after 600: the eastern empire of Byzantium; Christendom; and the Islamic empires, including the intellectual, religious, and cultural legacy of Sasanian Iran. And, we might add a fourth, the culture of rabbinical Judaism, which exerted powerful cultural influence despite the absence of territorial embodiment. A range of recent scholars has sought to introduce us to a reimagined era in which these cultures were far more conscious of and responsive to each other than earlier twentieth-century histories often implied, trading and exchanging ideas and artifacts, as well as fighting each other. (This reconsideration goes hand-in-hand with the previously mentioned revisionist accounts of the Middle Ages that challenge the narrative of decline or ignorance.) After all, the Roman empire to which Christendom was partial heir had included vast non-European territories, as was certainly understood in the Middle Ages.

Muslim culture is especially important in terms of the cultural history of medieval gardens: throughout our period, Muslim and Arab cultures seemed to the Latin West both fascinating and frightening: sophisticated, culturally and economically dynamic, comparatively stable and unified, and frighteningly ambitious, attempting to extend their reach into the heartland of Western Europe, from the Ummayad Caliphate's conquest of much of Iberia between 711 and 718, the Battle of Tours, just north of Poitiers, in 732, the conquest of Sicily in 827, and the Aghlabid sack of Rome in 846, to the ultimate capture of Constantinople in 1453. It is worth remembering how long the fear of being overwhelmed by Muslim forces remained in Christendom, with the Siege of Vienna in 1529, the Battle of Lepanto in 1571, and the Battle of Vienna that conclusively beat back the Ottomans from Habsburg lands in 1683. That fear continues to the present, as is witnessed by the resistance to the admission of Turkey to the European Union. For much of the Middle Ages—perhaps all of it—Latin Christendom is the peripheral culture, not the central. This does not mean that the history of its cultural products is unimportant, but that history should be cast in its correct proportions and in correct relation to the cultures of which it was conscious.

THE IDEA OF THE GARDEN IN THE LONG "MIDDLE AGES"

How does this affect the idea of the garden? In the period before 1000, and for some time after, the primary point is, perhaps, that for most people the garden is predominantly an idea rather than a reality. When we look at the representation of gardens in the earlier period, we are principally looking at representations of the garden as it appears in sacred scriptures, especially the Garden of Eden. It is striking that the representations of the Garden of Eden from later in the Middle Ages are iconographically so different from those dating from before 1000. Images of the Garden of Eden before the turn of the first millennium rarely show the garden as we would understand and expect. A good instance would be the Hildesheim Doors.[24] These constitute an extraordinary work of art, created at the height of the Ottonian Renaissance (c. 1010), imitating the art and architecture experienced on a visit to Rome by Bishop Bernwald of Hildesheim, and in particular the monumental carved wooden doors he encountered there, but also using the "lost wax" technique not seen on this scale since antiquity. The doors show sixteen panels in a chronological narrative of the main events of the Bible, beginning at the top of the left door with the creation of Adam and Eve and descending to end with the murder of Abel, and the right door beginning with, at its foot, the Annunciation and rising to the revelation of the risen Christ in the garden. There are clear typological relationships (horizontal, diagonal) as well as the vertical progression of narrative episodes. A substantial number of the panels include scenes set in gardens. The panels are remarkable for their vigor, with the divine and human figures in vivid and energetic poses, which are sometimes mirrored and amplified by an equal energy in the plant forms represented. But it is immediately striking how minimalist is the representation of the garden: a tree; stylized plant forms bordering the scene to left and right. Unlike images later in the medieval period, there is no border to the garden, no fence or hedge. There are no details of landscape or ornament. We might expect that of Eden as the archetypal garden, but it is equally true of the garden in which the risen Christ appears, gesturing to Mary and saying, "Noli me tangere." Even here, when the scene has changed from the remote myth of the fall of man to something validated much more as a credible historical moment dominated by Christ mistaken for a gardener, the panel makes no attempt to particularize its garden.

When one looks at representations of gardens in illustrated Bible texts before 1000, particularly those (among the first pandect Bibles) associated with Alcuin of Tours (c. 740–804, at times Charlemagne's principal ecclesiastical advisor and agent), one is surprised in these magnificent Carolingian illuminations by the absence of many of the features that we would consider essential to the representation of the garden.[25] In the British Library's Moûtier-Granval Bible,[26] a sequence of scenes achieves narrative progression in the same way as the Hildesheim Doors, and again the garden is simply represented as an undulating, lumpy grass area, with a few stylized trees; the landscape outside Eden is more hilly and has more plant forms in the grass. But there is no boundary wall; Eden has no interior fountain. In the book known as "Alcuin's Bible,"[27] the text of the Old Testament is preceded by a full-page image representing the key events of the Genesis narrative. The design is again of the comic strip or decorative frieze variety, with events depicted down the page, read left to right. There are no "tituli," written inscriptions attached to the scenes, such as are sometimes found in later, similarly structured images. What is striking is the representation of the Garden of Eden and the postlapsarian landscape: stylized trees punctuate the two-dimensional visual narrative. It has been suggested that this visual style descends from Roman decorative art in late antiquity, particularly glassware, and that there are strong connections with Byzantine representations of the events in the Garden of Eden, similarly episodic in structure, again with the symbolic representation of a garden but with no attempt at realistic depiction of the natural environment. For instance, the landscape of Eden in Bibliotheque Nationale Ms. grec. 1208[28] is signaled by outlined mounds and hills, with stylized trees. That it is Eden is indicated by the presence of a male half-figure holding a cornucopia from which surge four streams of water, clearly the four rivers of Eden. The figure equally clearly descends from antique river god figures. Like most biblical illustrations before 1000 in Western Christendom, this Byzantine illustration is iconographically spare, akin to a code rather than attempting realistic representation.

But this is all changed in the representations of Eden from the period of the High Middle Ages. In an image from a French translation of Boccaccio's *De casibus virorum illustrium* by Laurent de Premierfait,[29] the cycle of Adam's and Eve's lives in and expulsion from the garden is utterly different. The garden is surrounded by an elaborate wall, architecturally contemporary with the image. Within, the flowery lawn has elegant trees at its edges and at the centre is an elaborate fountain and basin. The shamed pair exit through a magnificent arched gateway that would grace a contemporary palace or castle.[30] More naïve in style but equally typical, a representation of Eve's fall while Adam sleeps, from nearer the end of the fifteenth century,[31] shows Eden again as a castle pleasure garden, with crenellated wall, towers at each corner, an elaborate gateway, an interior tower (perhaps to afford views within and beyond the garden), and two fine trees set in the lawn amid flowers.[32]

Both these images—and many more examples could be given—show that the illustrators imagine the Garden of Eden in ways radically different from the pre-1000 examples. My argument here is that the idea of the garden has changed as a result of social, political, economic, and cultural developments. These later illustrators now draw on actual gardens—their representations are no doubt idealizations, but the point stands—whereas the earlier creators of the Tours Bibles and the Hildesheim Doors had few existing gardens to fuel—or maybe constrain—their imaginations. The archetype of the garden, the garden's great original in the foundational text of the cultures of the book, has utterly changed in response to the history of what we call "the Middle

Ages." To adapt Richard Johnson's phrase, in these representations of the Garden of Eden we see "the social life of [a] subjective form," if not "at each moment of [its] circulation"—an impossible task over such a long period— then certainly at significant points. And that is what all the essays in this volume aspire to achieve.

CHAPTER ONE

Design

JOHN DIXON HUNT

Design would not have been a term, concept, or usage available to makers of gardens in the Middle Ages, since it is a word that only comes into existence gradually during the early modern period.[1] Nor did processes of design familiar to us now—notably the drafting of plans or the building of models—seem to have obtained.[2] Above all, while there were plenty of classical, Arabic, and medieval authorities to consult on a range of botanical and pharmaceutical matters, there was little available literature on how, practically, anyone could go about making a garden. On the other hand, it is obvious that medieval gardens were laid out according to certain conventions and established practices, even in mechanical ways that parallel more recent garden-making. We can deduce this from the many contemporary literary and graphic representations of gardens, where assumptions of organization, use, and even meaning become apparent, though they are rarely made explicit. It is therefore, while anachronistic, nonetheless pertinent to invoke a triad of concepts from a twentieth-century American landscape architect: Garrett Eckbo construed the activity of design as the consideration and production of "surface, enclosure, enrichment."[3]

ENCLOSURE

Since this is the prime characteristic of all medieval gardens and parks, it needs to be approached first. Enclosure keeps things in, and it keeps unwanted things out; it can focus the mind wonderfully inside a cloister, just as it can protect crops, poultry, and persons from the wild and hungry things that lurked outside the pale. The medieval act of enclosing garden spaces derived both from antecedent physical forms and from compulsions—cultural, climatic, and psychological—toward self-protection. Spatial organizations in classical times (above all, the Roman atrium and peristyle, and the adjacent garden courtyards that we now know from modern archaeological scholarship) were a format that must have continued to be the prime organizational unit of later gardens, lending itself above all in the Christian West to the ecclesiastical cloister, which is its earliest and the most pervasive form of medieval garden, as well as to the courtyard of a mosque like Cordova. The courtyard/atrium's suitability to all scales of establishment made it exceptionally versatile. In Venice is an early surviving example of a small cloister from the eleventh century at San Apollinario (originally S. Scolastica); its central space, now paved, would presumably have been grassed.[4] At the other extreme is the extensive cloistral enclosure at Mount Grace Priory in Yorkshire, with the added interest there of individual personal gardens attached to each of the monks' cells. The cloister, like its classical prototype in the peristyle, had the additional advantage of including some form of sheltered walkway around the edges, which thus mediated between the exterior space and the institution's interiors.[5]

But the geographical range of "the medieval garden" in Christendom also brought its makers and users into contact with Arabic traditions, particularly in Islamic Spain, Norman Sicily, and southern Italy; some northern cultures, such as the Venetian, also had intimate trading contacts with the eastern cultures of the Mediterranean basin.[6] Almost all the words used to describe gardens and gardening in Sicily, for example, have an Arabic root.[7] And in those worlds the courtyard, secular examples as well as those attached to mosques, were a prime spatial device: apt for the climate, yielding protection from both sun and desert winds, offering either privacy or communal foci in crowded urban settings for all conditions of the population, and in many cases centering upon some feature, well, or cistern, that contributed water essential to both religious ablutions and secular needs.

But as the ecclesiastical cloister in western Europe makes clear, the enclosure was a mode of self-protection, of turning away from the outside world—the divine territory of the sky was the only exterior landscape ever-present to those frequenting the cloister—and concentrating human activity inward.[8] The cloister garden was at the heart of the monastery or abbey, a symbolic centre of Christian existence, apart from the actual rituals within the church itself; accordingly, it was space carefully secured and just as lovingly decorated, however simply, to enhance the conduct of a cloistered life. This elaboration of garden spaces, however small, is a logical extension of their special and protected place in any community, and (as we shall see) the secular garden took those design elements to much greater heights than even the most well endowed and prosperous of ecclesiastical establishments. The very insistence on a garden's being enclosed—and the secular forms of this, as we shall see later, took various shapes—determined that what was inside acquired a special value; confinement elicited and authorized the elaboration and concentration of items that by the late Middle Ages seem to have characterized the concept and layout of gardens.

SURFACE

Eckbo was of course right to place surface before enclosure. The space or platform for a garden needs to be determined before it can be walled, hedged, or otherwise defended and surrounded. The major medieval treatise on gardening makes this clear at all points. Pier de' Crescenzi's *Liber ruralium commodorum* was written in the first years of the fourteenth century, first in Latin and then translated into Tuscan Italian in 1350; printed editions appeared from 1471 and in all came to number about sixty.[9] Since it also survives in over 100 manuscripts, some of which are illustrated, in four languages, it was clearly the premier instructional guide to gardening procedures in the late Middle Ages and beyond. Since, too, Crescenzi was by training a lawyer, well travelled throughout northern Italy, as well as well read in relevant ancient texts such as Columella's *De re rustica* or the mid-thirteenth-century *De vegetabilibus et plantis* of Albertus Magnus, we may presume his advice is both authoritative and encodes standard practices.

In his eighth book on the pleasure garden, Crescenzi makes clear that the essential preliminary to all garden-making is the selection of a level site with suitable soil and cleared of weeds and roots, of a workable shape ("square") and proportioned to the social status of "those who are expected to live there."[10] Peasants will have but a small lot. Middling folk have medium-sized plots, lords and kings more extensive ones that will include within their perimeter an enclosure for wild animals. But in every case, the selected surface is enclosed and careful instructions are given as to the various ways in which this can be achieved. Yet once the enclosure was set, the interior surface became the ground upon which the medieval gardener would set out a variety of other elements to further the programmatic needs of whatever size and status of garden were involved. These include rows of trees and vines; trees will be there for fruit or for shade, but Crescenzi advised against putting them in the middle of spaces for walking like lawns or "flowery meads," where the spiders' webs hung between the trunks would get in the faces of people as they strolled. They were be open areas of meadowland, groves, and bosquets, seats carved out of closely pruned bushes, pergolas and pavilions (the latter could be made out of weaving of tree branches and vines), and a fountain "in the middle of the garden." The central position of this important feature is (we can assume) driven by several design imperatives: its central position will facilitate irrigation of the entire surface of the enclosure, its craftsmanship will be the pinnacle of human intervention in the garden, and the extent of its elaboration will declare the social status of its owner; inevitably, it also allowed if it did not predicate certain symbolisms.

ENRICHMENT

Crescenzi's design advice for the treatment of a garden surface has already involved some elements of enrichment, though their installation is driven in almost every instance by practical reasons. He addresses the cultivation of "fine and delicate grasses" and the placing of odiferous herbs around the perimeter of the space. His design elements have also introduced, whether consciously or not, important vertical features to counter and enrich the horizontality of the place—besides the plants themselves, the fountain often rose in a pinnacle, the pergola took plants or fruit upward toward the sun as well as provided shelter from it for persons beneath, and there was eventually a repertoire of other vertical incidents like pilasters and railings to augment the surficial emphases of the layout. In a Netherlandish depiction of a garden space dedicated to archery, the long shooting area is marked by some up-standing trees, three pavilions with pointed roofs, and the ubiquitous posts and railing dividing the spectators from the archers.[11]

But the "enrichment" that is most crucial to the medieval gardener—or at least appears to be for his patron and the garden's visitors—was what we might call its meaning or significant associations.[12] While the practical business of horticulture and the garden's use for quotidian activities of leisure and social intercourse (to name the more respectable) were wholly physical, the medieval mind was also apt to seek metaphysical resonances in many of its cultural activities. What we cannot ascertain is the extent to which gardens, which in literary and painterly representations yielded an especially fruitful locale for such associations, were actually and in practice *designed* to promote them or whether it was just the interpretative instincts of its visitors that saw routine garden features as bearers of meaning, ideas, and concepts. Hispano-Arabic poetry, for instance, contains many passing allusions to the associations of gardens but little indication of whether any physical or design form had specifically triggered them: however, the verses are replete with associations that the rich legacy of Islamic gardening practice presumably endorsed. Thus, a description of Granada likens the city surrounded by flower gardens to a pretty face fringed with fair hair:[13] gardens are "clothed" like a sultan's retinue, or the boughs of trees hang with "jewels"; the waters of gardens are "like collars loosened from the necks of fair maidens"; souls are likened to "flower-filled gardens"; gardens are everywhere apt metaphors for the world of the mind and imagination ("a garden of thought"). Similar associations of gardens occur also in the Koran, but nowhere in these writings is there any sense that the design of such places was specifically geared to produce or elicit any of these projected meanings. On the other hand, the insistence upon richness and perfume and even privacy implies a concentration, a sensuous density of flowering plants and the safety of enclosure ("I withdrew from the world, and said to it . . . 'My garden is a small room' "), all of which must have been the result of deliberate design and maintenance.

But if the Christian maker of a medieval garden did seek to provide, or even to design, items that promoted larger significances than the practical, there were obvious texts to fuel his invention. A couple of influential and suggestive biblical passages on gardens—that of Eden and that in the Canticles or Song of Songs—certainly colored how gardens were understood in literature and visual imagery, so we can be certain that these too could at least have been the sources of practical design ideas, if such were sought in the actual creation of garden sites. There are, of course, other biblical narratives set in gardens—in the Old Testament, Bathsheba, bathing in the garden and watched by the old men, for example, or the Garden of Gethsemene, where Christ waits to be betrayed by Judas, in the New Testament; graphic representations of those scenes certainly tell us about how artists understood their own contemporary gardens, which they drew upon to give verisimilitude to the action. But in two important biblical passages, medieval garden makers would have found suggestions or hints of forms and layouts that they might believe were specific, originating, and "authentic." The passages are well-known but bear quotation again (from the "authorized" version of 1611). The first is found in Genesis 2:8–10:

And the Lord God planted a garden eastward in Eden; and there he put
the man whom he had formed.

And out of the ground made the Lord God to grow every tree that is
pleasant to the site, and good for food; the tree of life also in the midst
of the garden, and the tree of knowledge of good and evil.

And a river went out of Eden to water the garden; and from thence it was
parted, and became into four heads.

And the second comes in the Canticles, or the Song of Songs 4:12–16:

A garden enclosed is my sister, my spouse; a spring shut up, a fountain
sealed.

Thy plants are an orchard of pomegranates, with pleasant fruits; cam-
phire, with spikenard,

Spikenard and saffron; calamus and cinnamon, with all trees of frankincense: myrrh and aloes, with all the chief spices:

A fountain of gardens, a well of living waters, and streams from Lebanon.

Awake, O north wind; and come, though south; blow upon my garden,
that the spices thereof may flow out. Let my beloved come into his garden, and eat his pleasant fruits.

Admittedly, neither account is exactly what a modern designer would like to
have as a program for his or her proposals, let alone a thorough-going plants
list. But sufficient and intriguing hints are certainly there. Genesis establishes
a cluster of crucial design elements: that the garden was part of a larger landscape, Eden, situated in the east; that this garden was watered from a source
outside itself in the surrounding area and then that the water was conducted
throughout the garden before being released once again into the outside where
it split into four tributaries. Further, the garden was, like the human occupants,
"formed," with a specific centre marked by the tree of life, and was otherwise
planted with a complete conspectus of trees, just as (later in verse 19) we learn
it was stocked with every conceivable fowl and beast; it was also a worked
garden ("planted," "put," "made . . . to grow"). There is no mention of any
enclosure of the garden; that emphasis, of course, is added after the Fall, when

Adam and Eve are banished and any further access to the garden guarded by angels with fiery swords.[14]

The Song of Songs confirms some of these basic characteristics and adds a few more hints: the garden is now emphatically walled ("enclosed"). The Solomonic garden is, as Eden was said to be, a place *in relation to other territories*, as the emphasis upon the beloved entering the garden clearly implies, along with the spices, carried on the winds that waft out of it. Solomon's irrigation system is now executed ornamentally in a fountain or fountains ("a well of living waters"). Horticulturally, the place is replete with "all" fruits and with perfumed, even exotic plants; yet any emphasis on horticultural activity is lacking, if maybe presumed (though the presumption of maintenance would diminish the wonderful spontaneity of the poet's vision). The translation also speaks of an "orchard," though whether this is part of the garden itself or an adjunct of it is not clear. The garden is addressed as a person or personal thing, something to be possessed, unlike the more studiedly objective description of Eden, which of course recounted a site created before human occupation as well as one no longer inhabited. And the garden is associated principally with woman rather than with the whole of creation, an association that would have jibed with the making and use of many secular medieval gardens where the woman is the presiding presence as user, visitor, and often gardener. In much of this—the densely perfumed atmosphere, the association of gardens with a beautiful woman, the identification of the place as an expression of its owner—the parallels with Arabic poetry are (unsurprisingly) striking.

KEY DESIGN ELEMENTS REVEALED
IN VISUAL EXAMPLES

The designer of any medieval garden in Christendom would have understood that in the two key passages from the Bible, especially if they were somehow amalgamated in his mind typologically, he could find some fairly basic design elements for shaping his own site, though equally some of them would have urged themselves as practical necessities.[15] But at least they would have the authority of scripture. The key elements are enclosure, irrigation, and the provision of spaces for planting and other activities of the garden, including livestock and perhaps beehives, with the insistent sense that profusion and completeness were the essence of all gardens. And the basic infrastructures for the inhabitation of the space—shelters, seating, entrances—are necessarily implied, especially when the garden of the second passage is so emphatically occupied.

These same biblical texts of course generated a corpus of visual representations, along with literary commentary and glosses, but they also influenced
depictions of non-biblical gardens. Medieval artists, however, did not think of
themselves as observing historical accuracy:[16] on the contrary, they were drawing upon contemporary garden practice to furnish their readers and viewers
with convincing, familiar imagery, if only because in that way their narrative
and story-pictures will be more compelling. However, this makes illustrations
of medieval gardens the more useful in our search for the origins and practices
of what we now call garden design. Some caveats are, however, in order. In illustrating non-biblical texts by depicting plausible contemporary places, artists
simply refurbished conventional ideas and imagery derived from other sources:
biblical descriptions seeped into classical (Ovid particularly), agrarian merged
with amatory, devotional overlapped with horticultural, and the types were
conflated—later courtly love treatises drew upon them all. Another necessary
caution is that the majority of graphic representations of what we may take to
be medieval gardens are indeed executed often beyond the chronological limits
that one would normally set for the Middle Ages, but the relative conservatism
of gardening allows me (as it has allowed other scholars) the latitude to invoke
this imagery as indicative of well-established and older practice. The graphic
materials are numerous, too many for showing here.[17] But a few can be adduced to extend the rudimentary instructions found in Crescenzi, beginning
with familiar woodcuts that illustrated manuscripts and editions of Crescenzi
himself.

Designing Social Differences

Following the author's own discriminations about appropriate scale and
scope for different kinds of owners, Crescenzi editions illustrate a similar
social and cultural range. At the patrician end of the spectrum is the depiction in a French manuscript[18] of four women, along with two male bystand-
ers, occupying a high, brick-walled enclosure in which about ten raised beds
have been inserted; however, an earlier folio[19] presents an agrarian scene of
two small, peasant gardens enclosed with wattle fences, nearby a rich man's
orchard that is seemingly protected simply by occupying an island in the
river. This same manuscript also depicts a town garden,[20] with a doorway
in its high wall giving access to the street, squared beds and four gardeners,
and two women, one also working, but the other watching from the doorway of the house to which the garden is attached; a cistern is at the rear. Yet
another image[21] combines building operations of a fairly well-to-do sort in

FIGURE 1.1: Crescentius, circa 1485, British Library Add ms 19720, folio 20.

the foreground with a distant courtyard garden, its pattern of flower beds in the process of being surrounded by low railings, which a worker is installing.[22] Another image for Crescenzi, attributed to the Master of Margaret of York, shows a multi-squared set of raised flower beds being worked by six gardeners and entered under a simple archway set in a fence; the setting is a patrician manor or castle overlooking, in the far distance, an open landscape dotted with scrub.[23] The equally well-known frontispiece to the 1495 Venetian edition of Crescenzi shows a working farmyard enclosed with wattles, from which a gateway at the right leads into an orchard, fenced with railings along which plants are trained and where a pergola or arbor is conspicuous; another woodcut in the same edition focuses upon three gardeners tending fruit trees in an orchard now enclosed by a diamond-shaped fence trained with vines.[24] A further French edition (Paris 1486) depicts not only a house within its walled compound but reapers in a cornfield that is an island in a stream.[25] For even more elaborate and a more varied repertoire of enclosures, we need to look at other imagery.

Enclosures

Since *Le Roman de la Rose* is a story about the process and progress of the lover toward his beloved in the form of a symbolic route through landscapes and gardens, the artists who illustrated it not only utilize contemporary garden designs to make the intricate narrative clear, but in doing so also, inevitably, demonstrate modes of access to and movement through different sectors of a garden; patrician sites in particular are presented as places of restricted entry. A key depiction here is folio 12v of the British Library Harley 4425 ms where the lover appears at two different points in his itinerary. In one, he is about to be admitted to the walled garden through a stout door in its high brick wall; in the second, admitted and now walking inside the first enclosure, he seems to be looking over a latticework fence containing an archway under which we may assume he will soon pass toward an elaborate fountain around which ladies are listening to a musician playing his lute; we guess he will eventually be admitted to that final enclosure, but the series of thresholds to be navigated first is stressed. Not all representations are as elegant or elaborate as this. No doubt given the popularity and diffusion of *Roman* illustrations, they display a range of gardens and thus garden enclosures fitted to different social classes— from a castle with roses double-lining its battlements[26] to the rich, multilayered and decorated enclosure of the Harley image. Unlike the plausible spaces of this latter, the opening image of the earlier British Library Egerton ms 1069 is both cruder and aims rather to be more conceptual: an elaborately walled, castellated place, with allegorical bas-reliefs along its exterior walls—some elite places may have enjoyed such sculptural adjuncts like this, and a passage of Dante's *Divine Comedy*[27] suggests the same; inside are a pool and stream, a grassy meadow decorated with flowers, with a variety of trees and emblematic animals and birds.[28] In the rare French edition printed by Guillaume le Roy about 1487, where woodcuts were reused from an earlier publication of 1485, the lover is being admitted to the garden through a substantial gate set in an osier fence, but nothing of the garden is shown, and its entrance suggests a much less fancy design; in another edition of 1494–1495 where the woodcuts, printed on vellum, have been painted over with opaque colors, the lover is shown reading within the garden's wattle fence, with the door now open behind him, but again the scope of the site seems very restricted.[29]

Sir Frank Crisp's compendium of medieval garden imagery details the many forms of enclosure: the Mary garden of *Speculum Humanae Salvationis* is surrounded with its own battlements, but as it is also protected by a battery of angels with fiery swords, a post-Edenic enclosure merged with the Solomonic *hortus conclusus*, it is something that could only be imagined by an artist, not devised as a built work; the fountain, however, would be feasible.[30] Other gardens simply borrow the battlements of the fortified mansion in which to shelter;[31] brick walls could have elegant stone capping, essential to their better preservation;[32] and everywhere are wattles woven around stakes driven into the ground,[33] a pattern that lends itself well to the artist's pencil, but is obviously the cheapest item to make and to replace—it is usefully invoked when the figure of Christ as gardener is also depicted, for it recalls the work a gardener would have to do to protect his lot. Many wattle enclosures are depicted as too low to keep anything in or out, but the height of these structures is as much determined by the artists wanting their viewers to see over and beyond them into the depicted garden; indeed, some representations of enclosures make no pretence whatsoever to be accurate and effective—in one woodcut, the wattle fence is just a short length, sketched without any attempt to see it encircling the plot of land; it was presumably meant as a sample of what fencing would be. Open wooden railings, sometimes with panels of trelliswork, are used to divide spaces within gardens, generally to mark off beds,[34] but are clearly much less effective as outside boundaries. (Planting thorn bushes around the boundary, suggested by Crescenzi, never seems to be illustrated.) Later imagery shows fences constructed of closed planking.[35] There is some intriguing imagery that even shows the enclosures of a garden being extended, supervised by the owner (in one case, a woman directs the removal of a fence).

FIGURE 1.2: British Library Harley ms 4425, folio 12, verso.

Incorporating Larger Spaces

It is often said that medieval imagery shuts out anything but the carefully controlled and protected foreground and that medieval gardenists were especially fearful of anything that might be experienced as "wilderness." Certainly we do find several garden views that denote nothing save empty sky above and beyond the walls of their enclosure. But it is worth noting a contrary impulse: openness of the viewer inside a garden to some larger landscape beyond. Once again, it is impossible to know in most cases whether gardens were *designed* to take advantage of views of adjacent or distant land or, alternatively, designed specifically to exclude them. The location and physical circumstances of where gardens could be established within larger building complexes obviously determined whatever opportunities were available for such design decisions. In the Islamic world, however, the incorporation of views, distant prospects, into the designed spaces of a palace was routine and much sought after.

The *mirador* was a familiar vantage point within a palace from which to take in the surrounding countryside: it took many forms, but all were designed to control the view and therefore what could be seen. The palace-city of Madinat al-Zahra was established near Cordoba from the eighth to tenth centuries on huge, descending terraces, where contemporaries observed miradors and palaces on the upper level, with gardens and "a variety of trees" below; the design of this complex was evidently much influenced by Middle Eastern examples, where an emphasis on belvederes and viewing points was insistent (around Baghdad and at Samarra particularly).[36] The power of the gaze from such palace gardens was a physical manifestation of the ruling caliph's power over adjacent territory and was naturally exploited wherever the topography allowed. The later Alhambra and Generalife, at Granada, offered a variety of designs for larger views as well as beautiful examples of the enclosed garden type: vistas were opened from miradors high in towers or (at the Generalife) from terraced descents. The Court of the Myrtles at the latter is a long enclosed garden with a central pool, but through the Hall of the Ambassadors at its far end are openings that present a view across countryside and city, doubtless designed precisely to impress visiting delegations (for whose reception the space is named).

But Western gardens, too, seem to have taken advantage of views, to judge once more by available imagery. Jan van Eck's wonderful Madonna (Louvre, c. 1425) or Roger van der Weyden's *Virgin, Child and St Luke* (Munich, c. 1440) have their characters gazing across small enclosed garden spaces into a varied and busy townscape. The celebration of urban prosperity and mercantile pride

is evidently part of the enjoyment of a town garden. But views into a variety
of different countrysides are also shown: the far-off scrub landscape is not
blocked in the castle view of the Master of Margaret of York; the Memling
follower's painting of the *Virgin with Angels*[37] has a typical elite garden below
the open arcade where the figures sit. It has topiary trees, raised beds with trelliswork borders, or low fencing and plants set out in pots; but it also shows the
garden space spreading across a lawn toward a river that winds its way into
the far distance. So, a careful search among available imagery does suggest an
interest in the larger landscapes, especially among later paintings and drawings, as much as in the immediate and cloistered garden.

Some images incorporate the wider landscapes without necessarily showing them as an integral part of the experience from *within* a garden. Yet this
does demonstrate that wide expanses of open ground were not necessarily a
cultural no-man's land to be feared or avoided; indeed, many times it is groups
of women who have moved from the adjacent and walled garden into the open
landscape. The well-known calendar for "April" in the *Très Riches Heures* by
the Limbourg brothers shows a patrician gathering outside the high walls of
a garden (we catch a glimpse of its espaliered interior walls), which indicates
that the enjoyment of unconfined spaces was entirely possible. So, what this
suggests is that the garden is established, designed, and understood in deliberate and conscious opposition to its surrounding territory; it is a highly worked
space set apart, benefiting from conspicuous craftsmanship in the masonry, the
sculptural details of a fountain, and the often elaborate horticultural maintenance required. Crescenzi draws a similar distinction between the garden
where the aim is delight for its own sake and the delightful practicalities of
agriculture. (This deliberate contrast of a garden with its adjacent but less-
worked surroundings seems to be a given in many cultures and eras, but it
occurs often and even starkly in a good deal of medieval imagery.) Many gardens are represented as being established in the midst of a larger landscape:
sometimes with their accompanying manor or castle, like the fifteenth-century
Séjour d'Honneur by Octovien de Saint-Gelais;[38] sometimes as what appears to
be simply a walled garden in the midst of a landscape containing both cultivation and barren land, as with the famous work by Evard de Conty, *Le Livre
des Echecs Amoureux Moralisès*, where the protagonist is shown arriving at
the entrance to the Garden of Nature—another liminal moment—and where
a distant turret peeping over the far orchard hints at the nearest buildings.
Pictures of love gardens in particular seem to depict them deliberately as established away from the busier worlds of town or castle, set apart in the cultural
landscape, the better (one supposes) to accommodate their amorous activity.[39]

Even miniatures that could be cited as focusing wholly upon the inward garden world—like the elegant couple with their greyhound in a triply enclosed garden (castle walls, trellis fencing, brick embrasure) in the *Roman de Renaud de Montauban*—nevertheless hint at an exterior territory with tops of trees above the far wall and a sliver of scenery down the left side, which indicates the landscape immediately outside the main castle gateway.[40]

Some of these larger landscapes may well have been interpreted by contemporaries as areas still under human control, like hunting parks, which Crescenzi says could be attached to princely gardens, the whole estate amounting (he recommends) to around twelve acres. Such parks were often established as extensive, walled enclosures to keep in the animals reserved for patrician huntsmen, but some also contained smaller, garden-like enclosures within the much larger terrain, presumably as locations from which to observe the hunt or locations for retreat and refreshment of the hunt's spectators. A famous case is that of Hesdin in northern France, begun in the last decade of the thirteenth century: this large enclosure was entirely walled with five entrances, but also incorporated small walled gardens at its southern end and, toward the marshy north, a small enclosed garden with a tower as well as a nearby "pavilion" with automata—a rare medieval example of what had been a renowned Arabic hydraulic craft which would be revived in Europe during the Renaissance when Islamic and late classical texts became available or were rediscovered.[41] Crescenzi scatters his remarks on animal enclosures, devoting his tenth book to hunting (an activity, he notes, directly consequent upon the human expulsion from the Garden of Eden) and his ninth to the compounds where hares, stags, rabbits, and fish were kept within a palatial garden. Presumably, small creatures and birds were hunted within middle- and large-sized gardens, a practice that we know was common later in early Medici villas around Florence.[42]

Irrigation

Gardens need water, and those who lay them out have to devise ways to bring and distribute it within them. All the practical treatises, like Ibn Bassal's eleventh-century *Book of Agriculture*,[43] devote a section or chapter to water, its diffusion, and the placement of pools (he says they should be shaded by trees). Ibn Hawqal, travelling in Sicily in the year 977, observed the waters that came down from the western hills powered the mills and other agricultural zones, but above all fertilized "gardens of fruit" and were engineered into "a great number of gardens, with a large productivity."[44] In the late Middle Ages, the supply of waters to gardens in Palermo was regulated by an elaborate legal system,[45] that besides sustaining an advanced agricultural system also watered such royal castles as La Cuba and La Zisa, their richly decorated water channels extending outward from the *iwans* into courtyards and beyond, exploiting the Islamic partiality for longer vistas.

All communities needed to arrange their supply of waters: the thirteenth-century plan of the Christ Church priory precincts in Canterbury is well-known because it maps the water supplies as well as the gardens,[46] but hydraulic infrastructure must have been a necessary concern elsewhere. Both Genesis and Canticles insist upon the watering of the garden, one by rivers or irrigation channels, the other specifically featuring a fountain, and these texts must have assumed particular significance within religious communities. Several representations of Eden show a fountain, as if the Solomonic device had trumped the Edenic river (which in theological terms—merging Solomon's beloved with the Virgin Mary and typologically uniting Old Testament gardens with the new—was what had transpired). In one image in the early fifteenth-century Mandeville *Voyages*, the artist focuses entirely on the waters of Eden: within a hexagonal walled meadow (one side left open so our gaze is not impeded) is a tall fountain that releases its waters into a basin that in turn sends four jets onto the ground where they become the four rivers that are described in Genesis and are here shown exiting under the walls through small arches.[47] Clearly, artists enjoyed expending their creative energies upon fountains, which appear in many shapes and sizes, but one must assume, given the inventive forms depicted by the artists, that garden designers, too, saw the potential for their own skills in designing this salient feature.[48]

Of course, medieval garden makers did not need Genesis or the Song of Songs to instruct them about irrigation or fountains or wells. But illustrations to those and other texts suggest the range of possibilities. A curious image for a fifteenth-century *Roman de la Rose* has the lover, standing in a flowery mead within a circular wattle fence, gazing into a square tank with a pink headstone; a channel flows out of the pool and soon divides into two to flow in different directions.[49] This image suggests that small channels or conduits were as likely a way of distributing water within the garden, with illustrators well aware of how in contemporary gardens this infrastructure was geared to both the needs and the social standing of the garden's owner. The revered status of the Virgin Mary allowed her in many illustrations some splendidly wrought gothic fountains, whereas the town garden in British Library Add ms 119720[50] is provided with a simple round cistern. One must assume that simple tanks and cisterns to retain either spring water or water laboriously conveyed by hand into the garden were routine. Peasant gardens probably required that water be carried in buckets from a neighboring stream.

ENTRANCES, THRESHOLDS, SEATS, AND SHELTERS

Gardens are designed to be special places, distinct in some fashion from their surroundings, and accordingly places into which our entrance is both crucial and guided. Enclosures presuppose entrances (and, less importantly, exits: Adam and Eve are often depicted on their way out of Eden). Given high enough walls to keep things out, the disclosure of what was inside a garden would happen only as one crossed its threshold and was made aware of the scene or scenes within. That is what the narrative of *Le Roman de la Rose* is all about: making it past a series of obstacles, learning the next step in a navigation of its spaces. Accordingly, the artists who drew it took from the text exactly those moments when the lover encounters a doorway and its guardian or moves beyond where he has already established himself. Religious versions of the *Roman*'s liminal experiences also occur: often, the artist will depict an open door so as to represent the flowery mead and fountain within, which happens in the fifteenth-century "Garden of Virtuous Consolation," where the figure of Obedience is handing the little naked soul the keys of an already opened door.[51] A secular or at least amatory version of the same moment is available in *Le Livre des Echecs Amoureux Moralisès*, where Oiseuse (Idleness) greets the author with keys in her hand; behind them, an elaborate doorway gives access to a huge garden laid out in squares of raised beds across which lies the path to the courtyard of an immense, fortified manor.[52]

John Harvey pays little attention to design in his study of the European medieval garden, but he rightly notes that it consisted of a sequence of spaces ("each part, by a succession of proportionate scale, leads on to the next").[53] Movement through spaces also implies pathways, and illustrations certainly imply that routes were laid out through gardens to their adjacent buildings or land; Crescenzi's Book One writes of how paths should be used to divide segments of the larger estate, but offers nothing by way of instruction in their invention or creation.

Gardens need places to sit, to provide shelter and, for the privileged and elite, places from which to observe others in the gardens. Seats were made in brick, wood, turf, and—though it must have sagged under undue weight—clipped bushes. A German-illustrated Crescenzi has a woodcut of a gardener making a turf seat by filling the oblong wooden boards with earth prior to covering the top with turf.[54] Seats are inserted under pergolas, and pergolas are everywhere, providing both shelter and raising fruit toward the sun; they also provided some vertical elements in generally flat spaces. More elaborate and wealthy designs included pavilions, which, as Crescenzi explains, could have "roof and walls . . . densely woven from thick boughs." Such opportunities for elevating the garden's users so that they could enjoy cooling breezes and observe all around them were given by the Gloriet, usually a central pavilion in Islamic gardens (the word coming from Spanish out of Arabic). It provided a vantage point from which to enjoy the gardens below, an elevated platform on which to be seen by others, and (as late Islamic texts reveal) a secure spot for private or even political conversations—anyone approaching would have been quickly visible. But this measure of privacy, so essential in palaces, castles, and manors where crowds thronged and the layout of rooms yielded little of the personal space we are used to today, could be achieved as well in small, discrete gardens, where layouts shown in illustrations often imply a measure of personal seclusion. It was a seclusion clearly cherished and exploited by women, as evidenced by much literary reference and visual imagery and as equally authorized by courtly love narratives like the *Roman de la Rose* or by the Song of Songs, whose sexual fervor was handily typologized to celebrate and represent the Virgin Mary. A French manuscript from circa 1465 of the *Livre du Cuer d'Amours* illustrates an incident in Boccaccio's *Thesiad* of Emily alone and seated on turf benches against a trellis of double roses that screens her from the peering males in the adjacent castle: the little garden or herber has been created out of a small piece of leftover space within the battlements, and its representation (required by the tale it illustrated) makes clear both her privacy and the threat to it.[55]

FLOWER BEDS AND THE "FLOWERY MEAD"

Probably the easiest spaces to design and build in the medieval garden were those designated as meadows or, in the language of poetry and romance, the "flowery mead." The poet of the *Roman de la Rose* notes how the surface of a garden was "artfully decorated and painted with flowers of various colors and sweetest perfumes," and despite the artistic metaphor, this was clearly a specific gardening practice. Flowers were otherwise planted within contained beds, usually raised with brick or wooden surrounds, which made stooping to do the gardening work a little less strenuous; though in Islamic designs they were often sunken between paths, giving the effect of walking on carpets of flowers, or below the surface of waters.[56]

Beds for flowers and other plants are a central means of giving shape and pattern to spaces where they are inserted. Some visual evidence simply and predictably suggests that whatever space was available for plants was divided into regular beds, the width of which was determined by the need of the gardener to work it without stepping inside them.

For the flowery mead, careful preparation of the surface would have been followed by the sowing of grasses with wild flowers seeded among them, an effect that we can observe in countless paintings, not least because it challenged the artist's invention and skill in depicting it. Fra Angelico's Annunciations (in Madrid and in San Marco, Florence) observe the symbolism of an enclosed garden for the Virgin, but the detailed texture of flowery grass to the left of each of the loggias is lovingly painted, as is the flowery lawn below the Virgin and St Luke in van der Weyden's painting. A particularly lovely image comes appropriately enough at the start of the French book entitled *Le Livre des Propriétés des Choses* by Barthélémy L'Anglais, who depicts fruit trees, a hedge of flowering jasmine and roses, and a rich, green sward dotted with speedwell, daisy, and columbine.[57] Written texts, both literary and practical such as Crescenzi's, confirm this feature as the most ubiquitous and valued design element in medieval gardens. Just how this kind of open ground sustained people walking all over it is unclear, but in many cases one supposes that the numbers of visitors involved were relatively small; nevertheless, the maintenance of such areas would have been a continuous operation for the gardener.

* * * * * * * *

The size and elaboration of a medieval garden was determined by social status, which in its turn could be read into the final layout. While its forms were clearly directed—Crescenzi makes occasionally clear that the patrician owner would determine the disposition of elements, and in several illustrations of his text we are shown such a figure in conversation with somebody whom we might take to be an expert like Crescenzi himself or a steward—they were almost certainly not designed as we would now understand that term—that is, projected in advance by a specialist in garden forms. Local horticultural know-how and traditional and familiar procedures of husbandry were carried into the garden—Crescenzi twice explains how to use a cord for lining up trees, yet when it comes to proposing that a large estate be divided by two main and then subsidiary paths he offers no version of how they are to be formally disposed let alone laid down, implying that the making of paths was a familiar practice. The basic vocabulary of gardens, too, was established and reasonably concise, so that its deployment at different scales and on different sites responded to the

FIGURE 1.3: Crescenzi, *Livre des profits ruraux*, circa 1470, Pierpont Morgan Library, M 232, folio 157, recto.

available size and resources of the ground, to the needs of those who either gardened there (food, medicinal herbs, animal fodder, hunting) or who socialized and entertained themselves, and at the higher echelons of society, especially in the later Middle Ages, to an aesthetic delight in their secluded surroundings along with some responsiveness to the symbolical aspects of the place. In this respect, the fountain would bear the greatest freightage of meaning in its references to both the watering of Eden, the wells of Solomon's garden, and the sealed fountain of Mary Virgin (personifying the church); yet it was at the same time an essential practical adjunct to any well-maintained garden. It also seems (to the painter and so we must suppose to the fountain maker himself) to have been the most accomplished physical insertion in a garden, the recipient of exquisite carving and hydrology, though the creation and horticultural maintenance of trellis, pergola, pavilion, turf seats, and raised flower beds was no less crafted. Hard work, says Crescenzi, makes the garden, yet—for the rich and powerful, at least—places can be made that have many delights ("viridarium multam delectationem"[58]).

CHAPTER TWO

Types of Gardens

JAMES G. SCHRYVER

Discussions of the other have become sufficiently entrenched that the average undergraduate is now able to recite upon request the various relevant aspects, definitions, functions, and ideas of "otherness." The most relevant of these for our own present discussion revolve around the ways in which our image of "the other" helps us to define ourselves by virtue of the opportunity it presents to identify what it is that we consider ourselves *not* to be. The benefit of this when considering cultural products such as gardens is that attending to the other can help us to be more precise about what elements and ideas *are* and thereby also *are not* part of the gardens of medieval Western Europe. Unfortunately, however, it does not do too much for us in terms of how precisely we define, or understand, those "other" gardens. At its most innocuous, the projection of the notion of the other, intentionally or not, lumps all non-northwest European gardens together as the homogeneous products of some monolithic "East."

The most important other in the context of the medieval garden is the Islamic garden (though, as will be emphasized, this is itself a complex and debatable concept, not least because the term "Islamic" immediately suggests the preeminence of religious differentiation at the expense of, for instance, cultural conditions and inheritances, social and political structures, and climatological and geographic conditions). At its most harmful, the identification of this "other" can take on Orientalist tendencies and prevent us from recognizing everything from the diversity of gardens beyond the northwest European peninsula and islands, through the elements and ideas that they share with their counterparts in Eastern and Western Christendom, and the interchange and influence between garden cultures.

This chapter adopts a perspective deliberately different from the majority of writing on medieval gardens. What typology of gardens can we propose if we begin not in the northwest European peninsula but in the highly developed garden cultures of the rest of the known medieval world, particularly the civilizations of the Mediterranean basin? Can this view, beginning outside Western Christendom, enable us to look afresh? Instead of conceiving of medieval garden culture in a manner akin to the 1569 Mercator Projection, with the Low Countries, France, and Britain at the center, this chapter more resembles a *mappa mundi*, such as the Ebstorf or Hereford maps (both c. 1300, perhaps by the same "Gervase"), giving Jerusalem pride of place. In so doing, this chapter seeks to emphasize on the one hand the variety and diversity of these "other" garden cultures and, on the other, to point to connections with those of Western Christendom.

One powerful indicator of our difficulty in discussing these cultural differences is the inflexibility of our terminology: the Iberian peninsula is in Western Europe, but for much of our period Islamic culture dominates and so Spain is part of the "East." Constantinople and the Byzantine Empire are Christian cousins of the western realms of Christendom, but Byzantine garden culture is not at all the same as that of Western Christendom. "northwest European peninsula" is too laborious a term; "Mercator-land" too jocular. In this essay, therefore, I continue to use the shorthand of "West," meaning the heartland of Western medieval Christendom in the "northwest European peninsula," and "East," meaning the "other" gardens of Islamic cultures from Spain in the west to the Arabian peninsula.

Before looking at Christendom from this different perspective, it is useful to give an account of some of the garden cultures found beyond Christendom's borders. The cultural, natural, and psychological environments of many of the "other" gardens during the medieval period *were* different from many of those found in the West. As a product of these environments, the gardens themselves were also different, as is immediately clear in the example of the Islamic garden practice of placing the vegetation in sunken beds so that the viewer seated on the ground would look out upon the top surface of what looked like a carpet of plants and flowers.[1]

However, we should immediately challenge the notion that Islamic gardens composed a monolithic, homogeneous block; they were often very different

from each other. The foundations of these differences are often instructive in
that they direct our attention beyond the predominant Western and Christian
image of the Eastern garden as an earthly (and in Western eyes hedonistic) paradise. Many of the differences between various types of Eastern gardens stem
from their beginnings: the immediate cultural and environmental conditions
that gave them birth.

One of the first divisions that should be made is between the gardens of
Byzantium, Islam, and Persia. For example, the gardens of the early Byzantine Empire can be seen in a number of ways as continuations of the gardens
of the late Roman Empire. Ancient Persia had its own orientation and traditions to draw upon. Near Eastern Islamic gardens, meanwhile, seem to develop in response to a mix of these. But it should again be emphasized that
there are many different garden cultures within the territories of Islam in the
Middle Ages, and these respond differently to Roman and Persian influences
and are also conditioned by reflection on each other. The rise of the Islamic
Empire created an extremely complex and heterogeneous civilization.[2] We are
often tempted to group as a single phenomenon cultural products like gardens
produced in the lands that came under the control of the Umayyads and their
successors, but it is worth bearing in mind that these products and the cultures
that produced them represent a range in date roughly from the seventh to
the nineteenth centuries and a range in place from the steppes of Asia to the
Iberian peninsula.[3] And as in other art forms, local or regional differences even
within the medieval period created great variety among the gardens habitually
placed under the broader heading "Islamic."[4]

Challengingly for anyone trying to orient themselves within this wide field,
the range and variety of Islamic gardens is echoed in the scholarship that
seeks to analyze them.[5] Some areas and time periods such as Islamic Spain or
Mughal India have received a great deal of attention and are relatively well-
known, while others have seen a smaller number of publications and remain
less well understood, and this is itself a warning that we should avoid seeing
the "Islamic garden" as homogeneous. Few studies attempt to synthesize the
information available in scattered form.

GARDENS OF ISLAM

As noted earlier, it is inevitable in a volume of this kind that the focus of
most contributions will be Northwest Europe and, even within that, predominantly on France and England: European and North American scholarship has concentrated on the cultural, gardenist, and linguistic phenomena

most accessible and relevant to it. For this reason, it is important to give an overview of the "other" garden cultures, the products of the areas on the periphery of which stand the northwest European peninsula and its Atlantic archipelago.

Islamic gardens, as with Islamic art and culture in general, did not appear out of nothing, but were influenced by what came before.[6] Islamic civilization was born out of a mix of those of the classical world, the Near East, and Arabia.[7] In terms of gardens, it is important to ask what elements each of these civilizations might have provided to the development of what we are grouping under the title, valid or not, of Islamic.[8] In Arabia, the fourth through seventh centuries C.E. were marked by a transition from city life to nomadic life and an increase in the desertification of the landscape.[9] The few cities that survived seem to have been for the most part under Bedouin, as opposed to Greco-Roman or Persian, control.[10] Further north, in Syria and Persia, the formerly Bedouin tribes of the Ghassanians and the Lakhmites acted as clients of the Roman and Sassanian Empires, respectively, during the same general period.[11] Thus, different areas of the lands that were to fall to the adherents of the new religion in the seventh century C.E. already possessed different traditions concerning the uses and meanings associated with landscape and gardens. In the case of Mesopotamia, these traditions had already at this point a two thousand year history.[12] This does not mean that there were no areas of overlap with the Sassanian practices that inherited this tradition or Greco-Roman practices that seem to have been more dominant in the area of Syria. But we should recognize the force and potential influence of these traditions.

How and why might this be the case? The origins of what were to become the Byzantine and Islamic empires with their distinguishable cultural products, such as gardens, can in many instances be traced back to the Roman Empire. Particularly in the areas immediately around the eastern Mediterranean, the physical remains and structure of Roman agricultural practice were just as visible to peoples of the East as they were to those in the West. In Spain especially, but also in other areas traditionally belonging to the "other" during the medieval period, the remains of Roman hydraulic systems were put to good use wherever possible.

In addition, the reliance on classical knowledge surrounding all things agricultural and horticultural in late antiquity in the East can be seen in a remarkable parallel across centuries and cultures: in the sixth century, when the citizens of Honoratae wanted to present a gift to Anicia Juliana, an imperial lady, the book they chose was an herbal, now known to us as the Vienna Dioscorides.[13] Later, in the mid-tenth century, a copy of the same text was sent by the Byzantine emperor Constantine VII Porphyrogenitus to Abd al-Rahman III.[14]

Of course, one major difference from their pagan predecessors on both sides of the Mediterranean is the fact that the Byzantines could also cite biblical exhortations to eat "the fruit of the labor of your hands" (Psalm 128:2) and "plant gardens and eat their produce" (Jeremiah 29:5). This is especially interesting in light of the fact that many of the same people would have found certain aspects of the new religion quite threatening to their position in society in the first few centuries after its spread, as mentioned below. And although we must remain wary in the use of ekphrases as sources of information, the literary descriptions of gardens can often be traced back to classical and biblical models.

The acknowledgement of the strong role of history and tradition does not mean that these garden traditions were static: there certainly was continuous development both before and after the events of the seventh century. And after the initial spread of Islam, Arabic literature by the ninth and tenth centuries celebrated urban life and one's hometown, despite some nostalgia for the nomadic and "pure" life of the desert Bedouin.[15] Certainly, the achievements of city life came to be seen as superior to those of the nomadic past.[16] In the same way, the Byzantines, successors or continuers of the ancient Roman Empire, were not simply passive recipients of the classical heritage; and the same is true of Charlemagne and his successors, who surely did more than blindly copy, for all their focus on recreating the Western empire. Recognizing this oscillation between nomadic and urbanizing cultures in the Near East, with the consequent implications for gardens and the wider landscape, should alert us to the need to consider similar questions with regard to Northwest Europe and, indeed, the response to and reception of knowledge there of the urban and suburban garden cultures of al-Andalus, for instance, and of Byzantium.

Although Greece and Rome did play a significant role, not all scholars chart the origins of Byzantine and Islamic gardens in the Greco-Roman world. George Marçais is among those who credit Persia with introducing the Muslim world to the concept of landscape or garden architecture.[17] These scholars point out that the palaces of the Sassanid kings, such as the 'Imarat-I Khosrow and the Qasr-i Shirin of Chosroes II, looked out on extensive vistas of water and greenery.[18] In addition to tracing the roots of this practice to Iran, they also point out that Arabic terms such as *bustān* and *firdaws* derive from Persian.[19] Marçais goes even further and notes that those poets who best express the ideal of the garden are Persian.[20] He even interprets the influence of the Greco-Roman world through this lens. From this point of view, the Byzantine

influence on Islamic gardens in the eastern Mediterranean was simply a con-
duit for some of the ideas that Greece and Rome received from Persia.

   With the rise of the Abbasids in 750 and the transfer of their capital to Baghdad in 762 (later transferred to Samarra in 836), a shift in orientation occurred
away from the Mediterranean, the Byzantine Empire, and the Greco-Roman
heritage of the area, toward that of Persia and the areas further east; and this
applies also to gardens of the Muslim empire: a good deal of evidence points
to the Abbasid period as the real beginning of the Islamic garden. However,
there are traces of earlier Islamic gardens. A preliminary attempt at compiling
and synthesizing some of the scattered archaeological evidence for Umayyad
gardens indicates that these remained an important part of the environment in
which rulers chose to live.[21] Textual evidence for the role that gardens played
under the Umayyad rulers also exists and awaits proper study.

   From Persia, this garden culture spread westward along the same route
taken by the armies and influence of the new empire.[22] Thus, just as the
Tulunids (868–905) seem to have mimicked the art and architecture of contemporary Iraq during their rule of Egypt and Syria, their capital in Fustat was also
full of gardens modeled after those of their Abbasid overlords. From Egypt,
the Islamic garden spread to Tunisia together with the rule of the Aghlabid
emirs in the ninth century. Here, a palace was built at Raqqâda that contained
among its gardens an artificial lake, whose surface would have served to reflect
the pavilions and plants surrounding it.[23] As will be discussed below, this sort
of visual manipulation is something that, it is often argued, is also familiar in
certain Western gardens and landscapes, such as that of Bodiam Castle, in East
Sussex (though see the skeptical discussion of such interpretations in the final
chapter of this volume).

   Meanwhile, the gardens developed in Islamic Spain, which are undoubtedly
those which are the most familiar to scholars focused on Europe, seem to have
been of a slightly different sort than those found in Mesopotamia. A brief account of their history reveals once more the complexity of the interplay of sources
and influences at work. Although composed of many of the same elements, the
gardens of Islamic Spain seem to have been arranged on a much more modest
scale and to have been incorporated in many cases within the palace, as opposed to the opposite arrangement seen in the Abbasid capitals.[24] Much like the
Islamic gardens of North Africa, which can be seen as spreading together with
the conquests of the new religion, the gardens of Spain can be tied to the flight
of the remaining members of the Umayyad dynasty there and the establishment
of a new kingdom centered on Cordoba by the surviving Umayyad claimant to
the caliphate. In fact, there is clear evidence that the gardens incorporated in

Umayyad courtly centers or palaces such as Rusafa in Syria served as models for some of the early palaces and gardens of Umayyad Spain.[25] Other palace complexes, such as Madinat al-Zahra', show the influence of the palaces of Samarra.[26] Some Spanish gardens, such as those found in the Alhambra, in turn influenced later gardens in Morocco, the so-called *riâdh*, though it is unfortunately not clear when this occurred, and it may have been as late as the seventeenth-century expulsions of the Moslems from Spain.[27] The same may be true of some of the comparatively earlier gardens in Tunisia, such as the ones described by Anselme Adorne in 1470.[28] At the same time, however, these gardens were built on an existing Roman substructure that the Muslims in many cases took great pains to revive and put to good use.[29]

In the East, the gardens of Persia, including those of the Ilkhanid (1256–1353), Timurid (1370–1507), and Safavid (1510–1732) dynasties, developed in parallel to those of the middle and later Byzantine empires; considerable scholarship has been devoted to the written sources (agricultural manuals and literature) pertaining to these gardens.[30] Further to the west, and a bit earlier, there is also evidence that the Seljuqs of Rum (1071–1243) made use of suburban, royal walled gardens and palace parks centered around a pavilion or kiosk.[31] These were standard elements of the Persian gardens of the later dynasties. In addition to the various economic and sociopolitical functions, as one scholar has noted, "above all, the Persian garden was the product of the intensive, irrigated agriculture that characterized the urban oases of greater Iran and Central Asia."[32]

A TYPOLOGY OF FORM, STRUCTURE, AND PATRONAGE

The portrayal of gardens of the East as homogeneous masks the differences inherent in them; and understanding of the areas of overlap and similarity with the better-known "medieval garden" of northwest Europe constitutes an equally important casualty.

Looking at the issue from the ground up, so to say, one of the first places in which there seems a great deal more continuity between the medieval gardens of the East and those of the West than is typically acknowledged is in the area of patronage, especially in terms of where and why gardens other than kitchen gardens were constructed. The easiest place to begin an examination of this issue is with the gardens of Byzantium, which we might more pointedly label for the sake of the present discussion, "the gardens of the late Roman Empire". The divergence of the Western and Eastern medieval worlds can arguably be said to have begun at a number of points in the history of the Mediterranean. One date that stands out, however, is the year 395, when the Roman Empire was divided into a western and eastern half, upon the death of the emperor Theodosius I.[33] Nonetheless, as Averil Cameron has noted, part of what makes this period so interesting is the fact that it encompassed both instances of important change as well as of continuity.[34] Other scholars have gone further and focused on the similarities during this period, and in the case of Klaus Randsborg, have pushed the point of great change as late as the eleventh century.[35]

Amid the political changes instigated by the division of the empire into a western half and an eastern half, there were still groups among which social, and especially religious, change was resisted in the face of the rise of Christianity. As is often the case, the upper class would not have been overly eager to disregard the attitudes and practices that helped to form the basis of their status and power in society. In relation to our subject, it seems that there was a corresponding lack of immediate transformation in their attitudes toward gardens and gardening, at least during the period from the fourth to the seventh centuries C.E. discussed above. As many of the essays in the ancient volume show, for the Romans, from the end of the republic onward, agriculture and horticulture were considered to be gentlemanly pursuits, and these beliefs or opinions did not simply disappear with the political or administrative changes within the eastern half of the empire, but continued to be held by the Byzantine upper classes.[36] Looking further east at the Sassanian Empire and the Umayyad and Abbasid caliphates, it becomes clear that the ruling elites also saw a connection between their status and position in society and the use of gardens as appropriate markers of that status.

Not only the elites, but the emperors themselves also continued the practices of their predecessors related to the establishment of gardens and gardening. The seventh-century emperor Heraclius (610–641) is known to have created parks and vegetable gardens and the ninth-century emperor Theophilos (829–842) not only continued the trend in the construction of gardens, but tied parks and gardens to the creation of his palaces. In a move that seems to echo the frescoes of the Pompeian Second Style, he also encouraged the creation of wall mosaics displaying garden scenes.[37] At an even later date, Constantine IX Monomachus (1042–1055) was maligned for his constant manipulations of gardens and the landscape as he transformed hill into flowering field, to the amazement of some commentators.[38] Thus, in general, it seems that later emperors constructed a mix of hunting parks; formal, enclosed gardens associated with and integrated into their palaces; and combinations of both.[39]

For their part, the Abbasids, as seen in their palace complexes such as that uncovered at Samarra, took up the practices of their predecessors in Persia and caused them to flourish.[40] By the end of the ninth century, the garden of the Palace of the Pleiades (al-Thurayya), erected in Baghdad by the caliph Mu'tadid (892–902), was an integral part of the reasons for which it was to be praised. In addition to its battlements and other aspects:

> [It had] a garden and trees whose branches touch each other and that sprout out with fruit and green foliage. You see the birds cooing in their branches betake themselves from nest to nest . . . . Water-courses like (endless) chains are channeled to nurse the children of the sweet-smelling plants and flowers.[41]

That these gardens, much like the lordly landscapes of Anglo-Norman and later England, were meant to impress can be seen in the way in which important guests were made to tour them. The oft-cited account of the Byzantine ambassadors' experience during their mission to the Abbasid caliph al-Muqtadir in 917 C.E. makes this abundantly clear and reminds one of similar texts from the West. Having already been taken around the palace and offered snow-cooled water, sherbets, beer, and other refreshments at every turn, they entered what is called the "Park of the Wild Beasts":

> This was a palace with various kinds of wild animals therein, who entered it from the park and came up close to the visitors, sniffing them, and eating from their hands . . . Then the envoys passed to what was called the New Kiosk which is a palace in the midst of two gardens. In the center was an artificial pond of white lead, round which flows a stream of white lead more lustrous than polished silver. This pond was thirty cubits in length by twenty across, and round it were set four magnificent boats with gilt seats adorned with embroidery of Dabik, and the pavilions were covered over with the gold work of Dabik. All round this tank extended a garden with lawns with palm-trees, and it is said that their number was four hundred, and the height of each is five cubits. Now the entire height of these trees, from top to bottom, was enclosed in carved teak-wood, encircled with gilt copper rings. And all these palms bore full-grown dates, which were not quite ripe. Round the sides of the garden also are citrons and also other kinds of fruit. The ambassadors went out of this palace, and next came to the Palace of the Tree, where there is a tree standing in the midst of a great circular pond filled with clear water. The tree

has eighteen branches, every branch having a numberous [*sic*] twigs, on which sit all sorts of gold and silver birds, both large and small.[42]

If the ideas and coded messages within this tour seem familiar to those versed in Western medieval practices, they should. In a very similar manner, the constable of Dover Castle was ordered to arrange a similar tour, for a similar purpose, upon the arrival of Gaucher de Châtillon in 1247:

> When Gaucher de Châtillon shall come to Dover he shall take him into that castle and show the castle off to him in eloquent style, so that the magnificence of the castle shall be fully apparent to him, and that he shall see no defects in it. And Gaucher is to be allowed to enter the King's park of Elham, and to hunt there two or three does as a gift from the King.[43]

A TYPOLOGY OF SYMBOLISM AND MEANING

Beyond the simple continuation of practices of construction and patronage, a continuity significant in its own right, what is just as striking is the fact that some of the same reasons seem to lie behind these practices and the patronage of both the gardens of Western Europe and those of the East. In particular, the continuation of Roman garden traditions among the elite of Byzantine society, and certainly also among those who lived in late antique cities that happen to have been captured by the Umayyads in the first half of the seventh century, is closely intertwined with the imagery and the symbolism that came to be associated with gardens and other elements of created landscapes. Some of these meanings will be different from those dominant in the West—for example, the Byzantine interpretation of the garden as bride, or the specific connotations of paradise thought to have been associated with certain Islamic gardens.[44] However, much of the imagery associated with these Eastern gardens will seem strikingly familiar. The various interpretations of creation or renewal, for example, as well as the interpretation of the garden as not only a symbol of lordly status but also as a metaphor for creation, as a reflection of paradise, as a setting for achieving victory (military, moral, sexual, or otherwise), and even as a setting for romantic encounters all find parallels in the gardens coming out of these various traditions.

The further spread of the classical Mediterranean attitudes, if not necessarily the exact form and function of these gardens, to the early Islamic world (especially the Umayyad caliphate) might seem surprising at first considering the differences in culture, geography, and, in some cases, even climate. However, the following observation by Oleg Grabar that these gardens, especially when woven into a palatial context, would have been simply part of an international "class culture" does seem to explain what we see today when studying the various sources.

> The realm of the prince as it was made visible to others was, at this time, as unaffected by the faith as the prince's private palaces were earlier. Herein lies a key aspect of princely culture and hence of princely art. Because it was not modified or controlled by the faith and because it took its themes and practices from the enormous body of habits and motifs inherited from the classical and Near Eastern traditions, it created a system and vocabulary that could be understood by all comparable princely realms.[45]

Thus, when the Byzantine ambassadors were shown the gardens of the Abbasid capital in 917, they could read the message that was laid out before them. And although it has yet to be definitively proven one way or another, it is very tempting to think that embassies such as this would have led to a situation in which the various rulers and their circles were compelled to parallel one another's behavior in this arena, if not to attempt to outdo one another. If nothing else, it certainly would have led to the spread of ideas, sometimes in the form of books as noted above, between them. Whether or not these ideas spread to Christendom in the same manner is certainly worth asking in this regard. Status, at least, seems quite international when one is looking at medieval gardens.

A TYPOLOGY OF USE

The same princely culture of understanding seems true not just for the meaning of gardens but also for the activities took place within them. The lordly activity par excellence in medieval Europe was the hunt. As hinted at by the quotation above, the keeping and hunting of deer was a kingly prerogative, at least in England. Those who could afford it, or whose station required that they do so, went to great lengths and expense to impark land and fill it with game, especially deer. Although it is not certain how much the requests sent to the king for his permission to do so were simply pro forma, the tacit recognition of his dominion over this activity was certainly something that was a part of elite culture. The symbolism and the notion that this was an elite activity, not to mention the pure physical enjoyment, was also shared by those responsible for creating the appropriate landscapes for this activity in the East. And once again, we see the most overlap in Christendom of the early Middle Ages. For example, we have evidence from the fifth century of hunts organized on family estates.[46] Later centuries were to see the hunt become an integral part of imperial rhetoric and symbolism.[47] In this respect, Henry Maguire has noted that the beasts that served as game could represent either the emperor's internal demons or his external enemies.[48] Although they are far from being completely understood, one of the interpretations put forward to explain the function of the so-called desert palaces of the Umayyads is that they may have been used as hunting lodges.

AREAS OF FURTHER RESEARCH

Coming from the East, the aspects of medieval gardens that seem most interesting may be quite different than those appealing to scholars making their way along other paths. Among these issues, a number seem to offer especially fertile ground for future research. The first is ephemeral, the second symbolic, the third has to do with planning, and the fourth, with use.

First, although even more ephemeral than the combination of flowers of a particular season, the greenery used to accompany processions in the Byzantine Empire seems to have held an important place or role in the ritual. For example, in order to set the stage for a late ninth-century triumph of Basil I in Constantinople, the route was garlanded "with laurel and rosemary and myrtle and roses and other flowers . . . [and in addition, the ground] was completely covered in flowers."[49] The importance of processions for both the ecclesiastical and the secular nobility is well-attested in medieval Christendom. Did plants play an equally important role?

A second area that seems full of interesting potential is that of influence, as difficult as that term may be, of Eastern gardens and landscapes on those of the medieval West. Here, an obvious place to begin would seem to be Islamic Spain, whose gardens may have been known to various members of the noble class outside of that area to differing degrees of detail. One case in particular seems very deserving of more attention and may open up the field for further studies of its kind. Leeds Castle, in Kent, was substantially rebuilt during the 1280s under Edward I. Among the additions he constructed was a large ornamental lake and other bodies of water as well as a large tower from which the lakes could be viewed.[50] The fact that Edward I made frequent visits to the site is not necessarily of note. However, when coupled with the fact that he frequently made these visits together with his queen, Eleanor of Castile (in the Iberian peninsula), they become very interesting from the point of view of symbolism, use, and the shared culture of nobility as posited by Grabar and noted above.

I do not think I go out on a limb in claiming that traditionally, the assumption has been that in matters of both culture and material culture, medieval Christendom looked back at Rome as its source and inspiration. This was to a gross extent true and can be seen in any number of monuments from the palace chapel of Charlemagne at Aachen to the use of the imperial eagle atop the walls of Caernarvon castle. However, in both of these cases, the East played a role as well. Charlemagne received emissaries and the famous gift of an elephant and water clock (among others) from the Abbasid caliph Harun al-Rashid. He also sent three embassies of his own (797, 802, and 807). And in addition to the eagle, Edward I included the banded style of brick and stone in his fortification at Caernarvon for the express purpose of alluding to the walls of Constantinople. The automata in the garden of Hesdin in northern France represent another conscious importation.[51] Of course, one could argue that there are just as many examples of rulers and elites, if not more, who were ignorant of the lands, cultures, and practices of the East. The point is, however, that there was *some* familiarity with these practices and the related ideas in the West during the Middle Ages. As a result, in cases where it is warranted, the efforts put into exploring these connections more deeply look as though they would be positively rewarded.

One thing that is especially striking about the gardens of the eastern Mediterranean and of the Persian and later Islamic lands further east is the large amounts of integrative planning that went into them. More often than not, imperial landscapes were not simply developed piecemeal as an afterthought but were carefully integrated into a coherent whole with the architecture of the palace and surrounding complex. This third area looks to be an especially fertile ground for future research in the Islamic world, the Byzantine empire, and Christendom: with regard to medieval England and Wales, the work of scholars such as Oliver Creighton is showing that the landscape surrounding a castle was just as much a part of the projection of noble status as was the castle itself.

Lastly, in terms of the use of these gardens, there are interesting trends having nothing to do with the re-creation of paradise that might also serve as fruitful avenues of inquiry for the gardens of Western medieval Europe. In Byzantium, for example, there is evidence that the gardens of the elite were frequently the setting for various agricultural experiments.[52] One such insight is what seems to be a focus on the productive side of garden estates and plantations in the post-second century period, one that can perhaps be applied to more ancient examples with good harvest.[53] The medicinal gardens of hospitals and monasteries may also prove fertile especially if compared with their cousins in the West.[54] Practicality is something that is often lost in the focus on pleasure, although the latter is perhaps something that is timeless and not culturally specific.

The way in which these gardens were enjoyed also seems worth exploring. The temptation is, of course, to imagine that people in the Middle Ages enjoyed gardens in the same ways that we do today. But did they? Attributing modern notions to the past is a danger we constantly warn our students of as something to be avoided. So, what options does that leave us with?

Textual sources such as agricultural manuals, botanical treatises, historical descriptions, and poetry aid us in understanding how gardens were seen by those who used them.[55] The earthly paradise represented by the Islamic garden was something that was meant to be enjoyed with the senses. Poetry focuses on the visual experience, but mention is also made of the auditory and olfactory pleasures.[56] Thus, in addition to the contemplative joys of the garden, the sights, sounds, and scents were an important part of the experience, at least in the Islamic world. In this respect, Spain offers yet another enticing garden culture that may have provided a point of reference for certain Western gardens and their patrons. In Spain, such gardens would become places where people could enjoy the sensations a prodigious nature afforded them: "contemplation, the sounds of water and the nightingale's song, the scents of flowers, the cool feel of flowers against the skin, all in an atmosphere of Quranic paradise."[57]

In Persian gardens, as elsewhere, the relationship to contemporary miniature paintings, or those nearly contemporary, can only provide certain types of information about them such as architectural details and general use.[58] In terms of the latter, the frequent appearance of gardens as settings indicates that a great deal of court life took place in them.[59] Among the various other textual sources, travelers' accounts also seem to hold the promise of further information to help fill in the gaps. For example, such an exercise has helped to identify the remains of a possible Timurid garden built on raised terraces near Herat.[60] The use of raised terraces was tied into the hydrological engineering of the garden and was typical of Timurid gardens.[61]

Travelers' accounts also help us to understand the "variations on a theme" that marked the gardens of the Timurids. The visits of the "Spanish" ambassador Ruy Gonzalez de Clavijo to Samarqand, for example, help us to reconstruct a picture of gardens intricately connected to the palaces that they surrounded (and the large pools that reflected them), the pavilions that adorned their corners, and the pavilions that lay scattered throughout.[62] The gardens were surrounded by walls, filled with various fruit and shade trees and intersected by paths for enjoying the garden from different vistas. It is interesting that although Clavijo may have assumed that these paths were mainly for strolling about, and in fact may have used them for just this purpose, other evidence points to the fact that it was more common for people to sit and contemplate a garden in the Persian world, as opposed to walk through and around it. Another issue that is clear from the descriptions left by these visitors to various Persian gardens is the way in which water in the form of still reflecting pools as well as flowing streams and canals, and even fountains, was an integral part of the plan of the garden and the garden itself.[63] The more static uses of the Persian garden are especially interesting considering how much information we have for the active use of Western gardens, where they were the settings for activities such as jousts in addition to the hunt.

In sum, different as they may be from the gardens many of us may be familiar with from the world of medieval Western Europe, the medieval gardens of the East are equally different from each other. Not only do they refute any kind of homogeneous categorization, but their variety includes many types that are also found in the West during the Middle Ages. What is more, beyond the similarities in type are the similarities in areas such as patronage, use, and meaning. Most exciting of all, however, are the possibilities that a recognition of these similarities create for future research into "the other." Some of these possibilities hint that if we look hard enough, we may find bits and pieces of ourselves.

CHAPTER THREE

Plantings

REBECCA KRUG

It has often been observed that medieval gardens were planted to serve practical needs. Janet Ferrier's comments are representative: "Gardens in the fourteenth and fifteenth centuries were prized more for their utilitarian value than as places of recreation . . . it is clear that . . . the garden exists only to supply produce for the household."[1] Although medieval illustrations of gardens tend to represent small "pleasure gardens" or devotional spaces with a tiny "flowering mead," turfed garden bench, and herbs and flowers in beds, the consensus among garden historians is that medieval gardens were designed to be *useful*. Even pleasure gardens from the period included plants with alimentary and medical uses, and the botanical lists available are composed of plants that served practical needs. Necessary because they provided food, medicine, and a wide range of ingredients for household products, gardens have been studied as means for supplying basic needs throughout the Middle Ages.

The purpose of the present essay is to discuss the ways in which people in the Middle Ages thought about the act of planting a garden. I do not dispute the notion that medieval gardens were conceived of in relation to "utility." Rather, this essay explores the nature of the medieval garden's usefulness. How, I ask, did people in the Middle Ages conceive of this utility as they planted gardens, and, by extension, how did the idea of usefulness shape people's ideas about nature? I consider three approaches to the topic as it was articulated in the European Middle Ages. All offer an understanding of nature that is certainly utilitarian but that does not emphasize the garden's productivity exclusively or even as its primary function.

The first—common especially among writers interested in grafting—was that planting a garden was a way to fool nature. According to this way of thinking, gardeners needed to cheat nature, to find ingenious tricks to make it yield fruit more quickly and more interestingly. Although such writers clearly understood gardening as a practical art, and grafting was especially popular as a means of producing fruit quickly, these writers were more concerned with manipulating nature than with agricultural yield. The examples I use to illustrate this idea are taken from European treatises written by Nicholas Bollard and Geoffrey of Franconia in the later Middle Ages, and the idea began with Roman writers contemporary with Virgil. For these gardeners, nature could be thought of as an artistic medium and the gardener as a creative artist.

In contrast with these "ingenious" gardeners who sought to work around or reinvent nature are those who imagined themselves as cooperating with it. The early medieval poem *Hortulus* by Walahfrid Strabo serves as an example of one mode of cooperation. For Walahfrid, the act of planting a garden was a way to take part in nature's eternity. Although Walahfrid's poem is utilitarian, offering a catalogue of plants with their medicinal and alimentary uses, it refrains from discussions of maximizing the productivity of plants. Instead, Walahfrid describes gardening as interactive—as a dynamic process that establishes a personal relationship between the gardener and the plants in the garden. Planting a garden was, in the German poet's view, an ongoing process in which the gardener found spiritual renewal through his or her relationship with nature.

Finally, a third example in which the gardener cooperates with nature can be found in the household book written by the Menagier de Paris. For writers like the Menagier, planting a garden was about proper conduct, and the gardener's duty was to achieve a "feel" for nature's rules that was nearly second nature. Although the Menagier was clearly interested in making his and his wife's garden productive, the gardening treatise in his book conceives of the garden's utility explicitly in relation to ideas about the gardener's social behavior. For the Menagier, nature was an administrative "head" that coordinated forces such as soil conditions, weather, location, and calendar month. The gardener, as she is represented in the book's advice, is an agent responsible for fulfilling nature's agenda. He or she did this by learning rules that predicted nature's course and acting in response to these learned rules.

Based on these three cases, we can begin to see how diverse ideas about the utility of the garden were in the European Middle Ages. Planting a garden was not, it appears, obviously or exclusively about maximizing yield but, rather, extended to the creation of sustaining social and individual relationships between people, plants, and the natural world.

HOW PLANTING WAS DONE AND WHERE MEDIEVAL GARDENERS GOT THEIR PLANTS

Before turning to the three cases, a little background about gardening and the acquisition of plants and seeds in the European Middle Ages will be helpful. Medieval gardeners, like modern gardeners, built up their stock of garden plants in three basic ways: by planting seeds, by transplanting plants, and by using parts of already established plants, such as divisions from perennials.

Botanical materials—seeds, plants, and cuttings—were acquired in various ways. First, they could be purchased. Second, they could be found in one's own garden. Third, they could be gifts from friends and neighbors. John Hooper Harvey discusses the commercial aspects of planting a garden in his books *Mediaeval Gardens* (1981) and *Early Nurserymen* (1974).[2] He has traced records regarding seed and plant purchases by monasteries and royal institutions in order to demonstrate that trade in botanical materials was an important aspect of gardening in the later Middle Ages. Nurseries for seeds and fruit tree stock were an important source for medieval gardeners. Commercial gardeners also sold their wares at markets. In addition, as Harvey argues, at least some medieval gardeners found it advisable to acquire seed from sources outside of their own gardens even if they could reuse their own seeds. In Walter of Henley's treatise from the late thirteenth century, the author suggests that the gardener acquire seed "grown on other ground" than one's own plot because it will "bring more profit." The treatise is so committed to this idea that the author suggests the gardener run an experiment in which he or she should "plough two selions at the same time, and sow the one with seed which is bought and the other with corn you have grown: in August you will see that I speak truly."[3]

It is more difficult to find evidence concerning informal channels for acquiring botanical materials. Some gardening literature discusses how to save one's own seeds, and this was clearly a practice that people followed, as Henley's advice to do the opposite confirms. More difficult still to demonstrate is that gardeners shared plants and seeds, but there is some proof that this, too, was one of the ways gardeners acquired plants. Harvey mentions, for example, that the French poet Eustache Deschamps composed a ballad to the English poet Chaucer in which Deschamps explains that he had given the English poet plants for his garden at Chaucer's request.[4] Similarly, in the Menagier de Paris's treatise, it is assumed that the gardener may like to give her friends plants such as rosemary cuttings as gifts.[5] Plants, then, were acquired both commercially and informally. The medieval gardener could rely on commercial growers for some of his or her needs and also relied on friends for plants that, it seems, were particularly desired. Finally, the gardener found ways to grow plants from other plants, saving seed, making cuttings, and working with grafting stock.

ARTISTRY AND NATURE: GRAFTING AND THE INGENIOUS GARDENER

Grafting of fruit trees and roses was one of the primary means by which medieval people planted gardens. Grafting is a technique in which two plants are joined to form one plant. The "rootstock," the base plant, is generally a hardy cultivar; the "scion," the plant whose flower or fruit is the desired result, is grafted onto the rootstock. Modern, amateur gardeners do not think of grafting as a convenient way to increase the stock of plants in the garden; they consider it nothing like, for example, the division of perennials or planting of seeds. In contrast, medieval gardeners appear, given the body of literature on the subject, to have been fascinated by grafting, to have relied on the practice, and to have studied various, related techniques.

A number of treatises were written on the subject of grafting, and two that circulated widely across western Europe, one from the mid-fourteenth century by Nicholas Bollard, an English Benedictine, and the other from earlier in the century by Geoffrey (sometimes called "Gottfried") of Franconia, a native of Würzberg, are of particular interest on account of their combination of traditional learning and gardening experience. The two men apparently knew one another, and they seem to have thought of themselves *as* gardeners.[6] Geoffrey, for example, mentions information he gained both through his own experiences and from other gardeners including clerks, knights, monks, housewives, and Greek experts.[7] Bollard alludes to other "conyng men" (cunning men) who, like the author himself, possessed specialized knowledge of the sort that Bollard states he shares with his readers.[8]

Bollard and Geoffrey both wrote about various aspects of gardening, and both understood grafting as central to the gardener's experience. Their writing was influenced by the Roman author Palladius's discussion of grafting, and both Bollard and Geoffrey assume that their readers will accept the advantages of enlarging their gardening stock through grafting with little question.

In the medieval world, grafting was considered a valuable practice because it saved the gardener and farmer tremendous amounts of time. A translation of Palladius's treatise that circulated in vernacular translations in the later Middle Ages, for example, notes that nature does not mind "tarrying," but gardeners do: the treatise suggests that the gardener turn to grafting rather than starting fruit trees from seeds in order to speed up the process.[9] Similarly, as a prescription in a fifteenth-century edition of Bollard's work notes, one can "make a orchard in short space" if the proper methods are employed.[10] Grafting was, clearly, the most important of methods available.

Interest in horticultural techniques, as W. L. Braekman has noted, appeared to be widespread in the Middle Ages. Braekman observes that short prescriptions about grafting appeared in various manuscripts and not only in longer gardening treatises.[11] His conclusions are supported by the assumptions that underwrite the grafting treatises. For example, Geoffrey's treatise begins with the remark that "The manere of settyng of trees is manyfold and soo comon, that we wil not at this tyme shewe therof."[12] The Middle English term for grafting, "impe," was familiar, appearing in compound nouns describing places associated with grafting such as crofts, yards, and hills.[13]

Yet, although knowledge of grafting was apparently desirable for every gardener and not only for experts and professionals, the writing extant on the subject tends to be specialized. This is surprising since even the most basic grafting requires some technical knowledge on the gardener's part. Plant selection is one of the fundamental requirements for success. Not all plants can be grafted and not all of the ones that can accept grafts are compatible with one another. Pears, for example, are successfully grafted on quince rootstock but apricot scions have little success when grafted onto peaches. Medieval people seem to have thought of grafting in relation to trees and vines, so perhaps it was common knowledge that these were the plants to graft.[14] Still, it is worth observing that this meant that the run-of-the-mill gardener knew that some plants were excluded from this form of propagation.[15] Like plant selection, the fundamental fact that both the rootstock and the scion needed to be kept alive for the graft to take must also have been known to gardeners.

Yet, despite the importance of such basic information, writers such as Bollard and Geoffrey showed little interest in offering or expounding upon "common" knowledge. Rather, they wrote about specialized kinds of grafting and related techniques with the understanding that they were revealing *secrets* that were unknown to their readers. Books of secrets were popular throughout the Middle Ages. Such books often included recipes and prescriptions of various kinds: medical, culinary, magical, and, as we will see, horticultural.

The first paragraph of Bollard's treatise identifies his work with the most famous book of secrets, the pseudo-Aristotelian *Secretum Secretorum*: in Bollard's book the phrase "It seyth yn the Secretes of Aristotle" introduces the section on when to plant according to the astrological calendar. Similarly, Geoffrey's treatise presents itself as offering its readers special, secret information. Geoffrey states that the work will, at least in part, explore "the pryve workinges"—that is, the arcane secrets of planting and grafting trees.[16] Geoffrey and Bollard align their work with that by authors of books of secrets, and the treatises were clearly received by readers as offering specialized knowledge: the works were often found together in manuscripts including one known as the *Tollemache Book of Secrets*, a collection that includes magical charms, riddles, planting diagrams for "knot" gardens, and guides to mixing colors among many other items.[17]

Because Bollard and Geoffrey approach their subject as professional gardening "artists" whose interest is in the creative manipulation of nature, they offer advice about methods for "advanced" gardeners. They do provide some practical, basic instruction about gardening such as managing natural damage ("To distroye wormes in al manere trees"[18] is one heading in Geoffrey's book) and a little information about maximizing yield ("That the costard or quynche apple waxe grete" is another heading[19]), but their primary interest when they write about grafting is in creativity. Bollard refers to this as "meruellous graffyng," and the term accurately describes what the writer has in mind: "marvelous" grafting includes producing fruit without cores or stones, imparting the taste of one fruit on another and making sour fruit sweet, changing the color of the fruit produced, and growing unusual objects in the fruit (such as pearls in apples) or finding writing or pictures inside the stone of the fruit.

Grafting was meant to save time and increase the gardener's stock of plants, but for Bollard and Geoffrey it became, instead, a way to express ingenuity. For the marvelous grafter, gardening was an art form in which nature's materials might be transformed. The aim was to perform the astonishing. Nature, as their readers knew, only allotted one kind of fruit per tree. The grafting artist, on the other hand, sought to take nature's limited range and multiply his or her yields in terms of variety. For example, Bollard discusses trees that bear "diuers frutes of diuers colour and diuers sauour." Some of the directions he provides will, he states, make a cherry tree bear not just cherries but apples and, eventually, in "the second yere," red and white roses.[20] The instruction is false—cherries, apples, and roses cannot be grafted together successfully—but only because the examples chosen are not compatible. Cherries, apples, and roses would not work, but apples and pears can be grafted together, and a single tree might, in fact, produce different kinds and colors of fruit.

Bollard and Geoffrey's discussion of marvelous grafting reveals their express interest in complex operations that were inefficient and marginally productive. It would be apparent to any reader, for example, that making a "halfpeny" appear in a pear was not a way to save time or to maximize yield.[21] These writers' discussions about grafting reveal a fascinating aspect of horticultural practice in the period. Grafting, as an aspect of planting a garden, can be seen as a utilitarian practice, one in which the gardener manipulated nature, that was transformed by these writers into creative art. In the grafting treatises, an apparently straightforward technique for maximizing yield is reinvented as a means by which the gardener challenged nature's right to determine the nature of the gardener's art. For these writers, grafting plants as part of designing and planting a garden was a practice reserved for sophisticated horticultural artists.

RENEWAL AND NATURE: WALAHFRID STRABO'S HORTULUS

Like Bollard and Geoffrey's treatises, Walahfrid Strabo's ninth-century poem, referred to as the *Hortulus*, appears to be concerned with the utility of gardening.[22] The poem calls itself "liber de cultura hortorum," book on the cultivation of gardens, and it falls into two parts. The first seventy-five lines are explicitly about planting and caring for a garden. The remaining four hundred or so lines make up a descriptive catalogue of garden plants and their uses. The iris, for example, is used, according to Walahfrid, to freshen laundry; southernwood (artemisia abrotanum) relieves the pain of gout; melons are refreshing and easy to eat; betony has antiseptic qualities. Walahfrid's poem is clearly part of the medieval tradition of thinking about gardens in terms of use. Yet, although he writes about the utility of plants, especially their medical use, the poet conveys more than the sense that plants are needed to feed and heal people. In the *Hortulus*, garden plants *interact* with the people who grow and consume them, and planting a garden is about the joy, spiritual and emotional, the gardener experiences as he or she takes part in the process of nature's growth and renewal.

In the *Hortulus*, the gardener's aim is to take part in nature's fertility, a subject that Walahfrid adapts from Virgil's *Georgics*.[23] The *Hortulus* begins with references to Paestum and Priapus, allusions that appear just a few lines apart in Book IV of Virgil's highly influential poem, in order to emphasize the connection between human labor and nature's abundance. For Virgil, Paestum, a southern Italian town known for roses that bloomed twice a year, and Priapus, the god represented with an enormous erect penis whose statue was placed in gardens as a protective scarecrow, are linked together through their celebration of the fertility of the garden. They function as reminders that the poet has not had the chance to celebrate how "pinguis hortos quae cura colendi ornaret" (careful cultivation beautifies rich gardens).[24]

Although Virgil's narrator says he does not have time to write a song of praise, he describes an old man from Corycia, part of Asia Minor, who tended a poor, isolated piece of ground that, despite its lack of natural fertility, produced beautiful flowers and abundant fruits and vegetables. The old man planted carefully and tended to the needs of the land even during the brutal cold of winter. His success in gardening makes him feel, according to the poet, that his personal riches are equal to those of kings, "regum aequabat opes animis."[25] The poet concludes the celebratory passage with a catalogue of the old man's remarkably fruitful trees and suggests that other poets might consider writing to celebrate such gardening triumphs.

Walahfrid appears to have taken Virgil's recommendation to heart and used the earlier poet's aside as the basis for his own work. Walahfrid offers a meditation on the "riches" (*opes*)—the word appears in both Walahfrid's and Virgil's poems—of dedicating oneself to gardening. For Virgil, the gardener's triumph was measured largely in terms of yield: the old man's dedication pays off in terms of the quantity of vegetables produced and the early maturation of his apples and roses. Walahfrid, in contrast, takes up the subject of the gardener's dedication to explore the ways that such commitment is a guarantee, despite the variety of natural conditions, of nature's miraculous ability to renew itself. Planting and tending to a garden, for Walahfrid, is about taking part in the miracle of regeneration. For this reason, his discussion of the methods of planting sheds light both on practical aspects of gardening and on the meaning of planting in the period. In the *Hortulus*, planting a garden is about the ever-regenerating constitution of nature: plants renew themselves over and over again with the aid of the gardener.

The planting practices described by Walahfrid form part of the gardener's effort to understand the ways of nature, and the way to understand nature is, the poet argues, to understand oneself. The poem asserts the need to discipline the will first: the gardener must first resolve to work very hard before gardening success is assured. Natural conditions are various: soil can be sandy, barren, or moist; gardening sites can be on steep hillsides, on plains, or in valleys.[26] Yet, despite this variety, whatever sort of land one possesses, it will, the narrator asserts, support a garden as long as the gardener is neither lazy, "veterno," nor stupid, "stultis," about caring for the plants.[27] Walahfrid's poem lays great emphasis on the necessity of the gardener's dedication to his or her task, and the narrator discusses the labor required to make a garden succeed. The gardener must not hesitate to work outdoors or get dirty, or refuse to spread manure on the soil. Basing his authority on experience (*expertum*) along with information from books and general knowledge, the narrator tells the poem's readers that gardening is a struggle against the gardener's willful desires and, as he explains in the next passage, against the garden's natural enemies.[28]

Walahfrid's narrator imagines himself as Virgil's old Corycian. His little piece of ground, like the old man's, is less than ideal, and he emphasizes this point. Even though spring had restored the surrounding fields to their beauty, the narrator's own garden, as he tells the reader, was laden with weeds and unproductive. Covered with nettles, which the narrator describes as little spears tipped with poison, the garden seemed lost to nature's dark forces. It becomes the poem's narrator's mission to defeat the garden's natural enemies. He describes the process of digging up the nettles, which kept trying to come back, destroying the tunnels of another natural enemy, the moles, and building raised beds, whose soil he enriched with manure, to keep the rains from washing his garden away.[29]

It is at this point in the poem that the reader learns about methods for planting a garden. In contrast with modern accounts in which the science of gardening as it effects individual plants is emphasized, the poet's portrayal is imaginative and re-creative.[30] He represents the garden as an eternally renewing entity. Drawing on his immediate gardening experience, the narrator asserts that planting a garden is a process of reversing aging. Gardeners, he asserts, try to bring back the "youth" (*iuventae*) of plants whether they are grown from seed or from cuttings: "Seminibus quaedam tentamus holuscula, quaedam/ Stirpibus antiquis priscae revocare iuventae."[31] Transplants, similarly, are brought back to life. Taking plants that appeared almost dead and moving them to newly dug trenches, Walahfrid's narrator remarks that such actions make the garden green because the plants that were "lifeless" have come back to fruitful life.[32]

The narrator's methods for planting his garden are familiar to modern readers. He describes the act of transplanting—using divisions and cuttings— of grafting (although only in passing[33]), and of growing plants from seed. However, his planting differs from that of modern (and later medieval) gardeners in its eternal, self-contained nature. In Walahfrid's representation of the narrator's garden, plants seem to come from plants that are already growing at the monastery. This does not necessarily mean that monastic gardeners such as the poem's narrator did not purchase seed—we know that they did, and if Walahfrid is recording his own gardening experiences it seems likely that he did, too, given the diversity of plants in the garden—but, rather, that the poet is concerned with emphasizing renewal over acquisition.

This closed system excludes all others beside the gardener and his plants. So, for example, although the poem is dedicated to Walahfrid's teacher, Father Grimald, the relationship that is developed in detail in the poem is the one between the gardener and his plants. In this relationship, the plant, as the narrator explains in his description of gourds, is a guarantee of sorts for its gardener. Describing how his gourd grows (and he calls it his own— "mea . . . cucurbita"[34]), the narrator goes on to claim its seeds as pointing toward the future: the seeds promise another harvest as good as this one: "Quae tibi consimilen possunt promittere messem."[35]

These seeds of promise can be linked to the narrator's earlier discussion of hope for renewal and the planting of gardens. Earlier in the poem, after the narrator described how he had cleared his ground of weeds and planted seeds, he explains how he cared for his garden. He brought water to the raised beds in buckets and poured it gently over the plants. He did this with his own hands, drop by drop, "propriis infundere palmis/Guttatim,"[36] to keep the seed in its place in the garden bed. He describes his care to emphasize the optimism of gardening. The gardener's actions ensure that, despite the less than ideal conditions of his garden, including excess shade and lack of rain, what has been planted will succeed: his garden's sluggish, "pigro," soil is filled with, as he puts it, the hope, "spe," of growth, "crementi."[37]

This care of the seed is described in experiential terms: the narrator does not imagine a reader who would be unfamiliar with the act of planting a garden and spends little time describing technique except when it comes to elucidating the care and dedication that the gardener must show toward his or her plants. So, for example, when he describes sage, the first plant in his catalogue, he represents its nature and the ways it requires human intervention rather than detailing propagation methods, planting depth, or temperature for germination. Sage, the narrator asserts, is a plant divided against itself: its new growth needs to be cut away or it will choke the "parent" to death.[38] The gardener's work is to keep the sage eternally green, "Perpetuo viridi," so it can enjoy the perpetual youth, "iuventa," that it deserves. Similarly, the gardener's gourd is helped along by the gardener's placement of supports in the ground, which allow the vines to climb all the way to the top of the cloister.[39]

Walahfrid's narrator's role goes beyond simply tending to his plants. It is affection for his garden, love of each plant's traits and idiosyncrasies, that, most significantly, makes him part of the process of renewal. Describing the herb lovage, the narrator mentions that it is love, "amor,"[40] for his little garden, "parvi . . . horti,"[41] that compels him to promote this herb's fine qualities. Despite some seemingly negative qualities such as juice that can cause blindness, lovage, the narrator observes, should be praised for its use in blended cures. And even plants with few medicinal virtues, such as clary, which the narrator explains is rarely employed in cures, are honored: this herb's goodness lies in its strength as a plant that grows, branch and leaf, higher and higher, "ramosque comasque/Altius extollit,"[42] than others and its use in making a sweet-tasting drink. The poem suggests that one of the gardener's most important functions is to appreciate the plants for their best traits, no matter what those traits happen to be.

The lines of the poem associate the relationship between the gardener and plants, as described above, with that between savior and saved. The rose and the lily, the last two plants described, are identified with spiritual renewal. The narrator takes the rose, first, and remarks on the way the plant renews itself from year to year (a quality that is described in relation to many of the plants that precede the rose in the catalogue including catmint and tansy; tansy's name is taken from the Greek "athanasia," meaning "immortality," and the plant is also called "ambrosia," another word meaning "immortality"). He then goes on to associate the plant's renewal with spiritual regeneration. The rose and the lily, the narrator explains, are symbols of the Church. The rose signifies the blood of martyrs, of warfare, and of Jesus; the lily represents faith and peace. These two qualities, faith and peace, are, according to the poem, joined in the savior who is both rose and lily.[43]

The poem concludes with a dedication to the poet's teacher, Father Grimald, that links the planting of gardens, immortality, and education together. Jesus, in the lines above, *became* the lily and the rose that live in the poet's garden. The narrator makes this nearly literal when he chooses to assert that the rose takes its red color from Jesus's blood. Father Grimald, in contrast, cannot become a continuously renewing plant but must instead hope to achieve the eternity of nature through God's grace. Because he is not by nature "eternal," his pupil wishes that Father Grimald might win eternal life: "Te Deus aeterna faciat virtute virentem/Immarcescibilis palmam comprendere vitae."[44]

Although it may look as if this spiritual reward is finite (having a definite endpoint with Grimald's death), the poem treats it as part of the garden's regenerative and infinite qualities. The emphasis is on renewal and continuity: not only is the palm associated with his teacher "green forever," but Father Grimald himself also achieves a type of immortality through his relationship to his students. In the dedication, the poet imagines his teacher as sitting in his garden under fruit trees. Grimald's happy students, "ludentes pueri," surround him. They play in the garden, gathering apples. As Grimald imagines this scene, his former student, the poet, asks that his teacher accept the poem as a gift, looking on the poet's labors with favor, and, following the gardening metaphor, "pruning" its faults and enjoying its best qualities.

In the *Hortulus*, planting a garden has a practical component, but it is the spiritual engagement of the gardener with his plants that the poem underscores. For Walahfrid, nature becomes synonymous with the divine. Taking part in nature's eternity, by gardening and by teaching, offers the poet and his readers an opportunity to cooperate with forces that are larger than themselves.

PROPER CONDUCT AND NATURE'S RULES: LE MENAGIER DE PARIS'S GARDENING ADVICE

The Menagier de Paris's gardening treatise appears in a late fourteenth-century French household book written by the prosperous, presumably bourgeois author for his young wife. The book includes moral stories and devotional material as well as a number of treatises on subjects including cooking, hawking, horses, and gardening. The gardening treatise might, perhaps, be thought of as the most pragmatic section of the entire household book. It is organized by months of the year and under these groupings appears a rough "to do" list of gardening activities. In the treatise, there is little exposition, no moralizing, and no personal asides, features that occur throughout much of the rest of the book. The treatise's arrangement and inclusion of information is straightforwardly aimed at providing the young, inexperienced housewife with useful information about planting a garden.

However, despite the prosaic nature of the treatise, the Menagier's discussion reveals more about his sense of the importance of planting a garden than a simple acknowledgment that food and herbs were necessary for existence. Rather, the author's aim, as he tells his reader, is to teach his wife how to live an honorable life, and the practical advice that accompanies the spiritual and social commentary in the book is represented as integral to achieving this goal. In light of this purpose, it is possible to see the treatise on gardening as a conduct book in which nature's rules must be studied in order to lead an honorable life. Knowledge about gardening, like knowledge of the other practical arts, is valued in the book as a means by which one can accrue honor through disciplined action.

Janet Ferrier, the editor of the critical edition of the Menagier's book, remarks that the "advice [the author] gives is overwhelmingly concerned with the cultivation of fruit, vegetables, and herbs."[45] Ferrier goes on to refer to this as a "severely practical approach to horticulture" and observes that the author was concerned with "obtain[ing] the maximum return" from his plants.[46] Remarks about ensuring yield such as the advice to plant beans at various times from Christmas through early March "afin que se les unes sont gelees, que les autres ne le soient pas" (so if some of them freeze, the others will not) suggest that the Menagier was indeed concerned with making sure that the garden's productivity would be high regardless of, for instance, the variability of weather.[47]

However, at the same time, comments of this sort reveal more about the author's understanding of gardening than his concern with productivity. They demonstrate, beyond mere practicality, his keen sense of nature as following rules that the successful gardener must learn to accommodate. Beans cannot withstand freezing temperatures, but to get the highest yield possible over the greatest time period, the gardener needed to plant them before Paris was officially "frost free." Some years, the lucky gardener might be able to harvest beans in the early winter if temperatures stayed above freezing. The Menagier teaches his wife to think about gardening in terms of probability. Nature's course, the Menagier suggests, can be anticipated if not predicted, and the gardener who learns to do this will be more successful than the gardener who does not.

Both attention to timing and a sense of continuity over the years are introduced in the book as necessary components of an honorable life. The Menagier's book teaches his readers to think about time as allowing the completion of necessary duties. Time, in the treatise, is a quantity not to be wasted, and striking at the right time was necessary if the gardener wanted to work in concert with nature. This can be seen most clearly in the section concerned with the months that make up springtime. For the Menagier, spring was synonymous with opportunity, and the gardener needed to make the most of the fleeting period. The book conveys this sense of urgency by referring repeatedly to specific periods of time. For example, in February when "la gelee" comes to an end, "quinze jours aprez viennent les espinars" (fifteen days later spinach comes up).[48] Mention of spinach's swift appearance is followed by attention to the speed with which savory and sweet marjoram sprout in February: "et sont semees ou decours et ne sont que huit jours en terre" (and are sown at the waning of the moon and take just eight days to appear). Seeds come up quickly if planted at the right time. The gardener needs to be ready for these opportunities.

Along with the sense that the gardener must be ready to strike at the right moment on account of nature's course during a particular month, the author conveys the significance of applying this skill on a yearly basis. The Menagier signposts his advice about planting with religious holidays. Violets and gillyflowers (dianthus) are to be planted "a la saint Remy";[49] houseleeks (Sempervivum) are to be sown up through St. John's Day;[50] parsley that is planted "la veille de Nostre Dame en mars" (on the eve of the feast of Our Lady in March) comes up "a neuf jours."[51] The combination of number of days and annual religious holidays conveys a sense of time that is both finite and cyclical. The gardener must, each year, choose the right moment in which to plant. This cycle never ends, and the demands that it places on the gardener are strenuous.

The Menagier's sense of nature and its demands ranges from the large-scale model of seasons and months to the smaller scale requirements placed on the gardener by particular plants. Seeds seem to have struck the book's author as designed by nature to require special attention. He offers his wife some general principles concerning their functioning. For example, he distinguishes between planting shoots or transplants and seeds: "*Nota* que en temps pluieux fait bon planter, mais non mie semer; car la graine se retient au ratel" (Note: rainy weather is a good time for planting but not for sowing; this is because the seeds will stick on the rake).[52] Seeds, for the Menagier, are difficult on account of their constitution, and he offers this advice to readers unfamiliar with their physical properties.

The usefulness of this observation is matched by similar comments about planting individual types of seed. Lettuce seeds, for example, germinate quickly: "qu'elles n'arrestent point en terre et reviennent bien drues" (comes up rapidly and grows very thickly).[53] The general principle in this case is that seeds come up at different rates and with differing vigor. The gardener needs to know this and find ways to ensure productivity. As the Menagier explains, the way to do this for lettuce is to thin out the seedlings. For other seeds, various principles are important. His comments about cabbage seeds, for example, teach the reader about plant spacing. They, and other cole vegetables, are planted and then, when they have five leaves, the author explains, they should be dug up and replanted with a half foot between plants.[54] Those remarks about

"Roman" cabbage seed and round cabbage seed offer the reader constructive ideas about where seed for replanting can be found. For the round cabbage, the seeds grow out of a stalk from the top of the plant; for the Roman, they grow from the bottom.[55]

Like planting seeds, transplanting, dividing, and grafting were understood by the Menagier as practices in which the successful gardener exhibited her mastery of nature's rules. Transplanting of small seedlings took place throughout the gardening year. Although the Menagier does not refer to a nursery bed in which seedlings were raised before transplanting, he seems to have one in mind. Beets, for example, he explains, "quant elles sont levees de terre sont replantees par ordre" (when they have sprouted they are transplanted in rows).[56] The gardener needs to learn which plants need to be started in nursery beds and transplanted—beets, leeks, and various cabbages—and which were grown in situ—beans, lettuce, squash, spinach.

In other cases, plants are propagated through cuttings, division, and transplanting. Sweet marjoram, for example, can be sown and transplanted into a pot, but it can also be multiplied by taking cuttings: "les branches couppees fichees en terre et arrousees prennent racines et croissent" (branches cut from the plant, set in the ground, and watered take root and grow).[57] Marjoram is easy to care for, according to the Menagier, but some transplants and cuttings require more attention. Sorrel, for example, needs careful handling. To replant divisions, one must be sure not to disturb the roots too much: "il te convient replanter a toute sa terre qui est entour la rachine" (you need to replant it with all the soil that surrounds its roots).[58] The Menagier's description of the variety of demands placed on the gardener conveys the book's understanding of gardening as "proper conduct."

The housewife's gardening activities (or perhaps her supervision of gardening activities) extended beyond the planting of seeds and cuttings to grafting fruit trees and growing roses and rosemary. The Menagier includes, first, a short (and misinformed) discussion of grafting cherry and plum trees to vines, "grafting" a vine through a cherry tree, and grafting "various fruits" to an oak. Second, he concludes the gardening treatise with an explanation of how to preserve roses in winter and how to root rosemary and send it over long distances. Both the last section and the one on grafting are similar to the kinds of discussions found in books of secrets—one of the places where, as I discussed earlier, Bollard and Geoffrey's grafting treatises can be found. However, unlike those authors, the Menagier shows no interest in exposing secrets. His discussion of grafting techniques is as straightforward and didactic as his description of the proper way to plant beans. Rather than emphasizing the ingenious nature of these activities, the Menagier suggests that they are necessary accomplishments of the bourgeois housewife.

Planting a garden—growing fruits and vegetables successfully—was one aspect of proper conduct, but other gardening practices also formed part of this model. In particular, the author emphasizes the social significance of gardening. Gardening is "honorable" because, he suggests, it does more than provide food for one's family (as important as that was, of course). Proper gardening demonstrated one's affinity with the right kinds of people and practices. "Good" people, as far as the author was concerned, were gardeners.

This can be seen in the Menagier's encouragement of gardening activities that might, at first glance, seem to be frivolous or lacking in utility. For example, he encourages his young wife to grow flowers: "Et saichiez que je n'en pren pas desplaisir, mais plaisir, en ce que vous avrez a labourer rosiers, a garder violectes, faire chappeaulx, et aussi en vostre dancer et en vostre chanter" (Know that I take delight rather than displeasure in your cultivating rose bushes, caring for violets, and making chaplets, and also in your dancing and singing).[59] These activities are appropriate for her, he says, so long as she engages in them in the company of her social peers. They become markers of social status and demonstrate her association with things that are good, beautiful, and joyful. For the Menagier, planting a garden was clearly useful, but, like the authors of the grafting treatises and the poet Walahfrid Strabo, utility was not synonymous with productivity. Rather, the Menagier's gardening treatise demonstrates that gardening was useful because it was an aspect of proper conduct. Gardening, for the Menagier's wife, is recommended because it demonstrated important aspects of character and behavior. This is not to say that the family was unconcerned with growing produce to eat or providing medicinal herbs but, rather, to emphasize the ways in which gardening was inextricably bound up with ideas about conduct and social behavior in the later Middle Ages.

CONCLUSION

When modern scholars identify medieval gardening as simply utilitarian, they miss important information about life in the Middle Ages. The sense that medieval gardening was "only" useful has become a firmly entrenched view because, at least in some ways, it makes the Middle Ages a more manageable period for us to think about. Scholars concerned with garden history are, generally, interested in landscape and aesthetics. Writing about gardens in the

Renaissance, especially, tends to consider classical precedents for aesthetic decisions made by gardeners and designers. We think, in contrast, that medieval gardens and garden writers were merely concerned with productivity. What is especially interesting about this is the way that it tends to flatten out what, it turns out, was a vibrant, multidimensional concern of many medieval people.

It is no coincidence that modern scholars tend to write about medieval *gardens* rather than medieval *gardening*, and this is tied to our understanding of our sense that these gardens were useful. However, as we can see from the examples discussed in this essay, medieval gardeners thought about the usefulness of their endeavor in many ways. The utility of planting a garden in the Middle Ages was not limited to alimentary needs. Medieval gardeners thought of their efforts as creative, religious, and social, and the relationship between humans and plants in the period was dynamic. For people in the Middle Ages, planting a garden was a way of transforming their material and spiritual lives.

CHAPTER FOUR

Use and Reception

LAURA L. HOWES

As John Harvey noted, medieval gardens "could serve an aesthetic as well as a material purpose . . . The various motives involved were not mutually exclusive, but complementary."[1] Sylvia Landsberg elaborates: in the kitchen garden, where "many of the annual flowers such as borage, marigold, heartsease, langdebeef and poppy would have self-seeded endlessly, . . . the overall appearance of a mainly utilitarian garden in midsummer would have been one of surprising visual brightness, with a concentration of aromatic scents if a bunch were picked."[2] It is noticeable here that Landsberg avoids the anachronistic word "aesthetic"; nonetheless, she joins Harvey and others in emphasizing that the multiple uses of medieval gardens extend well beyond the production of plants for medicinal and food purposes. Gardeners' experiences throughout the ages confirm that pleasure derives from the cultivation of all sorts of plants, vines, shrubs, and trees. Gardens designed primarily for pleasure may prolong that pleasure over a longer period of time, but all cultivated space is potentially pleasurable, as well as productive, space.

Nonetheless, this chapter begins by focusing on gardens whose identifying function is production. With no medieval gardens surviving in anything like their original condition, historians are reliant to a significant degree on representations in visual art and literature (the subject of two other chapters in this volume). But such representations are addressed to highly selective audiences and contribute to the aspirational, imaginative life of their cultures.

The aspects of garden culture that get into such representations are limited. In particular, productive gardens tend to get short shrift, even though other kinds of evidence make it clear that these too could serve as the source not just of food and medicinal herbs but also of experiences of pleasure, comfort, social interaction, physical and mental recreation, and spiritual awakening.

Indeed, beyond the necessary production of food, medieval gardens served a variety of other functions during the European Middle Ages. The medieval garden in Northwest Europe drew on a variety of traditions, and horticulture was itself a medium of cultural transmission. Late Roman practice exerted clear influence; in particular, the cultivation of grapes and of medicinal plants in monastic communities carried classical horticultural knowledge to all corners of medieval Europe, as—less pervasively—did the garden cultures of the eastern Mediterranean and the Iberian Peninsula. These were supplemented by the cultural innovations of the twelfth century and the emergence in the twelfth century of elaborate pleasure gardens meant to telegraph their owner's wealth and exclusivity.

We find written evidence of a medieval horticultural sensibility as early as the ninth century. Walahfrid Strabo, Abbot of Reichenau (c. 808–849), in a series of twenty-seven short poems, *De cultura hortorum* (later retitled *Hortulus*), blended a botanist's observations with a clear sense of enjoyment. Describing in Latin hexameter twenty-three separate plants grown in his own garden, and mentioning a handful of other garden plants in the process, Walahfrid exhorts the reader to admire his plants, as though he were taking the reader on a tour of his garden:

> Nec minus abrotani pomptum est mirarier altae
> Pubentis frutices, et quas inspicat aristas
> Ramorum ubertas, tenues imitata capillos.[3]

> (Admire too the tall bushes of southernwood
> With their bloom of down, and the sharp spikes
> Which grow on its wealth of branches like finest hair.)[4]

Descriptions of plants using metaphorical language join advice on the care and cultivation of the plants. One must cut the new growth of sage back, or it will overtake the old stems,[5] and one should provide support for growing gourds[6] but let melons lie on dry ground.[7] Still, his appreciation for the flowers and

myriad shapes of his plants emerges in poetic metaphors as well as in straightforward descriptions of color, scent, and leaf patterns. Of the lily, he writes:

> Quorum candor habet nivei simulacra nitoris,
> Dulcis odor silvas imitatur flore Sabaeas.
> Non Parius candore lapis, non nardus odore
> Lilia nostra permit.[8]

> (Its white is the white of glistening snow,
> Its scent the scent of sweetest frankincense.
> Not Parisian marble in whiteness, not spikenard in fragrance
> Surpass our lily.)

Indeed, the art of describing a garden parallels and deepens an appreciation
of the art of the garden itself throughout the Middle Ages. Rhetorical treatises provide examples of verse forms and figures using the natural world—not
only gardens but also woodlands, such as the classical topos of a catalogue of
trees. To an educated viewer, a garden may also have recalled numerous poetic
passages.[9] In addition, as Oliver Creighton argues, "It was inherent . . . for
medieval people to disaggregate 'natural' surroundings and see flora and fauna
as symbols for higher things—in short, to transform the countryside into allegory."[10] But even where evidence for allegorical reading is scant, the potential
for multivalent meanings may be adduced in the simplest poetic descriptions
of gardens. Walahfrid dedicated his work to his mentor, Grimald, Abbot of
St. Gall, who, he says, also enjoyed a garden:

> Ut—cum consepto viridis consederis horti,
> Subter opacatas frondenti vertice malos,
> Persicus imparibus crines ubi dividit umbris,
> Dum tibi cana legunt tenera lanugine poma
> Ludentes pueri, schola laetabunda tuorum,
> At que volis ingentia mala capacibus indent,
> Grandia conantes includere corpora palmis.[11]

> (I can picture you
> Sitting there in the green enclosure of your garden
> Under apples which hang in the shade of lofty foliage,
> Where the peach-tree turns its leaves this way and that
> In and out of the sun, and the boys at play,

Your happy band of pupils, gather for you
Fruits white with tender down and stretch
Their hands to grasp the huge apples.)[12]

The orchard-garden alluded to here clearly serves many uses: it is a place of
repose for an adult, a space for childhood play, a productive component in
providing the monastery with its food, and a metaphor for the fruits of study
that the abbot cultivates in his students.

Several of the garden uses mentioned by Walahfrid—food production, the
growth of medicinal plants, a place for recreation and enjoyment—feature in
an early medieval plan of an ideal monastery and its grounds, produced at
Reichenau between 819 and 826.[13] The often-reproduced St. Gall Monastery
Plan, preserved in the monastic library of St. Gall (Switzerland), shows an
array of outdoor spaces, each with a specific use. While scholars remain uncer-
tain about the original purpose of this elaborate plan, which was designed for
the Carolingian Abbot Gozbert, but which, if built, could not have fitted into
the terrain at St. Gall, the plan identifies several different gardens, as well as the
ideal relationship among monastic structures and their grounds.[14] This plan,
with its rational organization of space, represents the various uses of early
medieval gardens in Europe and points to the development of similar gardens
in later periods.

Monastic communities have particular characteristics, and their garden
cultures are equally specific: monasteries tend to be isolated, with a particular inward concentration on the life of a religious community. Nonetheless,
the detail, elaboration, and encyclopedic qualities of the St. Gall plan make
it one of the key sources in interpreting the uses of medieval gardens in the
West. Using the St. Gall plan to organize this essay, we will consider first the
medicinal herb garden, the vegetable garden, and vineyards before moving
on to discussions of cloisters, entrances, the orchard, and the cemetery. The
chapter will then briefly consider gardens of the period from outside the
boundaries of Western Christendom. Finally, the pleasure garden, developed
later in the period with probable influence from the East, will occupy the last
section.

PRODUCTION OF FOOD AND MEDICINE

The medicinal herb garden (*herbularius*), located in the northeast corner of the
St. Gall Monastery Plan, adjoins the physician's quarters and sits just outside

the cloister for monks who are ill. The inscriptions on this garden plan list several plants still known for their medical properties, such as sage, cumin, pennyroyal, mint, and rosemary—along with others whose aesthetic properties distinguish them today, such as iris, lily, and rose, but which were also essential to the medieval physician.[15] The cultivation of plants with specific uses in treating patients—many of these plants being exotic non-natives—demonstrates the extent to which domesticated plants spread throughout Western Europe by human activity, with seeds and rootstock passing from hand to hand as valuable assets.[16]

The St. Gall *herbularius* is drawn as a set of eight symmetrical beds, themselves bordered by eight additional beds arranged along the inside of the garden's protective walls, with one entrance. Each bed is labeled with the name of a single plant, which corresponds to Walahfrid's description of his practice. After clearing his winter garden of nettles, and digging the ground so that worms emerged into the spring sun, Walahfrid tells us he constructed a series of raised beds:

Inde Noti coquitur flabris colisque calore
Areola et lignis, ne diffluat, obsita quadris
Altius a plano modicum resupina levatur.
Tota minutatim rastris contunditur uncis,
Et pinguis fermenta fimi super insinuantur.
Seminibus quaedam tentamus holuscula, quaedam
Stirpibus antiquis priscae revocare iuventae.[17]

(Then my small patch was warmed by winds from the south
And the sun's heat. That it should not be washed away,
We faced it with planks and raised it in oblong beds
A little above the level ground. With a rake
I broke the soil up, bit by bit, and then
Worked in from on top the leaven of rich manure.
Some plants we grow from seed, some from old stocks
We try to bring back to the youth they knew before.)[18]

In the herb garden, many plants useful for their medicinal qualities could be cultivated and more easily obtained than by collecting specimens in the open landscape, although collection in the wild continued to be necessary for certain plants that resisted domestication. Several pharmacological plants had analgesic properties and, in sufficient quantity, were poisonous. Keeping them sequestered in an enclosed garden kept them safe from grazing animals.[19]

The monastic practice of using herbal concoctions to treat ailments, represented on the St. Gall plan by the *herbarium*, probably dates from the Carolingian revival. Before this period, suspicion attended the use of herbs to treat disease, according to Paul Meyvaert,[20] and no early monastic rules mention the physic garden specifically. All mention vegetable gardens, however, and Meyvaert notes that "since medieval monasteries survived good times and bad, famine and plague, we can conclude that monastic gardeners must have been successful, on the whole, in their efforts to provide enough food to sustain life, even for large communities with many mouths to feed."[21]

Also along the eastern edge of the St. Gall plan, a vegetable garden (*hortus*), laid out next to the gardener's quarters and the houses for raising and keeping fowl, depicts a space larger than the *herbularium* (52.5 feet by 82.5 feet) also enclosed, and neatly divided into eighteen symmetrical beds, possibly also raised. The plant list for this garden, not surprisingly, lists primarily brassicas, root vegetables, lettuces, and the cooking herbs parsley, coriander, chervil, dill, and poppy.[22] Pottage, the daily vegetable stew that fed most people most of the time in Western Europe from the classical period onward, would have been cooked using these basic ingredients.

Indeed, the vegetable gardens of the European Middle Ages closely resembled those of classical Rome. As Linda Voigts notes,

> The cultivated garden plants of Rome became the cultivated garden plants of Europe, at least until 1560; and as recently as the nineteenth century an analysis of German peasant gardens concluded that the plants contained therein were of Greek or Latin origin, plants mentioned in Dioscorides, Pliny, and other antique writers.[23]

The typical home garden would include brassicas (colewort, similar to modern kale, and cabbage), root vegetables (garlic, leeks, onions, turnips, parsnips), and gourds.[24] Beans and peas were dried for storage, most commonly from field crops, but could also be eaten fresh from the garden in season. Salad vegetables included cress and lettuce, along with beet greens, celery, cucumbers, radishes, and herbs.[25]

Herbs contributed vitally both as seasonings and for their restorative qualities, and in the majority of gardens they would not have been grown separately from the vegetables. The fact that, at St. Gall, certain herbs were grown in a special *herbularius*, apart from the *hortus*, suggests the specialized quality of medical knowledge that developed within the monastic community. Herbs in widespread cultivation from Roman times onward include agrimony, bay, betony, catmint, chervil, coriander, dill, fennel, mint, mustard, parsley, pennyroyal, poppy, rue, sage, savory, and thyme. Fruit commonly grown included apples, sweet cherries, grapes, medlars, mulberries, peaches, pears, plums, and quince; for cultivated nuts, one could find chestnuts, hazelnuts, and walnuts.[26] One Henry Daniel, an English plantsman of the fourteenth century, describes in his herbal the following plants along with their uses:

> Borage, Mallows, three sorts of Orach [a salad green] and the root of Turnip were good for pottage; Chervil was used in pottages or meats; Chestnuts were "good meat roasted"; Colewort was "noble to meat"; Parsnip provided "wholesome food; the roots are good both baked and fried"; and there was no seed so good as that of the Vetch for . . . digestion ("so mykel helpeth me in mete . . . coct it meketh graue" [gravy] . . .); Chives "we eat . . . as cress or porret."[27]

Specialized knowledge of plants included their optimum uses in both culinary and medicinal concoctions.

We should also note that the neat garden beds depicted at St. Gall describe an ideal use of space. In practice, plants filled many other parts of a monastic compound. According to Meyvaert, "The account book of Beaulieu Abbey in Hampshire . . . makes it clear that all the intervening ground between the workshops was fully utilized . . . The monastic scene was therefore probably much less tidy and neat than the St. Gall plan might lead us to believe."[28] Landsberg surmises that the vegetable garden drawn on the St. Gall plan might have been a garden of seedlings, to be transplanted into larger plots outside the monastic walls.[29]

The St. Gall plan does not mark any space as a vineyard, but as with the majority of fruits, grains, and vegetables grown for a monastic community, grapes would most likely have been grown in fields outside of the enclosed space. The cultivation of grapes held an important place in Carolingian monastic and secular life. Charlemagne himself imported vine stocks from several different regions.[30] Grapes were grown in England by the time of Alfred the Great (c. 871–899)[31] and generally across Western Europe during the warm period which lasted about a century (1150–1300). William of Malmesbury describes how the countryside near Gloucester was "planted more thickly with vineyards than any other region in England, its fertility producing grapes which cropped more plentifully and were more pleasant in flavour, 'yielding nothing to the French in sweetness.' "[32]

But the so-called "Little Ice Age" that followed this warm period made cultivation of grapes for wine all but impossible in the northern latitudes.[33] Still, grapevines continued to be cultivated, even where they did not fruit. Ornamental grapevines at Michelmarsh, in Hampshire, are recorded in the early fourteenth century, and, as late as 1469 vineyards at Ely were still kept up, "though little wine had been produced over the previous 150 years."[34] At other locations, fruiting and nonfruiting varieties were maintained. In 1398, a plant inventory for the lavish garden of the French King Charles VI at Hôtel St. Pol lists 375 "gouais de morets," probably vines to be used to train over the tunnel arbors there.[35] The pragmatic and less material concerns of gardeners often overlapped; some plants that were prized as food or medicine later became cultivated for their pleasing appearances and scents. The grape vine, the lily, the rose, and the iris all followed this pattern.

LEISURE USES

In addition to the medicinal and vegetable gardens, three enclosed cloisters grace the idealized plan of the St. Gall monastery. The largest, 100 feet square, is built on the south side of the church and bordered by the Warming Room, Refectory, and the Cellar and Larder. The plan shows a square area divided by paths into quadrants, with a pool or other round object at its center, itself also enclosed in a square patio or garden. The smaller cloister for those who are sick is drawn on the St. Gall plan on the north side of the small chapel, not far from the physician's quarters and medicinal herb garden, and surrounded by rooms for the critically ill, for sleeping, and for storing materials. As with the larger cloister, a round pool or other object sits in the middle and four doors are drawn leading from the arcade into the cloister, but here no paths are depicted. The Cloister for the Novitiates occupies the same area on the south side of the small chapel, and, like its counterpart on the north side, it comprises about forty square feet.

For years, scholars believed that such spaces hosted a variety of plants in the Middle Ages, as they came to do in later periods. But archeological research has demonstrated that such spaces were typically turf lawns, divided by paths, and, as at St. Gall, focused on a central feature.[36] One may surmise that this form of cloister garth, intended as it was to be a meditative space, required less work to maintain, with the benefit that the garden laborers

created less disturbance. The plainness of a turf lawn would not disguise
the pattern of intersecting paths at right angles, perhaps symbolically representing the cross, and it would yield a more consistent view throughout the
year than an herb or flower garden, which is constantly changing its appearance with buds, blooms, and new stalks, followed by dead flowers and fallen
leaves.

We may also assume that enclosed spaces such as these were designed to
protect people within from extreme weather and the interference of outsiders.
But it is also worth noting that the privacy one gains from a walled garden or
cloister, with or without covered arcades, differs significantly from that of an
interior room. An outdoor room allows small meetings and solitary endeavors
to go on under the collective gaze of the larger community, all the while rein-
forcing that community and its collective endeavors. In this the cloister serves
a crucial function in monastic life. As Thomas Dale explains, "All physical
movement within the monastery is organized around [the cloister]." And while
its primary use was for

> quiet reading, it was also used by the *pueri* . . . who read aloud, and at
> other times of the day it served liturgical processions and more mun-
> dane tasks such as washing. It regularly functioned as a point of tran-
> sition between the life of prayer in the oratory and the more routine
> actions of eating, sleeping, and administration organized around its
> perimeter.[37]

Continuing with the St. Gall plan, we may note that the area just outside
the main church's entrance, the "West Paradise," and the long path leading
up to it may not have been planted as a self-conscious garden space, but their
relation to the church structure and their clear function as a well-conceived
entryway merit attention. The notation on the plan records two spaces with a
"parklike" nature (the etymological meaning of *paradisum*) and their importance to an individual's overall experience of the church itself. The first two
lines relate to the 200-foot pathway leading from the western edge of the compound up to the covered porch. The rest describe the West Paradise, enclosed
by walls but open to the sky:

> Here are provided the plans for a parklike space without a roof / From
> east to the west 200 feet / Here a roof extends supported by a wall and
> by columns / Between these columns count ten feet / Here stretches a

parklike space without a roof / This is the road of access to the church
in which all folk may worship and from which they may leave rejoicing /
Here all the arriving crowd will find their entry.[38]

A liminal space between the approach to the church and the church's interior, the West Paradise is both inside high masonry walls and outside—that is,
open to the sky above. A transitional space, prefatory to entry into the church
proper, the Porch and Paradise together heighten an entrant's awareness of the
church's sacred, interior spaces. Entrance from the west would entail passage
through three separate doorways, each one progressively closer to the altar
inside, creating in effect a series of boundaries to be passed through—the outer
Porch wall, the inner Porch wall, which leads to the Paradise, and finally the
door from the Paradise to the church's interior. Side entrances from north and
south lead directly into the walled paradise, but would still lead the pedestrian
through two separate doorways before his or her arrival inside the church. In
addition, the West Paradise at St. Gall connected not only to the main church,
but to two towers, estimated to be about 130 feet tall, one on each side of the
Paradise, which contained spiral staircases to elevated altars and observation
rooms:

> Ascent by a spiral staircase *to survey the entire orbit from above* / In the
> summit an altar dedicated to Saint Michael / Another of the same kind /
> At the top altar of the archangel Gabriel[39] (emphasis added).

These towers may be of special interest to garden historians, as they suggest, by the ninth century, the desirability of an elevated observation spot,
akin to the mirador (elevated window) in contemporary Islamic gardens.
And while towers were not an unusual feature of medieval structures, the
emphasis on their usefulness as viewing points over a planned landscape
(here both structures and gardens) is noteworthy. Later on, in the thirteenth
century, several gardens made by the English King Henry III were made to
stand under bedroom windows which, Harvey notes, "raises the question
of an early origin for ornamental plans giving rise to the later 'knot' of the
fifteenth and sixteenth centuries."[40] Archaeological research in England over
the last fifteen years has found several late medieval examples of elevated
observation hills.[41]

Finally, on the St. Gall plan, we find an orchard that serves also as a cemetery. Between the vegetable garden and the Cloister of the Novitiate, this
space performs triple duty as food source, as burial ground, and as a pleasing

outdoor space that may well be intended for private retreat and reflection, as is the orchard in Walahfrid Strabo's poem. As in other areas of the plan, symmetry prevails on the page, with a large central cross surrounded on four sides by fruit-bearing trees and grave sites. Notation on the plan lists "apple and pear / plum / service tree / mistletoe / laurel / chestnut / fig / quince / peach / hazelnut / [almond] / mulberry / walnut."[42] Such a variety of trees suggests that absolute visual symmetry is not paramount, as the trees would grow to varying heights and with varying crown sizes, and their progressive flowering in spring would change the orchard's appearance dramatically from week to week. Indeed, food production—over a relatively lengthy growing season— seems to dictate the variety of trees for cultivation on the plan, if not also a simple desire for an encyclopedic list. Locating the monks' cemetery among these trees, however, suggests a range of coexistent purposes and a clear meta- phorical resonance to the space. The inscription regarding the monastic plots reads:

> Inter ligna soli haec semper sanctissima crux est / in qua perpetuae . Poma salutis olent / Hanc circum laceant defuncta cadauera fratrum / Qua radiante iterm . Regna poli accipiant.
>
> (Among the trees always the most sacred of the soil is the cross / On which the fruits of eternal health are fragrant. / Around let lie the dead bodies of the brothers / And through its radiance they may attain the realm of heaven.)[43]

The radiance encountered here—the orchard in bloom, we might surmise, as well as the spiritual radiance of the cross—offers the monks a means to heaven. The cross, itself figured as the most sacred tree in the orchard, becomes here a part of the orchard that bears its own fruit, that of eternal salvation. This inscription promotes reflective, metaphorical thought in a space that is both cemetery and orchard. According to the plan, this is also the largest outdoor space of the entire compound, approximately 80 feet by 125 feet.

Orchards were widespread in medieval Europe. Fruit for eating and for making cider was grown on castle grounds, in monastic landscapes, and on many smaller outparcels. Larger orchards seem to have developed in tan- dem with pleasure gardens in the West, as early descriptions of orchards frequently mention their benefits to the spirit. Of the orchard established at the Cistercian abbey at Clairvaux, a description of the early twelfth century reads:

Within the precinct there is a wide level area containing an orchard of many different fruit-trees, like a little wood. Close by the infirmary, it is a great solace to the monks, a spacious promenade for those wishing to walk and a pleasing spot for those preferring to rest.[44]

In general, orchards appear to have been established adjacent to another garden feature or building: near the infirmary, as noted at Clairvaux; next to a smaller garden, from which one could walk into the orchard; or beside a particularly lovely building, as with the stone hall built by the mid-twelfth-century bishop Guillaume de Passavant at Le Mans in northern France:

Next the chapel [the bishop] laid out a hall, whose whole design and particularly that of its windows, was of such beauty . . . that there the architect might be thought to have outdone himself. Lower down . . . he had a garden planted with many sorts of trees for grafting foreign fruits, equally lovely; for those leaning out of the hall windows to admire the beauty of the trees, and others in the garden looking at the fair show of the windows, could both delight in what they saw.[45]

The most elaborate examples of orchards combined utilitarian function with ornamental features to a very high degree. Llanthony Priory ran the largest recorded English orchard in the period, at twelve acres, which Sylvia Landsberg estimates would have had between 400 and 1,000 trees.[46] Apples were the most important crop for most monasteries, but pears, cherries, hazelnuts, walnuts, and almonds were also grown, and in some cases the nuts were exported as a cash crop.[47] One hundred pear trees were planted in Henry III's royal garden, Rosamund's Bower, in 1268, and 139 apple trees were planted at Cuxham in Oxfordshire between 1298 and 1303. In these last two, personal preference appears to have dictated orchards of a single fruit, although we should not imagine an orchard monoculture, since at least sixteen varieties of pears and apples were available by the thirteenth century.[48]

In contrast to this practice of growing fruit trees in protected orchards, Hispano-Arab gardens followed more closely Arabic practice in which fruit trees would be integrated into an overall garden scheme, which "would be decorative in the center but . . . increasingly functional toward the periphery."[49] In the fourteenth century, Ibn Luyun prescribes that fruit trees be planted on the periphery of a garden and then inter-planted with grape vines and fig trees:

> And amongst the fruit-trees include the [common] grape-vine similar to a
> slim woman, or wood-producing trees . . . In the background let there be
> trees like the fig or any other which does no harm.[50]

The fruit-bearing trees and vines mentioned in several medieval texts, then, emphasize the restorative quality of time spent in the orchard, as well as its visual appeal. The well-managed orchard woodland could serve as a setting for tantalizing glimpses of irregularly shaped woody grapevines, as in Ibn Luyun's description, or of exotic animals brought in to roam freely within the orchard enclosure, many with their own symbolic meanings.[51]

Later evidence for Christian burial practice in orchards is difficult to come by. In contrast, the practice of garden burial in Muslim Spain, India, and Persia is well attested. According to James Dickie, the Arabic word *rauda* can mean both garden and mausoleum, and, further, "the custom of interment in a garden rests on an implied reciprocity between heaven and earth, a reciprocity whereby natural reality is plastically transformed into its supernatural counterpart."[52] The paradise of the earthly garden foreshadows the heavenly paradise of the afterlife for those alive, and for the dead provides a restful spot in which to spend eternity. "May rainclouds water his grave and revive it, and may the moist garden carry to him its fresh perfume" reads the epitaph of the Sultan Yusuf III.[53] A pleasure garden in Cordoba, known as Hair al-Zajjali, came to include the burial spot of the medieval poet Ibn Shuhaid (c. 1035) and his friend Abu Marwan al-Zajjali, the garden's owner in life,[54] so that the two friends' bodies might spend eternity together. It is worth reminding ourselves that the automatic association of the Islamic garden with the Koranic paradise has been forcefully challenged in recent scholarship, but when gardens included burial sites, the spiritual and religious meanings of the garden were clearly invoked.

ISLAMIC GARDEN DESIGN

In his 1981 study, *Mediaeval Gardens*, John Harvey asserted, "It was only in the Iberian kingdoms that, before the Renaissance, purely ornamental gardens were acknowledged as an end in themselves, even though this aim was implicit" in some of the written works of Latin Christian authors.[55] The notion that sybaritic pleasure reaches the European north via the Mediterranean and the (exotic) East certainly has a long pedigree. And it is worth noting that advances in plant cultivation, and the introduction of new plants from India and other eastern areas, did increase dramatically during the period of Arab expansion. Caliphs of Spain imported rare seeds and plants from as far away as India, and the history of botanic gardens begins in the Iberian peninsula, particularly at Toledo and Seville.[56] One of the most significant master gardeners, Ibn Bassal, "travelled widely and collected plants in Sicily, Egypt, at Mecca, in Khorasan in north-eastern Persia, as well as in various parts of Spain."[57] His *Book of Agriculture* (c. 1080) contains a great deal of information on soils, cultivation, water, planting, and grafting. That he pays special attention to several kinds of flowers indicates to Harvey that, by the late eleventh century, ornamental gardening in Muslim Spain was well established.[58]

But more recent research suggests that the line between utility and pleasure cannot be so easily fixed. Not only can primarily utilitarian gardens give pleasure to their inhabitants beyond that of food production—pleasures of scent, touch, and the visual—but gardens devoted to aristocratic pleasure and leisure may also bear actual fruit. Pleasure of taste can easily join the pleasures of sight, smell, touch, and of kinetic experience in a garden setting. In addition, an aristocratic sense of power over the landscape, a landscape that produces sufficient food for the assembled court and its servants, may well be represented by a garden that produces food *and* ornamental beauty concurrently.

The garden in Islam has long been considered "a reflection or rather an anticipation of Paradise," with the Arabic word "*firdaus* stand[ing] for both garden and Paradise."[59] But Islamic garden design arose in response to climate and other practical matters, according to Fairchild Ruggles. Islamic garden traditions emerged in arid regions, with irrigation and water control central to the horticultural enterprise. Thus, when comparing northern European gardens of the period to those of the Mediterranean region, one can readily discern the extent to which geography constitutes cultural difference and climate produces distinct cultural practices. Ruggles in particular foregrounds such considerations, arguing that religious and metaphorical meanings for gardens were superimposed on them later.[60] Thus, the quadripartite garden, the *charbagh* and its variations, with axial pathways that intersect in the garden's center, is the primary model in Islamic gardens because it successfully distributes water equally to all parts of the garden.[61]

In the *charbagh*, water was distributed by constructing raised walkways alongside water channels, both of which would border sunken beds. Bushes, flowers, and even trees in certain situations would be planted several inches or feet below a pedestrian's level. The water, contained in stone sluices running alongside the sunken beds, could then be opened at various intervals to flood the plants within a square or rectangular bed for a period of time. The flow of water to this bed could then be stopped and diverted to another such bed, as needed. This type of garden, a kind of inverse of the Northern European raised-bed garden described by Walahfrid and depicted in the St. Gall plan, answers the challenges of its originary places perfectly. As a response to the specific obstacles of growing plants in an arid climate, the Islamic garden focuses on water. Fountains, stonework that makes water ripple across it in interesting patterns, wells, reflecting pools, and bathhouses all highlight the crucial role of water in Islamic gardens from the earliest periods.

Some of the most ingenious uses of water occurred in al-Andalus, and this may account for the extraordinary developments there in garden design. Between 756 and 1031, Cordoba, the capital city, was ruled by Umayyad princes, and this political center was surrounded by farm estates, which both enriched the state and served ornamental and leisure functions.[62] Noteworthy examples include Madinat al-Zahra', begun in 936 by 'Abd al-Rahman III. Built on terraces at the base of a mountain, and using water piped from the mountain aquifer, Madinat al-Zahra' had at least three gardens:

(1) the small garden (or "Prince's Garden") on the uppermost terrace that was reserved for elite inhabitants of the palace, (2) a large quadripartite garden on the lowest terrace that has only partially been revealed through excavation, and east of this (3) a garden of equal dimensions and similar layout on the middle terrace, extending in front of the reception hall known as the Salon Rico. In the center of the Salon Rico's garden stood a pavilion surrounded by small rectangular pools of water. The deeply sunken garden quadrants were irrigated by channels that ran alongside the pavements marking the four-part plan.[63]

In addition, the Great Mosque of Cordoba had an unpaved courtyard from the eighth through the eleventh centuries, which was probably planted with palm and citrus trees spaced a regular intervals.[64] Later examples in southern Spain include Alhambra at Granada and the Generalife Palace, also outside of Granada, on a hill opposite Alhambra. The Court of Lions at Alhambra, built by Muhammad V in 1370–1390 consisted of a courtyard (28.5 by 15.7 m) with a chahar bagh of sunken quadrants . . . originally planted with orange trees . . . about 80 centimeters below the pavement surface so that from a seated position, a person's view would skim the tops of the garden's flowers. In the middle of the garden, water gushed forth from a jet in a basin borne on the backs of twelve stone lions, which also spewed water into a channel that encircled the fountain.[65]

At Velez Benaudalla, between Granda and Motril, the garden's central watercourse bends and changes levels, accommodating itself to the hilly terrain. These changes in elevation allowed for several fountains, as the water was driven by the force of gravity to squirt out in artful ways.[66] Most of these elaborately structured gardens continued in cultivation after the Reconquista, and in the same fashion. As Ruggles notes, "Mudéjar was not so much an imitation of Islamic style and techniques as it was a continuation of it, for although the patrons were Christian, the artisans were largely Muslims employed for their skill in stucco, glazed ceramics, and woodworking."[67]

The extensive use of water and of hydraulic pressure in al-Andalus and in other arid cultures led to the development not only of elaborate fountains that spouted streams of water, but also to the use of water pressure to run mechanical garden features. Mechanical birds made to whistle when air was forced through internal pipes, and animals with moving parts propelled by water moving over or through them, joined waterwheels and irrigation systems in al-Andalus. One of the earliest Arabic manuals on mechanical devices dates from the ninth century—*Kitab al-hiyal*—and the best-known treatise, al-Jaziri's *Book of Ingenious Mechanical Devices*, from the early thirteenth century, exists today in at least eleven copies, testifying to its popularity.[68]

The overall effect of a late medieval Islamic garden would thus include several features: the centrality of the watercourse; fountains and other water displays; moving mechanical devices to induce surprise and delight, particularly in guests to the garden; and carpet-like flower beds, aligned with the viewing surface. Ruggles identifies "a geometrical aesthetic that asks viewers to read visual forms as a series of interconnected flat surfaces, rather than as volumetric spaces." She continues:

> To a viewer seated on cushions on the ground, looking at a low angle toward the garden, each [garden] bed might appear as a horizontal surface

of evenly interspersed flowers, not unlike a carpet laid on a floor or the surface of still water in a large basin.[69]

Such visual pleasure accompanies both quiet conversation and convivial gatherings. Ibn Luyun's poem on agriculture emphasizes the privacy afforded by a garden:

In the centre of the garden let there be a pavilion in which to sit, and with vistas on all sides, / but of such a form that no one approaching could overhear the conversation within and whereunto none could approach undetected.[70]

Ibn Khaquan, describing the final resting place of Abu Marwan al-Zajjali and his poet friend Ibn Shuhaid, emphasizes the diversity of pleasures associated with the garden: "Fate gave him . . . whatsoever he desired, and the pleasures of sobriety and inebriation alternated with each other in his experience."[71] The Islamic garden's walls afforded a measure of privacy, which could be enjoyed in solitude or in leisurely company.

The walled privacy of the Islamic garden also provided opportunities for social gatherings that included feasts, gaming, drinking bouts, dance, music, and the performance of poetry. Medieval Arabic and Persian poetry often used imagery derived from the natural world, and the poems performed reflected the abundance of nature that surrounded the poet's audience. In fact, a new garden was often celebrated with an occasional poem produced especially for the event, further linking the garden and the poet in the context of the medieval *majlis* (court).[72] Dominic Brookshaw also recounts the practice in medieval Iran of leaving the enclosed spaces of the court for open gardens at a distance from the city: "verdant satellites, sometimes anchored to the urban nucleus by tree-lined walkways."[73] One account describes a group that left the city for the plains and split into different parties:

One group chose merry-making and horse-riding, another listened to music whilst dancing / One group drank wine in an orchard, another plucked flowers in a rose-garden / One group were seated on the bank of a river, another sat in the middle of a tulip-bed.[74]

This exploratory enjoyment of the cultivated landscape beyond the urban center points to an aspect of garden-related activity that is often neglected. In addition to hunting and feasting on the open plain, as described here, individuals chose from among a variety of pathways and outdoor endeavors. In so doing, they expand on the visual and olfactory pleasures associated with gardens and orchards to include the process of choice and the kinetic act of movement to and from specific spots. What we might understand as the pleasures of the pedestrian experience—movement through space, and the exercise of individual choice—thus join the other pleasures induced by a well-designed garden landscape.[75]

In all of these examples, we may discern the importance of large gardens as markers of aristocratic wealth and power. Scott Redford has traced the association between Seljuk gardens, with their distinctive wall color and patterning, and the assertion of dynastic affiliation to those outside the garden walls.[76] Even without such clear visual markings, similar messages are conveyed by gardens developed for the powerful al-Andulus as well as for northern princes, kings, and queens. The mere presence of a large enclosed space, where some are admitted but most are not, telegraphs the exclusivity of the space and signals its desirability.

PLEASURE GARDENS IN THE CHRISTIAN WEST

Pleasure gardens emerge as a distinct form in Western Europe by the twelfth century. But as noted above, gardens always served several purposes. Well before the twelfth century, orchards, cloister garths, and the specialized medicinal herb garden elicited pleasure responses from those who frequented them or found respite there. Still, the cultural forces that made possible Gothic cathedrals, the first European universities, and the wheelbarrow also drove an aristocratic fashion for elaborate pleasure grounds.[77] Both large and small, spaces designed primarily for pleasure provided a protected area for the private repose and enjoyment of their high-born residents, and they were used to impress visitors and viewers with the owners' importance and status.

We find evidence of elaborate pleasure grounds in England, France, Flanders, Italy, and Germany, in addition to Spain. Kings Charles V and VI of France both devoted extensive resources to a twenty-acre garden at Hôtel St. Pol in Paris. Count Robert II of Artois created the Park of Hesdin, famous for its automata but equally impressive for its grand size.[78] In France, the fourteenth-century Château de Mehun included several distinct gardens: Jardins de Vachon; Jardins de Bon Repose, which may have contained a dock on the adjacent river Yèvre and which abutted the Hostel de Bon Repos; and a smaller Jardin du Dauphin at some distance from the château.[79] By the mid-fourteenth century in Italy, we find large private gardens at Milan (at the palace of Azzo Visconti), at Parma (belonging to Petrarch), and outside of Florence, at the Villa Palmieri, where Boccaccio's storytellers retire to escape the plague.[80] The English Kings Henry I, II, and III all developed large pleasure grounds at royal residences. Beginning in about 1110, Henry I bought a large parcel of land outside Windsor Castle, which became the King's Garden; Henry II developed new herbers at Winchester and Arundel Castles; and Henry III made further improvements to Windsor as well as at Nottingham, Gloucester, Kempton (Middlesex), and Guildford.[81] Of special note is the compound at Woodstock, improved several times:

> where the great park had been enclosed for Henry I, [it] included after 1165 the walled pleasance of Everswell, consisting of an orchard with a series of pools fed by the natural spring. This was famous as Rosa-mund's Bower, and gave its name to a whole class of enclosed pleasure gardens. Here again Henry III had works carried out, in 1250 building walls about the Queen's garden and forming a herber by the king's pond where she could walk for recreation; ten years later a hedge was to be made around the King's garden and preserve . . . and the covered walk about the springs of Everswell . . . [were] repaired.[82]

The privacy afforded by Rosamund's Bower, an enclosed compound, said to have been built for the king's mistress, may stand for the privacy enjoyed gen-erally by these gardens' aristocratic owners. Removed from the gaze of other household members and beyond their earshot, individuals seeking privacy could find it in large garden settings with several different areas conducive to different forms of leisure, in different seasons, and under varying weather conditions. A late example of private use comes from Richard Layton, a com-missioner under Oliver Cromwell, who reported in 1535 that "the sub-prior of Warden Abbey had been apprehended in the vineyard [of his abbey] with a whore."[83]

Assignations and secret meetings join other, less clandestine uses. Out-door dining, reading aloud, or telling stories to a small gathering, conversa-tion, strolling, and gaming all occurred in pleasure gardens. Evidence found in manuscript illuminations and literary texts joins mention of such uses in the historical records. A few additional examples must suffice.

Literature records a range of leisure activities for gardens, including sto-rytelling, reading, singing, dancing, and walking. Twelfth-century examples include gardens depicted by Chrétien de Troyes. In his *Cligès*, a young woman

who has feigned her own death in order to enjoy her secret love affair with
the title character, Cligès, has been living secluded in a tower for over a year,
when she declares that she needs to go outside into the surrounding orchard
to "frolic":

> Biax amis chiers,
> Grant bien me feïst uns vergiers,
> Ou je me poïsse deduire.[84]

> (Dear sweet love," she said to him, "an orchard where I might frolic
>   would do me so much good.)

She asserts that this will do her much good and that with such access she
can live happily in her seclusion. In another of Chrétien's romances, *Yvain* or
The Knight with the Lion, the title character encounters a small family garden
scene on one of his adventures:

> Et mes sire Yvains lors s'en antre
> el vergier, aprés li sa rote;
> voit apoié desor son cote
> un riche home qui se gisoit
> sor un drap de soie; et lisoit
> une pucele devant lui
> en un romans, ne said de cui;
> et por le romans escoter
> s'i estoit venue acoter
> une dame; et s'estoit sa mere,
> et li sires estoit ses pere.

> (Sir Yvain entered the garden with his party following him. He saw a
>   noble man reclining on his side on a silk rug. In front of him a maiden
>   was reading from a romance—I do not know about whom. A lady
>   had come to recline there and hear the romance. She was the maiden's
>   mother, and the lord was her father.)[85]

About two centuries later, we find the similar example of Giovanni Boccaccio's
Decameron, in which ten well-born young men and women retreat from Florence to a country estate during an outbreak of the plague. While there, they

entertain each other by telling stories in and around the palace grounds. The ten begin by settling on a lush green meadow with a cooling breeze. There are olive trees nearby and chessboards and other games that the young men and women eschew in favor of their storytelling. Pampinea, chosen as "queen" for the first day, invites the others to join her on the lawn in the middle of the afternoon, saying:

> Come voi vedete, il sole è alto e il caldo è grande, né altro s'ode che le cicale su per gli ulivi; per che l'andare al presente in alcun luogo sarebbe senza dubbio sciocchezza. Qui è bello e fresco stare, e hacci, come voi vedete, e traolieri e scacchieri, e puote ciascuno, secondo che all'animo gli è piú di piacere, diletto pilgliare.[86]
>
> (As you can see, the sun is high in the sky, it is very hot, and all is silent except for the cicadas in the olive trees. For the moment, it would surely be foolish of us to venture abroad, this being such a cool and pleasant spot in which to linger. Besides, as you will observe, there are chessboards and other games here, and so we are free to amuse ourselves in whatever way we please.)[87]

On the third day of their retreat, the group explores the palace, eats a meal on a loggia overlooking a courtyard, and then progresses to a walled garden situated on one side of the palace. The detailed description of this garden includes wide paths overhung with grape vines in flower, a larger central lawn sprinkled with brightly colored flowers and bordered by lemon and orange trees, a white marble fountain with a strong stream of water that falls into a clear pool below, and numerous birds, rabbits, deer, and other animals, all of whom seem tame. In this garden the group sings, dances, eats breakfast at tables brought out to the fountain, reads romances, plays chess, throws dice, and later on settles in for the third set of ten stories, still "on the lawn near the fountain"[88] ("vicini alla fontana venutine"[89]). This setting corresponds to a tightening of focus in their storytelling topics, followed on day nine by a release from their proscribed topics and a physical venturing out to a "little wood, not very far from the palace"[90] ("infino ad un boschetto, non guari al palagio lontano"[91]) where they amuse themselves until the heat of the day, when they return to the palace grounds.[92] Similarly, we find Chaucer's young widow, Criseyde, retreating to her own garden with her three nieces and a "greate route"[93] of other companions, where they walk together "arm in arm"[94] [II.823] and listen to Criseyde's niece Antigone sing a song about love.[95]

In art, examples of people enjoying gardens abound, particularly in the later Middle Ages. The Virgin Mary is frequently depicted within a walled garden, symbolizing her inviolate nature. But many of these images, with their clear religious significance, also reveal the uses made of medieval gardens. An early fifteenth-century *hortus conclusus*, by a master painter of the Upper Rhine, depicts a music lesson in progress, an outdoor table set with food, fruit picking, reading, and drinking water from a cistern (The Garden of Paradise, Upper Rhineland, c. 1410–1420. Stadelsches Kunstinstitute, Frankfurt-am-Main). An early fifteenth-century image, this one from a French copy of the "Romance of Alexander," depicts a king and queen seated at an outdoor chess table, engaged in the game within a walled garden, while a gardener works in another part of the castle grounds.[96] In another depiction of a group enjoying the pleasures of the garden together, we see them making music around a large fountain.

Many seekers of private pleasure may also be found in gardens. Two examples must suffice: one from a manuscript of Christine de Pisan's work shows a man and woman engaged in conversation, seated apart from their companions, who are glimpsed through the trees in another part of the garden; and a second example, from a manuscript of *Livre des proffitz champestres et ruraulx* by Piero de'Crescenzi, depicts two lovers seated on a turf bench in the middle of a walled pleasure garden, clearly enjoying each other's presence.

Historical accounts of garden use tend to record their use for special functions and events, rather than as spaces of private reflection or enjoyment. The Bridge House in Southwark, first appearing in records for 1222–1223, served as "the nerve center for the many enterprises of London Bridge," itself central to the city's economic influence.[97] With a large staff, the Bridge House was run like a city within the city, and food from its grounds fed those who worked there. The expense accounts, kept by the Clerk of the Works beginning in 1381, record the cost of beans, onion sets, garlic, apple-tree grafts, and other seeds and plants, as well as a variety of garden tools. But in addition to a large vegetable garden and orchard, Bridge House also, from at least 1426, sported an herber that functioned as an outdoor parlor in good weather. Records show that it was used for the ceremonial annual audit of the Bridge House records: "In some instances lavish meals were prepared to mark the event, the open-air parlor on occasion hung with tapestries."[98] In similar fashion, at Winchester Palace, Bishop Henry Beaufort celebrated the wedding of his niece to James I of Scotland in 1424 with a reception in the palace and garden.[99]

On the continent, the Park of Hesdin was used to impress a group of English ambassadors in 1463, as recorded by the Burgundian chronicler, Georges Chastellein. The visitors to Hesdin first rode on horseback quite a long route, away from the castle to the far section of the park where they dined and drank, before being allowed to return to meet the duke at the castle,[100]clearly a gambit made to impress them with the duke's wealth and importance. Similarly, from a letter describing the visit of King François I and his charge Frédéric de Gonzague to Blois in 1516, we learn that some of the tunnel arbors built by the sixteenth century were quite large and impressive. At the early Renaissance garden at Château de Blois, the tunnel arbors in the "grand jardin" were roughly 300 steps in length and 10 steps wide and so tall that one could ride a horse through them.[101]

Whereas the gardens in al-Andulus sought to represent in miniature geometric forms the breadth of the caliphs' holdings outside the garden's walls,[102] these large pleasure gardens in Western Europe attempted to incorporate a variety of features that could emphasize the owners' ability to change and control nature on a grand scale. In the late twelfth century, Hugh de Noyers, the bishop of Auxerre, was praised specifically for the ways he had improved the landscape:

> He provided every pleasure and improvement that the industry of man could accomplish. The woods, beset with briars and undergrowth and thus of little value, he cleared and brought into cultivation. There he made gardens and planted trees of different sorts so that, apart from deriving pleasure from them, he also got great quantities of fruit. He surrounded a large part of the woods with a ring fence carried from the gate at the near end to the dam of the third pool, and enclosed within a pretty quantity of wild beats. These might be seen grazing in their herds by those in the palace, a pleasing sight.[103]

The transformation of wildwood into useful and beautiful gardens, the profits gained from programmatic cultivation, and the pleasure derived from seeing wild animals in the enclosed park all contributed to the accomplishments of the bishop in managing the land.

Indeed, it is useful to consider gardens within the larger landscapes and to acknowledge the ways in which the surrounding landforms could be manipulated to produce certain responses. Oliver Creighton identifies two scales available to large-scale garden designers to create differing effects: "the

creation of small-scale enclosed gardens . . . in the immediate vicinity" of
the castle or manor house, and the "large-scale redevelopment, typically including artificial water features, enclosed pleasure grounds and deer parks,"
adding that both contributed to the overall aesthetic aims of many castles.[104]
The smaller gardens might serve primarily as settings for small group gatherings and private reflection, while changes to the larger landscape were
probably undertaken primarily for the effects of grand vistas on visitors
to the site. Creighton further surmises that "where two parks are contem-
poraneous, they might have had distinct functions" whereby the smaller
ones, closer to castles, could have been "dedicated pleasure parks unsuited
to hunting but designed for the staging of other entertainment activities such
as tournaments and, perhaps, for aesthetic appeal," giving Fotheringhay
(Northamptonshire) as a prime example. The "Little Park" there included
as well an orchard, pond, and garden, while the "Great Park" stood at a
distance from the castle proper and was roughly ten times as large as the
Little Park.[105]

   Christopher Taylor and other British archeologists have discovered several
additional sites in England that show evidence of "dams, leats and other water-
management and control features . . . of such a scale or complexity that the
provision of sheets of water and other ponds and their arrangement . . . provide an ornamental outlook or approach." He continues:

> Most of them had associated deer parks, many also contained the re-
> mains of enclosed gardens and all seemed to be adjacent to high-status
> buildings. The majority seem to have been so arranged that they could be
> viewed from above, from local eminences, from the upper floors or roofs
> of the buildings, or from special "standings" or pavilions, often known
> as "gloriettes."[106]

Tom Williamson and Robert Liddiard cast a skeptical eye on the interpretation of
these landscapes in their essay on the wider landscape in this volume. Nonetheless, we should note the range of examples adduced by scholars as part of this
debate: Stow (Lincolnshire), Somersham (Cambridgeshire), Frandingham Castle
(Suffolk), Old Bolingbroke Castle (Lincolnshire), Ravenworth Castle (North
Yorkshire), Leeds Castle (Kent), and several smaller examples.[107] The visual pleasures attendant on such extensive grounds surrounding the castle may well
join more active pleasures. Taylor also suggests that hunting, as a social event,
would sometimes include "ladies, servants with food and furniture and even
chaplains with tented chapels and portable altars."[108]

An example of this sort of use can be found in a late Middle English romance, "The Awtyns of Arthure at the Terne Wathleyene," in which the Queen
Guinevere and Sir Gawain travel to a clearing in the woods to watch Arthur
and his men hunt deer.[109] They first cross "depe delles" (deep valleys)[110] in
order to reach the "forest frydde" (a legally protected forest)[111] where they
know the deer to be. The poet remarks that the deer are beautiful to see during the nonhunting season "in frithes and felles" (game-parks and pastures),[112]
and Gawain and Guinevere proceed along a path, beside a "grene well"[113] and
dismount beneath a laurel there near a "felle,"[114] or elevated stretch of open
pasture. Here they settle in, apparently to watch the hunt from a distance,
as Arthur and his men go off to their hunting stations. While not described
in detail, the landscape of the poem includes thickets where deer hide and
open space (woodland pasture) where deer are visible, along with an evergreen
bower fit for a queen and her escort.

As the Middle Ages came to a close, high-status gardens continued to
evolve, using more and more elaborate geometrical patterns, evident, for example, in several estates along the Thames River. Winchester Palace, the London residence of the Bishop of Winchester; Lambeth Palace, the Archbishop of
Canterbury's London residence; and further upriver from these two, Fulham
Palace, belonging to the Bishop of London all enjoyed extensive river-fed gardens, which evolved during the Middle Ages from a series of intensively productive farm-like gardens into manicured status settings for social gatherings
and events.[115] The river served as a highway for goods and people, as well as
a water source for various irrigation techniques. And, as Paul Christianson
notes, "A garden by the Thames, while seeming to exist for functional uses
and personal pleasure, also served to announce quite publicly by its prominent
river site the owner's exalted social position."[116]

THE GARDEN AS LIVING METAPHOR

The ninth-century poet Walahfrid Strabo metaphorically identifies real fruit
grown in a monastery garden and gathered by young pupils for their teacher,
with the knowledge gained by these same pupils under the teacher's tutelage.
The central cross drawn on the St. Gall cemetery plan is also associated metaphorically with the fruit trees around it and connected to a positive outcome,
in this case, eternal salvation. Landscapes can be constructed in order to remind the inhabitants of a particular idea, set of associations, literary allusions,
or fictional events. In this way, landscape features may be designed to be read,
or interpreted, as metaphors for something beyond themselves, by visitors to

the site and their hosts. Thus, in addition to the very real benefits of food and medicinal plant cultivation, medieval gardens provided an entree to social and spiritual benefits as well. Spaces that were intended for leisure, for contemplative use, for private meetings, and for social gatherings of all sorts, medieval gardens join their modern counterparts in satisfying a range of perceived needs. Their multivalent nature at times hides behind the names given to gardens with apparently specific uses. But we do well to remember that *herbularia* can also serve as meditative spaces, orchards are also often pleasure grounds, and hunting parks may also include private bowers fit for a queen.

CHAPTER FIVE

Meaning

ELIZABETH AUGSPACH

Refreshment and relaxation are the aim of all pleasure gardens, and during the Middle Ages the conscious model for the perfect garden, in Christendom at least, was the Bible. Descriptions of the gardens in the Bible are not specific, but the idea of perfection and well-being, of fulfillment of the soul, and of proximity to God—often manifested in nostalgia for lost innocence or sexual fulfillment and gratification of the senses or, more often, a mixture of both—is behind every medieval pleasure garden.

The Bible begins with the Garden of Eden and ends with the garden at the end of Revelation (22:1–5). This last is defined simply by a river and a Tree of Life that gives twelve fruits, each one in their respective months, and under which is the throne of the Lord.[1] In this sense, the notion of garden is linear rather than cyclical, since the final lesson is that one needs to transcend the garden of sensual pleasures in order to enter the garden of spiritual fulfillment. One garden stands to the other as fiction does to truth, a lesson further developed in the twelfth and even more in the thirteenth century, finding its expression in the way that Jean de Meun's simple garden at the end of the *Roman de la Rose* is overshadowed and transcends that of Guillaume de Lorris's in the first part, a garden whose door was opened by Idleness.

However, the garden that fired the medieval imagination was not the garden at the end of Revelation but rather that described in Genesis (2:8–14). Called a paradise (*paradisus*),[2] it is in the Orient, specifically in Eden, and holds all kinds of trees that are beautiful to the eye and delicious to the taste. Only two trees are identified: the Tree of Life and the Tree of Knowledge of Good and Evil, which are in the middle of the garden. There is also a river that issues from Eden and waters the garden, after which it branches into four rivers: the river Phison, which surrounds the land of Hevila, where gold, bdellium and onyx can be found; the river Gehon, which flows around Ethiopia, and the Tigris and the Euphrates, which flow in Mesopotamia.

There was much debate during the Middle Ages about Adam and Eve's activities in paradise: were Adam and Eve required to work, for idleness could lead either to sloth and the devil or to contemplation and God? For some, such as Adam of St. Victor, as we shall see later, the garden grew spontaneously, and work was one of the consequences of original sin. For others, namely Augustine and Thomas Aquinas, taking their cue from Genesis 2:15 ("The Lord took man and placed him in the garden of pleasure to dress and keep it"[3]), man was meant to work in paradise, albeit pleasurably, so that he would not be susceptible to evil.[4]

Isidore of Seville (c. 560–636) judged the Eden to be in the East because he believed the name "paradise" derived from the Greek for "garden."[5] Aquinas concurred: the East was "the most excellent part of the earth" because it is the "right hand of the heavens," just as "the right hand is nobler than the left."[6] For this reason, many a voyage was undertaken to reach the unreachable perfect garden, no doubt fuelled by the classical notion that only very special heroes were allowed to reach the otherworld. In Canto XXVI of the *Inferno*, perhaps the most famous example, Ulysses drowns striving to reach the mountain of purgatory on top of which lies the Earthly paradise.

The Bible's Garden of Eden appears stark, making all the more striking the influence it has exerted on the conception of all subsequent gardens of the Christian world. It is beautiful, but in a dry, intellectual way that does not appeal to the senses. Nevertheless, it carries with it the idea of a perfection, once ours and now lost, perhaps forever; there is an obvious connection with the classical myth of the golden age and with myths of origins in many cultures.

Yet when attempting to express the idea of lost perfection and well-being, it is impossible to do so without reference to the fulfillment of the senses. It is a sign of contradiction that on the occasions when gods and humans come together, the ineffable finds expression in sexual consummation[7]—that is, the yearning and fulfillment of the soul is explained through sensory experience. The result is a potentially explosive combination since, for many influential Christian writers of the period, the gratification of the senses is the primary tool of the devil, contrary to the ascetic way that leads to God.

What the Garden of Eden lacked in terms of sensual fulfillment was provided by another emblematic Biblical garden, the garden of the Song of Solomon (4:12–16):

> A garden enclosed, my sister, my spouse, a garden enclosed, a fountain sealed.
>
> Thy plants are a paradise of pomegranates with the fruits of the orchard, cypress with spikenard.
>
> Spikenard and saffron, sweet cane and cinnamon, with all the trees of Libanus, myrrh and aloes with all the chief perfumes.
>
> The fountain of gardens: the well of living waters, which run with a strong stream from Libanus.
>
> Arise, O north wind, and come, O south wind, blow through my garden, and let the aromatic spices thereof flow.[8]

Contrasting with the intellectual tranquility of the Garden of Eden, this is a veritable banquet of the senses, as form, in the shape of the beauty of the poem, follows function through the description of the splendor of the garden. This is no mere enumeration of the beauty and delicious fruits of the trees: sensory experience intoxicates and overcomes the reader.

Work has no place in this garden: it is an epithalamium combining the voices of Bridegroom and Bride with a choral interlude. The Bridegroom is jealous, just, and righteous. The Bride loves the Bridegroom but is susceptible to sin and infidelity. The Bridegroom chastises her, praises her, and loves her despite her faults, managing to bring her back to the right path. The lines quoted above are sung in praise of the Bride, the garden serving as metaphor for her beauty, sensuality, and virginity.

When confronted with this poem, Western exegesis labeled it a Wisdom Book and chose to interpret it as an expression of divine love rather than human sexuality. Woman and garden were glossed to signify the Church and the individual soul, and finally to stand for the one woman removed from fallen humanity, the Virgin Mary.

The idea of identifying woman with garden is anticipated in an age-old identification of woman with earth, beginning, for the Western world, with Hesiod's *Theogony*. In this work, Gaia, who is earth and female, is the great container and the great mother. The masculine principle, Uranos, is born spontaneously from her. Despite the fact that he is Gaia's son, Uranos quickly gains ascendancy over her—precisely by virtue of lying above her and encircling her, thus curtailing Gaia's active role. In effect, roles have been exchanged, for Uranos has become the container and Gaia, the contained. Uranos's lordship over Gaia is further demonstrated by the fact that she must couple with him in order to produce more children. In other words, the female earth now depends on the male sky in order to reproduce.[9]

The passivity of the earth and her marvelous generative abilities, upon whom the gardener had merely to drop a seed for it to bloom, undoubtedly contributed to the notions of conception that remained popular until well into our modern times. Earlier Greek theories, such as those of Empedocles and possibly Anaxagoras, had supported the notion of both male and female contributing seed to conception.[10] This theory was generally accepted in Europe during the ninth and tenth centuries and was the main reason why men were expected to marry women who were of equal or better station. In this way, the blood of the succeeding generation would not degenerate.[11]

Yet it was Aristotle's theory that gained acceptance when his works were translated from Arabic into Latin during the twelfth and especially the thirteenth centuries. In the *Generation of Animals*, Aristotle claims that the female provides the matter, while the male principle fashions it into shape.

Aristotle's thought formed the basis of the writings of Albert the Great and his student Aquinas, who inherited the obvious misogamy involved in this stance which is often labeled as typical of late medieval religious thought. And yet, many late medieval theologians were responsible for softening much of the misogynistic content inherited from classical Greek and Roman sources.[12] In their opinion, although inferior, woman was not a defective male, as Aristotle had claimed.[13] On the contrary, just like man she was called to be a perfect being at the General Resurrection.

Even though the prevalent opinion of medieval religious thought was that man's part in conception had less significance than it had had for Aristotle, by virtue of God's greater role in the act, woman's role remained essentially the same: she provided passive matter. In Canto XXV of the *Purgatorio*, Statius describes the medieval notions about conception: there are two principles, the active and the passive; the active is the semen and the passive is the menstrual blood. The semen activates the blood, coagulating and thickening it. This is how human life begins. Statius then discusses the formation of the different levels of the soul, vegetative and sensory. These two, however, are created without the intervention of God, who infuses the developing human being with a rational soul. This soul does not annihilate the previous ones but encloses them.

Clearly, then, woman was inextricably connected to earth, body, and passivity, while man was associated with sky, soul, and activity, and this notion was carried from ancient times into the Middle Ages and beyond. The transition from earth to garden was an easy one—a process of acculturation, in fact. The garden represents the manifestation of man's control over nature.[14] The same process of acculturation transforms a woman into a lady. A lady is precisely a woman who by accident of birth has been separated, controlled, and acculturated to move in a particular social environment.

Pleasure gardens and ladies share three features. In the first place, both women and gardens are mothers, a notion that is safeguarded by their common association with the earth; both are bearers who respond to the ministrations of man. Second, both gardens and women are ornamental and serve to delight the senses.[15] This is the sole source of power a woman has in relation to her lover and her husband. Since any ascendancy that a woman might have over man is rendered suspect, men were constantly being counseled against uxoriousness,[16] for a woman could indeed become a snare to her own husband, a thought that made the Fathers of the Church very uneasy. Third, women were prone to wander,[17] which meant they had to be watched and kept under control. In consequence, both garden and woman must be restrained so that neither of them becomes a whore. The garden may do so metaphorically, by becoming a forest or jungle. The woman may do so quite literally, by giving herself to someone other than her husband, or, if she is unmarried, to someone unsanctioned by other than her male relatives.

In early Western exegesis, then, the garden of the Song of Solomon was viewed as woman, but not as feminine. The feminine principle remained suspect, but the rise of the cult of the Virgin Mary offered the opposing image of an incorruptible woman. The woman in the garden was identified as the Church, protecting herself against the pollution of heresy. The figures of the *hortus conclusus* and the *fons signatus* were taken as metaphors for virginity, and because of the importance accorded by Christians to a permanent virginity, they gained much popularity.[18]

Perhaps the most important reason for the centrality of virginity within the Christian Church is that it is connected with pristine origin. Adam and Eve, according to some commentators, were virgins, until they committed original sin; then sex and death entered the world.[19] St Jerome writes the following to his friend, the nun Eustochium:

> That you may understand that virginity is natural and that marriage came after the Fall, remember that what is born of wedlock is virgin flesh and that

by its fruit it renders what in its parent root it had lost. "there shall come forth a rod [there is a pun here on the words virga, rod, and virgo, virgin] out of the stem of Jesse, and a flower shall grow out of its roots" [Is XI.1]. That virgin rod is the mother of Our Lord, simple, pure, unsullied; drawing no germ of life from without, but like God Himself fruitful in singleness.[20]

Even though not all the Christian commentators asserted that sex was the consequence of sin—and Augustine was among those who did not[21]—it is clear that all, including Augustine, connected sex with concupiscence and considered the choice of virginity more perfect, in accordance with the teachings of Paul.

Consequently, the most important quality women possessed was virginity, which provided some protection against all other sins associated with incontinence. The enclosure of the garden of delicious flowers and fruit was a perfect metaphor for any female figure, particularly any female figure who had taken a vow of virginity. However, prior to the fourth century, the Church Fathers preferred not to speculate concerning what lay beyond the enclosing boundary of the garden. Thus, in the *Patrologia Latina*,[22] the sensual contents of the garden, the spices, the fruits, the wind, all were largely ignored. Instead, the Church Fathers centered their writings on enclosure, linking it with virginity.

The idea of virginity as a wall that must not be breached carried into the notion of the pristine garden that can be seen in visions but not entered.

Pleasure groves lack the defining boundary. So in medieval texts, a lady in an open field is either fair game or a witch or some other sort of social outcast. When King Marc discovers Tristan and Iseult in a pleasure grove, for example, their position is that of outcasts. This notion will persevere throughout the Middle Ages. For instance, the Marqués de Santillana, a fifteenth-century Spanish poet, considers that since the women he encounters in open fields are peasant women (shepherdesses or otherwise), they are sexually available for a lusty lord. Open fields, like women of unremarkable background, are beautiful but without art, unsuitable for social living.[23] In general, ladies that seek recreation according to the rules of a man-made society are found in enclosed gardens adjoining the lord's castle.

Even though the Church in her virginity was most identified with the Bride of the Song, there were other possibilities. The Bride of the Song was sometimes understood as the individual soul striving for perfection. The soul had to guard its integrity/virginity in order not to be polluted by sin, as the Church had to guard itself against being polluted by heresy. Consequently, the figure of the hortus conclusus could just as easily be applied to the integrity of the soul as to the integrity of the Church.

However, it was Ambrose who in the fourth century played the most important role with respect to the development of the figure of the hortus conclusus.
Firstly, he considered what lay inside the garden. Like his predecessors, he
equated the walls of the garden with virginity. Unlike them, he went beyond
the walls to develop the contents of the garden. In his commentary on the Song
of Solomon, he claimed that the fountain in the garden reflects the image of
God, that the wall of the spirit fences virginity so that the wild beasts of the
world will not pollute anything within. Inside, inaccessible, are the violet, the
olive, and the rose, emitting delicious odors. The violet stands for religion,
the olive for peace, and the rose for virginity.[24]

But Ambrose made a more significant contribution. In the same commentary, he equated the hortus conclusus with the Earthly paradise. In fact, he
claimed that the Greek word *paradisus* was equivalent to the Latin word *hortus*.[25] Ambrose conflated the two gardens in such a way that the Earthly paradise acquired all the spices of the hortus conclusus of the Song of Solomon.
Now, striking descriptions of this garden avoided censure for sensual abandon
because God had fashioned it for the enjoyment of man in a purer state (before
original sin). It was a masculine garden, owned by God and derived from the
masculine gardens of antiquity, those the gods had bestowed upon privileged
humans, such as Alkinoos in *The Odyssey* and Aeetes in *The Argonautica*. It
spoke of closeness to God, tapping into nostalgia for a lost innocence. Seen in
this light, this garden posed no threat to the salvation of man.

On the other hand, the hortus conclusus was slow to gain the rich iconography that the Garden of Eden or Earthly paradise had developed free from every
restraint by its very association with God. It remained suspect because it was
irrevocably linked to woman and sensuality. One can appreciate the dangers
of elaborating on the interior of the garden if the walls are meant to stand for
virginity, particularly in reference to a woman, since the Bride is female. Thus,
the iconography of the Earthly paradise took upon itself the wall and the spices
of the hortus conclusus of the Song of Solomon, ignoring all sensual references
that abound in that text, particularly in connection with the hortus conclusus.

The Earthly paradise was not identified with a woman, other than the
Church or the soul, prior to the ninth century—and then only with a woman
who had been properly divested of any trace of sensuality. Paschasius Radber-
tus was the first to equate the hortus conclusus of the Virgin with the Earthly
paradise.[26] Previously, the Virgin had been called an hortus conclusus by Jerome (340–420),[27] but the title had referred only to her virginity and was taken
out of context from the Song of Solomon. Jerome was interested in the enclosure, not in what lay within the garden. Paschasius, on the other hand, saw the

relationship between the Virgin and the garden within, identifying the Virgin's garden as a hortus conclusus because from it flowed the delights of the Earthly paradise—that is, Christ.[28]

In a way, hymns anticipated the emotional note that became evident in the twelfth century, absent from the Church Fathers' commentaries. The hymns, particularly those addressed to the Virgin, seized the lover/beloved relationship literally present in the song, delighting in the emotional possibilities. Not surprisingly, much of the imagery used in Marian hymns derived from the Song of Songs. The lover is no longer Christ, and the beloved is not the Church. It is the individual soul that is the lover and the Virgin who is the beloved[29].

The title of hortus conclusus for Mary became one among many. The rich tapestry of the hymns was achieved by piling image upon image of praise, rather than by focusing on one figure and developing it. The result is that the hortus conclusus is not elaborated beyond a flowering spring garden, as exemplified in Adam of St. Victor's hymn LXXIV on the Nativity of the Blessed Virgin Mary:

> She is that sealed fount, ne'er drying,
> That walled garden fructifying
> By the good seed in it sown,
> She is that close-fastened portal,
> Shut by God 'gainst every mortal
> For some secret cause unknown.[30]

Commentaries from the twelfth and thirteenth centuries show a departure from earlier glosses on the hortus conclusus, as a result of the growing reverence for Mary, even though the association of virginity and the hortus conclusus remains. By the twelfth century, the title of hortus conclusus belonged primarily to the Virgin, one of her honorific titles. While the Bride of the Song of Solomon continued to be glossed alternately as the Church, the individual soul, and Mary, the title hortus conclusus, when taken independently from the Song of Solomon, became hers, signifying her virginity, virtue, and integrity, as well as her fruitfulness as mother of Christ.

By the thirteenth century, virginity was most often linked to a lily (and sometimes to a rose, as Ambrose had done—see above), while the violet stood for humility and the rose for charity.[31] Virginity was still chief among Mary's virtues, but as her cult developed and the excellencies of her person came to the fore, she and her garden grew beyond her womb to encompass her whole person. The hortus conclusus no longer alluded to the integrity of Mary's womb but to the integrity of her person.

The sublimated language of love applied to the Virgin Mary that encompassed her garden proved irresistible to secular poetry. Once the hortus conclusus left its Latin cradle to pass into the vernacular, and especially into romance, the immediate associations with Mary fell into the background. Instead, Mary and religious allegory became the subtext, while the text itself moved to include other women. A new form of poetry emerged, one that sought earthly rather than spiritual delights, but one that also needed to draw from the more readily available metaphors of religion in order to create its own language of love.

Since the perfect woman was the Virgin Mary and hyperbolic and metaphoric language had surrounded her in her roles of mother and lover, it was quite natural for secular writers to transfer Mary's ideal attributes to the lady of romance. This not only meant physical beauty and moral perfection but even Mary's miraculous interventions. In the same way that Mary saved the sinner, so the lady of romance could succor the lover confronted with earthly obstacles if only he would turn his thoughts to her.

The twelfth century is a century of literary ambiguity—at least from the point of view of modern readers who attempt to read the garden as either good or bad based on the elements it contains.[32] While the validity of that position cannot be entirely discarded, perhaps a more illuminating way of looking at these gardens is to see the relationships that are forged within them. The mix of religious and secular elements bewilders the modern reader, who is more comfortable with clear definitions of what is strictly religious and what is not. The twelfth century shows little discomfort with such blurrings. How else could the legend of the Holy Grail have come into being with its odd mixture of religious and secular elements?

By the thirteenth century, on the other hand, greater certainty seems to be demanded; literary texts are more rigorously explicated, often through an appeal to religious certainties. Tellings of the legend of the Holy Grail culminate in the *Vulgate Cycle* version, where every adventure is conveniently glossed by a priest or monk who happens to be at hand. Ferrante[33] has pointed out that while the goal of chivalric romances of the twelfth century is the lady, in the later part of the thirteenth the lady is displaced by religion. Woman has become the temptress who will lead the knight away from his true path.

During the twelfth century, then, secular love poetry borrowed from religion in order to develop its own language of love, and in turn, the religious poetry of the thirteenth century was influenced by secular love poetry.[34] The

Le Mans Commentary, composed in France at the close of the twelfth century, is a good example of the instability of meaning in the Song of Solomon. The anonymous author claims that it may be used to honor the Virgin or any other lady for that matter. The poem, written in octosyllabic rhyming couplets, delicately builds its theme of courtly love upon the religious subtext, thus successfully marrying secular love poetry with religious poetry. The mere fact that the poet has chosen to write this commentary in a vernacular romance language rather than Latin is a sufficient indication that it is not addressed to a learned and consequently largely masculine audience. The theme of love reinforces the notion that the authorial audience of this delightful work is feminine. The enclosed garden's traditional connotation of virginity is not foregrounded. Instead, the enclosure and the sealed fountain mark the secrecy that binds courtly lovers to one another.

Descriptions of gardens are as rare in twelfth-century romances as physical descriptions of knights and ladies. Even in uncommon occasions when the garden is highlighted, its shape, color, and types of flowers, plants and birds are imprecise. The poet prefers to evoke an archetype already present in his audience's minds. Chrétien de Troyes has very little to say about the gardens of his romances, despite the fact that he mentions them over thirty times. Only two receive closer scrutiny: the garden in the episode of the *joie de la cort* (joy of the court) in *Erec et Enide* and the garden that safeguards the lovers in *Cligès*. With respect to the contents of the garden, the former abounds in generalities (only one tree is mentioned by name) and the latter is specific only about the tree in its center, itself fraught with ambiguity. Likewise, Marie de France has nothing to say about the plants in the lady's garden in "Guigemar," nor about the garden in which the queen attempts to seduce the eponymous hero in *Lanval*. In the earliest surviving French play, the *Jeu d'Adam* (mid twelfth century), the Latin description instructs that paradise be on a high place and have scented flowers and leaves and trees with fruits hanging from them, and seem a beautiful place.

Social considerations also played a role in placing the lady of romance in the garden. The garden is a social space of recreation and relaxation, and ladies are naturally associated with pleasure. In fact, so intrinsic is the association lady/garden/pleasure, that the garden is often adjoined to the lady's chamber, so that it is necessary for the knight to pass through the garden simply to gain access to the chamber. Guinevere's garden in Chrétien's *Lancelot* is a case in point.[35]

The social body demanded that woman subordinate herself to man and that man lead her (Adam, the head, erred when he listened to Eve's counsel). Women were weak; men must therefore protect and circumscribe them and enjoin them to be chaste, humble, modest, silent, industrious, merciful.[36] Medieval law ratified the law of God, stating that married women and children were not recognized as full members of a society, being rather simply part of a man's household.[37] It was a man's duty to keep his wife under surveillance, though he could not very well imprison her. Those who attempted to imprison their wives were typically elderly and controlling, and they inevitably met with failure and ridicule.[38]

On the other hand, the man's space is the forest, the outskirts of civilization,[39] where he ventures to encounter the marvelous, so prevalent in medieval romance. The encounter with fantastic creatures such as giants, knights who defend rocks, magic castles with enchanted beds are tests of the knight's manhood. It is not in the confines of the castle and courtly life that Yvain will befriend a lion or that Perceval will meet the Fisher King. Liminal spaces and liminal times (twilight; the changing of the seasons) were often perceived as thresholds to the otherworld, where transformations are always a possibility.[40]

As social and civilized spaces reserved for ladies, gardens dot the landscape of medieval romance, but are not places of action. They are mostly intermediary resting places. Like the castle to which they are adjoined, they are markers of civilization, in sharp contrast with the unknown that lies in the forest and beyond. Ladies, like gardens, are the reminders of civilization and are circumscribed to a conquered space.

As we have seen, the enclosing walls of the garden were closely associated with virginity, thick, green marble walls off the garden-prison in Marie de France's "Guigemar." Marble (of unspecified colour) is also preferred in the wall of *Le Bel Inconnu*, and even though there is no detailed description of the carvings on this wall, we are told that these carvings represent everything to be found on earth. Undoubtedly, the walls that receive the most attention are the high crenellated walls in the *Roman de la Rose*, with their statues painted in gold and azure. The walls of the emir's garden in the French aristocratic versions of *Floire et Blanchefleur* are also elaborate. Even if they receive comparatively little attention with respect to the rest of the garden in the romance, they have turrets on each corner and that are painted in gold and azure, the same colors as on the walls of the *Roman de la Rose* and the most costly—in paintings, the Virgin's hair was often painted gold and her mantle blue.

The Middle English versions of *Floriz and Blauncheflur*, interestingly enough, substitute crystal walls for the gold and azure walls of the French aristocratic version, probably drawing on the association of crystal with purity, which is particularly appropriate for this romance.[41] Similarly, in the old Celtic romance of the "Voyage of Maildun," Maildun and his company arrive at an island that has four divisions with four walls. The gold wall separates the kings; the silver wall, the queens; the copper wall, the youths; while the crystal wall corresponds to the young maidens.

Gardens and cities, then, are protected by man-made walls, walls that are defined by their strength and beauty. These are masculine walls, whose chief purpose is to protect what lies inside. But gardens owned by women generally do not have such sturdy walls to define them. Instead, their protection derives from supernatural power. In the case of the Virgin's garden in the introduction to the thirteenth-century *Milagros de Nuestra Señora* by Gonzalo de Berceo, for instance, we know that there is a wall because there are four corners in the garden—and yet no wall is described. All indications point to a wall that is as invisible and permeable[42] as are the walls of the dangerous garden of the *Erec et Enide* episode of the *joie de la cort*.

Erec et Enide is a tale about the proper relationship between the knight, his lady, and society at large. When Erec marries Enide, he shuns all adventures and tournaments, preferring to stay by her side. Despite sly remarks at court, Erec turns a deaf ear until he accidentally overhears Enide's soft remarks. Waking from his dream of married bliss, he returns to manly activity but again without moderation, neglecting his proper duty to his wife, dragging her through the forests of adventure.

Once the situation between Erec and Enide has been resolved there is an additional final adventure that Erec must confront: the "Joy of the Court" episode, an uncommon adventure in that it takes place within an enclosed garden.

But this is no ordinary garden. It is not attached to a castle, although it is not far from one. More importantly, it is surrounded by stakes on which sit bright and shining helmets with heads within them. It is enclosed by a thick, impenetrable wall of air, with a single, gate-shaped, narrow entrance. The garden is full of flowers and ripe fruit, although these are not described or identified. They are imperishable, as in many enclosed gardens of romance. The fruit can only be eaten inside, if one is to ever find his way out. Other more typical features of the enclosed garden are also present. Although none are specifically identified, every singing bird that delights man is there, as are all spices and roots used for medicinal purposes.

Erec enters and follows a path that leads to a beautiful lady reclining beneath the shade of a sycamore tree. As he gazes upon her, a tall knight in vermillion arms issues forth, challenging Erec and telling him that he is not worthy of approaching the lady. Erec defeats him with difficulty and the mystery of the garden comes to light. It transpires that the challenger, Mabonagrain, had rashly vowed never to leave his lover's garden. Defeated, his vow is fulfilled and, after Enide comforts the lady (who turns out to be her cousin), Erec can lead Mabonagrain and his lady back to court, to everyone's intense joy.

In Mabonagrain, Erec finds a mirror image of himself, which he must confront once and for all. Mabonagrain has stayed too long in the garden—a place that should serve as refreshment but not as ultimate goal—to his own and society's detriment. Mabonagrain had given dominion to the woman just as Adam gave it to Eve; it is not Mabonagrain who owns the garden but the lady, and neither the lady nor the garden are subject to him. The fact that the lady commands is a commentary on the perils of *Frauendienst*: Mabonagrain's misgoverned manhood has itself become a destructive force, evidenced by the grotesque heads that mar the beauty of the garden.

It is only fitting that an adventure that involves dispossessing a controlling lady so as to place her in her proper social position should involve undoing the enchantment of the garden. Gardens that show women in control often have walls of air, as in Morgan le Fay's *val sans retour* (valley of no return) in the thirteenth-century *Vulgate* cycle of Arthurian romances. Knights who have been unfaithful to their ladies may wander into it, but are unable to leave. Although they enjoy the pleasures of the garden and of women, it is an unnatural situation that Lancelot must correct. The garden must be domesticated in the same way that the lady must be subjugated. The lady's and the garden's enchantments that make thralls of knights must be broken so that they may fulfill their duty to society at large.

Once Mabonagrain has been defeated, and ironically gained the upper hand over his lady, the lady herself is in despair. Enide gently consoles her with a lesson in social conventions. In contrast with their secret affair, unsanctioned by their parents, Enide tells of her own public, socially approved marriage. Enide's cousin learns the proper hierarchy of man and woman through words with a strong biblical ring: Erec is lord, while she is a "poor and naked" person who has been elevated by her husband so that she shares the honor that he has achieved. Enide physically leads her cousin out of the garden to be reintroduced into the social world.

The adventure reaffirms the universal social order in which ladies marry and become subject to their husbands and where husbands in turn protect and enjoy their wives without forgetting their duties as knights to the world at large. Gardens too are enclosed, attached to a castle, and owned by a knight.

In these stories, the unwitting knight is enticed into a life of pleasure and subordination represented by the woman in her enclosed garden. The invisible wall is simply a sign of what he does not see as he gravitates into feminine space. Men may enjoy a temporary sojourn there, often as a reward for heroic action, and they should defend the garden, but the knight must express his masculinity daily, and this can be done only in adventure, as Chrétien's Erec learns.

The Virgin Mary is the only one who can wield her power in the garden with impunity. She can do this because her power is not a threat to man. Indeed, her garden functions as a traditional hortus conclusus inscribed by men, as in Berceo's *Milagros de Nuestra Señora*. Men enter the garden for brief refreshment and then are free to leave. Their manhood is never imperiled. There are no battles or adventures to be fought in the garden. Instead, men relax briefly and then continue their adventure of life. Berceo the pilgrim never allows himself to forget that the respite provided by the Virgin's garden is only temporary. Man's final resting place is with God, and the virgin silently acknowledges her womanly position as temporary respite rather than final destination. She has, in fact, accepted her position as woman within a social scheme.

The female-dominated, traitorous, false garden comes into its own in the thirteenth century, a time when gardens real and ideal come of age. Sensuality is given free rein in the garden, which becomes more ornamental and opulent. Color and smell rule, and exotic and familiar plants are mentioned by name. Over twenty plants are mentioned in *Le Bel Inconnu*, and over thirty-five in Diversion's garden in the *Roman de la Rose*. The garden becomes part of the adventure; the achievement of control over it is the image of a righting of the disturbed hierarchy of society. In both religious texts and romance a close relationship between garden and woman exists, as if the beauty and peace of the garden were an extension of the lady herself.

An uneasy balance pits woman against man in the garden, precisely because this is the space where man delights in woman, given that both woman and garden provide sensual enjoyment. Yet this enjoyment must be on man's own terms: his masculinity must not be threatened. Enslavement to a woman was not only personally disastrous, but also damaged society as a whole, overturning divinely established order. In medieval misogynist texts there was steady enumeration of examples of even the wisest and strongest of men (Samson, David, and Solomon, as well as Adam) becoming enslaved by women.[43] Regardless of their virtue or intentions, women posed a threat to society unless kept under proper control.

The ambivalent nature of the garden in medieval literature extends to woman and to man's relationship to her. This is because sex, the woman, and the garden are intrinsically linked by the pleasure they produce (deemed suspect) and by their reproductive qualities (deemed good). But this is only one part of the equation. The other has to do with power, the controlling power that encloses both the woman and the garden. It is up to the owner of the garden, properly the woman's husband (or male relatives), to control space and what it contains. And it is for the woman and the garden to accept this control.

CHAPTER SIX

Verbal Representations

JOHANNA BAUMAN

Representations of gardens abound in the textual record of the Middle Ages. The garden descriptions may be short and oblique or long and involved. The gardens described range from small, simple, unadorned, and walled to sprawling, elaborate, and embedded in the larger landscape, replete with identifiable design features, plantings, and a sense of the garden as a functioning social space. Some of these sources approach the subject from the practical perspective of garden making, such as encyclopedic listings of plants and agricultural treatises; others approach the garden as an imaginary space in which meaning and symbolic significance take precedence over form and function, as seen in works associated with the literature of the medieval romance. As highly conventional descriptions that seem to refer in most cases to existing texts, these written representations would seem to reveal more about the history and continuity of literary traditions than of built gardens and landscapes.

The rhetorical nature of this literary tradition was addressed most famously by Ernst Curtius, who identified the locus amoenus as an ancient topos underlying landscape and garden descriptions in medieval poetic and epic texts. According to Curtius, these descriptions did not embody a true feeling for nature but functioned rather as a means to structure narrative,[1] posing a major challenge to garden historians seeking to discern from them evidence for the appearance and design of real gardens. If, however, one approaches these texts not as reflections of garden reality, but rather as another means of bringing

gardens into being, employing sometimes similar discursive strategies of or-
namentation and assembly, it is possible to see how, despite the fact that they
are deeply steeped in rhetorical traditions, texts about gardens can provide a
deeper understanding of how medieval garden culture was constructed.[2]

In this brief chapter, I will explore how a selection of practical and imaginary texts both reflect and participate in the construction of medieval garden
culture, beginning with the most commonly occurring garden topoi: paradise,
the locus amoenus, and the hortus conclusus. Practical and literary works will
then be considered separately, to show how the garden descriptions are framed
and invoked in each instance and draw on prevailing garden tropes.

GARDEN TOPOI

Paradise as a Garden

The Judeo-Christian conception and geography of paradise can be traced back
in part to the description of Eden in Genesis 2:8–10. Described as containing "every tree that is pleasant to the sight and good for food," Eden was an
orchard with a temperate climate. Located at the center of this landscape of
indeterminate scale was the tree of knowledge from which Adam and Eve were
forbidden to eat, and springing from the tree were four riverheads that flowed
out of the garden, whereby the tree came to be equated with a fountain, a fix-
ture in both actual and imaginary medieval gardens. A wall, another common
feature of medieval gardens, is never specifically mentioned in Genesis, but
the enclosure of Eden is implied by the presence of the angel guarding it with
a flaming sword after the expulsion. Eventually, the word *paradise*—derived
from the Persian *paraidaeza*, denoting a hunting park or royal enclosure—
was also used to refer to Eden, whereby the biblical ideal came to be associated with an existing landscape type with earthly connotations of luxury.[3]
This notion of paradise was later conflated with the golden age myths and
landscapes of Homer, Hesiod, Virgil, Horace, and Ovid, giving rise to the medieval notion of the earthly paradise of natural beauty and an eternally vernal
climate.[4]

Paradise, however, not only denoted a beautiful landscape or garden; it con-
jured up a way of life and a stage of historical development. In Eden—before
disobeying God's commandment not to eat from the tree of knowledge—man
and woman had dwelt simply and in harmony with all the beasts, unencum-
bered by sickness or strife; their responsibility was to "dress and keep" the
earth, but not, as after the expulsion, to till the ground and labor. In this ideal

state, there was no need for the arts that came to define humanity and ensure its survival in the face of such postlapsarian adversities as hunger, extreme climates, and sickness.[5] Eden also suggested a completeness that stood in marked contrast to the fragmentation of the world the first couple encountered after the expulsion.

Christian theologians and philosophers debated the meaning of Eden, its location, and whether or not it had been or continued to be a real place to which human beings might one day return.[6] From the tales of such "travelers" as John Mandeville and descriptions of the utopian Kingdom of Prester John, two distinct images of paradise can be discerned: firstly, Adam and Eve's primitivist state presented in the Eden of Genesis, where they lived simply in a beautiful natural landscape unmarked by human artifice;[7] secondly, the sumptuous earthly paradise of the Land of Cockaigne, characterized by excessive eating and drinking in a highly ornamented landscape or garden furnished with all manner of luxury goods and built structures.[8] Earthly paradises such as the Land of Cockaigne in many ways resemble the paradises of the Qur'an, which may have served as the model for these antitypes of the Old Testament Eden in the medieval period.[9]

Locus Amoenus

As described by Ernst Curtius, the locus amoenus is a structural element in medieval poetic and epic texts. It is a literary set-piece that describes a pleasant place found in the natural world that the protagonist of a romance happens upon accidentally in the course of his wanderings. Loci amoeni are often clearings with a brook running through them; they include singing birds, groves, meadows, flowers, shade, and fresh breezes. Curtius traces this tradition back to the works of such Latin writers as Ovid and Virgil, who in turn had taken their inspiration from descriptions of nature in Homer and Theocritus, whom Curtius credits with being the originators of pastoral poetry. According to Curtius, this topos was the setting for that particular moment in the narrative when the protagonist of the story seeks refuge from turmoil.[10]

In the Middle Ages, this naturally occurring place also came to be associated with gardens of love, a meaning that was reinforced by Isidore of Seville's false—but preferred—etymology in the *Etymologiae*: "According to Varro, 'pleasant places' (*locus amoenus*) are so called because they promote love (*amor*) only and, draw to themselves things that ought to be loved." The word *amoenus* relates more closely to the garden's lack of profit-making or public function, and Isidore presents this meaning in an alternate etymology: "According to Verrius Flaccus, they [*loci amoeni*] are so called because they are without a 'public function' (*munus*), nor is anything in them like business, as if the term were amunia, that is, without profit, whence no profit is rendered."[11] This etymology may be tied to Curtius's designation of such garden descriptions as rhetorical embellishment; the locus amoenus provides the author with an opportunity to describe a garden that will allow the reader, like the protagonist, to linger within a lovely, soothing place that exists for its own sake. The function of the device may be purely rhetorical, but—as will be elaborated below—it also appeals to the senses and soothes the mind, a power attributed in this period both to gardens and literature.[12]

Hortus Conclusus

The hortus conclusus is the garden topos that most overtly identifies the garden as a female space; an association that plays a particularly pivotal role in the gardens of medieval romances. The image of the hortus conclusus is derived from the fourth chapter of the Song of Solomon in the Old Testament. The poem may have been an epithalamium written for the marriage of King Solomon and is sometimes thought to be a description of Solomon's own garden.[13] In the dialogue between the bridegroom and his bride, the beauty of the garden is equated with the body of the bride, and in the fourth chapter of the text, the bridegroom declares:

> A garden enclosed (*hortus conclusus*) is my sister, my spouse; a spring shut up, a fountain sealed. Thy plants are an orchard of pomegranates, with pleasant fruits; camphire, with spikenard, Spikenard and saffron; calamus and cinnamon, with all trees of frankincense; myrrh and aloes, with all the chief spices: A fountain of gardens, a well of living waters, and streams from Lebanon (Song of Solomon 4:12–16).

From the earliest days of the Christian church, it was difficult for theologians to come to terms with the Song of Solomon as a biblical text. Its overtly sexual and sensual nature stood in marked contrast to the Christian code of moral conduct regarding sexual behavior. The early church fathers sought to accommodate the sexual content of the verses through allegory, equating the love of the bridegroom for the bride with the love of the believer for Christ.[14] It was not until the twelfth century, however, that the subject and garden of the story came to be inextricably linked to the Virgin Mary.[15] The enclosed but bountiful garden is an apt symbol for the Virgin and the miraculous birth of Christ from her chaste but fertile womb.[16] The fertility of earthly paradise, like the fertility of the Virgin as garden, is achieved miraculously and freely without furrowing the earth or sowing seeds. The Virgin Mary's chaste perfection makes her the antitype of two other women traditionally associated with gardens: Eve and Venus. Eve's temptation of Adam (perhaps sexual) leads to the expulsion from the "first" garden; and Venus presides over a bower as the goddess of love and an emblem of female fertility and fecundity which eschews Mary's chastity.[17]

The triumvirate of Eve, the Virgin Mary, and Venus and their association with gardens and nature mirror the complex role of women in the Middle Ages, inasmuch as women were simultaneously seen as temptresses, paragons of chastity and virtue, and bearers of children. With regard to the representations of gardens addressed below, there exists a correlation in some of them between the small, enclosed nature of the garden spaces and the hortus conclusus, on the one hand, and the exotic trees and plantings, on the other. In terms of meaning and function, the garden is often portrayed as the domain of women and as a setting for love. The women, like the gardens they inhabit, are simultaneously forces of nature and culture, inasmuch as both derive their power from the fertility and chaos associated with nature, but only achieve perfection when tamed by culture—or cultivated—either by Christian morality or the spade.[18]

PRACTICAL GARDENS

Traces of paradise, the locus amoenus, and the hortus conclusus can be identified in a number of practical texts about the making and keeping of gardens. Included among these are references to gardens in twelfth and thirteenth century encyclopedias and garden descriptions in such agricultural texts as Albertus Magnus's *De vegetabilibus* and Piero de'Crescenzi's *Liber ruralium commodorum*. These practical works draw on such Roman agricultural writers as Cato, Columella, Varro, and Palladius, as well as lists of plants from ancient herbals and works on medicine. The listings of plants provided in these contexts, however, should not be taken at face value. Plant names were often derived from existing works that were copied from others, such as the ninth-century *Capitulare de villis*, Charlemagne's famous decree that outlines how to maintain a rural estate.[19] The *Capitulare*, for example, included Mediterranean plants that would have been difficult to grow in the northern climes where the work was compiled. Although the texts provide clues regarding the components of a typical garden, how gardens were constructed on the ground, and how they could be used and enjoyed, they do not clearly describe garden layout and design. Even when garden practices or activities are illustrated, such as grafting and pleaching, the language of practical literature is ambiguous and vague, which begs the question of the function of these works. It is unlikely that these texts would have been read by practicing gardeners or farmers, their audience being more likely drawn from the educated strata of society, those with an abstract interest in practical pursuits: a monarch overseeing his subjects, an owner overseeing his estate, or a philosopher with an interest in the workings of the world.

Encyclopedic Texts: Gardens of Knowledge

References to gardens were often included in the works of such twelfth- and thirteenth-century encyclopedias as Alexander of Neckham's (1155–1217) *On the Nature of Things*, Thomas of Cantimpré's (1201–1275) *Book on the Nature of Things*, Bartholomäus Anglicus's (1190–1250) *On the Properties of Things*, and Vincent of Beauvais's (c. 1190—1264?), *Mirror of Nature*. As their titles suggest, the authors of these works sought to compile in one place a complete account of heaven and earth, which often began with God, the angels, spirits, and heavenly bodies, and continued with such earthbound subjects as human beings, creatures of the land and sea, plants, stones and minerals, geography and climate, and the four elements.[20] The information was presented in short entries on each subject and relied heavily upon existing authorities, including the Elder Pliny, whose first-century thirty-seven-volume *Natural History* originated the genre.[21] Isidore of Seville's *Etymologiae* is another important source. It was completed in the seventh century and presented information on the sum of human knowledge by using a method that relied on the origins of words or etymologies. The flurry of encyclopedic activity in this period may have been motivated by the rediscovery of Aristotle in the twelfth century, but it has also been suggested that the encyclopedists were influenced by Augustine's remark in the *Christian Doctrine* that it would be marvelous to assemble in one volume the nature of all things.[22]

Knowledge about gardens is found first and foremost in listings of plants and trees that outline their function and medicinal uses, and many of the references replicate what is found in herbals that can be traced back to Pliny and the medical writings of Galen and Dioscorides. Gardens need not be mentioned explicitly; Isidore includes in his list of plants such flowers associated with pleasure gardens as crocus, iris, narcissi, roses, lilies, and violets in the section aromatic and common plants.[23] All of these, Isidore says, should be planted in "a garden (*hortus*) [which] is so called because something always 'springs up' (*oriri*) there, for in other land something will grow once a year, but a garden is never without produce."[24] In keeping with Isidore, Alexander of Neckam describes plants grown in the garden without mentioning the garden's outward form; the plants with which, he says, the "garden should be ornamented" (*hortus ornari debet*) include flowers, herbs, and vegetables that are used for both medicinal and alimentary purposes, and fruit trees especially suited for a noble garden (*nobilis hortus*).[25] In the supplement to his main work, Alexander also describes a church garden, which he says is adorned with flowers of different colors, such as violets, lilies, and roses (*ecclesie variis ornatur floribus*).[26]

The type of completeness sought in these encyclopedias might be said to be paradisiacal, inasmuch as they strove—like Eden—to contain all things known to man. In this way, the garden tradition parallels the encyclopedic tradition: both seek to reassemble in one place what has been dispersed and divided across the globe.[27] These encyclopedias also provided a basis of knowledge about gardens and agriculture that would be mined by later writers. When ornamenting their literary texts with plants and gardens, poets and authors likely consulted the plant listings in encyclopedias for inspiration and information.

Albertus Magnus: Gardens of Health

Plants and agriculture constituted only a small part of the larger works of encyclopedists. Other authors, such as Albertus Magnus (1206–1280) and Piero de' Crescenzi (c.1233–c.1321), devoted entire treatises to these subjects and secured a special place for pleasure gardens in them. Albertus' *De vegetabilibus* of 1260 is in part an Aristotelian discussion of plant life, part herbal, and part agricultural manual.[28] The chapter on the pleasure garden—which he calls a *viridariorum* and may be roughly translated as green space—appears in the book on agriculture, which he defines as the art of transforming wild plants into cultivated ones. Here Albertus addresses the basic situation and layout of the pleasure garden, the types of plants it contains and how they should be arranged, and the function of the garden as a place of health.

The small garden, he writes, is "a place of no great utility or fruitfulness . . . lacking in cultivation," open to the healthy winds of the north and east and closed to the violent, unhealthy winds of the south and west.[29] At the center of the garden is a square patch of turf that has the texture and density of hair, around which are planted fragrant and flowering herbs, in addition to some flowering plants, such as violets, lilies, roses, and gladiolas. Between the central lawn and the herbaceous border is a raised turf-seat that is described as "flowering and pleasant" (*caespis florens et amoenus*)[30] evoking the locus amoenus, and on the periphery of the garden are trees and vines intended to cast shade on the occupants of the turf-seat. In addition to the recommended plants and trees, Albertus advises diverting a cool and pleasant stream into a stone basin at the center of the plot, whose beauty and purity will produce pleasantness. The pleasure garden Albertus describes appears to be an abbreviated or abstracted locus amoenus with its water features, bird song, abundant shade-giving trees, grassy turf, sweet-smelling flowers, and orientation to the most pleasant and healthful breezes.[31]

The functional aspects of Albertus's garden are deeply indebted to the doctrine of the four humors as outlined by Avicenna, according to whom all plants, climates, people, and things can be narrowed down to a balance between hot and cold and dry and wet properties or complexions.[32] A garden functions to keep the humors in balance in a variety of ways, and it refreshes the senses, in particular the senses of sight and smell. The sense of sight, Albertus says, is primarily refreshed by the green color of the turf, which, according to the Aristotelian color spectrum, occupies the mean position between the extremes of black and white.[33] As the mean between these two extremes, green most pleases the sense of sight because it allows the eyes to rest and be restored. The variety of sinewy and hair-like plants is also pleasing to the eye because it stimulates eye movement. This alternating between rest and motion is fundamental to keeping the humors in balance.[34] The sense of smell is pleased by herbs, flowers, and fragrant trees, but the most important function of trees is to provide shade, not fruit, as Albertus explicitly states. Another major benefit of the small herb garden is pleasant and fresh air, which in medieval medical theory was considered one of the most important means of ensuring good health.[35] Access to fresh air not only determines the situation of the garden vis-à-vis the cardinal directions but also dictates that trees not be planted too close to one another, since dense tree plantings would block the free flow of air through the garden.

The emphasis on health and the importance of the color green have paradisical connotations. The garden's healthful properties seek to restore the state of perfect health enjoyed by Adam and Eve in Eden, and the mode of perceiving color jibes with the symbolic meanings of green in a Christian context: refreshment and renewal, eternal life and resurrection.

Piero de' Crescenzi: Gardens of Delight

Although Piero de Crescenzi's *Liber ruralium commodorum* is greatly indebted to Albertus Magnus's *De vegetabilibus*, his overall approach to the subject of agriculture follows more closely the Roman agricultural writers. The treatise is divided into twelve books and provides direction for the management of an entire farming estate, from the construction and situation of the buildings to the domestication and maintenance of various plants and animals. Crescenzi sets himself apart from the Roman writers by drawing special attention to the pleasure garden where plants and trees are not arranged for obvious utility, but rather in such a way that they can give pleasure to the mind, which, in turn, has a positive effect on bodily health:

> In the previous books, trees and herbaceous plants have been discussed according to how they are of use to the human body; but now the same ones must be discussed according to how they give pleasure (*delectatione*) to a rational soul and consequently preserve the health of the body, since the humoric state of the body is always closely related to the disposition of the soul.[36]

The pleasure garden book consists of eight sections, three of which describe gardens as spaces and five of which provide practical recommendations for how to use trees, fields, vines, and herb gardens to pleasurable effect. The first section on the small herb garden is a gloss on Albertus Magnus's pleasure garden, but of greater interest are Crescenzi's descriptions of gardens for people of moderate means and gardens for kings and other lords, which cannot be traced back to specific sources, suggesting that they are based on Crescenzi's personal observations.[37] Unlike the small herb garden, defined primarily as a place to refresh and delight the senses, the medium-sized garden for large and moderate landowners is a place where trees are cultivated both for shade and fruit. It is composed of orchards and meadows and surrounded by a hedge of thorns and roses or pomegranates and other fruit trees. The trees are carefully ordered, arranged in rows according to type, and interspersed with vines that offer both delight and utility,[38] which is reminiscent of the encyclopedic impulse to collect and order information.

The garden for kings and wealthy lords is made up of a series of garden spaces connecting the castle and the hunting park.[39] Crescenzi recommends that such an abundant pleasure garden be located on twelve-and-a-half acres or more of well-irrigated, flat land surrounded by a high wall. Adjacent to the palace, which is located in the south, "will be made a pleasant garden (*loco amoenum*) and a Dominican herb garden, and a bee hive, and a columbarium, and an enclosure for young hares, which will serve a select community."[40] From the palace garden, members of the court have views directly into the northern section of the estate, which is made up of meadows and groves with a more natural appearance. This area is home to the wild animals that members of the court may observe flitting back and forth over well-placed alleys.[41] As a complement to the main palace, Crescenzi suggests building a summer palace constructed of trees. Such a pavilion with its leafy walks and bowers can be used in dry weather and will also provide shade in the summer months.[42]

In such a garden, with its delightful flora and fauna, Crescenzi says, "The king will not only take pleasure, but sometimes, after he has performed serious and obligatory business, he can be renewed in it, glorifying God on high, who is the origin and cause of all good and legitimate delights."[43] In the larger garden, the power of delight goes beyond the healthful benefits of the small garden: it provides an opportunity for contemplation and religious devotion. This is especially true for the king, who may retire here after performing his official duties, a purpose reminiscent of the classical ideal of retreating to one's villa to experience rural *otium*, or leisure, in preparation for the *negotium*, or business, of the city.[44]

Implicit in medieval texts about making gardens and cultivating the earth is the idea that in doing so one is creating a more perfect, rarefied space in which human beings, by imitating and working together with nature, can create a place that approximates the ideal of paradise. Similarly, encyclopedic treatises in which such gardens are represented are engaged in assembling dispersed fragments of knowledge with the goal of creating a complete world view, or, as in the case of Crescenzi's work, a complete view of agriculture. The audience for and creators of these texts belonged to the same elite, learned culture that had the means to design and maintain lavish gardens and estates, and exercised both aesthetic and economic control over the landscape. Their interest in these works is primarily recreational, for as Crescenzi's writes in the dedication of the *Liber ruralium commodorum* to Charles II of Anjou, the King of Jerusalem and Sicily, the treatise was intended for "the consolation and delight of his soul and the perpetual use of his subjects."[45]

LITERARY GARDENS

Gardens in practical texts may have imaginary features, but they are more likely to be ready literally. In literary works, by contrast, gardens exist as allegorical representations or function as a setting for a story in which the presence of the garden serves both to ornament and create meaning. Even so, direct parallels between practical and literary texts can be found when plantings or layouts are described and in the ways gardens are shown to relate to the physical and mental well-being of the fictional characters that inhabit them.

De Amore: Gardens of Love

Featured in the fifth dialogue of Andreas Capellanus's *De amore* (On Love) is an allegorical garden of love that displays many of the features and functions of the iconic and practical gardens described above. Andreas's work, which is often liberally and misleadingly translated as *The Art of Courtly Love,* was composed in France between 1170 and 1174. It consists of a series of exegeses on love and eight dialogues that give specific recommendations for how courtship between men and women of different classes should occur. The work has been interpreted as a manual on medieval courtship practices (the basis for the contested notion of "courtly love"), while others see it as a work of satire, based as it is upon Ovid's farcical *Ars amatoria* (Arts of Love).[46] The pleasure garden in the fifth dialogue is portrayed as the setting for courtship between members of the nobility,[47] and in attempting to convince the noblewoman not to be stingy with her love, the author invokes the image of a location in a beautiful meadow, "closed in on all sides by every kind of fruitful and fragrant tree, each bearing marvelous fruits according to its kind." The circular garden is divided concentrically into three distinct and walled-off areas with three entrances, to the south, west, and north that are guarded by women reflecting different approaches to love and its fulfillment. These women are also gate-keepers and determine who may or may not enter depending upon the humoral makeup associated with the cardinal directions over which they preside: the women at the western gate are excessively wet and hot and allow anyone to enter, those at the northern gate are cold and dry and allow no one to enter, and those at the southern gate exhibit a balance of these extremes and allow only the worthy to enter.

The three complexions represented by the women are reasserted in the three concentric rings of the space, which may be reached by means of a beautiful and temperate path that leads to the interior. *Siccitas,* the outer ring, is dry and hot, and its female inhabitants, "those who would not have pity on the soldiers of Love," are forced to sit on bundles of thorns to protect their feet from the heat, and the bundles shake causing their clothes and skin to be torn. *Humiditas,* the second ring, is hot and wet with plants growing in profusion and is filled with "common women," who, it is implied, are profligate with their affections. The central and culminating space—the ideal setting for love—is the garden of *Amoenitas,* or delightfulness, a garden presided over by the Queen of Love; its perfectly temperate climate represents a mean between the extremes of the outer rings. In the middle of the garden stands "a marvelously tall tree, bearing abundantly all sorts of fruits" from whose roots gush forth "a wonderful spring of the clearest water" tasting of "sweetest nectar" and filled with many varieties of fish. The tree as fountain conflates the tree of knowledge and the fountain at the center of paradise, from which brooks and rivulets flow out to water the whole garden. This delightful place—echoing the luxurious paradises of Islam and the Lands of Plenty—is perfectly suited for courtship and outfitted with couches on which lovely and comely women sit. The Queen of Love presides over perfectly balanced *Amoenitas*; it is her domain. The other unbalanced domains, however, are presided over either by women who give of themselves too freely or not freely enough. In medieval medical books, health and love were closely linked. While unrequited or overindulged physical love was thought to lead to poor health, sex, when practiced in moderation, was thought to have beneficial properties beyond procreation and the garden as an idealized expression of such moderate practices underscores its salutary function.[48]

Andreas's allegorical garden is an idealized space that is being used to make a didactic point about love, one of the primary themes associated with medieval gardens of the imagination. Here the Queen of Love echoes the Virgin Mary seated at the center of the hortus conclusus, presiding over a garden that is simultaneously fertile and chaste. The fountain and water channels in this garden bring to mind the water features proscribed for practical gardens, and the metaphor of the doctrine of the four humors that is employed throughout the garden description ties back to Albertus's and Crescenzi's focus on bodily health and the need for a temperate and pleasant climate in the garden. For Andreas, such a pleasant climate encourages courtship and love.

Roman de la Rose: Courtly Gardens

The *Roman de la Rose* is one of the most important works of medieval literature, influencing Chaucer, Dante, and Boccaccio, and contains, according to the protagonist, "the whole art of love."[49] Much like Andreas's *De amore*, it straddles the line between satire and allegory and has been read both as a primer on love and as a cautionary tale of its pitfalls. The story opens in the month of May—"the amorous month, when everything rejoices"[50]—and unfolds in a series of beautiful and fantastic landscapes and gardens peopled by allegorical figures who take turns guiding and thwarting the nameless lover on his quest for the rose, a complex metaphor standing for, among other things, his beloved. The book consists of two parts and was begun by Guillaume de Lorris in 1230 and completed by Jean de Meun over forty years later in 1275, and at the center of each are two very different but closely related gardens: the Garden of Delight and the Park of the Shepherd. Jean's text and garden are often characterized as more overtly erudite and less sensuous than Guillaume's, with its emphasis on didacticism and Christian morality.[51]

At the beginning of the first part, the lover comes upon the Garden of Delight after walking through a lovely landscape and washing his face and eyes in a stream. The "large and roomy garden, [is] entirely enclosed by a high crenellated wall, sculptured outside and laid out with many fine inscriptions"[52] and allegorical figures. Upon being let into the garden by Idleness, the lover declares that he thought he was "truly in the earthly paradise,"[53] and his attention is drawn to the multitude of singing birds and the beautiful dancing and music-making people. He describes the garden as "completely straight, regular, square, as long as it was wide,"[54] and the enumeration of its plantings evokes the image of an abundant orchard. In addition to at least one each of the most beautiful fruit trees, there are such ornamental trees as laurels, pines, olives, and cypresses, as well as branching elms and other shade trees planted in rows to maximize their shade-giving properties.[55] The entire space is densely covered with fine, green grass, dotted with fountains connected by brooks and channels, and filled with a profusion of flowers, such that "the earth was very artfully decorated and painted with flowers of various colors and sweetest perfumes."[56] It is here that the lover comes upon the fountain of Narcissus in which he espies a rose; he is pierced by the arrows of the God of Love, initiating his quest.

This garden, which becomes the stage for the interaction of allegorical figures and the education of the protagonist, contains many elements familiar from practical garden texts. The regularity of the rows of trees in the orchard is reminiscent of Crescenzi's garden for people of moderate means, which includes nearly all of the trees mentioned in the *Roman*. The poet specifies at what distance the trees should be planted from one another to allow for the best and most pleasing shade, a surprisingly practical detail to include when illustrating an otherwise fantastical space. The thick grass, sweet-smelling flowers, and fountains recall the central elements of the small garden of herbs. The meadow, replete with brooks and channels, is also filled with scampering animals and singing birds like those found in the garden for kings and lords.

The Park of the Shepherd, by contrast, is the place where Genius presents the Lover with the resolution of his fate in a sermon couched largely as a comparison with the Garden of Delight. Whereas the Garden of Delight is square and peopled with beautiful dancing figures, the Park of the Shepherd is round and occupied by a shepherd and his flock. This landscape is more rustic and natural, its beauty—according to Jean—more enduring than the vanity of the pleasure garden, which, in the words of Genius, contains "trifles and bagatelles" that are unstable and—like the dancers of the carols—will pass away and disappear. The deceptive fountain of Narcissus is contrasted with the purity of the fountain of the park from which "all good things well forth." It "waters all the enclosure," and "is so precious and health-giving, so beautiful, so clear, clean and pure," that sheep who drink from it will never be thirsty or sick and will live forever.[57]

This comparison makes clear that the Garden of Delight is a garden of vanity, deception, and earthly love, while the Park of the Shepherd is a garden of purity related to a more elevated spiritual love. As in the garden of Andreas, the *Roman* contains a debate between carnal and sexual love and spiritual and non-physical love that is expressed directly through the gardens represented. The gardens of the *Roman* can draw on some or all of the complex associations: they are places of cultivation, of culture, and of courtliness, but they are also places of nature and its potential carnality, with life-giving fertility and abundance. As members of an educated elite with an understanding of prevailing garden tropes, the audience for this work would have been able to discern their similarities and differences in understanding the poem's doctrines and meanings.

Remede de Fortune and *Floire et Blanchefleur:* ### Gardens of Artifice and Earthly Delights

Guillaume de Machaut's *Remede de Fortune*, completed in the mid-fourteenth century, also revolves around a protagonist who seeks solace in a garden-like landscape where he encounters Fortune with whom he enters into a dialog about love and its vicissitudes. Having recently left behind his lady, the protagonist of the *Remede* wanders around in search of answers to the woes of love and stumbles upon the Park of Hesdin. After finding the entrance in the high wall surrounding it, he enters:

> I walked along among the plantings, which were more beautiful than any I'd ever seen, nor will I ever see any so beautiful, so fair, so agreeable, so pleasing, or so delightful. And I could never describe the marvels (*merveilles*), the delights, the artifices (*ars*), the automata (*engins*), the watercourses, the entertainments, the wondrous things (*estranges choses*) that were enclosed within. Nonetheless I can well say that one could not seek any diversion in the air, the water, or on land that he'd not find there immediately, always ready to answer his wish.[58]

Rather than setting his story in a fictional landscape, Machaut invokes the Park of Hesdin, perhaps the most famous and extensive of the known medieval gardens thought by many contemporaries to embody paradise on earth. Located in northwest France, it was begun by Count Robert II of Artois around 1295 and carried on after his death in 1305 by his daughter, the Countess Mahaut of Artois.[59] The garden, which some scholars claim may have been created with the landscape of the *Roman de la Rose* in mind, remained in existence until the mid-sixteenth century and was probably best known for its mechanical marvels.[60]

It is unfortunate that Machaut enumerates but does not describe the *merveilles* he saw at Hesdin. He instead uses the trope of inexpressibility: the wonders cannot be described even though these are what draw him into the park, inciting him to take refuge by a "pure, clear fountain" where—reminiscent of the protagonist of the *Roman de la Rose*—he washes his face and eyes.[61] It is here that he will eventually encounter Hope, who offers him a consolation on the changeability of Fortune and the power of love. Machaut may be suggesting a correspondence between the artifice of the park and the artifice of his poem: both produce a sense of wonder and understanding.

In the fanciful French tale of *Floire et Blanchefleur*, in contrast to the *Remede de Fortune*, the automata in the garden spaces are described in great detail. The poem, which was originally transmitted orally throughout Europe, was written down between 1155 and 1170 and recounts the story of a love affair between Floire, a Saracen (i.e., Muslim) boy, and Blanchefleur, a Christian girl whose mother had been left behind during a raid on the Muslim kingdom.[62] The story of their love takes place in three gardens whose exotic plants and marvelous structures evoke the gardens of Islamic paradises, as well was the fragrant beauty of the garden in the Song of Solomon. Born to a captive mother upon whom the emir and his wife have taken pity, Blanchefleur becomes the childhood companion of Floire, and the children grow up and are educated together. Their love is born and blossoms in the garden of the emir, an "orchard fair" with "herbs and flowers of every kind and every color" and "shrubs and trees" filled with songbirds,[63] where they go daily to "take their ease, eat, drink, and play."[64]

Disapproving of their growing attachment, Floire's parents send the boy away and in his absence sell Blanchefleur to Babylonian merchants. To console the grieving Floire when he returns home, his parents set a jewel-bedecked tomb to her in a garden. The tomb is made of marble and set with inlaid gold and gems that evoke the heavenly Jerusalem. At the four corners of the tomb are "hollow pipes" that animate a wind-driven automaton of gold representing figures of Floire and Blanchefleur that embrace when the automaton is activated by the wind. The tomb is surrounded by four eternally blooming and fragrant trees: an "ebony tree" whose boughs are "always laden, bright with red and white flowers . . . fairer indeed than flowering rose," a fragrant "balm-tree," and a blooming "chrism." Like the orchard in which their love was born, this second significant garden of the story contains birds that "warble" such exquisite melodies that "no ear e'er heard the like of it."[65] This monument to their love does not, however, appease the grieving Floire. Realizing he has been deceived by his parents, he goes to Babylon in search of Blanchefleur.

Blanchefleur, meanwhile, has been imprisoned in the magical Tower of Maidens by an emir who annually selects and sacrifices a bride from his harem. This fantastical tower, like the tomb, is made of precious gems and metals and is driven by water-powered mechanical devices that move miraculously between all three levels of the tower. It is located in a garden surrounded by a wall with turrets bedecked with brass birds whose artificial singing is said to charm the tigers, lions, and leopards in the landscape beyond. The garden "blooms heedless of time" and lacks "no tree, be it rare or dear." It is a delight to all of the senses, filled as it is with flowering plants and crystalline streams (sight), sweet fruits (taste), singing birds (hearing), pleasant breezes and a moderate climate (touch), and fragrant spices (smell). Included among "other spices redolent" are pepper, cinnamon, frankincense, rosemary, and cloves. Together, these elements prompt the author to state that there is no country like it "from east to west" such that any "man" approaching it "might well believe that in some wise / He's been brought to Paradise."[66] Floire succeeds in rescuing Blanchefleur from this false paradise, which resembles both the Edenic orchard in which their love was born and the funerary garden containing Blanchefleur's illusive tomb.

The garden of the Babylonian king has all the trappings of an earthly paradise and evokes the exoticism of the Eastern gardens described in the Song of Solomon. Its geographical specificity conjures up images of the earthly paradises described in medieval travel literature, and the detailed descriptions of its orchards and spices hearken back to the practical literature of the encyclopedists and their listings of plants and trees. Automata, however, are rarely mentioned as garden features in the practical literature. While Crescenzi recommended including in the garden things that are "useless" (literally, *inusitatas*), he is most likely referring to horticultural marvels of grafting and not the mechanical marvels found more frequently in later Renaissance gardens.[67] The presence of such devices in literary gardens allows for reflection upon the relationship of art and nature and a celebration of human artifice. While the automata may be described as magical or supernatural, their inner workings are also revealed, which demonstrates how human ingenuity can harness such natural forces as wind and water to produce marvelous and pleasing works of artifice.[68] In the story of Floire and Blanchefleur, however, the automata are directly linked to the deception associated with the earthly paradise. The beautiful orchard in which their love blossoms contains only trees, flowers, and birds, whereas the gardens containing automata are false, dangerous, and impure.

Tristan: Gardens of Adventure and Romance

The romance of the child-lovers Floire and Blanchefleur takes place primarily in gardens. Such heroic stories as Gottfried von Strassburg's *Tristan* of the thirteenth century, however, are more likely to feature forests and hunting parks as backdrops for adventure and romance. Garden-like spaces exist primarily as respites from harm, havens for love, and settings for courtly activities and celebrations.[69] The story of Tristan begins with a festival set in the gardens of King Mark's Tintagel Castle. It is here that Rivalin (the brother of King Mark) and Blancheflor fall in love, eventually conceiving Tristan, the hero of the story. The guests are described as encamped in a "greensward," each according to the pleasures granted them by their station, in a manner reminiscent of Crescenzi's socially stratified approach to gardens:

> The princely camped in princely, the courtly in courtly, fashion: some were encamped under silk here, others elsewhere beneath blossoms. Lime-trees sheltered many: many were lodged in arbors made of boughs of leafy green. Neither household nor guests had ever been lodged so delightfully.[70]

The pergolas and other arboreal structures are reminiscent of those Crescenzi recommends for the gardens of kings and lords. But more importantly, Gottfried von Strassburg shows how each garden feature entertains and refreshes a different sense. The garden is filled with wood birds whose songs are a delight to the ears. The eye is pleased by flowers, grasses, leaves, and blossoms, which, in pleasing the eye, gladden the heart. The beautiful garden elements at Tintagel Castle interact with the eyes of the guests: "May's friend the greensward had donned a summer smock of flowers so lovely that they shone again from the dear guests' eyes."[71] In this way, the castle garden described by Gottfried meets the expectations of Albertus and Crescenzi as a place that delights all the senses, but especially the sense of sight.

Tristan, who eventually returns to Tintagel Castle, falls desperately in love with his uncle's wife, Isolde, and as the star-crossed lovers are drawn together, torn apart, and brought together again, they find themselves moving between a variety of garden-like settings that are alternately juxtaposed with the castle and the forest. When they are lodged in the castle, they meet secretly in an orchard located outside the castle walls into which a brook flows directly from Isolde's chamber. This garden is the setting for the well-known scene of the assignation by the brook, in which King Mark, attempting to catch the lovers in an act of infidelity, hides in a tree in the garden, but the lovers, seeing his shadow, deny their love and temporarily keep the jealous husband at bay. Eventually, however, the lovers are discovered and banished to the woods. Here their love is finally able to flourish in a marvelous cave filled with precious metals and gems and surrounded by a beautiful park-like space where,

> there were innumerable trees which cast the shade of their leafy boughs upon this mountainside . . . there was a level glade through which there flowed a spring—a cool, fresh, brook, clear as the sun . . . The bright flowers and the green grass, with which the glade was illumined, vied with each other most delightfully, each striving to outshine the other.[72]

In contrast to the more structured, courtly garden space outside Tintagel Castle, the ones located within the larger landscape appear firmly rooted in the tradition of the locus amoenus. They are settings for love that provide the protagonists with a brief respite from the reality of the insurmountable barriers to their affection. The garden's function as a haven from this reality is temporary, however, and after Mark finds the lovers in their cave of love locked in an embrace, they are finally and forever separated. They are drawn out of the respite of the garden and back into the harsh realities of the every day. They are, in effect, banished from paradise.

As I have shown in this selective sampling of medieval garden descriptions, there are a number of common features and themes that can be identified across a broad spectrum of texts. Writers will often place their protagonists in a garden or a garden-like landscape that they explicitly liken to an earthly paradise, or, as in the case of the practical garden texts, the texts themselves seek to replicate a paradisiacal completeness. Gardens are often embedded in a larger landscape and act as havens from the forest or the castle. As such, they may function as settings for lovers' trysts or places for relaxation and renewal; they exhibit such recurring features as fountains, watercourses, green turf, birdsong, and fresh breezes which evoke the locus amoenus. Gardens, finally, are frequently represented as the domain of women, as spaces of fertility, but also as spaces where through her civilizing force the idealized female is able to exert her power over the unruliness of men and nature. In many of these garden texts, the literary strategy of allegory is employed to inspire the reader to contemplate religious and spiritual meanings and reinforce moral codes and mores. Their function, as is often the case in medieval arts of all kinds, is to teach. In this way, the beauty of the texts and materials is a means to an end, not an end in itself, but the significance of the textual gardens extends beyond their role as mere reflections of prevailing tropes and traditions. Medieval writers used words to bring into being gardens of the imagination whose function in many ways mirrors that of built gardens. Literary works, like pleasure gardens, were created to please and delight an audience privileged and educated enough to appreciate and find solace in them.[73] The parallel between the pleasures of the garden and the pleasure of the text is nowhere as clearly drawn as in the *Decameron* (c. 1350) where Giovanni Boccaccio explicitly asserts the salubrious justification for both gardens and literature. He sets forth a justification for reading much as Albertus and Crescenzi asserted a justification for the pleasure garden.

It is plague time in Florence, and a group of seven young women and three men—known as the brigata—have fled the city of Florence and come to take refuge in a country villa that is filled with "gardens . . . meadows, and other places of great charm and beauty."[74] In these gardens, which exhibit features of paradise, the locus amoenus, and the hortus conclusus, they seek solace from the grim spectacle of the plague-ridden city by taking in the pleasant sounds of "birds singing," the pleasant sight of "fresh green hills and plains," and breathing in the "country air."[75] Once they have settled in the villa gardens, the brigata seek out activities that inspire cheerfulness, which, according to medieval medical theory, by refreshing the mind balance the humors of the body.[76] In the gardens, they indulge in such physical activities as weaving garlands, dining out of doors, playing games, singing songs of love, playing music, dancing, walking, and sleeping, but they agree that the best way to spend the hotter part of the next ten days will be in telling stories, from which "a great deal of pleasure and of profit is derived."[77] Boccaccio "preserves" on paper the 100 stories told over the course of ten days by ten different people. The garden setting and healthful function of the storytelling are reinforced in the framing device that introduces and concludes each day of stories, but even in the breaks between storytelling sessions, members of the brigata "overwhelmed by the beauty of their surroundings . . . remained where they were and whiled away the time in reading romances."[78] Romances filled, no doubt, with marvelously embellished passages describing gardens that provoke their readers to look up from their books and into the beauty of the surrounding landscape, refreshing their senses and delighting their souls.

CHAPTER SEVEN

Visual Representations

MICHAEL LESLIE

IMAGE, MATERIAL, AND CULTURAL HISTORY

No medieval garden survives in anything remotely like original form. Dimensions, structures, and materials can occasionally be confirmed from archaeological explorations; some nonfiction documents contain details from which one can deduce—often shakily—features of early gardens. Otherwise, we are principally dependent on contemporary literary and visual representations. But these latter come freighted with problems, as a glance at most works concerned with the medieval garden immediately suggests. The overwhelming majority of images date from the fifteenth century—and often later in that century— and they represent scenes and themes from religious myth or secular romance; their gardens are often stylized or schematized, often idealizations, frequently representing fictional locations accessible only to members of the social stratosphere. The manuscripts of Pier de Cresenzi's *Liber ruralium commodorum* (completed c. 1305) might be thought to be exceptions, since that work concerns the practicalities of estates and gardens, but these manuscripts are again elite productions, as are the surviving illustrated botanical lists and treatises (such as the *Tacuinum sanitatis*, the eleventh-century Arabic treatise available from the thirteenth century in Latin versions). The concentration of images is indisputable.

Equally problematic, especially in relation to the writing of cultural history, is the tendency of historical scholarship to read visual representations for the detail of garden features: turf seats are confirmed by this image, the structure of herbers by that. Almost all these representations come from manuscripts, largely of secular romances or Books of Hours. Some of these are so vivid, and so familiar, that there is the danger that we think it easy to reconstruct from them both gardens and the culture of their representation.

The garden elements featured in these images certainly existed but the ease of moving between representation and reality or representation and culture is illusory. Looking at many works on medieval gardens, it is as though we have access only to a scrapbook of illustrations torn from their original contexts; Frank Crisp's *Mediaeval Gardens* (1924) is invaluable but in this respect perilous. Representations of gardens need to be seen in their contexts since these release information otherwise unavailable. For instance, we need to attend to the physicality and properties of the object of which the image forms part. If a manuscript, where on the page does the image of the garden occur? What kind of volume does it occur in, where within the volume, and in relation to what other elements? How does the manuscript image relate to garden representations that form part of the wide range of other objects upon which gardens appear? What is the material of which a garden image is formed?

Even more importantly, what were the cultural uses of the object that made representation of a garden pertinent and what did the garden imagery mean in this context? Who owned such objects? Who saw them? Who bought them and gave them, why, when, and to whom? As Peter Burke, the doyen of cultural history, recently wrote, "who is representing what to whom, by what means and with what effects[?]"[1] In popular books on medieval gardens, so often the caption to an illustration says the equivalent of "Lovers on a turf seat"; but which lovers, sitting in which garden? In its original location, the image is precisely placed, surrounded by other signifying components. As William Blake, that latter-day creator of illuminated books, wrote, "Art & Science cannot exist but in minutely organized Particulars, / And not in generalizing."[2]

This chapter seeks the benefits of a modest degree of defamiliarization by approaching the visual representation of the medieval garden first by looking at largely non-manuscript examples and leaving direct consideration of the traditional topics of the *hortus conclusus*, the Garden of Love, and Marian iconography to its conclusion. The particular medieval iconographies of gardens need to be understood in terms of their locations (in the entrance porches of churches; on the walls of internal rooms as opposed to those on an exterior) and often with an eye to the nature of the object of which they form a key part.

Some objects are intimate and gain much of their value and meaning through degrees of exclusivity, while at the same time staging intimacy and exclusivity within wider social relations: betrothal gifts, such as a chest, or mirror-back, or comb.[3] The representation of gardens on these is culturally different from representations that are designedly more public, such as those in a grand Bible meant to be seen by many.[4] We should also recognize that even within a single category, distinctions must be made: the garden images of a small Book of Hours, for more personal use, may be different and have different cultural resonance from those in a grand display example, such as the *Très Riches Heures* of Jean, duc de Berry.[5]

Garden representations also occur in significant relation to each other and to other images, and their nature and meaning are often determined by such relationships. An obvious example is adjacent representation within the same volume of the Garden of Eden and the Annunciation, itself an event often staged as occurring across a threshold between garden and interior. In the *Très Riches Heures*, an Annunciation is paired with an exquisite image of the Garden of Eden, but this latter is tipped-in, added on a separate sheet.[6] That this conjunction of gardens is not fortuitous is confirmed by one of, if not, the first

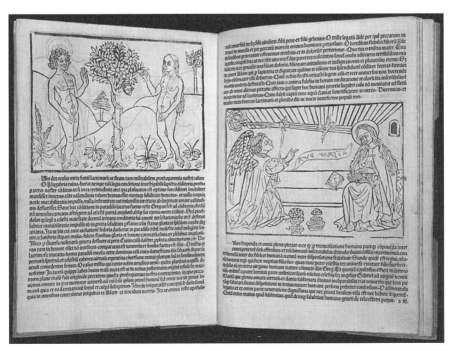

FIGURE 7.1: Juan de Torquemada's *Meditationes* (Rome, 1484). © Lessing J. Rosenwald Collection. Library of Congress.

printed illustrations of the Annunciation, which is juxtaposed in a single opening with the representation of Adam and Eve. The garden has been reduced to
mere potted plants, but the conjunction is striking nonetheless. It appears in
Juan de Torquemada's *Meditationes* (Rome, 1484), the first illustrated book
printed in Italy. Torquemada is commonly thought to have been instrumental
in introducing printing to the Papal States and (as is often the case with early
printed books) in form, structure, and arrangement of elements his *Meditationes* probably follows closely the model of manuscripts. The book clearly
continues a traditional iconographic pairing, in which the common garden
topos asks us to perceive connections and contrasts that reveal the meanings
of providential history: the Old Adam and first woman in their garden before
they sinned; the only immaculate woman, herself a garden, at the moment of
the incarnation of the New Adam of salvation.

SATIRE'S CLARITY: RETROSPECTIVE COMMENTARY ON IMAGES OF THE MEDIEVAL GARDEN OF LOVE

Visions of Harmony

Such significant relationships between images occur not only within a single
work but can also be historical, and nowhere is this clearer than in satire. An
example from the end of our period makes this point almost brutally.[7] The
engraver Master E.S. is famous for many images of young people, often lovers,
in gardens, and he draws with confidence and sophistication on the traditions
of representing the Garden of Love in the Middle Ages. "The Great Garden of
Love" (c. 1466) comes from early in the history of printing, a technology of
mass production and wide consumption, breaking away from the uniqueness
of manuscript illustration (even if manuscript illustrations followed patterns
and emerged from commercial workshops, and even if printed images were
often pasted into manuscript volumes in the fifteenth and sixteenth centuries).[8]
Information on the consumers of prints is very limited, but we know these
prints were produced in numbers for purchase.

Traditionally, the Garden of Love is a perfect place, populated by refined
young men and women engaged in cultured play, existing in an eternal spring,
focused only on their emotional relations, and largely without being subject
to moral judgment (Thomas Malory's refusal to brand as illicit Lancelot and
Guinevere's adultery—"love in those days was not as love is nowadays"—is an
example of the setting aside of judgment for such visions of love and celebrity);[9]

FIGURE 7.2: E.S. "The Great Garden of Love" (c. 1466) © The Cleveland Museum of Art. John L. Severance Fund 1993. 161.

and the elegance of the concept is encoded not least in the uniqueness of the representation and the rarefied material form: colorful hand-painted illustration on precious and expensive materials such as vellum. But the coming of the printed sheet introduces differences in material and manufacturing process that are inseparable from meaning. The Garden of Love presented by this print is a commentary on societal, cultural, and economic change. Instead of an elegant and expensive wall, hedge, or fence, this garden is enclosed within unadorned, rough paling. Three couples, none of elevated social standing, are engaged to different degrees in frank sexual acts. In the foreground, a woman grabs the coat of a grinning Fool, revealing his genitalia; he leers boldface at the viewer. Beyond the fence and, to indicate distance, higher up on the page is a contrasting scene: horse-riding nobles joust and hunt against the background of churches and towns. And high on a hill stands a castle, the architectural embodiment of a military aristocracy and the life of refinement and culture to which the social elite aspires and which is imaged so often in the Garden of Love.

But this printed version has only a sardonic interest in such vestiges of a hierarchical and deferential society; alcohol and sex are unabashedly and without euphemism or disguise on offer within its enclosure. Master E.S. here makes no attempt to claim the garden as encoding an ideal society through order, elegance, and harmony. There is no suggestion of the religious associations that often lurk in even the most secular garden representations. The print seems a derisive commentary on a long tradition of garden representation. It achieves its satire because viewers recognize the garden iconography of which it makes fun.

Perhaps most striking is the figure on the left, seemingly an itinerant musician, who looks into the garden and has one foot across the threshold, his unfinished, opportunistic motion energizing the image, but also suggesting that this garden is no longer characterized by separateness, no longer fascinating the viewer with impenetrability, where the surrounding wall might signal almost magical peace, security, and stability within. No unicorns will seek refuge here. In illustrations to the *Romance of the Rose* and other romances, courtly figures dance elegantly, their dancing an expression of restraint and, through it, order. The garden, as a space often dominated by and largely devoted to women, represented female chastity and was an icon of chastity's cult (the hortus conclusus). In the *Très Riches Heures*, a noble betrothal is represented[10] and, to the bride's right, a calm, ordered, enclosed, and unpopulated garden, seeming to represent her ideal femininity. But in Master E.S.'s print, the garden has become a place in which entertainments of all sorts, including sex, are commodities available to all who can pay a modest price. Its seats are not built of expensive and elegant brick; rather, the turf bench's sides are rough planks, held together with wooden uprights clearly nailed into place. Instead of a fountain, there is a small pool in which containers of wine cool.

The Pains, Excitements, and Delights of Exclusion

The promiscuous accessibility of Master E.S.'s "Great Garden of Love" (and correspondingly of the inexpensive print in contrast to the luxury manuscript) emphasizes by contrast what we see in the magnificent *Très Riches Heures* image for "April" by the Limbourg brothers: the garden is almost invariably represented as a world separated. Particularly towards the end of the Middle Ages and particularly in manuscript illustration, representations of the garden tend to emphasize enclosure within a fence or wall. Often there is a sense that what happens within the garden is "secret"; that word has its etymological roots in ideas of division and separation, just as do the words for *garden* (*jardin*, *Garten*, *hortus*, etc.) in various ancient and modern European languages.[11] If not secret in the modern sense, the viewer of the illustration and reader of the manuscript typically encounters these garden images from a world beyond a wall or fence that excludes us, looking in from a position sufficiently elevated that we can see over the barrier—there are few views *through* a gate or door, but the point of possible entry is frequently prominent in the foreground, often guarded or supervised. The consumers of manuscript images are clearly members of an affluent and cultivated elite; nonetheless, the images convey a sense that there is beyond the wall a yet more refined, yet more luxurious, yet more orderly, harmonious, and stable world that we can glimpse but not enter. It is worth noting the contrast, once more, with Master E.S.'s "The Great Garden of Love." There, our view of the merry-making is from within, the outer fence and gateway halfway up the print. Not so in images of the Garden of Eden, which we see from the (dis)advantage point of the fallen, the exiled. Such images often show the moment of the expulsion as well as the paradisial conditions of life before the Fall. That world is the one we, as children of Adam and Eve, lost at the moment our parents became mortal, to death devoted, as well as human; these images are suffused with nostalgia. In secular romances, the dominant emotion has less to do with loss (though Malory's deflection of judgment invokes the sense that the passage of time has exiled us from a simpler and nobler past), but the thrill still derives from the unattainability of an imagined perfection: personal, social, and environmental. Both the garden and its privileged occupants exist in perpetual spring, forever young, forever elegant, forever untroubled, or if troubled, with those perturbations that are proper to the young, elegant, and leisured.

The garden, then, is represented as a special place, a perfection from which one is, or has been, excluded; a place that contains the things one aspires to but knows unattainable. The garden is characteristically different, and its differences clarify the definition of the space one is currently in, from which one looks. Perfection comes in many forms: that of a prelapsarian paradise; of the immaculateness of the mother of God; of love and happy desire as paramount in human relations; of a world without the imperfections of mountainousness, aridity, sterility, barriers, or extremes of climate.[12] One of the most fascinating examples, here represented in a later but faithful copy (original c. 1448; copy, 1804), is the representation of the Garden of Eden as part of the world map by a Venetian monk, Fra Mauro. This delightful vignette shows a triply enclosed paradise with a single central tree, God to one side, Adam and Eve to the other. A pool beneath the tree is the source of the water that separates into the four rivers of Biblical myth, and the water flows under a bridge guarded by an angel into an entirely different landscape beyond. Outside the enclosing wall or fence are mountains, scrubby grassland, and a tree that leans alarmingly. Eden's tree stands erect and that garden's surface is smooth; that beyond is uneven, like the disorderly, lumpy grass of Master E.S.'s "Great Garden of Love."[13] Beyond Eden's walls is a landscape of sin, retribution, and pain; within the enclosing forms we can never repass lies a garden of perfection, purity, stillness, and safety.

Something of the same can be said of another splendid view of the Garden of Eden and the consequences of Adam and Eve's transgression. Modern readers know Boccaccio primarily as the author of the *Decameron*, a text that lent itself to illustration of gardens. But for fifteenth-century readers, especially in France, his history of the disasters that befall even virtuous people—*De casibus virorum illustrium* (c. 1355–1375)—was particularly magnetic. The 1409 translation of the work into French is by Laurent de Premierfait, secretary to Jean, duc de Berry.[14] It opens, necessarily, with Adam and Eve, and this inevitably produced images of the garden and the expulsion. In this manuscript (in which the first illustration shows the duc de Berry receiving the translation from Laurent de Premierfait), the creation occupies the upper portion, with the actors—human, divine, and snake—in a flowery mead, backed by single and clumped trees, with a terminal fortified wall. The tower of the wall is at the centre and is echoed by one of the two towers to the gate through which a disgraced Adam and Eve are being forced by the Archangel. This moment occupies the bottom left; to the right of the gate, Adam and Eve work, surrounded by domesticated animals (there are none in paradise, it seems). The landscape of the working world is notably less green than that of prelapsarian Eden.

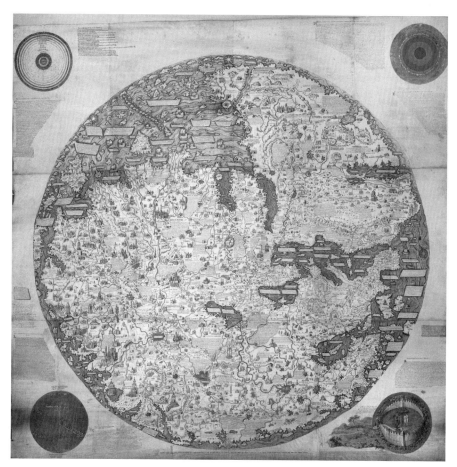

FIGURE 7.3: Fra Mauro, World Map British Library. ©The British Library Board, Add. MS 11267.

HORTUS EXCLUSUS, INCLUSUS, AND CONCLUSUS: THE IMAGE OF THE GARDEN AND THE ICONOGRAPHIES OF LOVE, BETROTHAL, MARRIAGE, AND SOCIETY

Form, Function, and Meaning: The Minnekästchen and the Image of the Garden

Enclosure, perfection, intimacy: the garden as a special space is a key reason for its prominence in the iconography of objects associated with betrothal and marriage, not least the medieval casket, the *Minnekästchen*. The "Talbot" Casket (c. 1400) in the British Museum, a leather box with embossed exterior decorations and painted interior scenes on the underside of the lid (the image on the base is likely to be a later addition, as is that inside of the Crucifixion and donor figures), is an expression of the culture of gift-giving and gift-acceptance in connection with affection, betrothal, wedding, and marriage customs. It embodies the complex constructions of and interplays between public and private worlds; the narratives, philosophies, and theologies of secular and divine love; the fashion for luxury materials and craftsmanship; and the emulation of sophisticated, exotic, often Muslim, cultures. The exact purpose of these caskets individually remains debatable, but they were clearly prized objects and their imagery is frequently focused on the garden.

The exterior scenes on the "Talbot" Casket show, *inter alia*, lovers meeting and wooing in gardens represented with economy and stylization. No one would use these images to reconstruct an actual medieval garden, but the garden iconography is no less significant for that: it is essential to the casket's cultural meaning and function.

On the top are shown two trees with six figures beneath playing a garden-based game; the principal figure is a woman placing her hands on a kneeling man's head. There is an inscription on the outer rim of the lid: *Ihesus autem transiens per medium illorum ibat ave maria gracia dominus tecum* (But Jesus passing through their midst went His way [Luke 4.30] [;] Hail Mary, full of grace, the Lord is with you [Luke 1.28]). This inscription is a common charm, also found on contemporary coins and amulets, and as is frequently the case it seems here to be a ward against theft. But there is a rich ambiguity about what might be stolen with regard to the "Talbot" Casket: the box, and/or its contents, and/or what the box and its images embody figuratively, a mutual realm of intimacy, humility, affection, self-offering, and possession. Hidden by the lid is another inscription, which only partially survives: "*AMOR IUSSAT ALLICE EST.*" This is an addition but seems to have been made very soon after the box's manufacture; it was probably added by the purchaser when presenting the casket as a gift to his betrothed. Around the sides of the casket are more lovers beneath trees, engaged in various stages of courtship, particularly strikingly on the front, to either side of the lock. So incorporated, the material fastening device takes on narrative and figurative meanings to do with boundaries, barriers, wooing, acceptance, betrothal, marriage, exclusiveness, and intimacy. Another late fourteenth-century casket, in the Musée Cluny, Paris,[15] again shows lovers in a garden on the front panel, the man separated from the woman by the casket's lock. In this instance, the woman is passing her belt beneath the lock, and the casket has a Flemish inscription: "Aen sien doe doet ghedenkren", "Looking at this will make you remember." Here again, there seems to be rich complexity to the object and its images: the casket and garden can contain those things deemed precious either because they are valuable in themselves or by virtue of their status as mementos. Both casket and garden stand for, are figurations of, remembering, places of memory.[16]

FIGURE 7.4: "Talbot" Casket exterior side. © The Trustees of the British Museum.

Details of gesture come freighted with meaning: the woman's intimate gift of the belt is a sort of anti-apple in the betrothal's Garden of Eden, an affirmation of trust and concord. There is gentle certainty to the woman's gesture; the obviously sexual metaphors of lock and girdle are left elegantly at one remove. On another, earlier, casket (British Museum), a Limoges enamel box of around 1180, the implications of garden and lock are different: here, to the right of the lock on the front panel a woman, standing amid plant forms, holds a leash securing her semi-kneeling lover.

From these scenes, it is impossible to identify a single textual narrative to which they might be alluding. However, the viewer is clearly meant to associate such representations with the many stories—verbal compositions but themselves frequently and most powerfully visual—in which key moments take place in gardens. The scenes could illustrate romances such as the *Châtelaine de Vergi* (see below for a summary) or one of the tellings of the Tristan and Isolde story (as on another casket [1350–1370] recently the subject of a re-evaluation by Henrike Manuwald and Nick Humphrey,[17] and another ivory "Tristan" Casket in the British Museum, from around 1200). The lovers appear in couples, elegantly attired, the male wooing, the female delicately accepting proffered love; the garden setting is essential and intrinsic.

Opening the "Talbot" Casket reveals a remarkable contrast. Inside the lid, bordered to left and right with plant-shaped arabesques in which sit birds, is a large scene of the Annunciation, with the Virgin, seated and reading, inside an architectural structure, an oratory; the angel greets her through a porch, substantially outside in an exterior space with plant forms, but with one knee on the threshold between the two realms. (Compare this with Domenico Veneziano [c.1410–1461]: "Annunciation" [c. 1445–1447; Fitzwilliam Museum, Cambridge], where the angel's lily is what visually joins the two worlds, the only thing that penetrates from the architectural to the hortus conclusus seen through a gateway.) Liminality is again significant, stressing the contrast between what is within and what is outwith, but the significance is utterly different from Master E.S.'s itinerant musician entering the satiric Garden of Love. The conjunction of scenes is also found in the Musée Cluny example: once opened, that casket again shows the Virgin seated within her enclosed garden.

In both instances, these caskets have interior and exterior representations of gardens, but the scenes contrast strikingly. The exterior is completely secular, alluding to human love and its social and physical expressions; the interior is entirely devoted to divine love and the moment of the incarnation.[18]

And that may be the point: garden and casket represent seemingly distinct versions of love, human and divine, as ultimately different facets (albeit far from equal) of a single phenomenon. The exterior scenes participate in the secular visual iconography of love, emphasizing competition, pursuit, game-playing, and the urge to physical consummation. Their gardens are the scene for process. But the interior scenes show the Virgin Mary in hieratic mode. Many images of the Virgin in the garden show her at full length, frontally facing the viewer, standing or seated in a throne-like chair, separate from those around her and engaged in an occupation that communicates self-possession and self-containment (she often reads). Human love in the caskets' garden images is dynamic, shown at a liminal, unstable moment, one moment in a process of becoming. By contrast, the Virgin and her garden are outside time, unchallengeable, beyond process and provisionality. The effect of combining these through the topos of the garden and in the single form of the casket, outside and inside, is to assert a seamless connection between the human game of love and the divine love that transcends it.

Casket and garden have tantalizing overlaps in form and signification: the casket with its lid and lock is physically an *arca conclusa*. The box as betrothal or wedding present connects with the action of grace at the Annunciation: both are associated with threshold moments between distinct phases of personal or providential history. Beyond the threshold, one enters a charged realm of commitment, fecundity, and intimacy, all achieved through the gift of love. This

FIGURE 7.5: "Talbot" Casket interior. © The Trustees of the British Museum.

cluster of associations is characteristic of much medieval garden iconography. The special, separate, and enclosed space of these gardens releases the significance of the actions and transactions imaged as taking place within and outside.

Manuscript representations of gardens and the *Minnekästchen* or *coffrets* resemble actual elite pleasure gardens in that they are precious, expensive, and available only to the few.[19] Such caskets often include images of the hunt and of the unicorn, again associated with both secular and sacred garden iconography. The properties of the object are not only physical but figurative: rich materials, finely worked, communicate the preciousness of what the caskets convey. These objects are delightfully self-conscious: form, function, and meaning all align. As, more perversely, with Master E.S.'s promiscuous print, the medium is the message.

Garden Imagery and Intimacy: Gardens on the Body
and the Body in the Garden

The *Minnekästchen* are among the most prominent examples of elite objects of which garden iconography frequently forms part. Others include such items as ivory mirror-backs and combs, brooches, belt buckles, belts and girdles themselves, and *aumônières*, the purses worn by or given to women, particularly married women who command households, from which to distribute alms. These last items often have a garden scene, again the setting for the negotiation or display of love.

These objects form a particular class: they are intimate in that they touch or are in close proximity to the body, particularly a woman's body, and they are often identified with her sexual and gender roles: as beloved, wife, mother, and centre of the household. And yet they are also worn on the exterior, and thus visible.[20] In Jean Renart's *Le Roman de la Rose ou de Guillaume de Dole* (early thirteenth century), the heroine, Liénor, contrives to make the villainous Seneschal look guilty of rape by sending him her belt, brooch, and purse, but convincing him to wear the belt concealed; when it is revealed and he cannot explain why he has it, Liénor uses this as evidence that he had stolen her possessions and her Virginity.[21] No one questions the association of the belt with the woman's sexuality. Girdles (worn immediately below the breasts) were common betrothal gifts, not only signifying possession and union but also frequently associated with fertility and successful childbirth: the childless wife of Francesco Datini, famous as the "Merchant of Prato," was encouraged to wear one.[22] Touching a fragment of the Virgin's girdle, one of the most prized of relics, was supposed to ward off miscarriage and stillbirth; the girdle is still displayed five times a year in the cathedral in Prato on the great Marian feast days.

The association of the garden with the woman and her sexuality results in frequent use of garden iconography on these intimate objects, such as a striking Siennese belt, probably a gift to a woman, now in the Cleveland Museum of Art.[23] Over two meters long and decorated with *basse-taille* enamel plaques, this is an elaborate and expensive accessory. It ends with an image of lovers embracing amid floral forms. Clearly, the position of the belt on the woman's body makes it an intimate item. The woman's sexual and marital self is circled by the garden iconography of the belt's plaques: she is herself the garden thus fenced and she is, in Milton's later phrasing, "the fairest unsupported flower" within the garden.

A similar association of garden iconography, circularity, and the commitment to marital fidelity and chastity can be seen in surviving betrothal or marriage brooches. This example shows the young couple within an enclosed garden, fenced with gold. Their hands are linked with a belt or girdle, one end held by the woman. The brooch is an object to be worn on the outside of clothing, a public display of a joining that is intimate but nonetheless not private, a

FIGURE 7.6: Marriage brooch, Kunsthistorisches Museum.

garden into which we can see but only the young couple enter. Their relationship constitutes the garden the brooch images.

   The same conjunction of images and associations is found on such items as
ivory mirror-backs and combs. In one mirror-back (c. 1390–1400), in the Walters Art Gallery[24] the lovers are shown standing beneath a stylized tree, with
architectural details to their left and right; this garden is in close proximity to
a castle or city. The man is making a gift to his beloved of a comb, an intimate
item. The carving is not detailed enough for there to be recognizable decoration on the depicted comb, but ivory combs themselves survive, and on these,
garden scenes are frequent, often illustrating the most recognizable moments
from the most well-known romances. In the most famous and influential of
such texts, the *Romance of the Rose*, Idleness appears holding a mirror:

> She hadde [in honde] a gay mirror,
> And with a riche gold tressour
> Hir heed was tressed queyntery.[25]

In this description, Idleness's hair does not sport a comb, though it is frequently
asserted that she does. Idleness is "Aqueynted . . . and pryve / With Myrthe,
lord of this gardyn."[26]

   A comb (c. 1320), now in the Victoria and Albert Museum, has garden
scenes on both the front and back, each showing three courting or sexual
scenes. At the centre of each side is an image of the lover kneeling; on the front,
the beloved crowns him with a circular object, a wreath or chaplet perhaps; on
the back, he may be offering the object to her. One of the panels on the back
also includes the circular object, which is being held by both lovers, standing, seemingly equal and in agreement. But the other panels show something
significantly more vigorous: the male lover appears to be making aggressive
sexual moves, reaching out for and grabbing the beloved. Again we see a bringing together of scenes of instability and process with those communicating
achievement and stability. With characteristic scholarship and acuity, Michael
Camille points out that such garden and garland scenes appear frequently on
combs and mirror-backs, and Camille connects this with a passage in the *Decretum Gratiani* (Gratian's *Decretum* or *Concordia discordantium canonum*),
a mid-twelfth-century harmonization of canon law that includes comments on
the meanings and dangers of gift giving; in one manuscript, these meanings
and dangers are illustrated with just such a scene of chaplet giving. The garden
iconography of all these objects images the processes of courtship and also
represents courtship's fulfillment in betrothal and marriage. As objects, as gifts,
they participate in the rituals of desire and consummation.

FIGURE 7.7: Mirror case with two lovers, anonymous, Italian, circa 1410, ivory. Photo © Walters Art Museum, Baltimore.

Similar scenes appear on the front panels of *aumônières*. These—like the belts, girdles, and brooches—again play with the iconography of the garden as an enclosed, private space, but do so publicly, displayed on a woman's body. Christine de Pisan's work (particularly *Le Livre de la Cité des dames*) pushed back against the misogynist strain in medieval literature, represented not least by the most influential and much illustrated garden-based work, Jean de Meun's *Romance of the Rose*. De Pisan asserts the virtue of women and the value of courtly conduct. In *Le Champion des dames*, Martin le Franc defends and supports her. Outside the garden, the author is dressed appropriately for a cleric, but once in this characteristically enclosed garden, in this illustration, he removes his clerical garment to reveal an inner self, courtly Superman

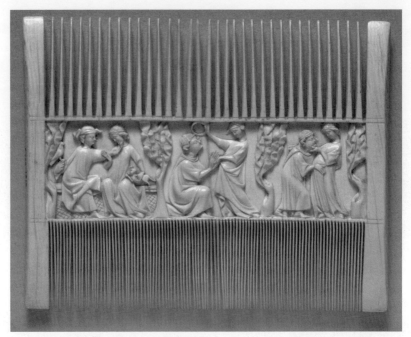

FIGURE 7.8: Comb, front. Photo © Victoria and Albert Museum, London.

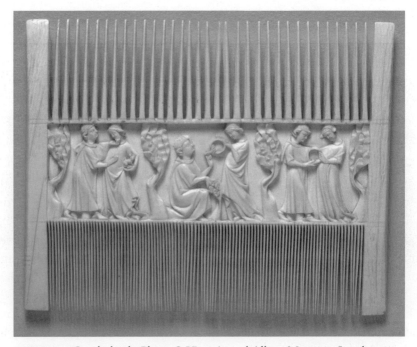

FIGURE 7.9: Comb, back. Photo © Victoria and Albert Museum, London.

to clerical Clark Kent: a fashionable young man whose body and clothes are those of the ideal long-legged, elegant-torsoed lover. Balancing his ink pot on his thigh, he writes with calm concentration in defense of women. Only in the special space of the garden can these different selves be reconciled.

FIGURE 7.10: *Le Champion des Dames*, par Martin Le Franc, Collection Bibliothèque Municipale de Grenoble Cliché BMG.

Martin le Franc's intentions are clear, but in interpreting the physical objects discussed, we should bear in mind their ambiguous status. Can they, as
gifts from man to woman, male suitor to beloved, husband to wife, manifest
an envisioning of garden space that represents mutual aspirations for com-
panionate affective marriage, the life of the newly married pair in Chaucer's
"Franklin's Tale" rather than the sad, hierarchical relationship into which they
descend as a nightmare result of the wife's careless vow? Or are they evidence
of male scripting of ideal female conduct and response? Dorigen's vow is made
in a "gardyn of swych prys," "verray paradys," "ful . . . of beautee with pleas-
aunce," and she is ultimately despatched by Arveragus back to that garden to
make good on her promise, which will involve the breach of commitments,
fidelity, and trust.[27] Chaucer is clearly drawing on the same associations of the
garden as the mirror-backs, combs, *aumônières*, and caskets, which depict the
imagined garden as the locale of a striking affectional equality, a mutuality in
the proffering of affection: "Love wol nat been constreyned by maistrie."[28]

Household Spaces and the Representation of the Garden

The objects discussed above are closely associated with what Anne Dunlop,
writing about the Palazzo Datini in Prato, calls "love at the intersection of
male and female realms."[29] The apparent feminization of household spaces
caused some anxiety in medieval Europe, not least in fourteenth and fifteenth-
century Piedmont and Tuscany, where frescos of garden scenes frequently decorate interior walls. We cannot be certain of the use of these spaces; they may
have served many functions. However, although Dunlop warns us that there
is no contemporary evidence for "the decorum of image placement within the
home,"[30] she goes on to quote Leon Batista Alberti giving broad guidance in
his treatise *De architectura* (c. 1450):

> [Painted subjects] which are the most majestic, will be appropriate for
> public works and for the buildings of the most eminent individuals; the
> second should adorn the walls of private citizens; and the last will be par-
> ticularly suitable for *horti*, being the most light-hearted of them all. We
> are particularly delighted when we see paintings of pleasant landscapes
> or harbours, scenes of fishing, hunting, bathing, or country sports, and
> flowery and leafy views.[31]

In general, Alberti is surely right, but garden imagery could, in some circumstances, appear on the walls of the residences of the eminent in the Middle

Ages and secular public buildings (garden scenes appear in decorative scenes at the entrances to churches, with the Garden of Eden prominent, for instance, in the mosaics of St Mark's Basilica in Venice). Here, they express power and status. Few cultures are as fascinating as medieval Sicily, with its unique combination of influences: Greek and Roman, Islamic, Byzantine, and Norman; the island's architecture expresses competition between, assimilation of, and reflection on all of these. In particular and in each of these cultures, Sicily's climate and environment gave particular status to the idea of the garden: the ability to create a flourishing garden despite aridity expressed the wealth and power of the ruler (the use of channeled water was here no less a statement of the ruler's authority, even over nature, than it was at Louis XIV's Versailles, and this Sicilian culture was also notable for its emphasis on the discovery and translation of Greek and Arabic technical texts essential to the manipulation of water and the great medical text, the *Tacuinum sanitatis*). In literature, Pietro da Eboli celebrates his monarch, the Holy Roman Emperor and king of Sicily Henry VI, by celebrating his realm as *Viridarium Genouard*, "the world's garden" (*Liber ad honorem Augusti, sive de rebus Siculis*). This perfect place has all the characteristics of an earthly paradise: never-ending flowering and fruiting achieved without any sign of labor; running with rivers sprung from the mythical source of pastoral poetry, the Arethusa fountain; unending happiness for its inhabitants. The kingdom of Sicily is the epitome of empire, and that perfection is expressed in the form and terms of the garden. The garden imagery of prosperity, power, and perfection is carried over into the interior decoration of the principal royal buildings of medieval Palermo (the city itself praised as a garden), not least the Palazzo Reale. In particular, the Zisa lodge (the name is derived from an Arabic term for "magnificence"), set in the royal hunting park, combined a real internal fountain with scenes of a perfect garden. These are too fragmentary to bear extensive analysis but make the point that the representation of the garden served political purposes associated with the world of male authority as well as communicated a sphere of life principally associated with the female. An inscription survives in the lodge in elaborate Arabic script: "In this exquisite palace you find the greatest king of the century . . . here we have a glimpse of the earthly paradise."[32]

Despite such instances, however, Alberti nonetheless judges that nonheroic scenes are most suitable for the household spaces of "private citizens," which women, by definition, were, and the most famous mural garden depictions are associated with those aspects of life in which women prominently participated.[33] At the Castello de La Manta, near Saluzzo, the fountain of love and other landscape scenes—more meadow than garden—appear high on the walls of interior rooms. In the loggia and courtyard areas of the Palazzo Datini in Prato, there are representations of heroes and the Worthies, but, high on the walls in the *camera delle due letta*, exotic trees and animals appear with the illusionistic representation of textile hangings below (such textile hangings—tapestries—themselves often represented garden and landscape scenes). The viewer has the sense of a privileged glimpse of things normally unseen: an intimate world away from the public sphere. To the modern eye, these scenes seem more forest than garden, and perhaps more fantastical than real, but Datini himself in correspondence calls them "gardens" and the exoticism probably connects them with his actual garden, known to have contained peacocks and unusual plants.

Perhaps the most fascinating and challenging series of scenes is that on the walls of the "nuptial chamber" of the Palazzo Davanzati in Florence. Here and elsewhere—on contemporary ivory caskets, for instance[34]—scenes from the startling, sanguinary thirteenth-century romance *La Châtelaine de Vergi* are depicted. To modern eyes, the opulence of the decoration may seem incongruous, but such chambers were not "private" in our sense; equally, the inappropriateness of the scenes depicted and the story of the romance may disappear when understood in the medieval context. This understanding requires us to step gingerly into the vexed territory of *amour courtois* and the complex arguments and ironies of one of the most celebrated medieval texts, Andreas Capellanus's *De amore* (c. 1185). Perhaps jokingly, Capellanus at some points seems to dissociate, even declare incompatible, love and marriage.[35]

La Châtelaine de Vergi, sometimes thought to be based on actual events at the Burgundian court, tells the story of a knight who enjoys a secret love affair with the married lady of the chateau of Vergi. The knight is sworn to absolute secrecy, but his position becomes difficult when he is propositioned by the wife of the duke, his feudal overlord. She, being rejected, tells her husband that the knight had attempted to seduce her. When the duke, who is also the chatelaine's uncle, reports to his wife that the knight has declared his innocence and that he is already engaged in a secret love affair, the duchess demands proof; the knight agrees to allow the duke to observe from the Lady of Vergi's garden. In the romance, the sexual encounters take place within a bedroom; the lover hides in a garden until the arrival of the chatelaine's dog signals that it is safe to enter. But in visual representations drawn from the romance, the meeting of the lovers moves outdoors, to the garden.

The duke was allowed to obtain his proof on the condition that the details were not disclosed to anyone, but he gives way to the duchess's demands for knowledge, making her promise absolute confidentiality. The duchess then discloses to the chatelaine that she knows of the affair, at which the lady dies of disappointment, the knight commits suicide, and the duke kills his wife and departs to fight in the Holy Land.

The key to the drama of the *Châtelaine de Vergi* appears to be the conflict between, maybe the incompatibility of, certain kinds of social bonds, each of which demands precedence. The lovers agree to absolute secrecy; the duke and his knight have sworn to a relationship of utter frankness and loyalty; the duchess insists that marriage entitles her to complete sharing of information with her husband.

Scenes from this perplexing romance unmistakably decorate what is accepted as a nuptial chamber in the Palazzo Davanzati.[36] The lower parts of the wall frescoes are designed to look like tapestries; the actual scenes are set within luxurious trees and greenery, with architectural details—towers, a stone ledge—marking the viewer's separation from the garden beyond, its inhabitants, and their story. The episodes are arranged in a manner similar to that found on the sides of the betrothal or marriage caskets previously discussed, separated by trees and the columns of arches. Such caskets, originating in French workshops, are known to have been offered as gifts in contemporary Tuscany.[37] The decoration of the Palazzo's chamber seems to be associated with the 1395 marriage of Francesco di Tomazzo Davizzi and Catalena (Italian for *chatelaine*) degli Alberti, and there is a contemporary manuscript of the *Châtelaine de Vergi* romance in the Biblioteca Riccardiana in Florence.[38]

To the modern eye it is not obvious why representation of scenes from this romance should have been thought suitable to a nuptial chamber: are they singularly disturbing warnings to a new bride about the perils of infidelity? But this is not a moral easily drawn from the poem. The chatelaine's adultery with her chevalier draws no censure from her uncle the duke, but the duchess's breaking of her promise and thus betrayal of her husband causes death in others and merits her own. The emphasis in the romance is on trust consecrated by mutual promises and mutual obligations—between woman and lover, vassal and lord, husband and wife—but the extravagant display of the chamber's decoration signals to the couple and their community that, through marriage, their obligations exist now not only within the intimate and special space of the garden/marriage but extend beyond and are crucial to the harmonious working of wider society. Such themes are explored in contemporary literary works, not only the *Châtelaine de Vergi* itself, but also works such as "The Franklin's Tale."

When we look at what is represented in the garden illustrations, it is clear that the focus is not only on the world of the lovers but on the ideal social world they represent and that surrounds them. As in the Palazzo Davanzati, refined love, courtship, and marriage are seen simultaneously as pertaining to individuals and to the wider culture of which they and their relationships inevitably form part and which their love, in some way, participates in constituting. In the *Romance of the Rose*, the dreamer's personal history is first set in the context of his entry into this sociable world, and illustrators seem to delight particularly in representing the Garden of Mirth and its inhabitants.

The emphasis in many of these images is on activity, but never on the actual work involved in creating and maintaining a garden. Rather, we gaze on the forms of social interaction: games are played, music is made, couples sit and converse, groups of young people—always *young* people—dance, sing, promenade, and eat alfresco meals. Like the garden's perpetual spring, its inhabitants are forever young, responding with elegance and decorum to ennobling passion. The garden is inextricably linked to this vision of a life of elegant and harmonious sociability, refined festivity in a world always temperate, and the images are frequently characterized by symmetries of form and color that convey the sense that all the elements of the garden—architectural, vegetable, and human—in their arrangement and occupation express an ideal order. The Dreamer in the *Romance of the Rose* surely desires his beloved, but perhaps he and we yearn even more to be admitted to that garden of sociable life lived without urgency and anxiety. We can imagine how fascinating and appealing such images must have been in the era of the Black Death and Boccaccio's *Decameron*, in which the young fugitives take refuge in a garden, escaping the chaos of plague and random death.

There are few instances in which the illustrator's attention is principally on the garden as separate from its human inhabitants. There is little attention to exotic plants (most identifiable plants come from a limited common stock, however beautifully represented) or idiosyncratic formal properties. The garden, whose elements are sometimes fantastic in their elegance, is nonetheless expressed simply: a fountain, one or more trees, a level lawn, flowers such as the rose and violet associated with the cult of love, somewhere to walk, somewhere to sit.

These images represent a special, separate space—not an agricultural landscape; not an urban townscape—marked by a barrier that preserves and protects. In manuscripts, positioning of the illustration on the page—mise-en-page—often incorporates a defining frame or border: we look through this apparent aperture to the garden beyond, gazing into that from which we are excluded. But in addition to the framing that is common in the structure of the book, images of gardens are almost invariably dominated by a fence or wall. The view we receive is often from a slightly elevated position, enabling us to see over that barrier into the different world within. Rather than a series of images representing episodes in the romance, in the manner of a cartoon as on the walls of the Palazzo Davanzati's "nuptial chamber," these images tend to mark set-pieces and moments of significant transition in the narrative and manuscript.

One exception to the representation of the physical labor of gardening occurs in the illustrations to manuscripts of Christine de Pisan's *Livre de la Cité des Dames*—an exception that may prove the rule. The work's title is perhaps a pun: the "city" built by Christine is the book itself, making its arrangement and mise-en-page all the more significant; but book and city are also an alternative society, equally if not better ordered, but on radically different principles. The women themselves wall in their garden, inevitably associating culture and cultivation. In Part 1, Lady Reason gives examples of women who have been pioneers in knowledge and the sciences, beginning with Minerva, goddess of arts and wisdom, Ceres the bringer of agriculture, and Isis the creator of gardens.

FIGURE 7.11: Christine de Pisan, *Cité des Dames*, © British Library Board (Harley 4431, f. 290).

THE BOOK OF HOURS AND GARDENS
IN RELIGIOUS IMAGES

Christine's city is represented as an enclosed space, often a garden with the women laboring within and on its walls. At the beginning of the third and final part, Lady Reason speaks of the greatest of women who inhabit the city's palaces, towers, and prominent buildings. Chief among these, inevitably, is the Virgin Mary, herself the hortus conclusus and the intense and culminating presence at the heart of the garden as a spiritual idea throughout this period. The pressure of the garden's religious associations can almost always be felt, even in the most apparently secular of contexts. The principal sources of those meanings are the gardens of the Bible (the Garden of Eden and the Garden of the Resurrection, when the risen Christ appears to Mary Magdalen), and, more figuratively but of equal power, the garden imagery of the Song of Songs, often implicitly or explicitly contrasted with Gethsemane, the Garden of Olives, infrequently represented, but when it is, as rocky and infertile, a sort of antigarden.

As in secular buildings like the Palazzo Davanzati and the Zisa hunting lodge, the representation of gardens occurs in significant spaces and on significant surfaces in religious buildings. Deriving from Byzantine usages, the area around the primary entrance to major churches was sometimes referred to as "paradise" (as on St Gall plan of an ideal monastery), and—as in the entrance mosaics at St Mark's Basilica in Venice—the association is stressed in garden representations found there, principally of Eden. The entrance to the House of God is clearly a special, liminal space, the very point at which the Christian moves from the realm of the Church Militant into the presence of the Living God, in the form of the consecrated host, joining the Church Triumphant. The primary Christian garden stories also centre on such decisive transitions—creation and resurrection—and on the union of God and his church, or the soul, derived from allegorical readings of the Song of Songs. The representation of the Garden of Eden at the entry points of churches heightens and intensifies our awareness that our individual and collective journey toward God and salvation has its place in that overarching providential history and that man's individual and collective journeys are prefigured in those of the Old Adam (and Eve) and Christ as the New Adam, in gardens.

There appears to be tantalizing evidence that different groups of religious adopted specific garden themes for their representations: orders, particularly enclosed orders, of female monastics appear to have been particularly enthusiastic about images of the Virgin within a walled or fenced garden, both in the hortus conclusus and herself that miraculous place.[39] Similarly, there appears to be a concentration of images of the risen Christ as a gardener in works associated with such orders as the Benedictines. Horticultural and agricultural labor were central to the life of these orders; Christ the gardener typically carries identifying cultivating implements and stands in an ordered and productive space.

However, two image types dominate religious representations of the garden: the Garden of Eden and the hortus conclusus associated with the Virgin Mary. Images of the Virgin place her, first, within an enclosed and fertile garden, clearly deriving from the emotional quality, if not the details, of the Song of Songs. She is usually centrally placed, and it is striking that she is so often represented full length, either standing or, more frequently, seated as on a throne, as *Regina Coeli*. There is typically a sense of conscious formality in her pose; she is aware that she is participating in the creation of meaning through ceremony and pose. Others watch her reverently. She appears in rich clothing, sometimes alone, sometimes holding the Christ child, reading or gazing calmly at the viewer, but rarely interacting with other figures (besides the child). These images are not social in the same way as those characteristic of the gardens of the romances. The Virgin often appears to preside over a different kind of society: a garden of the Virtues, for instance, or as the patron figure dominating a garden of saints. She does not need to *do* anything in this garden nor does she need to interact; her presence and identity guarantee the safety, structure, and nature of the garden. These gardens are often full of flowers (again deriving from the imagery of the Song of Songs), and there is a sense that the floral plenitude represents her fertility both as the mother of Christ and as the intercessive representative of a redeemed humanity. The floral plenitude often extends beyond the formal boundaries of the image, filling the margins of manuscripts to create an overwhelming image of the beauty and fullness of creation.

The representation of the garden as a site and symbol of female chastity meant, as (with a certain irony) in Master E.S.'s "Great Garden of Love" print, that gates and entrances assume particular significance. In image after image, the Annunciation takes place in a garden setting, with the Virgin inside and the angel addressing her through a doorway. This iconography seems to be derived, not least in its ambiguity, from extra-biblical texts concerning the incarnation, notably the Protevangelium of James from about 150 C.E. and the Homilies on the Annunciation by Gregory Thaumaturgus (third century). In the *Très Riches Heures*, there is a conjunction within a single opening between an image of the Annunciation[40] and, immediately preceding it, the Garden of Eden[41] with its inevitable and essential representation of Adam and Eve being expelled through the gates into a harsh world beyond. Significantly, this latter image was added to the book on a separate sheet, the symmetry with difference between two of the key events in providential history being insisted on. The Limbourgs seem to have intended the reader to consider the correspondences between the two images and the two gardens: the angles of the Virgin's head and gaze at the kneeling archangel are echoed in those of Eve offering the fateful apple to the kneeling Adam. The moment at which the original humans become "mortal," departing forever from paradise through that gate, parallels the moment at which the divine becomes human to defeat death, as the archangel speaks to the Virgin literally astride her gateway, his knee in the green world outside, his foot planted on the lintel. These images also occur at a crucial, liminal point in the object of which they are part, forming the transition to the Hours of the Virgin: the reader may be being encouraged to pause and prepare, to reflect on time and providential history, on the dramas of the expulsion and the Annunciation, so vividly expressed in the Virgin's hand raised in surprise at the archangel's exclamation: "Ave gratia plena." Hands create correspondences within and between these images: Eve raises hers to the serpent (as often, this has her own facial features) acquisitively; Adam raises his—in alarm? in anticipation?—as Eve proffers the apple; he again raises his in a gesture that most corresponds to that of the Virgin as the fiery angel drives him from the garden.

The mystic marriage between Christ and his Church, a theme often found in the Song of Solomon, picks up on the iconography of the Virgin and the garden in the *Très Riches Heures* and elsewhere: Mary is *Ecclesia*, the Church, and the garden; Christ is the lover who gains entrance and weds the bride, the beloved.

Images of gardens appear frequently in the Book of Hours, the special devotional book developed in the later Middle Ages for the laity, and itself often portable, like the objects discussed earlier. Inspired by the breviaries used by clergy, the lay Book of Hours is structurally freer: owner, creator, or patron could determine what it contained, choosing texts more or less close to the formal liturgy. Characteristic of the later fourteenth and fifteenth centuries, the Book of Hours is a product of the rise of lay devotion, a phenomenon that also produced the intense piety of the *devotion moderna*, the Brethren of the Common Life, and such works as Thomas Kempis's *Imitation of Christ* (early fifteenth century). Kempis did not write a work devoted to the Virgin, but devotion to the cult of the Virgin is everywhere in his writings. Similarly, the Book of Hours is usually dominated by the Hours of the Virgin, modeled on but different from the "Little Office of the Blessed Virgin Mary" found in the breviaries and missals of the clerics. The Book of Hours as a form comes into being at just the same time as Marian devotion becomes one of the principal features of Western Christianity, from the twelfth century onward. As an illustrated form, the Book of Hours is largely concentrated in northwest Europe—there were fewer illustrated Books of Hours in the southern Christian lands of Italy and Spain. Although Books of Hours were produced in France and elsewhere, the centre of production seems to have been the commercial and trading centers of the Low Countries, particularly Bruges and Ghent. In these cities, at the centre of so much political, commercial, and trading life in the High Middle Ages and also at the centre of the generation of the new forms of intense lay devotion, the creation of the constituent elements of the Book of Hours, particularly of illustrations, seems to have become almost industrialized.

The Book of Hours was in origin an object for private use: small and discrete. It was also a class-based object and somewhat gendered; Books of Hours were often given to the wives of the affluent. Until the end of the fifteenth century, when printing renders it available to a much wider audience, possession of even a simple Book of Hours was a marker of wealth and social status, often appearing in wills as the sole book owned by the testator.

Because the Hours of the Virgin dominate the form, because Books of Hours are particularly associated with women, especially new wives, and because these books grow out of an intense, private, lay devotional culture, it comes as no surprise that they are dominated by the image of the garden, especially the hortus conclusus, substantially derived from the Song of Songs. Eventually the Book of Hours will yield place at the end of the fifteenth century to the yet-simpler form of the Rosary, itself represented visually at the end of the Middle Ages and, because of its name, closely associated with plants—the Virgin as mystic rose—and the garden.

The association of the Virgin with enclosures and their entrances is unsurprising: she is herself not only *Regina coeli*, queen of heaven, but also *porta coeli*, the gateway to eternal life. The Virgin was also connected with the figure of *Ecclesia*, the church in both its human and architectural forms and the *paradisum* entryway is often dominated by a representation of Mary.

The most famous Book of Hours is the *Très Riches Heures* (c. 1410) of Jean, duc de Berry, previously discussed. Exceptional in quality, complexity, and lavish illustration by the Limbourg brothers at the beginning of the fifteenth century and then by Jean Colombe around 1485, it is also complex because of the person for whom it is created. The *Très Riches Heures* is clearly different from the more modest Book of Hours, even though its quasiliturgical components may be the same: it is an assertive display version of what is otherwise often an intimate object.

The most interesting and famous garden illustrations are the calendar images by the Limbourg brothers, dating from the beginning of the fifteenth century. These are ravishing, offering details of courtly and country life, representations of princely castles and palaces, portraying the customs and habits of the aristocracy and, to a limited degree, their peasants (river swimming in "August,"[42] for instance). These images conjure up a yearly cycle of timeless, unvaried harmony: the peasants labor in orderly, curving lines, creating symmetrical mounds of hay; the nobles encounter each other with a perfect ceremoniousness. Even the materials with which the illustrations are created contribute to the ecstasy: unimaginably expensive pigments and gold leaf transmute the everyday features of the garden and its inhabitants into impossible luxury and perfection.

But we know that this book was created for a man in the middle of turmoil: civil war; the murder of his nephew sanctioned by another uncle; invasion by the English which would culminate in national defeat at the Battle of Agincourt (1415); and most of all the increasingly obvious replacement of an aristocratic model of society with a much more plural and complex one in which a dynamic, predominantly urban, commercial class played an essential role. Ironically, given their name, the Limbourgs never depicted town life.[43] The Limbourg illustrations to the *Très Riches Heures* are irredeemably nostalgic, offering the reader then and now an escape from a world of change to one that, perhaps, had never existed. Millard Meiss famously wrote that the world presented "is a garden, beautiful and secure,"[44] but it is not, as he suggested, the revelation of "contemporary France" in "naturalistic calendar scenes."[45] As John White wrote of the near-contemporary "new realism" developing in Northern Italy, this "new style associated with Giovanni dei Grassi is essentially a court art," even in the seeming depiction of "ordinary life."[46] The imaging of the garden here, and through it a world of hierarchy and order, is in keeping with the nature of the Book of Hours as a form that married the rotation of the seasons with the liturgical cycle of months, weeks, days, and hours. But both the *Très Riches Heures* and the *Visconti Hours* associated with the workshop of Giovanni dei Grassi marry the iconography of the seasons with idealized labors of the year. The *Très Riches Heures* conjures up an unending, uninterruptible, and unchanging cycle, figuring longed-for stability, the garden equivalent of "these endless cloisters and eternal aisles" painted by Robert Browning's anonymous medieval painter.[47] But by the time Jean Colombe completes the illustrations, the luxury manuscript is losing its competition with the printed book and the Limbourgs' gardens of perfect stasis are being challenged by Master E.S.'s satiric "Great Garden of Love." Browning's Pictor Ignotus would shrink from its unstable, vulgar dynamism, but not his harbinger of the Renaissance: "I always see the garden and God there / A-making man's wife."[48]

CHAPTER EIGHT

Gardens and the Larger Landscape

ROBERT LIDDIARD AND TOM WILLIAMSON

Medieval gardens did not exist in a vacuum, and their character cannot be fully understood without some appreciation of the countryside within which they existed. This might provide distant views, or it might be rigorously excluded, but either way this wider environment formed the context within which gardens were viewed and experienced. Moreover, many scholars have argued that wide tracts of land beyond the garden were themselves manipulated, on an extensive scale, on largely aesthetic lines. Whether we think of the wider countryside simply as a context for the garden, or as the raw material for more ambitious and extensive schemes of landscape design, we need to know something about its physical layout and appearance, and about the accumulated social meanings attached to the various structures and features found within it: for the medieval landscape, like all landscapes, possessed an iconography, widely understood at the time but today only recaptured with a conscious effort.

Medieval Europe was characterized by a wide range of landscapes, agricultural practices, and societies. A detailed discussion of all these local and regional variations would mean that a brief chapter such as this would become a mere catalogue, with little scope for analyzing the strength and character of the various forces shaping the physical environment. We have therefore decided to use medieval England as an example, although we are acutely aware that in so doing we are, to some extent, perpetuating a well-entrenched tendency to consider separate "national" landscapes as distinct from one another, a tendency fostered by independent academic traditions, each with their particular emphases and scholarly concerns. Volumes such as this will, we hope, encourage greater cross-cultural consideration in the future.

We concentrate on three main issues. We begin by examining the character of what we have called here the "working countryside," of productive agricultural land, considering in particular how far regional variations in field systems and settlement patterns were a function of social, economic, tenurial, or environmental factors. Secondly, we consider the elite exploitation of a specialized range of animals, both by hunting and through what we have termed systems of "intermediate exploitation"; the landscapes and structures associated with these practices; and the meanings—ideological and aesthetic—with which they came to be invested. Lastly, we examine the difficult question of how far the landscape was directly shaped in the Middle Ages, as it was in postmedieval times, by abstract aesthetic concerns.

In considering all of these matters, use must be made of interpretative strategies drawn from a wide range of disciplines, and a wide range of evidence must be employed: documents and visual representations; the results of archaeological surveys and excavations; and the numerous remnants of the medieval countryside, which still survive within the modern landscape. We suggest that, when such evidence is employed to consider the medieval landscape as a whole, the arguments often advanced for large-scale ornamental landscape "design" seem problematic. This is not to say that such arguments are necessarily wrong, but a review of the evidence, and of the strategies used to interpret it, vividly reveals the need for more caution and due qualification.

THE WORKING COUNTRYSIDE OF MEDIEVAL ENGLAND

By the twelfth century, and probably for a long time before this, the essential structure of the English landscape—patterns of settlement, the layout of agricultural holdings—displayed an almost infinite degree of local variation. Yet above and beyond this, this essential structure also exhibited a broader pattern of regional differences. Of particular importance was the distinction between what later, sixteenth- and seventeenth-century topographers were to describe as "woodland" and "champion" regions. The latter formed a broad band of territory, running from Yorkshire, through the Midlands to the south coast. Here, the majority of people lived in nucleated villages and most of the arable land lay

in extensive "open fields," in which the holdings of particular farmers lay intermingled in narrow strips and across which highly communal systems of farming were imposed.[1] Sometimes there were two great fields, more often three: in
which case one would lie fallow each year, while one was planted with spring-
sown crops, and one with winter-sown. The fields themselves were subdivided
into units called furlongs, within which cultivators were normally obliged to
grow the same crop each year. Such champion landscapes themselves displayed
much variation. On lighter lands, as on the Wessex chalk, the Cotswolds, and
the Wolds of Yorkshire and Lincolnshire, there was generally very little woodland, but extensive tracts of common grazing usually existed beyond the arable
fields. The "hungry" soils of these districts were easily leached of nutrients and
needed to be regularly fertilized by flocks of sheep, grazed on the downs and
heaths by day and systematically folded by night on the arable, after harvest
or when it lay fallow: here they dunged the soil, the areas of unplowed ground
thus operating, in effect, as nutrient reservoirs.[2] On the heavier and more fertile
soils of the Midlands, in contrast—in counties like Leicestershire, Northamptonshire, and in the northern parts of Buckinghamshire—areas of pasture and
other grazing were generally in short supply. The majority of the land in these
districts was under arable cultivation, with the individual strips often ploughed
in ridges to facilitate drainage on this heavy, intractable land. In many townships, only the enclosures around the village and the hay meadows (which often
formed important components of the landscape) remained unplowed.[3] Woodland was again usually in very short supply, except in areas of royal forest such
as Rockingham and Salcey, where tree cover might locally be extensive.

   To either side of this broad belt of champion land, the various kinds of
woodland landscape could be found, the term deriving from the fact that these
areas were generally well endowed with trees, whether growing in hedges or
in woods and wood pastures. Settlement in such districts was much more dispersed than in champion areas, with numerous hamlets and isolated farms as
well as (or in some districts, instead of) nucleated villages. Open fields were
again a prominent feature of the landscape, but they here took rather different forms. Particular hamlets often had their own diminutive field systems,
and even where they did not, holdings were generally grouped close to the
farm from which they were cultivated, rather than being scattered throughout
the territory of a particular township, and the organization of agriculture was
generally less rigidly communal in character. Indeed, in addition to open fields
many woodland areas, even in the twelfth and thirteenth centuries, could boast
some land farmed "in severalty," as hedged closes occupied by single individuals and largely free of communal controls.[4] More importantly, "woodland"

areas generally possessed more diverse environments than the champion lands, especially those in the Midlands. Areas of common grazing, woods, and wood-pastures were often abundant.

Woodland and champion are useful terms, if oversimple ones, for discussing lowland landscapes. The upland areas of England had their own range of countrysides. In major valleys, nucleated villages could often be found, but where the terrain was more broken, settlements were often small and scattered and field systems were generally complex and irregular. There were usually very extensive areas of common grazing, mainly in the form of upland moors.

The origins of these and other variations in the countryside of medieval England are a source of considerable debate amongst landscape historians, archaeologists, and historical geographers. The reason for the marked differences between "woodland" and "champion" regions has been a matter of particular concern. While these different kinds of landscape seem to have emerged during the tenth, eleventh, and twelfth centuries, their determinants remain elusive. Some scholars still characterize woodland districts as late-settled tracts of forest, only broken up and settled to any extent in the eleventh, twelfth, and thirteenth centuries.[5] The scattered settlements were the homes of pioneers, the woods and commons the remnants of once more continuous wastes. While this kind of explanation may make sense in some of these districts, such as the Chiltern Hills to the northwest of London, most woodland areas seem to have been as densely settled by middle and later Saxon times, or even more densely settled, than champion ones. Indeed, to judge from such sources as Domesday Book, the woodland areas of East Anglia and across much of Essex and Hertfordshire, were the most populous districts in England. Other researchers, in contrast, favor ethnic and social explanations for regional variations in the landscape, some for example interpreting champion districts as being more manorialized—that is, more dominated by local lords—than woodland ones.[6] Again, there is little evidence to support such views. The distribution of the different kinds of landscape does not seem to correlate well with known variations in the social or tenurial structure of medieval England—with the size of manors, the number existing in each township, or the density of free peasants, for example.

While not denying the importance of social and tenurial factors, the main determinants of variations in settlement patterns and field systems were probably environmental and agricultural in character. Given particular social and tenurial developments—the emergence of local lordships as large estates fragmented during the ninth, tenth, and eleventh centuries, and the adoption of a heavier plough pulled by a large team of oxen—it simply made more sense for farmers to adopt highly communal forms of agriculture and to live together in large villages in some areas than in others. Districts of light soils and permeably geologies, for example, were invariably characterized by nucleated villages farming extensive open fields. In such areas, good supplies of water were usually limited to river valleys and spring lines, leading naturally to some clustering of farms. The organization of the folding flocks, so necessary to keep the fields in heart, became increasingly complex as the population increased: a landscape of intermingled strips developed as holdings were divided, by inheritance or sale, and as land formerly used as grazing was brought into cultivation. Farmers were obliged to organize communal flocks and impose communal rotations across their splintered and scattered farms, and, with a growing need to coordinate their farming operations, new farms tended to fill the spaces between existing dwellings, leading to the emergence of nucleated villages.[7]

Yet champion landscapes were also, as we have seen, a feature of the Midlands, an area of particularly heavy and intractable clays. Here, other practical factors probably encouraged the development of communal fields and villages. In such areas, communal plow teams needed to be organized rapidly to make the most of relatively short windows of opportunity when the soil was in the right condition for winter plowing—assembling the draft oxen might be difficult where farms lay widely scattered around the landscape. Champion landscapes are also usually found in districts where wide river floodplains, characterized by gravel or alluvial substrates, provided abundant meadow land. By concentrating farms in large villages, labor and equipment could be turned onto the meadows at short notice, to cut and turn the hay, another important activity that needed to be carefully timed, in accordance with the weather conditions: "Make hay while the sun shines." In addition, the availability of large reserves of hay for winter fodder may have encouraged farmers to expand their arable at the expense of grazing land, something that presumably explains why, in many Midland townships, most of the land was under the plough, with grazing limited to the fallow fields.[8]

Woodland landscapes tend to be found where none of these various conditions applied to any significant extent. Not only were farmers thus able to live in scattered farms and small hamlets, and to organize their farming on less communal lines. In addition, a general shortage of land suitable for hay obliged communities to leave extensive areas of land unplowed, as greens, commons, and woods, to provide additional grazing for the livestock, late into the autumn or even over the winter months.

Whatever the precise explanations for variations in the farming landscape, these were unquestionably correlated much more closely with types of soil and terrain than with patterns of land ownership. The villages and field systems within any one medieval estate, that is, were laid out like those in the surrounding area, not along lines decided by particular owners, lay or ecclesiastical. And this in turn is a clear enough indication that the majority of land in medieval England, in woodland as in champion areas, was under the de facto control of local peasant communities. True, manorial lords generally retained a significant minority of their property as a *demesne*, or "home farm," but in many cases this lay intermingled with the strips of villagers and was generally farmed with them: even where it was not, cultivation usually followed the dictates of local custom. Local lords and great magnates drew rents, in labor or in cash, from their tenants but they did not, for the most part, get too closely involved in the dirty business of practical agriculture.

Whatever the precise character of the medieval working landscape, it was everywhere untidy and irregular in appearance. A minority of villages, especially in the north east of England, appear to have been laid out to a measured plan, but for the most part this was a disordered world, with none of the straight surveyed lines and regularity that came to characterize, for example, the landscapes created in the eighteenth and nineteenth centuries by large scale parliamentary enclosures. It was perhaps partly for this reason that medieval gardens were so frequently enclosed, by walls and hedges. The abstract aesthetic forms of the garden, created by a cultured and privileged elite, had to be clearly separated from the formless disorder of the working countryside, created by the peasantry. All this said, there was a significant minority of land in England that was under the direct control, and management, of the feudal elite. Such land took a variety of forms and was exploited in a variety of ways which often had particular connotations of status. Toward such land, the feudal elite appears to have had a rather different aesthetic response.

WOODLAND AND DEER PARKS

The steady increase in population, and the expansion of farmland, in the course of the tenth, eleventh, and twelfth centuries led to a gradual reduction of the area of woodland in England. In early Saxon times vast tracts of wooded "waste" had existed in the country. By the thirteenth century, probably less than 5 percent of England was tree covered. This process of destruction went furthest in some champion areas, although in many of these areas discrete pockets of wooded ground—usually, as we have noted, areas of royal forest—continued to exist. But even in woodland regions, the extent of ground under trees seems to have declined, as arable expanded and as common woodland often degenerated, under intense grazing pressure, to treeless heath and pasture. All this placed a particular value on surviving areas of woodland and on the various resources, including wild animals, which such areas contained.

As the extent of woodland dwindled, many remaining areas were enclosed from the common wastes by manorial lords and exploited more intensively, as coppice-with-standards. In this form of management, the majority of trees and shrubs were cut down to at or near ground level every few years in order to produce a regular crop of straight poles suitable for firewood, fencing, and a host of other uses.[9] Timber trees or *standards* were comparatively few in number in order to avoid shading out the coppice stools. Such woods were usually enclosed with substantial banks and fences or hedges in order to protect the regenerating coppice stools from browsing livestock. But these perimeter earthworks were often much larger than would be necessary for this purpose, and they clearly also functioned as displays of ownership and authority. The association of woodland and lordship was close and became closer as, with the passing centuries, common woods continued to degenerate to open pasture.

In early and middle Saxon times, the natural woodlands had provided the habitat for many of the creatures most regularly hunted by the elite: for as in most agricultural societies, the exploitation of wild resources was unnecessary for survival, and hunting was essentially a social action restricted to a small number of people and thus expressive of status.[10] Hunting continued to be a key activity of lords, lay and ecclesiastical, through the later Saxon period and into post-conquest times. But we must be careful not to draw too stark a distinction between hunting and farming. By the twelfth century, and for a long time afterward, much investment was poured into forms of livestock management that lay somewhere between the hunting of truly wild animals and the farming of fully domesticated ones.[11] These various forms of "intermediate exploitation" were, as much as true hunting, largely if not entirely restricted to the landed elite. They generally involved the creation and maintenance of specialized facilities and landscapes that themselves became important symbols of status.

The most important of these, without question, were deer parks: large enclosures, bounded by some combination of earthwork bank, fence, and hedge. Parks have been much studied by landscape historians and historical geographers and clearly took many forms. Some were "compartmentalized" in the sense that they were divided into relatively open areas, known as *launds*, that were managed as wood pastures and areas of coppice, enclosed by fences to prevent damage by browsing stock. In contrast, "uncompartmentalized" parks consisted entirely of wood pasture, without a coppiced understory. This distinction was not always clear-cut, however, and it was possible to alter the parkland regime when it was deemed necessary by, for example, planting or removing coppice. The need to surround the park with a substantial deer-proof bank and fence ensured a relative degree of security, and it was common for other demesne assets, such as fishponds and warrens, to be placed within these parks. Lodges for the use of the park keeper provided further security and, in some cases, accommodation for hunting parties. While the term *park* was synonymous with *deer* throughout the Middle Ages, a wide range of other activities took place within the pale, ranging from forestry to iron working and even mining.[12] Recent scholarship has tended to emphasize such economic and functional diversity, without lessening the importance of parks as places where a particular range of semidomesticated animal might be hunted or harvested.

In the twelfth and thirteenth centuries, the majority of parks were located on the fringes of agricultural territories (like coppiced woodland, they represented a way of guaranteeing lordly rights over the diminishing reserves of the common waste[13]). For this reason, they usually lay at a distance from manor houses. Of greater importance for the history of garden design, however, were a minority of more extensive parks owned by the greatest magnates, for these generally lay close to, or beside, great secular and ecclesiastical residences, castles and palaces. This close relationship between parks and great residences can be traced back at least to the eleventh century. We know, from later documentary evidence, that a number of the parks recorded by Domesday Book lay close to castles, as at Benington in Hertfordshire, Rayleigh in Essex, and Eye in Suffolk, although not immediately adjacent to them. This in turn was probably a reflection of pre-conquest practice. A number of recent studies have shown the close congruence between pre- and post-conquest hunting grounds, and while continuity is extremely difficult to prove, Norman developments often started from a significant pre-conquest base.[14]

The twelfth and thirteenth centuries saw a dramatic increase in the number of parks, with the twelfth century in particular a period of rapid expansion.[15] But as a consequence, greater attempts seem to have been made to distinguish parks found in association with elite residences from those created by the generality of minor landowners. Zooarchaeological evidence suggests, in particular, that both the numbers, and the variety, of parkland animals—including smaller mammals and game birds—increased dramatically over the course of the twelfth century.[16] It was at this time, moreover, that fallow deer—rare and exotic foreign imports—started to appear in some numbers in English parks.

Moreover, many parks that had been close to castles or palaces were now expanded, or relocated, so that they lay immediately adjacent to them. The growing importance of the park as a feature of the seigniorial *capita* can be seen at a number of places where castles were newly constructed in the first half of the twelfth century. At Devizes in Wiltshire, for example, the castle raised in 1120 by the Bishop of Salisbury was placed directly between the new park and borough; at Restormel in Cornwall in circa 1130, the castle, which also probably served as a lodge, was situated within its surrounding park; at Castle Rising in Norfolk, the principal apartments in the chamber of the donjon, built around 1140, overlooked the park, while at Kenilworth in Warwickshire in the 1120s, the attention given to the location of the park within the overall landscape setting is clearly indicated in the foundation charter of Kenilworth Priory, where Geoffrey de Clinton made sure that the endowment for the monks was delineated from land "reserved for my castle and my park."[17] The twelfth century was thus a key time in the general history of parks: at the highest social levels, the park was being thought of as an integral part of the "experience" of the residence.

This importance is also suggested by the apparent care taken, at a number of places, in the management of the views from the residence across the park. At Ludgershall Castle in Wiltshire, for example, the northern boundary of the park disappears over the skyline, seemingly to enhance its size when viewed from the castle apartments.[18] Such an arrangement seems to prefigure the situation at castles like Okehampton in Devon, where, in the fourteenth century, the rebuilding of the main range of buildings offered what was, in effect, a grandstand view over the adjacent park.[19] As we shall see, it remains a moot point as to whether such arrangements constitute landscape "design," but there can be little doubt that prospects across the park from the mansion, and views of a residence in a parkland setting, were now of paramount importance to noble builders.

If the eleventh and twelfth centuries witnessed the spatial convergence of park and residence, then the thirteenth and fourteenth centuries saw a growing complexity and sophistication in park landscapes and a general increase in their size. In some respects, the fourteenth century can be seen as the "golden age" of the park, with monarchs such as Edward II and Edward III spending vast sums on the creation of parks, and on the construction of lodges and other facilities within them: works probably associated with a heightened interest in venery in the royal court.[20] But the extent to which parks were used for hunting deer, as opposed to functioning primarily as venison farms, has been a source of much debate, in part because of a failure, on the part of historians, to appreciate the great variety both in the size and character of parks, and in the practice and organization of hunting.[21] Hunting *par force de chiens* ("by strength of hounds") and its many variants, which involved the hunting down of a single animal over an extensive area, would have been impractical in most parks—but the hawking and coursing of deer and, in particular, bow and stable hunting from stands, were practices eminently suitable to the park environment. In some cases, the layout of parks was manipulated for the purposes of hunting: at the large royal park at Clarendon in the 1270s, for example, *trenchea* (presumably rides) were cut to facilitate hunting on horseback.[22] This said, it is likely that some parks, and especially the smaller ones, may have served more as venison farms than as hunting grounds, although almost all seem to have been used for hunting to some extent.

A diversity of roles probably explains why a number of separate parks could be found around some residences, especially, once again, at the highest social levels. But this issue is complicated by a distinction frequently encountered in medieval documents between "great" and "little" parks, as, for example, at Fotheringay Castle, Windsor Castle, and Eltham Palace. In some cases, "little" was simply a tag used to differentiate a smaller area of enclosed wood-pasture from a larger one, but it is curious that, wherever the evidence allows us to see their topographic relationship, the "little" park often lies closer to the mansion and the "greater" park, at a distance. "Little" is thus another term for "inner" or "home" park, but, while the full implications of the distinction are currently the matter of some debate and research, there is accumulating evidence that little parks were in some sense pleasure grounds, physically resembling deer parks, but more like gardens in terms of their function. In literary texts such as the *Roman de la Rose*, depictions of gardens often describe woody areas containing deer, and these are rather different from the enclosed, formal *herber* type garden usually seen in manuscript illustrations. Great medieval residences and their surroundings were to some extent gendered spaces, and gardens were associated with the feminine. So too, it appears, were little parks. In John Coke's *Debate between the Heralds*, for example, it is explicitly stated that such parks "are made only for the pleasure of ladies and gentlewomen."[23] These landscapes were clearly different from "great parks," which had a range of productive functions but were also used for hunting—here a male activity. But in addition, the great park was perhaps associated in the medieval mind with the dwindling forests, and the little park may thus have occupied a liminal position between the order of the *caput* and the "wilderness" of the landscape beyond.[24]

The later Middle Ages was a period in which the association between park and residence moved down the social scale: increasing numbers of lesser land-owners placed their homes within, or beside, a park. Of course, we should not exaggerate the extent of this development. Parks continued to be expensive features—indeed, they became increasingly expensive as labor costs rose in the later fourteenth and fifteenth centuries, leading to some reduction in their overall numbers. Parks thus continued to be a symbol of elite status, and where new parks were created in the fourteenth and fifteenth centuries, they were often laid out around the homes of new arrivals in the knightly class, individuals whose wealth had been made in the expanding textile industry. By the end of the Middle Ages, the park still retained its position as a marker of status and was, perhaps more than ever, seen as the proper setting for an important residence. This role was to continue, and develop, over the next four centuries or more.

WARRENS, FISHPONDS, AND DOVECOTES

Deer parks have received much attention over the years from historians. The structures and facilities associated with other forms of "intermediate exploitation" have, in contrast, been rather neglected, in spite of the fact that they, too, were often a source of considerable income and prestige. This is especially true of rabbit warrens. Rabbits were introduced into England soon after the Norman Conquest and widely kept as semidomesticated animals in enclosures.[25] Some of these were small fenced areas beside great residences; larger examples lay in deer parks or on manorial wastes. Where a manorial lord possessed a right of free warren—a royal grant, conveying the exclusive right to hunt a range of wild animals across a particular tract of countryside—he was legally permitted to establish a rabbit warren on the manorial commons, even though the rabbits would there compete with the livestock of the commoners for the grass and other herbage.[26] Warrens have a complex and sophisticated archaeology. Many were equipped with breeding mounds called buries (which often contained purpose-built, stone-capped tunnels), boundary banks or walls, and lodges, to provide accommodation for the warrener and a place to store carcasses, skins, and equipment.[27] Warrens, as well as producing meat and fur, also afforded some recreational hunting—rabbits were not highly esteemed quarry, yet nor were they entirely neglected—and some warren lodges, such as that at Thetford (Norfolk), almost certainly provided bases for lordly hunting parties.

Warrens were probably resented more than deer parks by the wider population. The rabbits frequently escaped, causing considerable damage to crops.
In 1388 at Wilton in Norfolk, for example, a survey noted that sixty acres of
arable were "worth nothing by the year because of destruction of the coneys of
the Duke of Lancaster's warren there."[28] More importantly, when established
on commons, the rabbits competed with the livestock of commoners for the
grazing, often stripping the vegetation. Not surprisingly, warrens were a regular target for rebels and rioters, and many of the incidents that legal documents
present as attacks by armed poachers were probably, in reality, acts of social
protest—as in 1306, when a large group of people broke into the warrens
of the Earl of Surrey at Methwold, Thetford, Castle Acre, and Sculthorpe in
Norfolk and carried away rabbits.[29] But warren breaking was often a symbolic
act, a sign of generalized opposition to inequality and authority, rather than a
protest against warrens *per se*. During the Peasants' Revolt of 1381, the rebels
in St Albans placed one of the abbot's rabbits, liberated from one of his many
warrens, in the town pillory.[30]

Warrens were thus detested as symbols of lordly privilege, but *as* symbols
of lordly privilege, they were also proudly displayed in the immediate vicinity of great mansions. Indeed, in the course of the thirteenth, fourteenth, and
fifteenth centuries, the two were steadily brought into closer spatial association, as the parks within which many warrens were located came to be placed,
in increasing numbers, beside elite residences. Some archaeologists have suggested that warrens also carried a religious symbolism, and it is true that they
were often very publicly displayed in monastic precincts, as at Sawtry Abbey
in Cambridgeshire or Bruton in Somerset.[31] Rabbits were symbolic of man's
redemption through Christ and the church, an association that continued into
the Reformation period, and this explains, for example, the elaborate trian-
gular lodge, with three gables, three stories, and three-sided chimneys built
within the rabbit warren a short distance from Rushton House in Northamptonshire by the Catholic recusant Thomas Tresham in the 1590s. This provided
both a pun on Tresham's name and a statement of his faith in the tridentine
mass. But for the most part, warrens seem to have had a more straightforward, prosaic symbolism of lordly control over resources, and they continued to feature prominently in the landscapes laid out around country houses
right through the sixteenth and seventeenth centuries, as at Ascott House
near Wing (Buckinghamshire); Quarrendon (Buckinghamshire); Chatsworth
(Derbyshire); Shrubland Park (Suffolk); or Sopwell House (Hertfordshire).[32]

Fishponds were another form of elite food production and again an important marker of status.[33] Purpose-built fishponds may have existed from

the early Middle Ages, but they unquestionably increased in both numbers, and sophistication, from the thirteenth century, when carp—another foreign import, like rabbits and fallow deer—became the principal fish kept within them.[34] Fishponds took a variety of forms, but there was a broad distinction between the large ponds or *vivararia*, which were substantial affairs, often with large retaining dams, and the smaller, usually rectangular *servatoria*, or holding ponds.[35] The latter were located close to manor houses and castles and by the sixteenth century were certainly doubling as garden features; the former often lay at a distance, frequently placed (like rabbit warrens) within deer parks, where they could be more effectively protected from poachers.

In addition, medieval landowners usually kept dovecotes or *columbaria*, a privilege reserved by law to manorial lords, mainly because pigeons gorged indiscriminately on the fields of landowner and neighbors alike. Dovecotes provided a good source of year-round protein, for each pigeon produced two chicks between eight and ten times a year for six or seven years.[36] They also afforded a good supply of rich fertilizer. It was partly for this reason that dovecotes were often located within easy reach of gardens. But it was also to protect the pigeons from poachers and above all because of their considerable symbolic significance: reserved by law to the elite, dovecotes became, inevitably, a badge of elite status. Their importance in this respect again continued into the postmedieval centuries, and sixteenth- and seventeenth-century illustrations frequently show dovecotes proudly displayed beside the principal facades of country houses.

Features and structures associated with hunting, or with various forms of "intermediate exploitation," were thus carefully positioned beside great residences. They were symbols of lordly status because they were restricted to the feudal elite by virtue of cost, or by law. Indeed, with the increasing association of deer parks with local manor houses in the course of the fourteenth and fifteenth centuries, such associations became closer and more common. But, as we have noted in the case of enclosed and coppiced woodland, other features of the landscape were strongly associated with lordship and thus became emblematic of it. This might include structures as apparently functional and practical as corn mills: for in England, as across much of Europe, mills were a major item of investment and in most areas a seigniorial monopoly. It was probably for this reason, as much as for practical convenience, that mills—especially water mills—were frequently located close to manor houses, monasteries, and castles. In many medieval contexts, it is hard to distinguish the ponds created to hold fish from those constructed to provide a supply of water for a mill; in some places the distinction is arbitrary, a body of water serving both functions. Once again, the symbolic importance of mills continued into the postmedieval period: Jan Kip and Leonard Knyff's engravings, for example, made at the start of the eighteenth century, frequently show examples close to great houses. Indeed, even when the "landscape" style came to be widely adopted in the course of the eighteenth century, mills were still occasionally used as eye catchers, rebuilt in a suitably classical or picturesque mode, as, for example, at Rousham or Chatsworth.

DESIGNED LANDSCAPES

A range of features in the medieval landscape, symbols of lordship, were thus ostentatiously displayed in the immediate vicinity of great mansions. Considerations of practical convenience and security also played a part in this, while in addition some of these features and facilities also had a recreational role: extensive water bodies, beside containing fish, also provided opportunities for boating. Over recent decades, however, a number of landscape archaeologists and art historians have suggested something rather more surprising: that these and other elements were manipulated on a grand and sophisticated scale to create "designed landscapes" similar, in many respects, to those of the eighteenth or nineteenth centuries. These featured, in particular, irregular bodies of water, extensive prospects of grass casually scattered with trees, and complex, circuitous approaches. Numerous examples of such landscapes have been published over the last two decades, associated with a wide range of castles and palaces. Indeed, they are now expected as the norm whenever high-status sites of the period are studied or surveyed. Nevertheless, it is arguable that the idea of "medieval designed landscapes" has been taken too far, and at the very least needs to be subjected to rather more critical scrutiny than it has so far received.

One problem with this widely held belief concerns the recognition of intent. How can we be sure that prospects or arrangements that we might find aesthetically appealing were really the consequence of conscious decision, rather than chance? Or to put it another way, how much of the evidence of medieval design resides in the eye of the beholder, rather than in the actions of contemporaries? A case in point is Bodiam Castle in Sussex. The castle—erected in circa 1385 by Sir Edward Dalingridge—achieved some notoriety in the 1990s when it became the "touchstone" in the debate over the military role of the castle.[37] Research by Charles Coulson downplayed Bodiam's possible role as a defense against the French and highlighted instead its character as a residence built in a martial style—it was "an old soldier's dream house."[38] At the same time, the Royal Commission on the Historic Monuments of England (RCHME) survey of the castle's surroundings suggested that extensive and substantial earthworks were the remains of "elaborate gardens and water features all intended to enhance the visual appearance of the building."[39] The arrangement included a "contrived approach," wending in a circuitous manner between extensive water bodies, from which the castle and its landscape were displayed to maximum effect. Earthworks on the low hill to the north known as the Gun Garden were interpreted as a detached pleasure garden or viewing terrace from which a view across this whole elaborate prospect could have been enjoyed.

Bodiam is endlessly quoted in the literature as an incontrovertible example of a medieval designed landscape, but closer scrutiny suggests a number of problems. The argument for the carefully laid out circuitous approach rests in part on an interpretation of the earthworks—gaps between the various ponds and the wide retaining banks of the moat itself can be used to chart the line of a drive or track—and in part on the observation that, when the proposed approach is followed, the castle appears to rise dramatically from the ponds and moat, and to "float" on the water. But the latter is close to being a circular argument (if the suggested route is followed then a particular effect is experienced; therefore, the approach to the castle must have followed the suggested route), while the various gaps and terraces allow for a number of alternative routes to the castle gate. One has in fact been proposed, from the north, which would have made the castle's main entrance appear more visually imposing.[40] Equally important is the fact that detailed work on the local tenurial geography suggests that the southern section of the approach would have crossed the land of a neighboring manor, which was not Dalingridge's property.[41] There is thus no clear-cut, unequivocal evidence that the castle was approached in the manner suggested and some reason to doubt that it was. Slightly different problems surround the Gun Garden, for its broad terrace is offset from the main façade of the castle so that the visitor sees the castle neither in direct alignment, where the symmetry of the building could be best appreciated, nor from a point specifically intended to bisect its symmetry. The location of the Gun Garden vis-à-vis the castle may or may not suggest a desire to enjoy views of the latter from above, but these views do not seem to have been contrived in a very complex or sophisticated manner. Above all, there are problems with the interpretation of the various water features around the castle as being primarily aesthetic in character. While considerable efforts were evidently made to create these ponds, their form or disposition does not display, in any very obvious way, thoughtful aesthetic intent. The two to the northwest of the castle are part of a natural valley that has been dammed and, resembling normal fishponds, they do not seem to have been "landscaped" in any meaningful sense.

All the other ponds display a range of shapes, none obviously either geometric or serpentine in character, and these likewise appear to have been for keeping fish, with the exception of the large pond to the south, which was evidently to supply a mill. The "designed landscape" may, in fact, represent nothing more than a concentration of fishponds and a mill in the vicinity of the castle: visually pleasing, no doubt, to owner and visitors, convenient, and redolent of lordly status, yet hardly a designed landscape as William Kent or Lancelot Brown might have understood this concept.

A similar range of problems surrounds many if not all of the numerous castles and palaces where large-scale landscape design has been asserted, especially that of how we decide whether particular visual effects were intentional or fortuitous. This is particularly the case given that these designs fail to follow a single coherent set of "rules," beyond a general preference for associating the residence with parkland and water, allowing archaeologists considerable latitude in their interpretations. Features or spatial relationships that might indicate aesthetic intent at one site can be conspicuously absent from another, which is nevertheless likewise deemed to be "designed." As already noted, at Ludgershall Castle in Wiltshire the line of the north park pale ran over a small section of skyline, thus making the park look larger than it really was when viewed from the residential buildings.[42] But at Ravensworth in Yorkshire, where the castle is surrounded by a watery landscape and the whole enveloped by a park, the latter does *not* disappear over the horizon; rather, the church that stands beyond its boundaries is interpreted as a "feature" on the skyline, which thus serves to emphasize the park's limits.[43] Restormel in Cornwall is different again. Here, the boundary of the park is clear when viewed from the castle, but once in the valley below, it disappears, creating an impression of an unbounded wilderness dominated visually by the residence, with the castle coming in and out of view as hunters rode in the park.[44] In short, archaeologists thus usually have at least two bites at the interpretative cherry when identifying "design."

Proponents of "designed landscapes" have also, it can be argued, elided two connected but nevertheless distinct concepts: the symbolic connotations that medieval elite landscapes were capable of sustaining, on the one hand, and the processes by which landscapes were manipulated for aesthetic effect, on the other. There is little doubt, as we have emphasized, that contemporaries found parks, ponds, and warrens visually pleasing. But this does not necessarily mean that the form or disposition of these landscapes was altered, in sophisticated and complex ways, to improve the appearance. The appeal of these landscapes arose from their function and in so far as they were designed, it was to allow them to fulfill this most effectively. At Clarendon Palace, for example, the park took a "typical" medieval form, displaying the familiar mixture of launds, enclosed blocks of coppice, and wood-pasture: it was "managed almost exclusively for fallow deer".[45] The principal landscape setting for this important residence was largely, if not entirely, molded by its role in deer management, rather than by abstract aesthetics. This is not to deny that the park at Clarendon was considered visually appealing. But that appeal was derived from its function as a game reserve, not from any special planting, creation of vistas, or alteration of land forms, or any of the other activities that, in the eighteenth century, would have been involved in the design of parkland.

Eighteenth-century landscape parks developed, in part, from their medieval predecessors, and perhaps this very historical continuity has encouraged many to assume that both were equally designed and perhaps in similar ways. The kinds of circuitous approaches suggested for Bodiam, and detected at a range of other sites, seem strikingly similar to the drives created by mid- and late eighteenth-century landscape designers such as Lancelot "Capability" Brown, along which the visitor was presented with "a series of interesting effects and contrasting views" before the mansion itself was revealed.[46] In a similar way, the irregular water bodies and sylvan scenes that form the main elements in most published examples of medieval designed landscapes have much in common with the landscapes of Nathaniel Richmond, "Capability" Brown, Richard Woods, and their ilk, and it is significant that Richard Muir, among others, has argued that "the medieval determinants of landscape taste were not greatly different from those of the 'great masters' of postmedieval landscape design."[47] Yet it is strange that proposed medieval designs should so closely resemble these "naturalistic" landscape gardens and parks, rather than the more clearly and obviously designed layouts of the sixteenth and seventeenth centuries, with their structured geometric formality, straight avenues, and rigid linear vistas. We should thus at least consider the possibility that the surroundings of medieval residences exhibited the same "un-designed" appearance as a Brownian composition because they were not, in fact, designed.

But perhaps, in part, the question is one of semantics, of what we mean by "landscape design." In postmedieval times, this meant altering a considerable tract of ground according to some predetermined plan, an activity that involved careful consideration of the visual relationships between various features and of the relationship of the whole to the residence itself. This in turn usually required, prior to its execution, the creation of some representation of the intended scheme—if only to communicate to those undertaking the work what precisely was expected from them. Complex schemes of landscape design would not have been absolutely impossible in a medieval world that lacked plans, maps, and perspective drawings. But it is arguable that the creation of such "Cartesian devices," and the redrawing of entire landscapes to a predetermined design were closely related practices, and ones that were far more at home in a postmedieval, capitalist society, in which land was measured, valued, and owned as private property, than in a medieval, feudal one.

CONCLUSION

The aristocracy of medieval England evidently found deer parks, fishponds, warrens, and other markers of lordly status visually pleasing and tended to place them in prominent locations around their residences. These markers might figure prominently in views from the mansion, and doubtless from the ornamental gardens. In some cases, the form of such facilities may have been modified or exaggerated in order to make the facilities more conspicuous, and sometimes no doubt their size was increased far beyond the needs of ordinary household production. But whether the aesthetic manipulation of the wider landscape, beyond the garden, went much further than this is perhaps a more open question than many landscape historians currently suggest.

NOTES

Introduction

1. J. Milton, *Paradise Lost*, ed. A. Fowler (1968; 2nd ed., London: Longman, 1998), Book 9, lines 28–29.

2. There are notable attempts, including various works by J. Harvey (see Bibliography) and several by G. Gibault, including "L'ancienne corporation des maîtres jardiniers de la ville de Paris," *Journal de la Société nationale d'horticulture de France* 18 (1896): 153–74; and "La condition et les salaires des anciens jardiniers," *Journal de la Société nationale d'horticulture de France* 20 (1898): 65–82.

3. For an overview, see E. A. Clark, *History, Theory, Text: Historians and the Linguistic Turn* (Cambridge, MA: Harvard University Press, 2004).

4. For two recent views, see R. Johnson, "Historical Returns: Transdisciplinarity, Cultural Studies and History," *European Journal of Cultural Studies* 4 (2001): 261–88; and C. Robertson, "The Archive, Disciplinarity, and Governing: Cultural Studies and the Writing of History," *Cultural Studies <=> Critical Methodologies* 4 (2004): 450–71.

5. P. Burke, "Afterword: Exploring Cultural History. A Response," in *Exploring Cultural History: Essays in Honour of Peter Burke*, ed. J. P. Rubiés, M. Calaresu, and F. de Vivo (Aldershot: Ashgate, 2010), 351–58, 353.

6. P. Fridenson, L. Niethammer, and L. Passerini, "International Reverberations: Remembering Raphael," *History Workshop Journal* 45 (1998): 246–60, 256.

7. For two recent studies, see M. Alexander, *Medievalism: The Middle Ages in Modern England* (New Haven: Yale University Press, 2007); and J. M. Ganim, *Medievalism and Orientalism: Three Essays on Literature, Architecture and Cultural Identity* (New York: Palgrave Macmillan, 2008). For later gardens in particular, see P. Henderson, "Clinging to the Past: Medievalism in the English 'Renaissance' Garden," *Renaissance Studies* 25 (2011): 42–69.

8. R. Johnson, "What Is Cultural Studies Anyway?" *Social Text* 16 (1986–87): 38–80, 62.

9. For a summary, see L. Boia, *Forever Young: A Cultural History of Longevity* (Reaktion Books, 2004), 48–51.

10. See A. L. Matthies, "The Medieval Wheelbarrow," *Technology and Culture* 32 (1991): 356–64; and M.J.T. Lewis, "The Origins of the Wheelbarrow," *Technology and Culture* 35 (1994): 453–75.

11. As Peter Burke makes clear, Clifford Geertz's example looms large in cultural history ("Afterword," 351). For a brief discussion of an approach based on Geertz's practice, see my contribution to "'Whither Garden History?': The Hard and the Soft: Interdisciplinarity and Cultural History in Landscape Studies," *Studies in the History of Gardens & Designed Landscapes* 27 (2006): 91–112.

12. F. Bacon, *The Essayes or Counsels, Civill and Morall* (1625), 266.

13. For a recent set of discussions, see A. Lee, P. Péporté, and H. Schnitker, eds., *Renaissance? Perceptions of Continuity and Discontinuity in Europe, c.1300–c.1550* (Leiden: Brill, 2010); and for Vasari's use of the terms *media aetas* and *rinascita*, see the essay by M. Burioni, "Vasari's *Rinascita*: History, Anthropology, or Art Criticism?," 115–27.

14. P. S. Wells, *Barbarians to Angels: The Dark Ages Reconsidered* (New York: W. W. Norton, 2008), 200. See also K. Randsborg, *The First Millennium AD in Europe and the Mediterranean: An Archaeological Essay* (Cambridge: Cambridge University Press, 1991); P. Brown, *The Rise of Western Christendom: Triumph and Diversity, A.D. 200–1000*, 2nd ed. (Oxford: Blackwell, 2003); P. Horden and N. Purcell, *The Corrupting Sea: A Study of Mediterranean History* (Oxford: Blackwell, 2000); and M. McCormick, *Origins of the European Economy: Communications and Commerce, A.D. 300–900* (Cambridge: Cambridge University Press, 2001).

15. P. Brown, *The World of Late Antiquity: AD 150–750* (London: Thames & Hudson, 1971).

16. P. Brown, G.W. Bowersock, and O. Grabar, eds., *Interpreting Late Antiquity: Essays on the Postclassical World* (Cambridge, MA: Harvard University Press, 1999).

17. G. Fowden, "Contextualizing Late Antiquity: The First Millennium," in *The Roman Empire in Context: Historical and Comparative Perspectives*, ed. J.P. Arnason and K.A. Raaflaub (Oxford: Wiley-Blackwell, 2011).

18. B. Wittrock, "The Meaning of the Axial Age," in *Axial Civilizations and World History*, ed. J. P. Arnason, S.N. Eisenstadt, and B. Wittrock (Leiden: Brill, 2005), 51–85, esp. 81–82.

19. P. Heather, *Empires and Barbarians: The Fall of Rome and the Birth of Europe* (New York: Oxford University Press, 2010), 610–11.

20. Wells, *Barbarians to Angels*, 199–200.

21. Heather, *Empires and Barbarians*, 547.

22. For a fascinating contemporary analysis of this question, still so much a live issue, see D. Marquand, *The End of the West: The Once and Future Europe* (Princeton, NJ: Princeton University Press, 2011), especially chapter 5, "Which Boundaries? Whose History?," 141–76, and the work he praises, J. Zielonka, *Europe as Empire: The Nature of the Enlarged European Union* (Oxford: Oxford University Press, 2007).

23. Heather, *Empires and Barbarians*, 517.
24. See H. Stahl, "Eve's Reach: A Note on the Dramatic Elements of the Hildersheim Doors," in *Reading Medieval Images: The Art Historian and the Object*, ed. E. Sears and T. K. Thomas (Ann Arbor: University of Michigan Press, 2002), 162–75.
25. See especially the works of H. L. Kessler, *The Illustrated Bibles from Tours* (Princeton: Princeton University Press, 1977); *Spiritual Seeing: Picturing God's Invisibility in Medieval Art* (Philadelphia: Pennsylvania University Press, 2000), 158ff. for the Moûtier-Granval Bible; and *Pictorial Narrative in Antiquity and the Middle Ages* (*Studies in the History of Art*, XVI), ed. with M. S. Simpson (Washington, D.C.: National Gallery of Art, 1985).
26. British Library Add MS 10546, folio 5v; circa 840.
27. Bamburg Staatsbibliothek Misc. class. Bibl. 1.
28. Folio 47.
29. *De cas des nobles homes et femmes*, c. 1420; Paris, Bibliothèque nationale, ms. Fr. 226, f.6v.
30. Illustrated in É. Antoine et al., *Sur la terre comme au ciel: Jardins d'Occident à la fin du Moyen Âge* (Paris: Éditions de la Réunion des museés nationaux, 2002), 31–32.
31. Paris, Bibliothèque nationale, ms. Fr. 111, f.260v.
32. Illustrated in M.-T. Gousset, *Eden: Le jardin medieval à travers l'enluminure, XIIIe-XVIe siècle* (Paris: Albin Michel, 2001), 38.

1 Design

1. Thus in the late seventeenth century, John Evelyn saw that "design is of things not yet appearing; being but the pictures of ideas only": C. F. Bell, ed., *Evelyn's Sculptura with the Unpublished Second Part* (Oxford: Clarendon Press, 1906), 104–6.
2. These characteristic modern assumptions about design process were not even available in the early Renaissance period: see R. F. Giannetto, *Medici Gardens: From Making to Design* (Philadelphia: University of Pennsylvania Press, 2008).
3. G. Eckbo, *Landscape for Living* (New York: McGraw-Hill, 1950), 6.
4. J. H. Harvey argues that there is no continuity between Roman and mediaeval designs, yet San Apollinario so resembles the survivals of atria and garden courtyards in Pompeii and Herculaneum that one must be skeptical of that assertion.
5. See C. Higounet, ed., "Jardins et vergers en Europe occidentale (VIIIe-XVIIIe siècles)," *Flaran 9* (1989), for more details of French ecclesiastical complexes.
6. See D. Howard, *Venice and the East: The Impact of the Islamic World on Venetian Architecture 1100–1500* (New Haven, CT: Yale University Press, 2000).
7. See H. Bresc, "Les jardins de Palerme (1290–1460)," *Mélange de l'Ecole francaise de Rome* 84 (1972): 62, 81, passim.
8. Cf. "the real room for movement in Carthusian life lies within": T. McLean, *Medieval English Gardens* (London: Collins, 2004), 51.
9. See T. Alfonsi and R. Bozzoli, *Pier de' Crescenzi (1233–1321). Studi e documenti* (Bologna: Copelli, 1933); J. Bauman, "Tradition and Transformation: The Pleasure Garden in Piero de' Crescenzi's *Liber ruralium commodorum*," *Studies in the History*

of Gardens and Designed Landscapes 22 (2002): 99–141 (whose translations are used here); G. L. Gaulin, *Crescenzi et L'agronomie en Italie XIII-XIV siècles* (Paris: Thèse de l'Université de Paris I, 1990).

10. Crescenzi, *Trattato dell'agricoltura*, 2 vols. (Naples, 1724), vol. 2, 93; author's translation.

11. Bodleian ms Douce 93, folio 101; illustrated in M. Stokstad and J. Stannard, eds., *Gardens of the Middle Ages* (Lawrence, KS: Spencer Museum of Art, 1983), 43.

12. I trespass here upon the territory of Chapter 7 but do so largely to set out the design programs that may have driven garden layouts that in their turn enabled or authorized meanings.

13. A.R. Nykl, ed., *Hispano-Arabic Poetry and its Relations with the Old Provencal Troubadors* (Baltimore, MD: Furst, 1946), 364; the following references are to 298, 287, 157, 138, 117, 203.

14. See P. Morris and D. Sawyer, eds., *A Walk in the Garden: Biblical, Iconographical and Literary Images of Eden, Journal for the Study of the Old Testament*, supplement series 136 (Sheffield: JSOT Press, 1992), for other considerations and interpretations of Eden.

15. I leave aside the whole iconography of heaven, for which see J. R. Rhodes and C. Davidson, "The Garden of Paradise," in *The Iconography of Heaven*, ed. Clifford Davidson (Kalamazzo, MI, 1994), 69–109, largely because it may be understood as being more speculative than the two "historical" gardens. However, like Eden itself, it was physically represented in mediaeval drama, of which records of sets and staging survive.

16. A useful indication of this lack of interest in (maybe ignorance of) historical or cultural accuracy is the illustrated Marco Polo that shows his arrival in the port of Curmos (Bandar Abbas) where people inhabit gardens during the hot summers: the garden shown is a purely European affair, with trellis fencing and a vine-covered pergola and people swimming in the river (see M.-T. Gousset, ed., *Eden. Le jardin médiéval à travers l'enluminure XIIIe-XVIe siècle* [Paris: Albin Michel/Bibliothèque nationale de France, 2001], 75).

17. Various authors who have written about the mediaeval garden draw extensively upon the corpus, so the reader is directed to work by F. Crisp, J. H. Harvey, and *Eden* (Paris: Albin Michel, 2001), the small compendium of imagery from French collections by M.-T. Gousset.

18. British Library Add ms 119720, folio 214.

19. British Library Add ms 119720, folio 117.

20. British Library Add ms 119720, folio 165.

21. British Library Add ms 119720, folio 27.

22. Respectively, these four types are illustrated by Stokstad and Stannard, *Gardens of the Middle Ages*, 26, 44, 52, 46.

23. Stokstad and Stannard, *Gardens of the Middle Ages*, catalogue #28

24. Stokstad and Stannard, *Gardens of the Middle Ages*, 55.

25. Stokstad and Stannard, *Gardens of the Middle Ages*, catalogue #29

26. Stokstad and Stannard, *Gardens of the Middle Ages*, 30.

27. See D. Aligheri, *The Divine Comedy*, tr. C. S. Singleton (Princeton, NJ: Princeton University Press, 1973), "Purgatorio" Canto 10, lines 31 et seq. I am grateful to my

colleague Victoria Kirkham for elucidating this passage where Dante sees *basso-rilievi* that instruct in the "goads" to good action: so, on the terrace of pride he sees the humility of the virgin receiving the angel of the Annunciation (in a garden, of course).

28. Dante, *Divine Comedy*, 24.
29. Dante, *Divine Comedy*, catalogue 356, 357.
30. F. Crisp, *Mediaeval Gardens*, vol. 1 (London: John Lane The Bodley Head, 1924), fig. 11.
31. Crisp, *Mediaeval Gardens*, vol. 1, fig. 35, and for the next example, fig. 36.
32. References are given to illustrations in Crisp's volumes: here vol. 1, 36.
33. Modern versions of this wattling can be seen in the many modern French recreations of mediaeval gardens (see Gousset, *Jardins Médiévaux en France* [Rennes: Editions Ouest-France, 2003]).
34. Crisp, *Mediaeval Gardens*, vol. 1, 31, 38, 39.
35. Rhodes and Clifford, "The Garden of Paradise," 81, 102, propose some symbolic connections between garden palings and the wood of the cross.
36. I rely hereon discussions by D. F. Ruggles, *Gardens, Landscape, and Vision in the Palaces of Islamic Spain* (University Park: Penn State University Press, 2003), 62, 88, seriatim (see index under "mirador").
37. Interestingly, given the Islamic concern with view the landscape, this painting is now in the Capilla Real at Granada.
38. Illustrated Gousset, *Eden*, 80, and *Jardins Médiévaux en France*, 60.
39. Two such are illustrated in J. Bauman, "Tradition and Transformation," figs. 5, 9.
40. Paris Arsenal ms 5072, folio 71 verso; illustrated Harvey plate VIIB and Gousset, *Jardins Médiévaux en France*, 61.
41. See A. Hagopian van Buren, "Reality and Literary Romance in the Park of Hesdin," in *Medieval Gardens*, ed. E. B. MacDougall (Washington, D.C.: Dumbarton Oaks, 1986), 115–34. Walled hunting parks were also a feature of Middle Eastern elite, and some also contained smaller and decorated enclosures.
42. See D.R.E. Wright, "Some Medici Gardens of the Florentine Renaissance. . . .," in *The Italian Garden: Art, Design and Culture*, ed. John Dixon Hunt (Cambridge: Cambridge University Press, 1996), 34–59.
43. See J. H. Harvey, *Medieval Gardens* (London: Batsford, 1981), 40.
44. Quoted in G. Bellafiore, *Parchi e Giardini della Palermo normanna* (Palermo: Flaccovio, 1996), 6–8 (my translation from the Italian).
45. See Bresc, "Les jardins de Palerme."
46. Variously reproduced (see A. Jennings, *Medieval Gardens* [London: English Heritage, 2004], 18).
47. Illustrated Gousset, *Eden,* 34–35, with transposed caption.
48. However, we need to observe caution, here and elsewhere: fountains were associated with the Eucharistic chalice and may well have been depicted with that typology in mind rather than as drawing upon the likeness of a plausible contemporary fountain (see E. Underhill, "The Fountain of Life: An Iconographical Study," *Burlington Magazine* 17 [1910]: 99–109).
49. Underhill, "The Fountain of Life," 91. The Narcissus fountain reflects not the lover's face but a quincunx of roses, the emblem of his love—again, not exactly a feasible design move.

50. Folio 165.
51. Illustrated Gousset, *Eden*, 49.
52. Gousset, *Eden*, 42.
53. Harvey, *Mediaeval Gardens*, 142.
54. Stokstad and Stannard, *Gardens of the Middle Ages*, catalogue #37.
55. Gousset, *Jardins Médiévaux en France*, 61.
56. Noted by Harvey, *Mediaeval Gardens*, 44.
57. Illustrated Gousset, *Eden*, 85.
58. Bauman, "Tradition and Transformation," 102.

2 Types of Gardens

1. For a good, general discussion of this practice, see D. F. Ruggles, *Islamic Gardens and Landscapes* (Philadelphia: University of Pennsylvania Press, 2008), 73–74.
2. Among many who have noted this, see G. L. della Vida, "Pre-Islamic Arabia," in *The Arab Heritage*, ed. Nabih Amin Faris (Princeton, NJ: Princeton University Press, 1946), 25. For a discussion of this issue in relationship to art, see O. Grabar, *The Formation of Islamic Art* (New Haven, CT: Yale University Press, 1973), chapters 1 and 2.
3. For a discussion of this issue see Grabar, *Formation of Islamic Art*, 19–44.
4. This is summed up quite nicely in Petruccioli's statement: "Giardino Islamic, dunque, o giardini del mondo islamico?" See A. Petruccioli, "Introduzione," in *Il Giardino Islamico: Architettura, natura, paesaggio*, ed. A. Petruccioli (Milan: Electa, 1994), 9.
5. This was recognized already over thirty years ago by scholars. R. Ettinghausen, "Introduction," in *The Islamic Garden*, ed. E. B. Macdougall and R. Ettinghausen (Washington, D.C.: Dumbarton Oaks, 1976), 3. The most thorough and useful discussion of the historiography of Islamic gardens is Petruccioli, "Introduzione," 7–11.
6. Cf. S. E. Petersen, *The Paradise Garden and the Desert* (Copenhagen: Royal Danish Academy of Fine Arts, 1995), 8.
7. Della Vida, "Pre-Islamic Arabia," 25–26, 39.
8. See again, Petruccioli, "Introduzione," 9.
9. Della Vida, "Pre-Islamic Arabia," 41–45, esp. 43–55, 55. In terms of the advent of Islam, della Vida notes the following: "In a way, the Islamization of Arabia was directed against the nomadic pattern of life. All that was characteristic in it and dear to the Bedouin's heart was bitterly assailed in Muhammad's preaching: the tribal organization, the individualistic freedom, and the coolness towards regular worship" (55–56).
10. Della Vida, "Pre-Islamic Arabia," 51. The author does note that Mecca was somewhat different (52).
11. Della Vida, "Pre-Islamic Arabia," 46.
12. See D. Stronach, "The Royal Garden at Pasargadae: Evolution and Legacy," in *Archaeologia Iranica et Orientalis: Miscellanea in honorem Louis Vanden Berghe*,

ed. L. De Meyer and E. Haerinck, vol. 1 (Gent: Peeters Press, 1989), 475–502; and "The Garden as a Political Statement: Some Case Studies from the Near East in the First Millennium B.C.," *Bulletin of the Asia Institute* 4 (1990): 171–80.

13. A. R. Littlewood, "Gardens of the Palaces," in *Byzantine Court Culture from 829 to 1204*, ed. H. Maguire (Washington, D.C.: Dumbarton Oaks, 1997), 17. This occurred shortly after 512 C.E.

14. See the chapter by Fabiani Giannetto in this volume.

15. G. E. von Grunebaum, "Aspects of Arabic Urban Literature Mostly in the Ninth and Tenth Centuries," in *Themes in Medieval Arabic Literature*, vol. 4, ed. D. S. Wilson (London: Variorium Reprints, 1981), 280–84.

16. Von Grunebaum, "Aspects of Arabic Urban Literature," 284. The relationship was actually a bit more complex. For a very brief treatment of the relationship of the new and neo-classic strains of poetry in the Abbasid empire, see von Grunebaum, "Aspects of Arabic Urban Literature," 289–91. For the role of Abū Tammām in ushering in the change from pre-Islamic poetry of the desert to that of the urban court of the 'Abbasids, see S. P. Stetkevych, *Abū Tammām and the Poetics of the 'Abbāsid Age* (Leiden: E. J. Brill, 1991).

17. See G. Marçais, "Bustān," in *Encyclopedia of Islam*, vol. 1 (Leiden: E. J. Brill, 1960), 1345–47, and "Les jardins de l'Islâm," in *Mélanges d' Histoire et d'Archéologie de l'Occident Musulman*, vol. 1 (Alger: Imprimerie officielle, 1957), 235.

18. Marçais, "Bustān," 1345.

19. Marçais, "Bustān," 1345, and "Les jardins," 235.

20. Marçais, "Les jardins," 235.

21. For the evidence at Rusafa/Resafa, see T. Ulbert, "Ein umaiyadischer Pavillon in Resafa- Resafa-RuṢāfat Hišām," *Damaszener Mitteilungen* 7 (1993): 213–31; for the evidence at Khirbat al Mafjar, see R. W. Hamilton, *Khirbat al Mafjar: An Arabian Mansion in the Jordan Valley* (Oxford: Clarendon Press, 1959), 111–21.

22. Marçais, "Les jardins," 236.

23. Marçais, "Les jardins," 236.

24. Marçais, "Les jardins," 237–39.

25. For the influence of Rusafa (also spelled Resafa) on the palace of al-Ruṣāfa outside of Cordoba, see T. Ulbert, "Ein umaiyadischer Pavillon," 230–31, with further pertinent bibliography.

26. D. F. Ruggles, "The Mirador in Abbasid and Hispano-Umayyad Garden Typology," *Muqarnas* 7 (1990): 73–82.

27. Marçais, "Les jardins," 239–40. Marçais sees the *riâdh* as the culmination of Islamic gardens; the perfect balance of organization and order with spontaneity and freedom.

28. Marçais, "Les jardins," 242.

29. D. F. Ruggles, *Islamic Gardens and Landscapes* (Philadelphia: University of Pennsylvania Press, 2008), 39–49, esp. 40–41.

30. For an overview of medieval Persian agricultural manuals, see Ž. Vesel, "Les traits d'agriculture en Iran," *Studia Iranica* 15, no. 1 (1996): 99–108. For an exploration of the relationship between these manuals and actual medieval Persian gardens, see M. E. Subtelny, "Agriculture and the Timurid Chahārbāgh: The Evidence from a

Medieval Persian Agricultural Manual," in *Gardens in the Time of the Great Muslim Empires: Theory and Design*, ed. A. Petruccioli (Leiden: Brill, 1997), 110–28.

31. S. Redford, "Thirteenth-Century Rum Seljuq Palaces and Palace Imagery," *Ars Orientalis* 23 (1993): 219.

32. Subtelny, "Agriculture and the Timurid Chahārbāgh," 110.

33. The seminal treatment of this division remains A. Cameron, *The Mediterranean World in Late Antiquity AD 395–600* (London: Routledge, 1992), 1–11.

34. Cameron, *The Mediterranean World*. For a similar discussion, but from the point of view of Byzantium, see A. Kazhdan and A. Cutler, "Continuity and Discontinuity in Byzantine History," *Byzantion* 52 (1982): 429–78.

35. K. Randsborg, *The First Millennium AD in Europe and the Mediterranean: An Archaeological Essay* (Cambridge: Cambridge University Press, 1991).

36. Littlewood, "Gardens of the Palaces," 16. L. Brubaker and A. R. Littlewood, "Byzantinische Gärten," in *Der Garten von der Antike bis zum Mittelalter*, ed. M. Carroll-Spillecke (Mainz am Rhein: P. von Zabern, 1992), 230.

37. Littlewood, "Gardens of the Palaces," 17, 33, with further references. The author also provides further examples on these pages.

38. M. Psellos, *Chronographie*, vol. 2, ed. E. Renauld (Paris: Les Belles Lettres, 1928), 56–63, 70–71, for the passages and their context.

39. The most useful discussion of the location and appearance of the gardens and parks of Constantinople is H. Maguire, "Gardens and Parks in Constantinople," *Dumbarton Oaks Papers* 54 (2000): 251–64.

40. Marçais, "Les jardins," 235–36.

41. Adapted from the translation given in Von Grunebaum, "Aspects of Arabic Urban Literature," 287.

42. The most accessible version of this "itinerary" can be found in Grabar, *Formation of Islamic Art*, 168–71. The section quoted here is from 169–70. For a discussion of the archaeological reality of this description, see E. Herzfeld, "Mitteilungen über die Arbeiten der zweiten Kampagne von Samarra," *Der Islam* 5 (1914): 197–203, esp. 197–98; quoted verbatim and translated into English in K.A.C. Creswell, *Early Muslim Architecture*, vol. 2 (Oxford: Oxford University Press, 1940), 232. The relationship between Herzfeld, Creswell, and the more recent work carried out at Samarra is discussed in the following interesting work: A. Northedge, "Creswell, Herzfeld, and Samarra," *Muqarnas* 8 (1991): 74–93.

43. C. Coulson, "Structural Symbolism in Medieval Castle Architecture," *Journal of the British Archaeological Association* 132 (1979): 73–90, at 75. As quoted in R. Liddiard, *Castles in Context* (Macclesfield, Chesire: Windgatherer Press, 2005), 139–40.

44. This is not to say that every Islamic garden or garden in the Islamic world was always interpreted as a vision of paradise. Although the notion of paradise was certainly important, I tend to agree with the cautionary statement made by Gülru Necipoğlu concerning the tendency to exaggerate paradise symbolism. See G. Necipoğlu, "The Suburban Landscape of Sixteenth-Century Istanbul as a Mirror of Classical Ottoman Garden Culture," in *Gardens in the Time of the Great Muslim Empires: Theory and Design*, ed. A. Petruccioli (Leiden: Brill, 1997), 46n2. On the

inherent Orientalism of some of the statements used to explain this, see Necipoğlu, "The Suburban Landscape," 46n3. This thought is echoed in Subtelny, "Agriculture and the Timurid Chahārbāgh," 119, 124n178.

45. Grabar, *Formation of Islamic Art*, 171–73, at 173. Page references will differ in different editions of this book.

46. J. J. Rossiter, "Roman Villas of the Greek East and the Villa in Gregory of Nyssa *Ep.* 20," *Journal of Roman Archaeology* 2 (1989): 101–10, at 103, with further references.

47. H. Maguire, "Imperial Gardens and the Rhetoric of Renewal," in *New Constantines: The Rhythm of Imperial Renewal in Byzantium, 4th–13th Centuries*, ed. P. Magdalino (Aldershot: Variorum, 1994), 181–98, at 191–93.

48. Maguire, "Imperial Gardens," 192.

49. As quoted in Maguire, "Imperial Gardens," 187. The triumph occurred in 878.

50. Liddiard, *Castles in Context*, 98.

51. See John Dixon Hunt's chapter in this volume.

52. Brubaker and Littlewood, "Byzantinische Gärten," 214, 216.

53. An example of this is the way in which Anthony Littlewood divided his recent discussion of the current scholarship concerning Byzantine gardens into two sections on pleasure gardens and productive gardens. See A. Littlewood, "The Scholarship of Byzantine Gardens," in *Byzantine Garden Culture*, ed. A. Littlewood, H. Maguire, and J. Wolschke-Bulmahn (Washington, D.C.: Dumbarton Oaks, 2002), 13–21.

54. For a discussion of Byzantine monastic horticulture, see A.-M. Talbot, "Byzantine Monastic Horticulture: The Textual Evidence," in *Byzantine Garden Culture*, ed. A. Littlewood, H. Maguire, and J. Wolschke-Bulmahn (Washington, D.C.: Dumbarton Oaks, 2002), 37–67; Y. Hirschfled, *The Judean Desert Monasteries in the Byzantine Period* (New Haven, CT: Yale University Press, 1992).

55. D. F. Ruggles, among other scholars, makes particular use of surviving manuals and treatises.

56. G. Schoeler, *Arabische Naturdichtung* (Beirut: Orient-Institut der Deutschen Morgenländischen Gesellschaft, 1974), passim.

57. J. Dickie, "The Hispano-Arab Garden: Notes Towards a Typology," in *The Legacy of Muslim Spain*, ed. S. K. Jayyusi (Leiden: E. J. Brill, 1992), 1017.

58. Subtelny, "Agriculture and the Timurid Chahārbāgh," 116. See also J. L. Wescoat Jr., "Picturing an Early Mughal Garden," *Asian Art* 2, no. 4 (1989): 59–79. Wescoat discusses the famous miniature painting (Victoria and Albert Museum) of Babur laying out his Mughal Garden.

59. L. Golombek and D. Wilber, "Gardens and Garden Structures," in *The Timurid Architecture of Iran and Turkey*, vol. 1, ed. L. Golombek and D. Wilber (Princeton, NJ: Princeton University Press, 1988), 174.

60. W. Ball, "The Remains of a Monumental Timurid Garden outside Herat," *East and West* 31, nos. 1–4 (1981): 79–82.

61. D. Wilber, *Persian Gardens and Garden Pavilions* (Rutland, VT: Tuttle, 1962), 64; Golombek and Wilber, "Gardens and Garden Structures," vol. 1, 181. See also a slightly different discussion of the same point in A. U. Pope and P. Ackerman,

"Garden," in *Survey of Persian Art*, vol. 2 (Oxford: Oxford University Press, 1939), 1432–34. The authors discuss the relation of the mountain to the same cosmological view that divides the universe into four parts as well as, indirectly, its relationship to the flow of water.

62. Golombek and Wilber, "Gardens and Garden Structures," vol. 1, 175–77, 181.

63. Golombek and Wilber, "Gardens and Garden Structures," vol. 1, 175–77.

3 Plantings

1. G. E. Brereton and J. M. Ferrier, eds., *Le Menagier de Paris* (Oxford: Clarendon Press, 1981), xli. Ferrier's comments refer to the gardening treatise in the Menagier de Paris's household book.

2. J. H. Harvey, *Mediaeval Gardens* (London: B. T. Batsford, 1981), and *Early Nurserymen* (London: Phillimore, 1974).

3. Harvey, *Mediaeval Gardens*, 78. Walter of Henley, *Boke of Husbandry* (London: Wynkyn de Worde, 1508), available through *Early English Books Online* (http://gateway.proquest.com/openurl?ctx_ver=Z39.88-2003&res_id=xri:eebo&rft_id=xri:eebo:citation:99843839). Henley's treatise was first written in the 1280s. *STC* 25007 includes a tract offering advice on planting trees and vines and grafting.

4. Harvey, *Mediaeval Gardens*, 87.

5. Brereton and Ferrier, *Le Menagier de Paris*, 124.

6. W. L. Braekman, ed., *Geoffrey of Franconia's Book of Trees and Wine*, Scripta 24 (Brussels: OMIREL UFSAL, 1989), 45.

7. Braekman, *Geoffrey*, 27. I cite the text internally, using Braekman's edition, from this point.

8. J. Griffiths, A.S.G. Edwards, and N. Barker, eds., *The Tollemache Book of Secrets: A Descriptive Index and Complete Facsimile* (London: Roxburghe Club, 2001), 98. This book of secrets includes versions of Bollard's and Geoffrey's treatises. I introduce it here to demonstrate the connection compilers saw between the two.

9. Palladius's treatise circulated widely throughout the Middle Ages. A late Middle English version (c. 1420), used in the present chapter, was printed by the Early English Text Society (EETS): B. Lodge, ed., *Palladius on Husbondrie* (London: N. Trübner, 1872; reprint, Millwood, NY: Kraus, 1973), 86–87. For a selection of Roman garden writers including Palladius, see J. Henderson, *The Roman Book of Gardening* (London: Routledge, 2004).

10. W. L. Braekman, "Bollard's Middle English Book of Planting and Grafting and Its Background," *Studia Neophilologica* 57 (1985): 25. Braekman includes a transcript of the version of Bollard's text found in British Library MS Harley 116, fols. 162–65v.

11. Braekman, "Bollard," 23–26.

12. Braekman, "Bollard," 62.

13. See the *Middle English Dictionary*, s.v. "impe."

14. Plants tended to be identified by single features and not by total morphology until 1682 when John Ray composed his *Methodus Plantarum Nova* and introduced the

"new method." The distinction between monocotyledons and dicotyledons was introduced by Theophrastus (c. 370 B.C.E.), but up until the late seventeenth century plants were generally divided into three groups based on external features: for example, trees, vines, and herbs.

15. They knew, for instance, that the plants we now refer to as monocots could not be grafted, even if they did not refer to them as monocots. Monocots or monocotyledons are flowering plants whose seed contains one cotyledon, or embryonic leaf. Dicotyledons are those that contain two. Grasses, corn, lilies, and irises are some common monocots; tomatoes, beans, roses, and basil are well-known dicots.

16. Braekman, *Geoffrey*, 62.

17. Griffiths, Edwards, and Barker, *The Tollemache Book*. See also W. Eamon, *Science and the Secrets of Nature: Books of Secrets in Medieval and Early Modern Culture* (Princeton, NJ: Princeton University Press, 1994), 84–86.

18. Braekman, *Geoffrey*, 59, 74.

19. Braekman, *Geoffrey*, 75.

20. Braekman, "Bollard," 33. Cherries, apples, and roses belong to the same botanical family, Rosaceae. Grafting between genera in the same family is sometimes possible, but not in this case.

21. Braekman, *Geoffrey*, 68.

22. W. Strabo, *Hortulus* (Pittsburgh: Hunt Botanical Library, 1966). This is a facsimile and parallel text edition.

23. D. Ferry, trans., *The Georgics of Virgil* (New York: Farrar, Straus, and Giroux, 2005). This is a parallel text edition.

24. Ferry, *The Georgics of Virgil*, 148.

25. Ferry, *The Georgics of Virgil*, 150.

26. Strabo, *Hortulus*, lines 5–8.

27. Strabo, *Hortulus*, lines 10–11.

28. Strabo, *Hortulus*, lines 15–18.

29. Strabo, *Hortulus*, lines 36–50.

30. Modern gardening literature tends to particularize the needs of specific plants in terms of soil type, light, and moisture requirements.

31. Strabo, *Hortulus*, lines 51–52.

32. "Quin potius, quae sicca fere et translata subactis / Suscepit scrobibus, redivivo plena virore / Restituit reparans numeroso semina fructu"; Strabo, *Hortulus*, lines 70–72.

33. Strabo, *Hortulus*, lines 51–52.

34. Strabo, *Hortulus*, line 112

35. Strabo, *Hortulus*, line 135.

36. Strabo, *Hortulus*, lines 59–60.

37. Strabo, *Hortulus*, line 69.

38. Strabo, *Hortulus*, lines 80–82.

39. Strabo, *Hortulus*, lines 122–25.

40. Strabo, *Hortulus*, line 230.

41. Strabo, *Hortulus*, line 230.

42. Strabo, *Hortulus*, lines 276–77.

43. Strabo, *Hortulus*, lines 427–28.
44. Strabo, *Hortulus*, lines 442–43.
45. Brereton and Ferrier, *Le Menagier de Paris*, xli.
46. Brereton and Ferrier, *Le Menagier de Paris*, xlii.
47. Brereton and Ferrier, *Le Menagier de Paris*, 118. This advice is repeated in the discussion of planting peas and beans in October and November.
48. Brereton and Ferrier, *Le Menagier de Paris*, 119.
49. Brereton and Ferrier, *Le Menagier de Paris*, 119.
50. Brereton and Ferrier, *Le Menagier de Paris*, 119.
51. Brereton and Ferrier, *Le Menagier de Paris*, 119.
52. Brereton and Ferrier, *Le Menagier de Paris*, 118.
53. Brereton and Ferrier, *Le Menagier de Paris*, 120.
54. Brereton and Ferrier, *Le Menagier de Paris*, 121.
55. The editors of the critical edition speculate that "Roman" cabbage is what we now call "Savoy" cabbage. See Brereton and Ferrier, *Le Menagier de Paris*, 301.
56. Brereton and Ferrier, *Le Menagier de Paris*, 121.
57. Brereton and Ferrier, *Le Menagier de Paris*, 119.
58. Brereton and Ferrier, *Le Menagier de Paris*, 120.
59. Brereton and Ferrier, *Le Menagier de Paris*, 1.

4 Use and Reception

1. J. H. Harvey, *Mediaeval Gardens* (Beaverton, OR: Timber Press, 1981), 2. See also O. H. Creighton, *Designs Upon the Land: Elite Landscapes of the Middle Ages* (Woodbridge: Boydell, 2009), 7: "It would be misleading to create a false dichotomy between what might be labelled 'landscapes of pleasure and leisure' and 'landscapes of production.' The boundaries between the two were mutable rather than fixed . . . and many of the components of landscapes . . . manifestly meet both definitions."
2. S. Landsberg, *The Medieval Garden* (New York: Thames and Hudson, 1995), 28.
3. W. Strabo, *Hortulus,* tr. Raef Payne (Pittsburgh: Hunt Botanical Library, 1966), 91–93.
4. Strabo, *Hortulus*, 91–93, 32–33. See also J. P. Migne, ed., *Patrologia Latina* (Paris, 1841–55), vol. 114, columns 1119–30B.
5. Strabo, *Hortulus*, lines 80–83.
6. Strabo, *Hortulus*, lines 110–14.
7. Strabo, *Hortulus*, lines 152–56.
8. Strabo, *Hortulus*, lines 250–53.
9. For example, see Matthew of Vendôme, "Ars versificatoria," in *Les Arts Poétique du XIIe et du XIIIe Siècle*, ed. E. Faral (Paris: Campion, 1958), 106–93, esp. I.iii. For additional examples of the classical *locus amoenus*, see E. R. Curtius, *European Literature and the Latin Middle Ages* (Princeton, NJ: Princeton University Press, 1953), 195–200.
10. Creighton, *Designs Upon the Land*, 7.
11. Strabo, *Hortulus*, lines 432–8.
12. Strabo, *Hortulus*, 64–65.

13. See the extensive website, "St. Gall Monastery Plan," at http://www.stgallplan.org/en/index.html, and the definitive *The Plan of St. Gall: A Study of the Architecture and Economy of, and Life in a Paradigmatic Carolingian Monastery*, by W. Horn and E. Born, 3 vols. (Berkeley: University of California Press, 1979); also useful is L. Price's *The Plan of St. Gall in Brief* (Berkeley: University of California Press, 1982).

14. For a discussion of the plan as an aid to memory, see M. Carruthers, "The Poet as Master Builder: Composition and Locational Memory in the Middle Ages," *New Literary History* 24 (1993): 881–904, 895.

15. For the medicinal uses of many medieval plants, see T. Scully, "A Cook's Therapeutic Use of Garden Herbs," and P. M. Jones, "Herbs and the Medieval Surgeon," both in *Health and Healing from the Medieval Garden*, ed. P. Dendle and A. Touwaide (Woodbridge: Boydell Press, 2008), 60–71, 162–79.

16. Trade in seeds increased dramatically in the reign of Edward I. See Harvey, *Mediaeval Gardens*, 78–79. But throughout history, plants and seeds have been exchanged as valuable commodities. See Harvey, *Mediaeval Gardens*, 58 for examples of monastic houses requesting and receiving seeds, cuttings, and plants from one another.

17. Strabo, *Hortulus*, lines 46–52.

18. Strabo, *Hortulus*, 28–29.

19. J. Bond, *Monastic Landscapes* (Stroud, Gloucestershire: Tempus, 2004), 158. See also P. M. Jones on the surgeon's use of herbs: "Herbs and the Medieval Surgeon," in *Health and Healing from the Medieval Garden*, ed. P. Dendle and A. Touwaide (Woodbridge, Suffolk: Boydell and Brewer, 2008), 162–79.

20. E. B. MacDougall, ed., *Medieval Gardens* (Washington, D.C.: Dumbarton Oaks, 1986), 39.

21. Mayveart, "Monastic," 31.

22. "cepas / aleas / p[o]rros / ascolonias / apium / petrosilium / coliandrum / celefolium / anetum / lactuca / papauer / sataregia / radices / pestinachas / magones / caulas / betas / gitto" (onion / garlic / leek / shallots / celery / parsley / coriander / chervil / dill / lettuce / poppy / pepperwort / radish / parsnip / poppy / cabbage / chard / fennel), http://www.stgallplan.org/StGallDB/plan_components/public_list_berschin_english (accessed March 12, 2009).

23. L. E. Voigts, "Anglo-Saxon Plant Remedies and the Anglo-Saxons," *Isis* 70, no. 2 (1979): 250–68, 264.

24. Harvey, *Medieval Gardens*, Appendix 3: "Plants of the Middle Ages: A Dated List," 163–80; see also F. E. Crackles, "Medieval Gardens in Hull: Archaeological Evidence," *Garden History* 14, no. 1 (1986): 1–5; and H. M. Leach, "Plant Categories and the Significance of Meaning Changes: The Case of Herbs and Related Terms," *Garden History* 23, no. 1 (1995): 126.

25. Landsberg, *Medieval Garden*, 28.

26. Harvey, *Mediaeval Gardens*, Appendix 3.

27. Harvey, "Henry Daniel, A Scientific Gardener of the Fourteenth Century," *Garden History* 15, no. 2 (1987): 81–93, 89.

28. Meyvaert, "Monastic Garden," 35.

29. Landsberg, *Medieval Garden*, 29.

30. Harvey, *Mediaeval Gardens*, 28.
31. Harvey, *Mediaeval Gardens*, 34. The Domesday Book in England mentions thirty-eight vineyards in 1086 (Harvey, *Mediaeval Gardens*, 54).
32. Bond, *Monastic Landscapes*, 166.
33. J. Harvey, *Mediaeval Gardens*, 2–3, on climate change. See also R. S. Bradley M. K. Hughes, and H. F. Diaz, "Climate Change: Climate in Medieval Time," *Science* 302 (October 17, 2003): 404–5.
34. Bond, *Monastic Landscapes*, 176.
35. Harvey, *Mediaeval Gardens*, 92–93, 114.
36. Bond, *Monastic Landscapes*, 156.
37. T. Dale, "Monsters, Corporeal Deformities, and Phantasms in the Cloister of St.-Michel-de-Cuxa," *The Art Bulletin* 83, no. 3 (2001): 402–36, 409–10.
38. "HIC SINE DOMATIBUS PARADISI PLANA PARANTUR / AB ORIENTE IN OCCIDENTEEM LONGITUDO PEDUM CC / HIC MURA TECTUM IMPOSI-TUM PATET ATQUE COLUMNI / Has interque pedes denos moderare columnas / HIC PARADISIACUM SINE TECTO STERNITO CA[M]PUM / OMNIBUS AD SANCTUM TURBIS PATET HAEC UIA TEMPLUM QUO SUA UOTA FERANT UNDE HILARES REDEANT / Adueniens aditum populus hic cunctus habebit," http://www.stgallplan.org/StGallDB/plan_components/public_list_berschin_english.
39. "ascensus per cocleam ad uniuersa superinspicienda / in summitate altare sancti michaehelis arch / alter similis / in fastigo altare sancti gahelis arch" http://www.stgallplan.org/StGallDB/plan_components/public_list_berschin_english.
40. Harvey, *Mediaeval Gardens*, 80.
41. O. H. Creighton, *Designs Upon the Land: Elite Landscapes of the Middle Ages* (London: Continuum, 2002), 190–92.
42. "M[alus] uel perarius / prunarius / sorbarius / mispolarius / laurus / castenarius / ficus / gudunarius / persicus / auellenarius / amandelarius / murarius / nugarius" http://www.stgallplan.org/StGallDB/plan_components/public_list_berschin_english.
43. Please see http://www.stgallplan.org/StGallDB/plan_components/public_list_berschin_english.
44. Quoted in Harvey, *Mediaeval Gardens*, 8.
45. Quoted in Harvey, *Mediaeval Gardens*, 10.
46. Landsberg, *Medieval Garden*, 17.
47. Bond, *Monastic Landscapes*, 165.
48. Landsberg, *Medieval Garden*, 17–18, 20.
49. J. Dickie, "The Hispano-Arab Garden: Its Philosophy and Function," *Bulletin of the School of Oriental and African Studies, U London* 31, no. 2 (1968): 240.
50. Quoted in Dickie, "The Hispano-Arab Garden," 241.
51. See Creighton, *Designs Upon the Land*, 100–21 for several examples of animals introduced into the landscapes of elite estates.
52. Dickie, "Hispano-Arab Garden," 239.
53. Dickie, "Hispano-Arab Garden," 239.
54. Dickie, "Hispano-Arab Garden," 240. See also D. F. Ruggles, *Islamic Gardens and Landscapes* (Philadelphia: University of Pennsylvania Press, 2008), 107.
55. Harvey, *Mediaeval Gardens*, 48.

56. A. Touwaide, "The Legacy of Classical Antiquity in Byzantium and the West," in *Health and Healing from the Medieval Garden*, ed. P. Dendle and A. Touwaide (Woodbridge: Boydell Press, 2008), 26–27. See also Dickie, "The Hispano-Arab Garden" on Arab plantsmen, 246–48.

57. Harvey, *Mediaeval Gardens*, 40.

58. Harvey, *Mediaeval Gardens*, 40–41.

59. Dickie, "Hispano-Arab Garden," 238.

60. Ruggles, *Islamic Gardens and Landscapes*, 13–27. See also Y. Tabbaa, "Control and Abandon: Images of Water in Arabic Poetry and Gardens," in *Rivers of Paradise: Water in Islamic Art and Culture*, ed. S. Blair and J. Bloom (New Haven, CT: Yale University Press, 2009), 59–79; and T. F. Glick, "Tribal Landscapes of Islamic Spain: History and Archaeology," in *Inventing Medieval Landscapes: Senses of Place in Western Europe*, ed. J. Howe and M. Wolfe (Gainesville: University Press of Florida, 2002), 113–35, on water as a source of political power.

61. Ruggles cautions against identifying this scheme solely with Islam. Versions of the irrigated axial design appear earlier in both pre-Islamic Persian and Mediterranean cultures (*Islamic Gardens and Landscapes*, 40).

62. Ruggles, *Islamic Gardens and Landscapes*, 18.

63. Ruggles, *Islamic Gardens and Landscapes*, 152–53.

64. Ruggles, *Islamic Gardens and Landscapes*, 152. See also her "From the Heavens and Hells: The Flow of Water to the Fruited Trees and Ablution Fountains in the Great Mosque of Cordoba," in *Rivers of Paradise: Water in Islamic Art and Culture*, ed. S. Blair and J. Bloom (New Haven, CT: Yale University Press, 2009), 81–103.

65. Ruggles, *Islamic Gardens and Landscapes*, 154. See also Dickie, "Hispano-Arab Garden," 242–45.

66. Dickie, "Hispano-Arab Garden," 246.

67. Ruggles, *Islamic Gardens and Landscapes*, 157.

68. Ruggles, *Islamic Gardens and Landscapes*, 82.

69. Ruggles, *Islamic Gardens and Landscapes*, 73–74. See also Dickie, "Hispano-Arab Garden," 245.

70. Quoted in Dickie, "Hispano-Arab Garden," 241.

71. Quoted in Dickie, "Hispano-Arab Garden," 240.

72. D. P. Brookshaw, "Palaces, Pavilions, and Pleasure-Gardens: The Context and Setting of the Medieval *Majlis*," *Middle Eastern Literature* 6, no. 2 (2003): 202.

73. Brookshaw, "Palaces, Pavilions," 204.

74. Quoted in Brookshaw, "Palaces, Pavilions," 205. For examples of similar garden use in medieval Byzantine gardens, see C. N. Constantinides, "Byzantine Gardens and Horticulture in the Late Byzantine Period, 1204–1453: The Secular Sources," in *Byzantine Garden Culture*, ed. A. Littlewood, H. Maguire, and J. Wolschke-Bulmahn (Washington, D.C.: Dumbarton Oaks, 2002), 87–103, and available at www.doaks.org/etexts.html.

75. For additional discussion about the kinesthetic experience of space, see L. L. Howes, " 'The Slow Curve of the Footwalker': Narrative Time and Literary Landscapes in Middle English Poetry," *Soundings: An Interdisciplinary Journal* 83, no.

1 (2000): 165–81; and Howes, ed., "Introduction," *Place, Space, and Landscape in Medieval Narrative*, Tennessee Studies in Literature, vol. 43 (Knoxville: University of Tennessee Press, 2007).

76. S. Redford, "Rum Seljuk Gardens: Typology and Tradition," in *Landscape and the State in Medieval Anatolia: Seljuk Gardens and Pavilions of Alanya, Turkey,* BAR International Series 893 (Oxford: Archaeopress, 2000), 91–114.

77. See Harvey for the probable influence of the "horticulture of the Near East" on the development of the European pleasure garden (*Mediaeval Gardens*, 22, and his Chapter 3).

78. See M. Charageat, "Le parc d'Hesdin, création monumentale du XIIIe siècle," *Société de l'historie de l'art français, Bulletin* (1950): 94–106, and A. H. van Buren, "Reality and Literary Romance in the Park of Hesdin," in *Medieval Gardens*, ed. Elisabeth B. MacDougall (Washington, D.C.: Dumbarton Oaks, 1986), 117–34.

79. P. Bon, "Les Jardins du Duc de Berry et les Préceux de Mehun-sur-Yèvre," in *Flore et Jardins: Usages, Savoirs et Représentations du Mond Végétal au Moyen Age*, ed. Pierre-Gilles Girault (Paris: le Léopard D'Or, 1997), 39–50.

80. Harvey, *Mediaeval Gardens*, 51.

81. Harvey, *Mediaeval Gardens*, 10–11.

82. Harvey, *Mediaeval Gardens*, 11.

83. James Bond, *Monastic Landscapes*, 170.

84. Chrétien de Troyes, *Les Romans de Chrétien de Troyes: Cliges,* ed. A. Micha (Paris: Champion, 1966), lines 6271–73; D. Staines, trans., *The Complete Romances of Chrétien de Troyes* (Bloomington: Indiana University Press, 1990), 164.

85. Chrétien de Troyes, *Les Romans de Chrétien de Troyes: Yvain*, ed. A. Micha (Paris: Champion, 1966), lines 5354–64; Staines, *Complete Romances*, 320–21.

86. G. Boccaccio, *Opere*, ed. Cesare Segre (Milan: Morsia & Col, 1966), 27; *The Decameron*, trans. G. H. McWilliam (New York: Penguin, 1972), 67–68.

87. Boccaccio, *The Decameron*, 67–68.

88. Boccaccio, *The Decameron*, 234.

89. Boccaccio, *The Decameron*, 177.

90. Boccaccio, *The Decameron*, 681.

91. Boccaccio, *The Decameron*, 569.

92. G. Chaucer, "Troilus and Criseyde," in *The Riverside Chaucer*, ed. L. D. Benson (New York: Houghton Mifflin, 1987), Book II, line 818.

93. Chaucer, *Troilus and Criseyde*, Book II, line 823.

94. Bodleian Library ms Bodley 264; folio 258.

95. See R. F. Giannetto, *Medici Gardens: From Making to Design* (Philadelphia: University of Pennsylvania Press, 2008), 117–31, for an examination of gardens in *Decameron*: "Gardens can be regarded as narrative elements that materialize the actions and passions of multiple selves" (124).

96. For further discussion of Criseyde's and Deiphebus's gardens, see Howes, *Chaucer's Gardens*, 64–82.

97. C. P. Christianson, *The Riverside Gardens of Thomas More's London* (New Haven, CT: Yale University Press, 2005), 28.

98. Christianson, *The Riverside Gardens*, 29.

99. Christianson, *The Riverside Gardens*, 180.

100. Van Buren, "La Roulotte de Philippe le Bon," *Liber Amicorum: Études Historiques Offertes à Pierre Bougard* (Arras: Revue du Nord, hors serie: collection histoire 3, 1987), 115–22.

101. C. Gratias, "Le Pavillon d'Anne de Bretagne et les Jardins du Château de Blois," in *Flore et Jardins: Usages, Savoirs et Représentations du Mond Végétal au Moyen Age*, ed. Pierre-Gilles Girault (Paris: le Léopard D'Or, 1997), 132–33.

102. Ruggles, *Islamic Gardens and Landscapes*, 44.

103. Quoted in Harvey, *Mediaeval Gardens*, 10, from V. Mortet, *Recueil de Textes relatifs à l'Historie de l'Architecture . . . XI—XII siècles* (Paris: Alphonse Picard et fils, 1911).

104. Creighton, *Castles and Landscapes*, 73.

105. Creighton, *Castles and Landscapes*, 190.

106. C. C. Taylor, "Medieval Ornamental Landscapes," *Landscapes* 1 (2000): 39.

107. Taylor, "Medieval Ornamental Landscapes," 39–42. See also M. Leslie, "An English Landscape Garden before 'The English Landscape Garden'?" *The Journal of Garden History* 13 (1993): 3–15, on the example of Bodiam Castle (Sussex) and its water features.

108. *The Awntyrs off Arthure at the Terne Watheleyne*, ed. R. Gates (Philadelphia: University of Pennsylvania Press, 1969), line 6. For additional discussion of this forest, see L. L. Howes, "Ingulwood Forest in Two Middle English Romances," *Neophilologus* 96, no. 3 (2012; Online First Publication March 3, 2012).

109. *The Awntyrs off Arthure*, line 6.

110. *The Awntyrs off Arthure*, line 7.

111. *The Awntyrs off Arthure*, line 27.

112. *The Awntyrs off Arthure*, line 32.

113. Taylor, "Medieval Ornamental Landscapes," 50.

114. R. J. Gates, ed., *The Awntyrs off Arthure at the Terne Watheleyne: A Critical Edition* (Philadelphia: University of Pennsylvania Press, 1969).

115. Christianson, *The Riverside Gardens*, 48. See also M. Leslie and T. Raylor, *Culture and Cultivation in Early Modern England: Writing and the Land* (Leicester: Leicester University Press, 1992), 3.

116. Christianson, *The Riverside Gardens*, 107.

5 Meaning

Portions of this chapter have been taken from E. Augspach, *The Garden as Woman's Space in Twelfth- and Thirteenth-Century Literature* (Lewiston: Edwin Mellen Press, 2004).

1. "Et ostendit mihi fluvium aquae vitae, splendidum tamquam crystallum, procedentem de sede Dei et Agni. In medio plateau eius, et ex utraque parte fluminis lignum vitae, afferens fructus duodecim, per menses singulos, reddens fructum suum, et folia ligni ad sanitatem gentium" (*Biblia Sacra iuxta Vulgatam Clementinam* [Madrid: BAC, 1994]).

2. There have been many studies related to the history of paradise and the origin of the word. It derives from *paridaeza*, an old Persian term (*pari*: around,

daeza: wall) and was used to designate a royal park of a Persian king. The Hebrews adopted the word as *pardes*, to signify park in a more general term, while in Greek it retained its meaning of royal park. Nevertheless, in the *Septuagint* the term *paradeisos* acquires a lexical extension, since it now means both park and heaven. Jerome's *Vulgate* retains the Latinized version of the word, *paradisum*. For further information, please see G. Luttikhuizen, ed. *Paradise Interpreted: Representations of Biblical Paradise in Judaism and Christianity* (Leiden: Brill, 1999).

3. "Tulit ergo Dominus Deus hominem, et posuit eum in paradiso voluptatis, ut operaretur, et custodiret illum" (*Biblia Sacra iuxta Vulgatam Clementinam*).

4. T. Aquinas, *Summa Theologica*, first part, question 102, art. 3. *Newadvent.org*, May 20, 2008, http://newadvent.org/summa/1102.htm.

5. Isidore of Seville, *Etimologías. Edición bilingüe*, 2 vols. (Madrid: Editorial Católica, 1982–83), vol. 2, book 14, chapter 3, 166–67.

6. Aquinas, *Summa*, first part, question 102, art. 1.

7. See, for instance, the poetry of St. John of the Cross and St. Theresa of Avila.

8. "Hortus conclusus, soror mea, sponsa,/ Hortus conclusus, fons signatus./ Emissions tuae paradisus malorum punicorum,/ Cum pomorum fructibus, cypri cum nardo./ Nardus et crocus, fistula et cinnamomum,/ Cum universes lignis Libani;/ Myrrha et aloe, cum omnibus primis unguentis./ Fons hortorum, puteus aquarum viventium,/ Quae fluunt impetu de Libano./ Surge, aquilo; et veni, auster;/ Perfla hortum meum, et fluant aromata illius" (*Biblia Sacra iuxta Vulgatam Clementinam*).

9. Some believe that society was originally matriarchal, pointing out that it was women who were concerned with generation, who tended agriculture and ensured the propagation of the species. Men were essentially onlookers, called upon to occasionally participate in ritual copulation in praise of the Goddess. He adds that the change from a matriarchal to a patriarchal society, governed essentially by sky gods, went hand in hand with the development of tools for agriculture, trade and commerce (P. Shephard, *Man in the Landscape: A Historic View of the Esthetics of Nature* [College Station: Texas A&M University Press, 1991], 101).

10. P. Allen, *The Concept of Woman: The Aristotelian Revolution 750 BC–1250 AD* (Montreal: Paradise Press, 1985).

11. G. Duby, *The Knight, the Lady and the Priest: The Making of Modern Marriage in Medieval France* (Chicago: University of Chicago Press, 1993), 37. Duby says that "the purpose of marriage was to unite a valiant progenitor to a wife in such a manner that his legitimate son, bearer of the blood and name of ancestor, should be able to bring that ancestor to life again in his own person. But all depended on the wife. She was not regarded as a mere passive terrain, as she is even today in some black African cultures. In Carolingian and post-Carolingian Europe people believed that women produced sperm, or at least that both the man and the woman contributed to the act of conception, and that the immediate effect of sexual intercourse was to mingle indissolubly the blood of the two partners."

12. V. L. Bullough, "Medieval Medical and Scientific Views of Women," *Viator* 4 (1973): 485–501. Christianity did not accept all of Aristotle's teachings on women. Aristotle taught that women were defective, that they were incomplete males. He claimed that "the female, in fact, is female on account of an inability of a sort, viz.

It lacks the power to concoct semen out of the final state of nourishment (this is either blood, or its counterpart in bloodless animals) because of the coldness of its nature." Thomas Aquinas disagreed. He believed that women are passive and inferior to man, who is active by nature, but they are also part of God's plan and can therefore not be defective by nature.

13. See Aquinas, *Suma Contra los Gentiles*, ed. and tr. J. M. Pla Castellano et al., vol. 2 (Madrid: BAC, 1952). In discussing the resurrection of the bodies, Aquinas says in book 4, 88: "Similiter etiam nec infirmitas feminei sexus perfectioni resurgentium obviat. Non enim est infirmitas per recessum a natura, sed a natura intenta. Et ipsa etiam naturae distinctio in hominibus perfectionem naturae demonstrabit et divinam sapientam, omnia cum eum quodam ordine disponentem" (Similarly, the weakness of the female sex is not inconsistent with the perfection of the resurrection. Because the weakness is not a departure from nature, but is intended by nature. This natural differentiation which exists in human nature shows its perfection, and, at the same time, divine wisdom that arranges creation according to an order [trans. p. 920].)

14. R. B. Riley, "Flowers, Power and Sex," in *The Meaning of Gardens: Idea, Place and Action*, ed. M. Francis and R. T. Hester Jr. (Cambridge, MA: MIT Press, 1990), 67.

15. While it is true that we often encounter beautiful gardens that do not include women, such as the garden where King Darius inspires his troops to battle in the Spanish *Libro d'Alixandre*, these gardens have a minor role. Their purpose is to serve as frame to the world of ideas. Sensory experience takes a back seat to intellectual rumination. Their inspiration comes primarily from Virgil's Elysian fields.

16. See K. M. Wilson and E. M. Makowski, *Wykked Wyves and the Woes of Marriage: Misogamous Literature from Juvenal to Chaucer* (Albany: State University of New York Press, 1990). The authors show how throughout the Middle Ages misogamy prevailed, yet constantly evolved in its character and address in accordance with the changing times.

Furthermore, The sacralization of marriage had been gradual, and even though it had come to be accepted as a sacrament by the middle of the twelfth century, it never quite lost the negative connotations naturally associated with sex. Its only function was to protect against sin. Though on the whole quite advanced for its time, Gratian's controversial *Decretum* finds that marriage is a means of protecting oneself from sin. "The first institution of marriage was effected in Paradise in such a way that there would have been, 'an unstained bed and honourable marriage' [Hebrews, xiii.4] resulting in conception without ardor and birth without pain. The second, to eliminate unlawful movement, was effected outside Paradise in such a way that the infirmity that is prone to foul ruin might be rescued by the uprightness of marriage. This is why the apostle, writing to the Corinthians says, 'On account of fornication let each man have his own wife and each woman her own husband' [I Corinthians, vii.2]" (Gratian, "On Marriage (dictum post c 32, 2.2)," in *Medieval Sourcebook*, ed. P. Halsall [New York: Fordham University, 1999], http:www.fordham.edu/halsall/source/gratian.html).

17. Dinah, Jacob's daughter, was the example of the defiled female who was raped when going for a walk to visit the "daughter's of the land." The episode is related in Genesis 34. For a full commentary of the need to watch over wandering females,

see C. Casagrande, "The Protected Woman," *A History of Women: Silences of the Middle Ages* (Cambridge, MA: Harvard University Press, 1998).

18. St Ambrose compared this with the Vestal Virgins, who 'retired' from virginity after thirty years: in *De Virginibus*, he wonders what sort of religion can it be that expects your girls to be modest and old women immodest. J. P. Migne, ed., *Patrologia Latina Database* (Alexandria, VA: Chadwick-Healey, 1995), Col. 0408B.

19. M. Warner, *Alone of All Her Sex* (New York: Vintage, 1983), 51. Warner adds that John Chrysostom held this idea, although Augustine and Aquinas did not support it, believing that the first couple enjoyed untainted sex "for otherwise why would God have bothered to create a woman and not a man to be Adam's companion?" (Warner, *Alone of All Her Sex*, 52).

20. Et ut scias virginitatem esse naturae, nuptias post delictum: virgo nascitur caro de nuptiis in fructu reddens, quod in radice perdiderat. "Exiet virga de radice Iesse et flos de radice ascendet." Virga mater est domini, simplex, pura, sinceris nullo extrinsecus germine cohaerente et ad similitudinem Dei unione fecunda (Jerome, *Select Letters of Saint Jerome* [Cambridge, MA: Harvard University Press, 1991], 92).

21. In *City of God*, 14:23, Augustine states that, sex took place in Paradise but without the passions that resulted from Original Sin. Sex, therefore, is not the consequence of Original Sin, but lust is. *City of God Against the Pagans*, vol. 4 (Cambridge, MA: Harvard University Press, 1988).

22. Migne, ed., *Patrologia Latina Database* (Alexandria, VA: Chadwick-Healey, 1995).

23. In the fourteenth-century *Libro del Buen Amor* the poet speaks of four encounters with women in open country. These women are ugly, rude, and ready to mate.

24. "Eo quod in hortis ejusmodi impressam singaculis imaginem Dei, sinceri fontis unda resplendeat, nec volutabris spirtualium bestiarum sparsa coeno fluenta turbentur. Hinc ille murali septus spirtu pudor clauditur, ne pateat ad rapinam. Itaque secut hortus furibus inaccessus, vitem redolet, flagrant oleam, rosam renidet; ut in vite religio, in olea pax, in rosa pudor sacratae virginitatis inolescat" (*Patrologia Latina* 15, Col. 1910B).

25. *PL* 15, Col. 1911A—1911C.

26. M. L. D'Ancona, "L'Hortus Conclusus nel Medioevo e nel Rinascimento," *Miniatura* 2 (1989): 121–29.

27. Epistola XLVIII, seu Liber Apologeticus, ad Pammachium, pro Libris contra Jovinianum, *PL* 22, Col. 1510.

28. Itaque hortus conclusus, quia uterus Virginis modis omnibus integer atque incorruptus fuit. Hortus autem ideo est apellatus, quia universae deliciae paradisi in eo effloruerunt, et signatus est venter pudoris, ubi fons emicuit nostrae redemptionis. Signatus, inquam, quia incontaminatus atque incorruptus existit sanguis, ex quo manavit liquoris (Expositio in Evangelium Matthaee II, *PL* 120, Col. 0106C–0107A).

29. See, for instante, Alcuin of York's Carmina CLXXIV, *PL* 101, Col. 0771B. Alcuin of York (735–804) was one of the most learned men of his time and Charlemagne's minister of education. His poetry anticipates the *Dolce Stil Novo*.

30. Haec est ille fons signatus,/ Hortus clausus, fecundatus/ Virtutum seminibus./ Haec est illa porta clausa,/ Quam latente Deus causa/ Clauserat hominibus (Adam of St. Victor, *The Liturgical Poetry of Adam of St. Victor* [Oxford: London, 1881], 33–38).

31. D'Ancona shows that the figure of the *hortus conclusus* becomes fixed in the Patrologia Latina in the thirteenth century.

32. D. W. Robertson Jr., "The Doctrine of Charity in Mediaeval Literary Gardens: A Topical Approach through Symbolism and Allegory," *Speculum* 26, no. 1 (1951): 24–49.

33. J. Ferrante, *Woman as Image in Medieval Art* (New York: Columbia University Press, 1975).

34. T. Hunt, "The Song of Songs and Courtly Literature," in *Court and Poet: Selected Proceedings of the Third Congress of the International Courtly Literature Society*, ed. G. S. Burgess (Liverpool: F. Cairns, 1980), 193. See also B. Cazelles, *The Lady as Saint: A Collection of French Hagiographic Romances of the Thirteenth Century* (Philadelphia: University of Pennsylvania Press, 1991), 31. In describing hagiographic romances of the twelfth and thirteenth centuries, Cazelles shows that while secular literature borrowed from religion in order to give courtly love a mystical aura, so hagiography was forced to turn to secular romances in search of devices of composition that would attract the audience.

35. Chrétien's Lancelot is a case in point: Sanz conpaignie et sanz conduit/ molt tost vers le vergier s'an va,/ que conpaignie ne trova/ et de ce li est bein cheü/ c'une piece del mur cheü/ ot el vergier novelemant./ Par cele fraite isnelemant/ s'an passe, et vet tant que il vient/ a la fenestre, et la se tient/ si coiz qu'il n'i tost, n'esternue,/ tant que la reine est venue/ en une molt blanche chemise" (4568–79). Alone and unobserved, he [Lancelot] went straight to the orchard. He had the good fortune to discover that a part of the orchard wall had recently fallen. Through this breach he quickly passed and continued until he reached the window, where he stood absolutely silent, careful not to cough or sneeze, until the queen approached in a spotless white shift (263). C. de Troyes, *Les Romans de Chrétien de Troyes: Le Chevalier de la Charrete*, vol. 3 (Paris: Librairie Honoré Champion, 1965).

36. Casagrande, "The Protected Woman," *A History of Women*, vol. 2 (Cambridge, MA: Harvard University Press), 102

37. M. C. Howell, *Women, Production and Patriarchy in Late Medieval Cities* (Chicago: University of Chicago Press, 1986), 15. "Whether it was considered as owned communally or separately, family property was legally under the management of husbands, but husbands did not own the assets outright. Instead, they managed family property with duties towards all dependent family members, including their wives. A man's responsibilities for the property on which his family members depended was part and parcel of his general responsibility for them, a responsibility which derived from his position as head as household" (15).

38. Consider, for example, January's experience in Chaucer's "The Merchant's Tale."

39. For further information, see C. Saunders, *The Forests of Medieval Romance: Avernus, Broceliande, Arden* (Rochester, NY: D. S. Brewer, 1993).

40. M. Camille, *Image on the Edge: The Margins of Medieval Art* (Cambridge, MA: Harvard University Press, 1992), 16.

41. G. H. McNight, ed., *King Horn, Floriz and Blauncheflur, the Assumption of Our Lady* (London: Oxford University Press, 1962).

42. Invisible walls can indeed be quite spiritual. See W. von Grafenberg, *Wigalois: The Knight of Fortune's Wheel* (Lincoln: University of Nebraska Press, 1977). In this thirteenth-century High Middle German work, believed to have a French source, we find the following garden: "In front of the gate, upon a broad rock by the road, was a grassy plot with a tree—beautiful without measure—which shaded the whole area. From its sweet blossoms came a delightful odor which gave one strength and happiness" (von Grafenberg, *Wigalois*, 155). When Wigalois's guide, a stag, enters the garden, he becomes a man again. He turns out to be the father of Wigalois's beloved, who has been wrongfully killed. This is his little paradise, preserved for him by God. Wigalois "wanted to go to the man and dismount, but the plot, though without walls, was so enclosed by God's wondrous power that he could not approach the man who was right in front of him and whom he saw quite clearly" (von Grafenberg, *Wigalois*, 155).

    This *hortus conclusus* stands for paradise, the reward of the faithful. The *Wigalois* is tinged with religious fervor but also with supernatural elements of folklore such as dragons, giants, and dwarves. The gardens enclosed by air that are controlled by women, as described above, are suspect because the marvelous occurs within the garden. On the other hand, in the *Wigalois*, the garden is one of the many fantastic elements within the tale, so it cannot be regarded with much suspicion. It serves as a reminder that the evil that remains sealed off from it—which is represented by the hellish images in the castle nearby and the dragon that besieges all knights—cannot touch it. While not an hortus conclusus in the traditional sense of inscribing the lady, it remains tied to biblical tradition and representations of paradise and the resurrection.

43. For more on this topos, see S. L. Smith, *The Power of Women: A Topos of Medieval Art and Literature* (Philadelphia: University of Pennsylvania Press, 1995).

6 Verbal Representations

1. E. R. Curtius, *European Literature and the Latin Middle Ages* (New York: Curtius, 1953), 192–202.

2. See for example, D. Thoss, *Studien zum Locus Amoenus im Mittelalter* (Vienna: Wilhelm Braumüller, 1972), passim; P. Piehler, *The Visionary Landscape* (London: Edward Arnold, 1971), passim.

3. For a discussion of the connection to the Persian hunting park, see A. B. Giamatti, *Earthly Paradise and the Renaissance Epic* (Princeton, NJ: Princeton University Press, 1966), 10; J. Delumeau, *History of Paradise: The Garden of Eden in Myth and Tradition* (New York: Continuum, 1995), 3–6.

4. Giamatti, *Earthly Paradise and the Renaissance Epic*, 33–49; Delumeau, *History of Paradise*, 6–15.

5. There is a comprehensive literature on the relationship of the mechanical arts of necessity to an attempt to recreate Edenic perfection through the human arts.

See for example, E. Whitney, *Paradise Restored: The Mechanical Arts from Antiquity through the Thirteenth Century* (Philadelphia: American Philosophical Society, 1990), passim; G. Ovitt, *The Restoration of Perfection: Labor and Technology in Medieval Culture* (New Brunswick, NJ: Rutgers University Press, 1987), passim.

6. For a useful characterization of the various sides of this debate, see G. Boas, *Primitivism and Related Ideas in the Middle Ages* (Baltimore, 1948), 154–74.

7. Boas, *Primitivism and Related Ideas*, 161–64.

8. For a comprehensive look at the meaning of the Land of Cockaigne and related stories of earthly paradises, see H. Pleij, *Dreaming of Cockaigne: Medieval Fanatasies of the Perfect Life* (New York: Columbia University Press, 2001), passim.

9. For a description of Muslim paradise, see A. Schimmel, "The Celestial Garden in Islam," in *The Islamic Garden* (Washington, D.C.: Dumbarton Oaks, 1976), 13–39; for the possible connection between the lavish earthly paradises of Europe and Muslim paradise, see also Pleij, *Dreaming of Cockaigne*, 209–13.

10. See Curtius, *European Literature and the Latin Middle Ages*, 192–202.

11. This translation and all subsequent references to Isidore's *Etymologies* are taken from S. A. Barner, W. J. Lewis, J. A. Beach, and O. Berghof, trans., *The Etymologies of Isidore of Seville* (Cambridge: Cambridge University Press, 2006); this citation: XIV, viii, 33.

12. For the role of wonder and the hygienic justification of literature, see G. Olson, *Literature as Recreation in the Later Middle Ages* (Ithaca, NY: Cornell University Press, 1982), 87–88.

13. S. Stanley, *The Enclosed Garden* (Madison: University of Wisconsin Press, 1966), 4.

14. W. E. Phipps, "The Plight of the Song of Songs," in *The Song of Songs*, ed. Harold Bloom (New York: Chelsea House Publishers, 1988), 9–21.

15. R. Fulton, "Mimetic Devotion, Marian Exegesis, and the Historical Sense of the Song of Songs," *Viator: Medieval and Renaissance Studies* 27 (1996): 87.

16. B. E. Daley, "The 'Closed Garden' and the 'Sealed Fountain': Song of Songs 4:12 in the Medieval Iconography of Mary," in *Medieval Gardens*, ed. E. Macdougall (Washington, D.C.: Dumbarton Oaks, 1986), 259–63. See also, A. W. Astell, *The Song of Songs in the Middles Ages* (Ithaca, NY: Cornell University Press, 1990), 42–72.

17. E. Augspach, *The Garden as Woman's Space in Twelfth- and Thirteenth-Century Literature* (Lewiston: Edwin Mellen Press, 2004), 31, 36.

18. Augspach, *The Garden as Woman's Space*, 7.

19. D. Herlihy, "The Carolingian capitulary, *De Villis*," in *Medieval Culture and Society* (New York: Harper & Row, 1968), 42–52.

20. R. Collison, *Encyclopedias: Their History throughout the Ages* (New York: Hafner Publishing, 1964), 36–37.

21. Collison, *Encyclopedias*, 21.

22. See L. Thorndike, *A History of Magic and Experimental Science*, vol. 2 (New York: Macmillan, 1923–58), 531.

23. Barner, Lewis, Beach, and Berghof, *The Etymologies of Isidore of Seville*, XVII, ix, 4–19.

24. This etymology is reminiscent of Varro's false etymology of "prata," which he traces back to *parata*, or being ready at hand. Varro, *De rustica*, vol. 1 (Cambridge,

MA: Harvard University Press, 1934), 7, 10–12; this citation: Barner, Lewis, Beach, and Berghof, *The Etymologies of Isidore of Seville*, XVII, x, 1.

25. A. Neckam, *De naturis rerum, Libri Duo, CLXVI: De herbis et arboribus et floribus horto crescentibus* (Liechtenstein: Kraus Reprint LTD, 1967), 274–75.

26. A. Neckam, *Suppletio Defectuum, Book I : Alexander Neckam on Plants, Birds and Animals: A Supplement to the Laus Sapientie Divine* (Florence: SISMEL edizioni del Galluzzo, 1999), 351–65, 29.

27. For a discussion of the paradisical foundation of later botanical gardens, see J. Prest, *The Garden of Eden: The Botanic Garden and the Re-Creation of Paradise* (New Haven, CT: Yale University Press, 1981), passim.

28. His entire work consists of seven books, and its purpose was to act as a commentary on the pseudo-Aristotelian *De plantis*, which was probably written by Nicolas of Damascene, a late Hellenistic (first century B.C.) historian, scholar, and writer. See the entry on "Nikolaus Damaskenos" in *Paulys Realencyclopädie* 17, no. 1, especially 423–24.

29. I, 2, 2. Translated and quoted in J. Harvey, *Mediaeval Gardens* (London: B.T. Batsford, 1981), 6. For a complete text of the original Latin, see Albertus Magnus, *Alberti Magni ex ordine praedicatorum de Vegetabilibus libri VII : historiae naturalis pars XVIII / editionem criticam ab Ernesto Meyero coeptam : absolvit Carolus Jessen* (Berlin: G. Reimeri, 1867), 636–38.

30. Albertus Magnus, *Alberti Magni ex ordine praedicatorum de Vegetabilibus libri VII*, 637.

31. Thoss, *Studien zum Locus Amoenus im Mittelalter*, 4.

32. N. G. Siraisi, *Medieval and Early Renaissance Medicine: An Introduction to Knowledge and Practice* (Chicago: University of Chicago Press, 1990), 101–4.

33. For Aristotle's discussion of color, see his *Parva Naturalia* (Cambridge, MA: Harvard University Press, 1936), 245.

34. For a discussion of motion and rest as one of the non-naturals, see Olson, *Literature as Recreation in the Later Middle Ages*, 42–44.

35. Siraisi, *Medieval and Early Renaissance Medicine*, 128–29; Avicenna was one of the most important proponents of fresh air as a requirement for good health, see Avicenna in O. C. Gruner, *A Treatise on the Canon of Medicine of Avicenna: Incorporating a Translation of the First Book* (London: Luzac, 1930), 175–76.

36. All subsequent translations of Crescenzi were made by the author, J. Bauman, and published in "Tradition and Transformation: The Pleasure Garden in Piero de'Crescenzi's *Liber ruralium commodorum*," *Studies in the History of Gardens and Designed Landscapes* 22 (Summer 2002), XVII, preface.

37. A comprehensive annotated edition of the *Liber ruralium* was compiled from the original manuscripts by Will Richter and posthumously published by his daughter Reinhilt Richter-Bergmeier. Petrus de Crescentiis, *Ruralia commoda. Das Wissen des vollkommenen Landwirts um 1300*, 3 vols. (Heidelberg: Universitätsverlag C. Winter, 1995–98).

38. Crescentiis, *Ruralia commoda*, XVIII, 2, 1–3.

39. Crescentiis, *Ruralia commoda*, XVIII, 3, 1.

40. Crescentiis, *Ruralia commoda*, I, 7, 3.

41. Crescentiis, *Ruralia commoda*, XVIII, 3, 1.

42. Crescentiis, *Ruralia commoda*, XVIII, 3, 4.

43. Crescentiis, *Ruralia commoda*, XVIII, 3, 6.

44. See J. Ackerman, "The Typology of the Villa," in *Villa: Form and Ideology of Country Houses* (Princeton, NJ: Princeton University Press, 1990), 9–34.

45. "*Epistula missa ad Karolum regem secundum*" (Crescentiis, *Ruralia commoda*, 2).

46. For more on the role of courtly love see the introduction to A. Capellanus, *The Art of Courtly Love* (New York: Columbia University Press, 1941), 1–23; for a discussion of the disputed significance of the term courtly love itself, see the introduction in J. M. Ferrante and G. D. Economou, eds., *In Pursuit of Perfection: Courtly Love in Medieval Literature* (Port Washington, NY: Kennikat Press, 1975), 3–12.

47. All translations and references below appear in Capellanus, *The Art of Courtly Love*, 73–83.

48. For a discussion of the role of coitus in relieving illnesses and balancing the humors, see the chapter "Medicine and the Art of Love," in D. Jacquart and C. Thomasset, *Sexuality and Medicine in the Middle Ages* (Princeton, NJ: Princeton University Press, 1985), 87–138.

49. G. de Lorris and J. de Meun, *Romance of the Rose*, trans. C. Dahlberg (Princeton, NJ: Princeton University Press, 1971), 31.

50. de Lorris and de Meun, *Romance of the Rose*, 31.

51. P. Zumthor, "Narrative and Anti-Narrative: Le Roman de la Rose," *Yale French Studies* 51 (1974): 184.

52. de Lorris and de Meun, *Romance of the Rose*, 32.

53. de Lorris and de Meun, *Romance of the Rose*, 39.

54. de Lorris and de Meun, *Romance of the Rose*, 48.

55. de Lorris and de Meun, *Romance of the Rose*, 48.

56. de Lorris and de Meun, *Romance of the Rose*, 49.

57. de Lorris and de Meun, *Romance of the Rose*, 328–38.

58. G. de Machaut, *Le Jugement du roy de Behaigne and Remede de Fortune* (Athens: University of Georgia Press, 1988), lines 783–823, 214–17.

59. For the most recent reconstruction of the park and critique of the literature on Hesdin, see A. Hagopian van Buren, "Reality and Literary Romance in the Park of Hesdin," in *Medieval Gardens*, ed. E. MacDougall (Washington, D.C.: Dumbarton Oaks, 1986), 125–29.

60. Hagopian van Buren, "Reality and Literary Romance in the Park of Hesdin," 15.

61. de Machaut, *Le Jugement du roy de Behaigne and Remede de Fortune*, lines 838–39.

62. J. M. Hubert, "The Romance of Floire and Blanche-fleur: A French Idyllic Poem of the Twelfth Century," *North Carolina. Studies in the Romance Languages and Literatures* 63 (1966): 13–19. All references to the text below are taken from this edition.

63. Hubert, "The Romance of Floire and Blanche-fleur," lines 235–63.

64. See also, J. Price, "*Floire Et Blancheflor*: The Magic and Mechanics of Love," *Reading Medieval Studies* 8 (1982): 12–33.

65. Hubert, "The Romance of Floire and Blanche-fleur," lines 598–627.

66. Hubert, "The Romance of Floire and Blanche-fleur," lines 1748–819.

67. Interestingly, in a 1548 Latin edition of the *Liber ruralium commodorum*, the word *inusitatas* was inaccurately rendered as *musicatas* (or musical things) suggesting that for a sixteenth-century author there is a continuity between grafting and horticultural experiments and such marvels as the Organ Fountain at the Villa d'Este.

68. For a discussion of the role of automata in medieval literature, see M. Sherwood, "Magical Mechanics and Medieval Fiction," *Studies in Philology* 14 (1947): 567–92.

69. Augspach, *The Garden as Woman's Space*, 1.

70. G. von Strassburg, *Tristan* (Harmondsworth: Penguin Books, 1960), 49.

71. von Strassburg, *Tristan*, 48–49.

72. von Strassburg, Tristan, 261–62.

73. In his *Literature as Recreation in the Later Middle Ages*, G. Olson convincingly argues that by the late Middle Ages literature and reading were considered to have medical benefits that justified their otherwise secular and "entertaining" qualities.

74. G. Boccaccio, *The Decameron*, tr. G. H. McWilliam (Harmondsworth: Penguin, 1972), 66.

75. Boccaccio, *The Decameron*, 110.

76. Olson, *Literature as Recreation in the Later Middle Ages*, 49–55.

77. Olson, *Literature as Recreation in the Later Middle Ages*, 68.

78. Olson, *Literature as Recreation in the Later Middle Ages*, 233–34.

7 Visual Representations

1. P. Burke, "Afterword: Exploring Cultural History. A Response," *Exploring Cultural History: Essays in Honour of Peter Burke*, ed. J. P. Rubiés, M. Calaresu, and F. de Vivo (Aldershot: Ashgate, 2010), 351–58, 353.

2. W. Blake, *Jerusalem, Emanation of the Giant Albion*, Plate 55, lines 62–63.

3. See M. M. Sheehan, "The Formation and Stability of Marriage in Fourteenth-Century England: Evidence of an Ely Register," in *Marriage, Family, and Law in Medieval Europe: Collected Studies*, ed. J. K. Farge (Toronto: University of Toronto Press, 1996), 38–76, 56.

4. See C. A. Fleck, *The Clement Bible at the Medieval Courts of Naples and Avignon: A Story of Papal Power, Royal Prestige, and Patronage* (Farnham: Ashgate, 2010).

5. See similar points made by M. H. Caviness in "Reception of Images by Medieval Viewers," in *A Companion to Medieval Art: Romanesque and Gothic in Northern Europe*, ed. Conrad Rudolph (Oxford: Blackwell, 2006), 65–85.

6. Such addition of separate sheets was not unusual, though this does nothing to lessen the sense that the duc de Berry's Book of Hours is being rendered unique. See J. Alexander, *Medieval Illuminators and Their Methods of Work* (New Haven, CT: Yale University Press, 1992), 141. Alexander details regulations to prevent import of single leaf illustrations, which clearly threatened those manufacturing whole manuscript Books of Hours in the fifteenth century (125).

7. Another example would be Hieronymus Bosch's *Garden of Earthly Delights* in the Prado. But this probably dates from 1500, rather late for this volume, and its magnificent idiosyncrasy distracts from a simpler point.

8. It is clear that the production of images for the Books of Hours was a commercial trade by the fifteenth century, and Books of Hours produced toward that century's end include printed plates with hand-colouring; nonetheless, mass-production in the modern sense differs.

   Writing about the coming of the print as a "revolution" has been rightly questioned by Peter Schmidt, who points out the limited nature of the evidence available and the dependence for this argument on many unexamined assumptions ("The Multiple Image: The Beginnings of Printmaking, between Old Theories and New Approaches," in P. Parshall and R. Schoch, eds., *Origins of European Printmaking: Fifteenth-Century Woodcuts and their Public* [Washington, D.C.: National Gallery of Art, 2005], 37–56). But it is clear that there was a different and wider audience for printed images on paper; determining how to interpret that remains a live scholarly issue.

9. For a modern reading of the "Garden of Love" tradition, see R. Barnett, "Serpent of Pleasure: Emergence and Difference in the Medieval Garden of Love," *Landscape Journal* 28 (2009): 137–50.

10. *Très Riches Heures*, "April," folio 4v.

11. *Oxford English Dictionary* (a. F. *secret* adj. and n. [OF. also *secré*: see *SECRE a.* and *n.*], ad. L. *sēcrētus* adj. [neut. *sēcrētum* used subst., a secret], orig. pa. pple. of *sēcernēre* to separate, divide off: see *SECERN v.* Cf. Pr. *secret*, Sp. *secreto*, Pg. *secreto*, *segredo*, It. *secreto*, *segredo* [all used as adj. and n.].)

12. See J. Prest, *The Garden of Eden: The Botanical Garden and the Re-Creation of Paradise* (New Haven, CT: Yale University Press, 1981), 96.

13. See P. Barber and T. Harper, *Magnificent Maps: Power, Propaganda and Art* (London: British Library, 2010), 52–53; A. Cattaneo, *Fra Mauro's World Map and Fifteenth-Century Venetian Culture* (Turhout: Brepols, 2010).

14. Bocace, Des cas des nobles homes et femmes (ms. 860) chute d'Adam et Eve (f. 7).

15. Musée Cluny Cl. 17506.

16. See M. J. Carruthers, *The Book of Memory: A Study of Memory in Medieval Culture* (Cambridge: Cambridge University Press, 1990), 40–55.

17. H. Manuwald and N. Humphrey, "A Painted Casket in the Victoria and Albert Museum, London," *The Antiquaries Journal* 90 (2010): 235–60.

18. Interpretation of the iconography of such objects is inevitably tentative. Some scholars have argued that we must read them as ironic ("these gestures and postures have a symmetry that enlarge [*sic*] the ironies of the relationship" [P. Barnet, ed., *Images in Ivory: Precious Objects of the Gothic Age* (Detroit: Detroit Institute of Arts in association with Princeton University Press, 1997), 243]), but it is hard to think irony alone is an adequate explanation of their emotional tone.

19. The "Talbot" Casket's covering layer is embossed leather, a luxury material associated with the sophisticated and high-value products of Islamic Spain. Even while fearing and fighting Islam, the cultures of Christendom were fascinated by the more sophisticated garden and artistic culture to their south and east. Like their Moorish models, the caskets are made of painted and gilded wood, ivory, or leather; intricately carved ivory caskets, prized at the Umayyad court, for instance, found their way north to Christian owners. There is a reason why the decorative forms of the interior of the "Talbot" Casket are called arabesques (or the earlier form: *Rebeske*).

20. All these objects are acknowledged and authorized as gifts between lovers by Andreas Capellanus's countess of Champagne in the 1180s. The countess judges that
"a lover may freely accept from her beloved these things: a handkerchief, a hair
band, a circlet of gold or silver, a brooch for the breast, a mirror, a belt, a purse, a
lace for clothes, a comb, a keepsake of the lover, and, to speak more generally, a
lady can accept from her love whatever small gift may be useful in the care of her
person, or may look charming, or may remind her of her lover, providing, however,
that in accepting the gift it is clear that she is acting quite without avarice" ([Bk 2,
Ch 7: De variis iudiciis amoris, paragraph 49] *Quaesitum quoque fuit a Campa-
niae comitissa quas res deceat amantes a coamantibus oblatas accipere. Cui taliter
inquisitioni comitissa respondit: "Amans quidem a coamante haec licenter potest
accipere, scilicet orarium, capillorum ligamina, auri argentique coronam, pectoris
fibulam, speculum, cingulum, marsupium, lateris cordulam, pectinem, manicas,
chirothecas, anulum, pyxidem, species, lavamenta, vascula, repositoria, vexillum
causa memoriae, et, ut generali sermone loquamur, quodlibet datum modicum
quod ad corporis potest valere culturam vel aspectus amoenitatem, vel quod potest
coamantis afferre memoriam, amans poterit a coamante percipere, si tamen dati
acceptio omni videatur avaritiae suspicione carere*).

21. J. Renart, *The Romance of the Rose or Guillaume de Dole* (Philadelphia: University of Pennsylvania Press, 1993).

22. E. Muir, *Ritual in Early Modern Europe* (Cambridge: Cambridge University Press,
2005), 17.

23. Cleveland Museum of Art accession No. 1930.742[0]; 1375-1400.

24. Walters Art Gallery PL2 71 269.

25. Chaucer's translation in F. N. Robinson, ed., *The Works of Geoffrey Chaucer* (London: Oxford University Press, 1957), lines 567–69.

26. Chaucer's translation in Robinson, *The Works of Geoffrey Chaucer*, 600–601.

27. "The Franklin's Tale," in Robinson, *The Works of Geoffrey Chaucer*, 137.

28. "The Franklin's Tale," in Robinson, *The Works of Geoffrey Chaucer*, 1764.

29. A Dunlop, *Painted Palaces: The Rise of Secular Art in Early Renaissance Italy*
(University Park: Pennsylvania State University, 2009), 39.

30. Dunlop, *Painted Palaces*, 26.

31. L. B. Alberti, *On the Art of Building in Ten Books* (Cambridge, MA: MIT Press,
1988), 299; summarized by Dunlop, *Painted Palaces*, 26.

32. N. Büttner, *The History of Gardens in Painting*, tr. Russell Stockman (New York:
Abbeville Press, 2008), 30.

33. Modern notions of the "private" can mislead and the question of privacy is much
debated among historians of social life. For a recent commentary, see S. McSheffrey, "Place, Space, and Situation: Public and Private in the Making of Marriage
in Late-Medieval London," *Speculum* 79 (2004): 960–90; and B. J. Harris, *English Aristocratic Women, 1450–1550: Marriage and Family, Property and Careers*
(New York: Oxford University Press, 2002).

34. For the surviving ivory caskets illustrating the *Chatelaine de Vergi* romance, see
Barnet, *Images in Ivory: Precious Objects of the Gothic Age*, 242–44.

35. C.D.A. Monson, *Andreas Capellanus, Scholasticism, and the Courtly Tradition*
(Washington, D.C.: Catholic University of America Press, 2005).

36. The most recent consideration of this room is J. M. Musacchio, *Art, Marriage, and the Family in the Florentine Renaissance Palace* (New Haven, CT: Yale University Press, 2009). See also P. Watson, *The Garden of Love in Tuscan Art of the Early Renaissance* (Philadelphia: Art Alliance Press, 1979), 48–50.

37. Musacchio, *Art, Marriage, and the Family*, 100.

38. E. Borsook, *The Mural Painters of Tuscany from Cimabue to Andrea del Sarto*, 2nd ed. (Oxford: Clarendon Press, 1980), 55–56.

39. *Sur la terre comme au ciel: Jardins d'Occident à la fin du Moyen Âge*, ed. É. Antoine et al. (Paris: Réunion des Musées Nationaux, 2002), 53.

40. *Très Riches Heures*, folio 26r.

41. *Très Riches Heures*, folio 25v.

42. *Très Riches Heures*, folio 8v.

43. Cathleen Hoeniger makes a similar point concerning the nearly contemporary *Tacuinum sanitatis* illustrations for Giangaleazzo Visconti, comparing these to the Visconti *Book of Hours*:

    In assembling the prototypes for the *Tacuinum* illuminations, Giovanni dei Grassi strove to capture a world of fertile fields, orchards, and gardens on a perfectly run feudal estate intended to echo the Visconti's own. Just as the famous prayer book, the *Visconti Hours*, initiated by Giovanni dei Grassi's workshop, showed that count as devout, chivalric, and a worthy successor to the Roman emperors, so, too, the *Tacuinum* illustrations portrayed the peaceful, orderly, bountiful world such a ruler would enjoy . . . The reality was, however, something quite different. The period 1340 to 1400 was one of famine, disease, and warfare in northern Italy . . . At a time when so many were starving, the wealthy and powerful class gained the popular title "*il populo grasso*," the fat people. Knowing this context, it is hard to take utopian landscapes of the *Tacuinum* paintings, with their bountiful harvests and cheerful laborers, at face value. Ultimately, the celebration of an abundance of food in the *Tacuinum sanitatis* manuscripts must be interpreted in part as an assertion of power and class by the Visconti rulers. Eating well and hopefully was their privilege ("The Illuminated *Tacuinum sanitatis* Manuscripts from Northern Italy *ca.* 1380–1400: Sources, Patrons, and the Creation of a New Pictorial Genre," in *Visualizing Medieval Medicine and Natural History, 1200–1550*, ed. J. A. Givens, K. Reeds, and A. Touwaide [Aldershot: Ashgate, 2006], 51–82, 81–82).

44. M. Meiss, preface to *Les Très Riches Heures du Duc de Berry*, eds. J. Longnon and R. Cazelles (London: Thames & Hudson, 1989), 13.

45. Meiss, *Les Très riches heures du Duc de Berry*, 10, 11.

46. G. dei Grassi, *Art and Architecture in Italy, 1250–1400* (New Haven, CT: Yale University Press, 1993), 583.

47. R. Browning, "Pictor Ignotus," *The Poems*, vol. 1, ed. J. Pettigrew (Harmondsworth: Penguin, 1981), lines 59–61.

48. Browning, "Fra Lippo Lippi," lines 266–67.

8 Gardens and the Larger Landscape

1. T. Williamson, *Shaping Medieval Landscapes: Settlement, Society, Environment* (Windgather: Macclesfield, 2003).

2. E. Kerridge, *The Common Fields of England* (Manchester: Manchester University Press, 1992), 74–86.

3. D. Hall, "The Open Fields of Northamptonshire," *Northamptonshire Record Society* 38 (1995); Williamson, *Shaping Medieval Landscapes*, 62–72.

4. D. Roden, "Field Systems of the Chiltern Hills and Their Environs," in *Studies of Field Systems in the British Isles*, ed. A.H.R. Baker and R. A. Butlin (Cambridge: Cambridge University Press, 1973), 325–74; M. R. Postgate, "Field Systems of East Anglia," in *Studies of Field Systems in the British Isles*, ed. A.H.R. Baker and R. A. Butlin (Cambridge: Cambridge University Press, 1973), 281–324.

5. B. K. Roberts and S. Wrathmell, "Peoples of Wood and Plain: An Exploration of National and Local Regional Contrasts," in *Landscape: The Richest Historical Record*, ed. D. Hooke (London: Society for Landscape Studies, 2000), 85–96; C. Lewis, P. Mitchell-Fox, and C. Dyer, *Village, Hamlet and Field: Changing Medieval Settlements in Central England* (Macclesfield: Windgather, 2002).

6. B.M.S. Campbell, *English Seigniorial Agriculture 1250–1450* (Cambridge: Cambridge University Press, 2000).

7. Kerridge, *The Common Fields of England*; Williamson, *Shaping Medieval Landscapes*, 123–40.

8. Williamson, *Shaping Medieval Landscapes*, 160–79; Campbell, *English Seigniorial Agriculture*, 75–76.

9. O. Rackham, *Trees and Woodland in the British Landscape* (London: Dent, 1976); and *The History of the Countryside* (London: Dent, 1986).

10. N. Sykes, "The Dynamics of Status Symbols: Wildfowl Exploitation in England AD 410–1550," *Archaeological Journal* 161 (2004): 82–83; S. Kent, *Farmers as Hunters: The Implications of Sedentism* (Cambridge: Cambridge University Press, 1989); Y. Hamilakis, "The Sacred Geography of Hunting: Wild Animals, Social Power and Gender in Early Farming Societies," in *Zooarchaeology in Greece: Recent Advances*, ed. E. Kotjabopoulou, Y. Hamilakis, P. Halstead, C. Gamble, and V. Elefanti (London: British School at Athens, 2003), 239–47.

11. Williamson, "Fish, Fur and Feather: Man and Nature in the Post-Medieval Landscape," in *Making English Landscapes*, ed. K. Barker and T. Darvill (Bournemouth: Bournemouth University School of Conservation Sciences Occasional Paper 3, 1997), 92–117.

12. P. Stamper, "Woods and Parks," in *The Countryside of Medieval England*, ed. G. Astill and A. Grant (Oxford: Basil Blackwell), 128–48; S. Moorhouse, "The Medieval Parks of Yorkshire: Function, Contents and Chronology," in *The Medieval Park: New Perspectives*, ed. R. Liddiard (Macclesfield: Windgather, 2007), 99–127.

13. L. M. Cantor and J. M. Hatherly, "The Medieval Parks of England," *Geography* 64 (1979): 71–85.

14. D. Hooke, "Pre-Conquest Woodland: Its Distribution and Usage," *Agricultural History Review* 37 (1989): 113–29; A. Richardson, "'The King's Chief Delights': A Landscape Approach to the Royal Parks of Post-Conquest England," in *The Medieval Park: New Perspectives*, ed. R. Liddiard (Macclesfield: Windgather, 2007), 27–48; T. Beaumont-James and C. Gerrard, *Clarendon, Landscape of Kings*

(Macclesfield: Windgather, 2007); K. Mew, "The Dynamics of Lordship and Land-scape as Revealed in as Domesday Study of the *Nova Foresta*," *Anglo-Norman Studies* 23 (2000): 155–66.

15. R. Hoppitt, "Hunting Suffolk's Parks: Towards a Reliable Chronology of Impark-ment," in *The Medieval Park: New Perspectives*, ed. R. Liddiard (Macclesfield: Windgather, 2007), 146–64.

16. Sykes, "Animal Bones and Animal Parks," in *The Medieval Park: New Perspec-tives*, ed. R. Liddiard (Macclesfield: Windgather, 2007), 49–62.

17. M. W. Thompson, *The Rise of the Castle* (Cambridge: Cambridge University Press, 1991), 141–42.

18. P. Everson, G. Brown, and D. Stocker, "The Castle Earthworks and Landscape Context," in *Ludgershall Castle, Wiltshire: A Report on the Excavations by Peter Addyman, 1964–1972*, ed. P. Ellis (Devizes: Wiltshire Archaeological and Natural History Society, 2000), 97–119.

19. R. A. Higham, J. P. Allan, and S. R. Blaylock, "Excavations at Okehampton Castle, Devon, Part Two: the Bailey," *Proceedings of the Devon Archaeological Society* 40 (1982): 19–151.

20. Richardson, " 'The King's Chief Delights.' "

21. Rackham, *The History of the Countryside*; A. Pluskowski, "The Social Construc-tion of Park Ecosystems: An Interdisciplinary Perspective," in *The Medieval Park: New Perspectives*, ed. R. Liddiard (Macclesfield: Windgather, 2007), 63–78; S. A. Mileson, "The Sociology of Park Creation in Medieval England," in *The Medi-eval Park: New Perspectives*, ed. R. Liddiard (Macclesfield: Windgather, 2007), 11–26.

22. Richardson, " 'The King's Chief Delights,' " 38.

23. J. Cummins, *The Hound and the Hawk: The Art of Medieval Hunting* (London: Weidenfeld & Nicolson, 1988), 7.

24. Pluskowski, "The Social Construction of Park Ecosystems."

25. M. Bailey, "The Rabbit and the Medieval East Anglian Economy," *Agricultural History Review* 36 (1988): 1–20; J. Sheail, *Rabbits and their History* (Newton Abbot: David and Charles, 1971).

26. J. E. Harting, *The Rabbit* (London: Longman, 1898), 37.

27. Williamson, *Rabbits, Warrens and Archaeology* (Tempus: Stroud, 2007).

28. *Calendar of Inquisitions Post Mortem*, vol. 16, 7–15 Richard II (London: Public Records Office, 1974), 235.

29. *Calendar of Patent Rolls: Edward I*, vol. 4 (London: HMSO, 1901), 476.

30. C. Oman, *The Great Revolt of 1381* (Oxford: Clarendon Press, 1903), 65.

31. D. Stocker and M. Stocker, "Sacred Profanity: The Theology of Rabbit Breeding and the Symbolic Landscape of the Warren," *World Archaeology* 28 (1998): 269.

32. Williamson, *Rabbits, Warrens and Archaeology*, 164–75.

33. C. Dyer, "The Consumption of Fish in Medieval England," in *Medieval Fish, Fish-eries and Fish Ponds in England*, ed. M. Aston (Oxford: British Archaeological Reports, 1988), 27–38.

34. C. K. Currie, "The Early History of the Carp and its Economic Significance in England," *Agricultural History Review* 39 (1991): 97–107.

35. M. Aston, ed., *Mediaeval Fish, Fisheries, and Fishponds in England, Parts 1 and 2* (Oxford: British Archaeological Reports, 1988).

36. G. G. Astill and A. Grant, eds., *The Countryside of Medieval England* (Oxford: Blackwell, 1988), 186–87; J. McCann, *The Dovecotes of Suffolk* (Ipswich: Suffolk Institute of Archaeology and History, 1998).

37. D. Stocker, "The Shadow of the General's Armchair," *Archaeological Journal* 149 (1993): 415–20.

38. C. Coulson, "Some Analysis of the Castle of Bodiam, East Sussex," in *Ideals and Practice of Medieval Knighthood,* vol. 4, ed. C. Harper-Bill and R. Harvey (Woodbridge: Boydell Press, 1992), 51–107.

39. C. Taylor, P. Everson, and R. Wilson-North, "Bodiam Castle, Sussex," *Medieval Archaeology* 34 (1990): 155.

40. T. E. McNeill, "The View from the Top," in *Melanges d'archeologie medieval. Liber amicorum en hommage à André Matthys,* ed. J. de Meulemeester (Liège: Mardaga, 2006), 122–27.

41. C. Whittick, "Dallingridge's Bay and Bodiam Castle Millpond: Elements of a Medieval Landscape," *Sussex Archaeological Collections* 131 (1993): 119–23.

42. Everson, Brown, and Stocker, "The Castle Earthworks."

43. P. Everson, "Medieval Gardens and Designed Landscapes," in *The Lie of the Land: Aspects of the Archaeology and History of the Designed Landscape in the South West of England,* ed. R. Wilson-North (Exeter: Mint Press, 2003), 24–33.

44. P. Herring, "Cornish Medieval Deer Parks," in *The Lie of the Land: Aspects of the Archaeology and History of the Designed Landscape in the South West of England,* ed. R. Wilson-North (Exeter: Mint, 2003), 34–50.

45. A. Richardson, *The Forest, Park and Palace of Clarendon, c.1200–c.1650: Reconstructing an Actual, Conceptual and Documented Wiltshire Landscape* (Oxford: British Archaeological Reports, 2005), 54.

46. D. J. Turner, "Bodiam Castle: True Castle or Old Soldier's Dream House?," *England in the 14th Century: Proceedings of the 1985 Harlaxton Symposium*, ed. W. Ormrod (Woodbridge: Brewer, 1986), 267–77.

47. R. Muir, *Ancient Trees, Living Landscapes* (Stroud: Tempus, 2005), 133.

BIBLIOGRAPHY

Aberg, F. A., ed. *Medieval Moated Sites*. London: Council for British Archaeology, 1978.

Acidini Luchinat, C., ed. *Jardins des Médicis: jardins des palais et des villes dans la Toscane du Quattrocento*. Arles: Actes Sud, 1997.

Ackerman, J. "The Typology of the Villa." In *Villa: Form and Ideology of Country Houses*. Princeton, NJ: Princeton University Press, 1990.

Adam of St. Victor. *The Liturgical Poetry of Adam of St. Victor*. Oxford: London, 1881.

Alberti, L. B. *On the Art of Building in Ten Books*. Cambridge, MA: MIT Press, 1988.

Albertus Magnus. *Alberti Magni ex ordine praedicatorum de Vegetabilibus libri VII : historiae naturalis pars XVIII / editionem criticam ab Ernesto Meyero coeptam : absolvit Carolus Jessen*. Berlin: G. Reimeri, 1867.

Albertus Magnus. *De vegetabilibus, Lib. VII, Historia naturalis, pars XVII*. Frankfurt: Minerva, 1982.

Albertus Magnus. *Opera Omnia Ad Fidem Codicum Manuscriptorum Edenda, Apparatu Critico, Notis, Prolegomenis, Indicibus Instruenda Curavit Institutum Alberti Magni Coloniense, Bernhardo Geyer Praeside*. Aschendorff: Monasterii Westfalorum, 1951.

Albrecht, M. R. "La flore des tapisseries de l'Apocalypse." *L'Information scientifique* 19 (1964): 196–205.

Alexander, E. J., and C. J. Woodward. "The Flora of the Unicorn Tapestries." In *Journal of the New York Botanical Garden*, 2nd ed. New York: New York Botanical Garden, 1974.

Alexander, J. *Medieval Illuminators and Their Methods of Work*. New Haven, CT: Yale University Press, 1992.

Alexander, M. *Medievalism: The Middle Ages in Modern England*. New Haven, CT: Yale University Press, 2007.

Alfonsi, T., and R. Bozzelli. *Pier de' Crescenzi (1233–1321). Studi e documenti*. Bologna: Copelli, 1933.

Allen, P. *The Concept of Woman: The Aristotelian Revolution 750 BC–1250 AD*. Montreal: Paradise Press, 1985.

Allen, T., and J. Hiller. *The Excavation of a Medieval Manor House of the Bishops of Winchester at Mount House, Witney, Oxfordshire*. Oxford: Oxford Archaeology, 2002.

Amherst, A. "A Fifteenth-Century Treatise on Gardening. By 'Mayster Ion Gardener.'" *Archaeologia* 54 (1894): 157–72.

Amherst, A. *A History of Gardening in England*, 2nd ed. Detroit, MI: Singing Tree, 1969.

Amt, E. *Women's Lives in Medieval Europe: A Sourcebook*. London: Routledge, 1992.

Anderson, F. J. *Herbals through 1500: The Illustrated Bartsch 90*. New York: Abaris, 1984.

Anderson, F. J. *An Illustrated History of Herbals*. New York: Columbia University Press, 1977.

Anderson, H. J. "The Terrestrial Paradise: A Study in the 'Intermediacy' and Multi-Levelled Nature of the Medieval Garden of Eden." PhD diss., University of New York at Buffalo, 1966.

Andreas Capellanus. *The Art of Courtly Love,* ed. and tr. John Jay Parry. New York: Columbia University Press, 1941.

Anon, C. A. "La literature de jardines en el sigl XVI. Del Hortus al Jardin de las Delicias." In *À proposito de la agricultura de los jardines de Gregorio de los Ríos Perez*, ed. J. F. and I. G. Tascón, 81–101. Madrid: Tabapress, 1991.

Antoine, E. "Jardins de plaisance." In *Paris et Charles V: arts et architecture*, ed. F. Pleybert, 151–65. Paris: Action artistique de la ville de Paris, 2001.

Antoine, E. *Le Jardin médiéval*. Paris: Réunion des musées nationaux, 2000.

Antoine, E., et al. *Sur La Terre Comme au Ciel: Jardins d'occident à la fin du Moyen Âge*. Paris: Éditions de la Réunion des musées nationaux, 2002.

Anzelewsky, F. "A propos de la topographie du parc de Bruxelles et du quai de l'Escauté à anvers de Durer." *Bulletin des Museés royaux des beaux-arts de Belgique* 6 (1957): 87–107.

Aquinas, T. *Suma Contra los Gentiles*, vol. 2, ed. and tr. J.M. Pla castellaao, et al. Madrid: BAC, 1952.

Aquinas, T. *Summa Theologica*, first part, question 102, art. 3. *Newadvent.org*, May 20, 2008, http://newadvent.org/summa/1102.htm.

Arber, A. *Herbals: Their Origin and Evolution. A Chapter on the History of Botany, 1470–1670*, 3rd ed. Cambridge: Cambridge University Press, 1938.

Archer, R. B. "'How Ladies . . . Who Live on Their Manors Ought to Manage Their Households and Estates': Women as Landholders and Administrators in the Later Middle Ages." In *Woman Is a Worthy Wight: Women in English Society, c. 1200–1500*, ed. P.J.P. Goldberg, 149–81. Wolfboro Falls, NH: Straud, 1992.

Arden, H. "The Slings and Arrows of Outrageous Love in the *Roman de la Rose*." In *The Medieval City Under Siege*, ed. I. A. Corfis and M. Wolfe, 191–205. Woodbridge: Boydell, 1996.

Arens, F., ed. "Die ursprüngliche Verwendung gotischer Stein- und Tonmodel, mit einem Verzeichnis der Model in mittelrheinischen Museen." *Mainzer Zeitschrift* 66 (1971): 106–31.

Arisi, F. *La Galleria Alberoni di Piacenza*. Piacenza: Artioli, 1991.

Aristotle. *Parva Naturalia*. Cambridge, MA: Harvard University Press, 1936.

Armstrong, J. *The Paradise Myth*. London: Oxford University Press, 1969.

Ashbee, J. A. "'The Chamber called *Gloriette*.' Living at Leisure in Thirteenth and Fourteenth-Century Castles." *Journal of the British Archaeological Association* 157 (2004): 17–40.

Ashbee, J. A. "Cloisters in English Palaces in the Twelfth and Thirteenth Centuries." *Journal of British Archaeological Association* 59 (2006): 71–90.

Ashbee, J. A. "The Royal Apartments in the Inner Ward at Conwy Castle." *Archaeologia Cambrenis* 153 (2004): 51–72.

Aspinall, A., and J. A. Pocock. "Geophysical Prospecting in Garden Archaeology: An Appraisal and Critique Based on Case Studies." *Archaeological Prospecting* 2 (1995): 61–84.

Astell, A. W. *The Song of Songs in the Middle Ages*. Ithaca, NY: Cornell University Press, 1990.

Astill, G. G., and A. Grant, eds. *The Countryside of Medieval England*. Oxford: Blackwell, 1988.

Aston, M. "Earthworks at the Bishop's Palace, Alvechurch, Worcestershire." *Transacitons of the Worcestershire Archaeological Society* 3, Series 3 (1970–72): 55–59.

Aston, M., ed., *Mediaeval Fish, Fisheries, and Fishponds in England, Parts 1 and 2*. Oxford: British Archaeological Reports, 1988.

Augspach, E. *The Garden as Woman's Space in Twelfth- and Thirteenth-Century Literature*. Lewiston: The Edwin Mellen Press, 2004.

Augustine. *City of God Against the Pagans*, vol. 4, ed. and tr. O. S. Wiesen. Cambridge, MA: Harvard University Press, 1988.

Avril, F. "Jean Le Tavernier, un nouveau livre d'heures." *Revue de l'art* 126 (1999): 9–22.

Avril, F., and N. Reynaud. *Les Manuscrits à peintures en France, 1440–1520*. Paris: Flammarion/Bibliothèque nationale, 1994.

Azzi Visentini, M., ed. *L'arte dei giardini. Scritti teorici e pratici dal XIV al XV secolo*. Milan: Il Polifilo, 1999.

Bacon, F. *The Essayes or Counsels, Civill and Morall* (1625).

Ball, W. "The Remains of a Monumental Timurid Garden outside Herat." *East and West*, n.s., 31, no. 1–4 (December 1981): 79–82.

Bailey, M. "The Rabbit and the Medieval East Anglian Economy." *Agricultural History Review* 36 (1988): 1–20.

Barber, P., and T. Harper. *Magnificent Maps: Power, Propaganda and Art*. London: British Library, 2010.

Barnatt, J., and T. Williamson. *Chatsworth: A Landscape History*. Macclesfield: Windgather, 2005.

Barner, S. A., W. J. Lewis, J. A. Beach, and O. Berghof, trans. *The Etymologies of Isidore of Seville*. Cambridge: Cambridge University Press, 2006.

Barnett, P., ed. *Images in Ivory: Precious Objects of the Gothic Age*. Detroit, MI: Detroit Institute of Arts, 1997.

Barnett, R. "Serpent of Pleasure: Emergence and Difference in the Medieval Garden of Love." *Landscape Journal* 28 (2009): 137–50.

Barnwell, P. S., and P. Everson. "Landscapes of Lordship and Pleasure: The Castle and its Landscape Setting." In *Helmsley Castle,* ed. J. Clarke, 24–25. London: English Heritage, 2004.

Bauman, J. "Tradition and Transformation: The Pleasure Garden in Piero de' Crescenzi's *Liber ruralium commodorum.*" *Studies in the History of Gardens and Designed Landscapes* 22 (2002): 99–141.

Baumann, F. A. *Das Erbario Carrarese und die Bildtradition des Tractatus de herbis.* Berne: Benteli, 1974.

Bayard, T. *Sweet Herbs and Sundry Flowers. Medieval Gardens and the Gardens of the Cloisters,* 2nd ed. New York: Metropolitan Museum of Art, 1997.

Beaumont-James, T., and C. Gerrard. *Clarendon, Landscape of Kings.* Macclesfield: Windgather, 2007.

Beaune, C. "Le langage symbolique des jardins médiévaux." In *Jardins du Moyen Age,* 63–75. Paris: Léopard d'or, 1995.

Beck, B. "Jardin monastique, jardin mystique. Ordonnance et signification des jardins monastiques médiévaux." *Revue d'histoire de la pharmacie* 88 (2000): 377–94.

Beck, C., and P. Beck. "La nature amenagée. Le parc du château d'Aisey-sur-Seine (Bourgogne, XIVe-XVIe siècles)." In *L'homme et la nature du Moyen Âge, actes du Ve congrès international d'archéologie médiéval,* ed. M. Colardelle, 22–29. Grenoble: Errance, 1993.

Beck, C., and M. Casset. "Résidences et environnement : les parcs en France du Nord (XIIIe-XVe siècles)." In *Château et nature, colloque des rencontres d'Histoire et Archéologie de Périgueux (Septembre 2004).* Bordeaux: Ausonius Publications, 2005.

Beck, C., P. Duceppe-Lamarre, and F. Duceppe-Lamarre. "Les parcs et jardins des ducs de Bourgogne au XIVe siècle." In *"Aux Marches du Palais." Actes du VIIe colloque international d'archeologie médiévale 1999,* ed. A. Cocula and M. Combet, 97–112. Universite du Maine: Publications du LHAM, 2001.

Behling, L. "Das italienische Pflanzenbild um 1400. Zum Wesen des pflanzlichen Dekors auf dem Epiphaniasbild des Gentile da Fabriano in den Uffizien." *Pantheon* 24 (1966): 347–59.

Behling, L. *Die Pflanze in der mittelalterlichen Tafelmalerei,* 2nd ed. Cologne: H. Böhlaus Nachfolger, 1967.

Bek, L. " 'Ut ars natura, ut natura ars': le ville di Plinio e il concerto del giardino nel Rinascimento." *Analaecta Romana Instituti Danici* 7 (1974): 109–56.

Belding, L. "Betrachtungen zu einigen Dürer-Pflanzen." *Pantheon* 23 (1965): 279–91.

Bell, C. F., ed. *Evelyn's Sculptura with the Unpublished Second Part.* Oxford: Clarendon Press, 1906.

Bell, C. "New College Mound, Oxford: An Archaeological Investigation." *Garden History* 22 (1994): 115–19.

Bellafiore, G. *Parchi e Giardini della Palermo normanna.* Palermo: Flaccovio, 1996.

Bénetière, M.-H. *Jardin. Vocabulaire typologique et technique.* Paris: Éditions du patrimoine, 2000.

Benoit, F. *Histoire de l'outillage rural et artisanal.* Paris: Lafitte, 1947.

Berenson, B., and M. R. James. *Speculum humanae salvationis, Being a Reproduction of an Italian Manuscript of the Fourteenth Century*. Oxford: Oxford University Press, 1926.

Beresford, M., and J. Hurst. *Wharram Percy: Deserted Medieval Village*. London: Batsford/English Heritage, 1990.

Berger, R., and D. Hammer-Tugendhat, eds. *Der Garten der Lüste: Zur Deutung des Erotischen und Sexuellen bei Künstlern und ihren Interpreten*. Cologne: DuMont, 1985.

Berry, A., and H. Legrand. *Topographie historique du Vieux Paris. I, Le Louvre et les Tuileries, 1200–1928*. Paris: Imprimerie Nationale, 1868–86.

Bertaud, É. "*Hortus, Hortulus*, jardin spiritual." In *Dictionnaire de spiritualite ascetique et mystique*, vol. 7, columns 766–84. Paris: Beauchesne, 1969.

Bettey, J. H. *Estates and the English Countryside*. London: Batsford, 1993.

Bevers, H. *Meister E. S. Der Grosse Liebesgarten*. Frankfurt: Schmidt, 1994.

Beylier, H., and B. Leclerc. *Treillages de jardin du XIVe au XXe siècle*. Paris: Centre des monuments nationaux, 2000.

Biblia Sacra iuxta Vulgatam Clementinam. Madrid: BAC, 1994.

Bilimoff, M. *Promenade dans des jardins disparus. Les plantes au Moyen Âge d'après les Grandes Heures d'Anne de Bretagne*. Rennes: Editions Ouest-France, 2001.

Birrell, J. "Deer and Deer Farming in Medieval England." *Agricultural History Review* 40 (1992): 112–26.

Bliss, D. P. "Love Gardens in the Early German Engravings and Woodcuts." *The Print Collector's Quarterly* 15 (1928): 90–109.

Blunt, W., and S. Raphael. *The Illustrated Herbal*. London: Weidenfeld and Nicholson, 1979.

Boas, G. *Primitivism and Related Ideas in the Middle Ages*. Baltimore, MD: Johns Hopkins University Press, 1948.

Boccaccio, G. *The Decameron*. New York: Penguin, 1972.

Boccaccio, G. *Opere*. ed. Cesare Segre. Milan: Mursia & Co., 1966.

Boia, L. *Forever Young: A Cultural History of Longevity*. London: Reaktion Books, 2004.

Bon, P. "Les jardins du duc de Berry et les préaux de Mehun-sur-Yèvre." In *Flore et jardins: usages, savoirs et représentations du monde végétal au Moyen Age*, ed. P.-G. Girault, 39–50. Paris: Léopard d'Or, 1997.

Bond, J. "Forests, Chases, Warrens and Parks in Medieval Wessex." In *The Medieval Landscape of Wessex*, ed. M. Aston and C. Lewis, 115–58. Oxford: Oxbow, 1995.

Bond, J. *Monastic Landscapes*. Stroud, Gloucestershire: Tempus, 2004.

Bond, J. "Water Management in the Rural Monastery." In *The Archaeology of Rural Monasteries*, ed. R. Gilchrist and H. C. Mytum, 83–112. Oxford: British Archaeological Reports, 1989.

Borsook, E. *The Mural Painters of Tuscany from Cimabue to Andrea del Sarto*, 2nd ed. Oxford: Clarendon Press, 1980.

Botineau, M. *Les plantes du jardin médiéval*. Paris: Belin, 2003.

Bouillerie, F.-A. de la. *Études sur le symbolisme de la nature, interprété d'après l'Écriture sainte et les Pères*. Paris: Gaumes and Duprey, 1866.

Boureux, C. *Les Plantes de la Bible et leur symbolique*. Paris: Le Cerf, 2001.

Bourgeois-Comu, L. *Les Bonnes Herbes du Moyen Âge*. Paris: Publisud, 1999.

Bousmanne, B. *"Item a Guillaume Wyelant, aussi enlumineur": Willem Vrelant. Un aspect de l'enluminure dans les Pays-Bas meridionaux sous le micenat des dues de Bourgogne Philippe le Bon et Charles le Temeraire*. Tournhout: KBR, 1997.

Bouvet, F. *Le Cantique de cantiques, Les chefs d'oeuvre de la xylographie*. Paris: Éditions de minuit, 1961.

Bouvier, J.- C. "*Ort* et *Jardin* dans la littérature médiévale d'Oc." In *Vergers et jardins dans l'univers médiéval [Senefiance 28]*, 41–51. Aix-en-Provence: C.U.E.R.M.A., 1990.

Bradley, R. S., et al. "Climate Change: Climate in Medieval Time." *Science* 302 (October 17, 2003): 404–5.

Braekman, W. L. "Bollard's Middle English Book of Planting and Grafting and Its Background." *Studia Neophilologica* 57 (1985): 19–39.

Braekman, W. L., ed. *Geoffrey of Franconia's Book of Trees and Wine Scripta* 24. Brussels: OMIREL, 1989.

Branca, V., ed. *Boccaccio visualizzato. Narrare per parole e per immagini fra Medioevo e Rinascinamento*. Turin: Giulio Einaudi, 1999.

Brereton, G. E., and J. M. Ferrier, eds. *Le Menagier de Paris*. Oxford: Clarendon Press, 1981.

Bresc, H. "Gènese du jardin meridional. Sicile et Italie du Sud, XIIe-XIIIe siècles." In *Jardins et vergers en Europe occidentale (viiie-xviiie siècles)*, 97–113. Auch: Comité départmental de Tourisme du Gers, 1989.

Bresc, H. "Les jardins de Palerme (1290–1460)." *Mélanges de l'Ecole française de Rome. Moyen Âge et Temps moderns* 84 (1972): 55–127.

Bresc, H. "Les jardins royaux de Palerme." *Mélanges de l'École française de Rome. Moyen Âge et Temps modernes* 106 (1994): 239–58.

Brinkmann, B. "Neues vom Meister der Lübecker Bibel." *Jahrbuch der Berliner Museen* 29–30 (1987–88): 123–61.

Brinkmann, B. *Die Flamische Buchmalerei am Ende des Burgunderreichs, der Meister des Dresdener Gebetbuchs und die Miniaturisten seiner Zeit*, 2 vols. Turnhout: Brepols, 1997.

Brookshaw, D. P. "Palaces, Pavilions, and Pleasure-Gardens: The Context and Setting of the Medieval." *Majlis' Middle Eastern Literature* 6 (2003): 199–223.

Brown, P. *The Rise of Western Christendom: Triumph and Diversity, A.D. 200–1000*, 2nd ed. Oxford: Blackwell, 2003.

Brown, P. *The World of Late Antiquity: AD 150–750*. London: Thames & Hudson, 1971.

Brown, P., G. W. Bowersock, and O. Grabar, eds. *Interpreting Late Antiquity: Essays on the Postclassical World*. Cambridge, MA: Harvard University Press, 1999.

Brownlow, M. *Herbs and the Fragrant Garden*. New York: McGraw Hill, 1963.

Brubaker, L., and A. R. Littlewood. "Byzantinische Gärten." In *Der Garten von der Antike bis zum Mittelalter*, ed. M. Carroll-Spillecke, 213–48. Mainz: von Zabern, 1992.

Brunet, M. "Le parc d'attraction des ducs de Bourgogne à Hesdin." *Gazette des beaux-arts* 78 (1971): 331–42.

Brut, C., and Lagarde, F. "Une fosse du Bas Moyen Age au 4, rue de la Collegiale, Paris. Etude du materiel." *Cahiers de la Rotonde* 14 (1993): 91–120.

Bullough, V. L. "Medieval Medical and Scientific Views of Women." *Viator* 4 (1973): 485–501.

Burioni, M. "Vasari's *Rinascita*: History, Anthropology, or Art Criticism?" In *Renaissance? Perceptions of Continuity and Discontinuity in Europe, ca. 1300–1550*, ed. H. Schnitker, P. Péporte, and A.C. Lee, 115–27. Leiden: Brill, 2008.

Burke, P. "Afterword: Exploring Cultural History. A Response." In *Exploring Cultural History: Essays in Honour of Peter Burke*, ed. J. P. Rubiés, M. Calaresu, and F. de Vivo, 351–58. Aldershot: Ashgate, 2010.

Büttner, N. *The History of Gardens in Painting*, tr. Russell Stockman. New York: Abbeville Press, 2008

Byvanck, A. W. *La Miniature dans les Pays-Bas septentrionaux*. Paris: Éditions d'Art et d'Histoire, 1937.

Cahn, W. "Medieval Landscape and the Encyclopedic Tradition." *Yale French Studies* 80 (1991): 11–24.

Calkins, R. G. "Piero de' Crescenzi and the Medieval Garden." In *Medieval Gardens*, ed. E. MacDougall, 156–73. Washington, D.C.: Dumbarton Oaks, 1986.

Cambornac, M. *Plantes et jardins médiévaux*. Paris: Edipso, 1996.

Cameron, A. *The Mediterranean World in Late Antiquity AD 395–600*. London: Routledge, 1992.

Camille, M. *Image on the Edge: The Margins of Medieval Art*. London: Reaktion, 1992.

Camille, M. *The Medieval Art of Love: Objects and Subjects of Desire*. New York: Harry N. Abrams, 1998.

Campbell, B.M.S. "Commonfield Origins—The Regional Dimension." In *The Origins of Open-Field Agriculture*, ed. T. Rowley, 112–29. London: Croom Helm, 1981.

Campbell, B.M.S. *English Seigniorial Agriculture, 1250–1450*. Cambridge: Cambridge University Press, 2000.

Cantor, L. *The Medieval Parks of England: A Gazetteer*. Loughborough: Loughborough University of Technology, 1983.

Cantor, L.M., and J. M. Hatherly. "The Medieval Parks of England." *Geography* 64 (1979): 71–85.

Cardini, F. "Il giardino del cavaliere, il giardino del mercante. La cultura del giardino nella toscana tre-quattrocentesca, *Mélanges de l'École française de Rome.*" *Moyen Âge et Temps modernes* 1 (1994): 259–73.

Cardini, F., and M. Miglio. *Nostalgia del Paradiso. Il giardino medieval*. Rome, Bari: GLF editori Laterza, 2002.

Carolle-Spillecke, M., ed. *Der Garten von der Antike bis zum Mittelalter*. Mainz am Rhein: Von Zabern, 1992.

Carru, D. "La vaisselle consommée à Avignon à la fin du Moyen Age: mutations, influences et sources d'approvisionnement." In *La Céramique médiévale en Méditerranée*, 487–95. Aix-en-Provence, 1997.

Carruthers, M. *The Book of Memory: A Study of Memory in Medieval Culture*. Cambridge: Cambridge University Press, 2008.

Carruthers, M. "The Poet as Master Builder: Composition and Locational Memory in the Middle Ages." *New Literary History* 24 (1993): 881–904.

Casagrande, C. "La Femme Gardée." In *Histoire des Femmes en Occident,* 2: *Le Moyen Age*, ed. G. Duby and M. Perrot, 83–116. Paris: Plon, 1991.

Casagrande, C. "The Protected Woman." *A History of Women: Silences of the Middle Ages.* Cambridge, MA: Harvard University Press, 1998.

Cattaneo, A. *Fra Mauro's World Map and Fifteenth-Century Venetian Culture.* Turnhout: Brepols, 2010.

Cavallo, A. S. *Medieval Tapestries in the Metropolitan Museum of Art.* New York: Metropolitan Museum of Art / H. N. Abrams, 1993.

Caviness, M. H. "Reception of Images by Medieval Viewers." In *A Companion to Medieval Art: Romanesque and Gothic in Northern Europe*, ed. Conrad Rudolph, 65–85. Oxford: Blackwell, 2006.

Cazelles, B. *The Lady as Saint: A Collection of French Hagiographic Romances of the Thirteenth Century.* Philadelphia: University of Pennsylvania Press, 1991.

Cazelles, R., and J. Rathofer. *Illuminations of Heaven and Earth: The Glories of "Tres Riches Heures du Duc de Berry."* New York: H. N. Abrams, 1988.

Chalmin-Sirot, É. "Les jardins des maisons de la petite noblesse rurale (comtés de Savoie et de Genève, XIVe- XVIIe siècle)." *Cadre de vie et manières d'habiter (XIIe-XVIe siècle)*, ed. D. Alexandre-Bidon, F. Piponnier, and J.-M. Poisson, 283–90. Caen: Publications du CRAHM, 2006.

Chamblas-Ploton, M. *Jardins médiévaux.* Paris: La Maison Rustique, Flammarion, 2000.

Charageat, M. "De la maison Dedalus aux labyrinths." In *Actes du XVIIe Congrès d'histoire de l'art français*, 345–50. La Haye: Imprimerie Nationale des Pays-Bas, 1955.

Charageat, M. "Le parc d'Hesdin, création monumentale du XIIIe siècle." *Bulletin de la Société de l'histoire de l'art français* (1951): 94–106.

Charron, P. "Quelques bibliophiles de la cour de Bourgogne et le maître du Champion des dames (ca. 1465–1475)." In *L'artiste et le commanditaire aux derniers siècles du Moyen Age (XIIIe-XVIe siècles)*, ed. F. Joubert, 191–207. Paris: Presses de l'Université de Paris-Sorbonne, 2001.

Cherry, J. "The Talbot Casket and Related Medieval Leather Caskets." *Archaeologia* 107 (1982): 131–40.

Chrétien de Troyes. *Complete Romances of Chrétien de Troyes*, tr. D. Staines. Bloomington: Indiana University Press, 1990.

Chrétien de Troyes. *Les Romans de Chrétien de Troyes: Cligès.* Paris: Champion, 1975.

Christianson, P. *The Riverside Gardens of Thomas More's London.* New Haven, CT: Yale University Press, 2005.

Clark, E. A. *History, Theory, Text: Historians and the Linguistic Turn.* Cambridge, MA: Harvard University Press, 2004.

Clark, J. "Bill Hooks." *Tools and Trades History Society Newsletter* 12 (1986): 41–43.

Clarke, C.A.M. *Literary Landscapes and the Idea of England, 700–1400.* Cambridge: Brewer, 2006.

Colardelle, M., ed. *L'Homme et la nature au Moyen Âge.* Grenoble: Errance, 1996.

Collins, M. *Medieval Herbals: The Illustrative Traditions.* London: British Library, 2000.

Collison, R. *Encyclopedias: Their History throughout the Ages*. New York: Hafner, 1964.

Colvin, H. M. *The History of King's Works*. London: Ministery of Public Building, 1963.

Colvin, H. M. "Royal Gardens in Medieval England." In *Medieval Gardens*, ed. E. MacDougall, 7–21. Washington, D.C.: Dumbarton Oaks, 1986.

Comet, G. *Le Paysan et son outil. Essai d'histoire technique des céréales (France, VIIIe–XIe siècle)*. Rome: Ecole française de Rome, 1992.

Comet, G. "Les calendriers médiévaux, quelques questions." *Iconographie et histoire des mentalités*, 170–74. Paris: Centre national de la recherche scientifique, 1979.

Comito, T. *The Idea of Garden in the Renaissance*. New Brunswick, NJ: Rutgers University Press, 1978.

Commeaux, C. *La Vie quotidienne en Bourgogne au temps des ducs de Valois, 1364–1477*. Paris: Hachette, 1979.

Conan, M. *Dictionnaire historique de l'art des jardins*. Paris: La Maison rustique, 1997.

Constantinides, C. N. "Byzantine Gardens and Horticulture in the Late Byzantine Period, 1204–1453: The Secular Sources." In *Byzantine Garden Culture*, ed. A. Littlewood, H. Maguire, and J. Wolschke-Bulmahn, 87–103. Washington, D.C.: Dumbarton Oaks, 2002.

Cooper, M.P.K. *The Early English Garden: Medieval Period to 1800 AD*. Nashville, TN: Trinity Press, 1984.

Cooper, S. "Ornamental Structures in the Medieval Gardens of Scotland." *Proceedings of the Society of Antiquaries of Scotland* 129 (1999): 817–39.

Contreni, J. J. "Charlemagne." In *Medieval Germany: An Encyclopedia*, ed. J. M. Jeep, 98–102. New York: Routledge, 2001.

Coulet, N. "Jardins et jardiniers du roi René à Aix." *Annales du Midi* 102 (1990): 275–88.

Coulet, N. "Pour une histoire du jardin. Vergers et potagers à Aix-en-Provence: 1350–1450." *Le Moyen Âge* 73 (1967): 239–70.

Coulson, C. "Bodiam Castle: Truth and Tradition." *Fortress* 10 (1990): 3–15.

Coulson, C. *Castles in Medieval Soceity: Fortresses in England, France and Ireland in the Central Middle Ages*. Oxford: Oxford University Press, 2003.

Coulson, C. "Some Analysis of the Castle of Bodiam, East Sussex." In *Ideals and Practice of Medieval Knighthood*, vol. 4, ed. C. Harper-Bill and R. Harvey, 51–107. Woodbridge: Boydell Press, 1992.

Coulson, C. "Structural Symbolism in Medieval Castle Architecture." *Journal of the British Archaeological Association* 132 (1979): 73–90.

Council for British Archaeology. "Ornamental Water Garden Found at Cheshire Castle." *British Archaeology* 24 (1997). Available at http://www.archaeologyuk.org/ba/ba24/BA24NEWS.HTML.

Cox, E.H.M. *A History of Gardening in Scotland*. London: Chatto & Windus, 1935.

Crackles, F.E. "Medieval Gardens in Hull." *Garden History* 14 (1986): 1–5.

Creighton, O.H. *Castles and Landscapes: Power, Community and Fortification in Medieval England*. London: Equinox, 2005.

Creighton, O. H. *Designs Upon the Land: Elite Landscapes of the Middle Ages*. Woodbridge: Boydell, 2009.

Creighton, O.H., and R. A. Higham. "Castle Studies and the 'Landscape' Agenda." *Landscape History* 26 (2004): 5–18.

Crescentius, P. *Opus Ruralim Commodorum*. Venice, 1495.

Crescentius, P. *Ruralia commoda. Das Wissen des vollkommenen Landwirts um 1300*, 3 vols., eds. W. Richte and R. Richter-Bergmeier. Heidelberg: Universitätsverlag C. Winter, 1995.

Creswell, K.A.C. *Early Muslim Architecture*, vol. 2. Oxford: Clarendon Press, 1940.

Crisp, F. *Mediaeval Gardens: "Flowery Medes" and Other Arrangements of Herbs, Flowers and Shrubs Grown in the Middle Ages, with Some Account of Tudor, Elizabethan and Stuart Gardens*. London: Bodley Head, 1924.

Crossley-Holland, N. *Living and Dining in Medieval Paris: The Household of a Fourteenth-Century Knight*. Cardiff: University of Wales Press, 2000.

Cummins, J. *The Hound and the Hawk: The Art of Medieval Hunting*. London: Weidenfeld & Nicolson, 1988.

Cummins, J. *"Veneurs s'en vont en Paradis*: Medieval Hunting and the 'Natural' Landscape." In *Inventing Medieval Landscapes: Senses of Place in Western Europe*, ed. M. Wolfe, 33–56. Gainesville: University of Florida Press, 2002.

Currie, C.K. "The Early History of the Carp and its Economic Significance in England." *Agricultural History Review* 39 (1991): 97–107.

Currie, C.K. "Fishponds as Garden Features *c.* 1550–1750." *Garden History* 18 (1990): 22–46.

Currie, C.K. "St. Cross: A Medieval Moated Garden?" *Hampshire Gardens Trust Journal* 11 (1992): 19–22.

Curtius, E.R. *European Literature and the Latin Middle Ages*. London: Routledge and Kegan Paul, 1953.

Dale, T. "Monsters, Corporeal Deformities, and Phantasms in the Cloister of St.-Michel-de-Cuxa." *The Art Bulletin* 83, no. 3 (2001): 402–36.

Daley, B. E. "The 'Closed Garden' and the 'Sealed Fountain': Songs of Songs 4:12 in the Late Medieval Iconography of Mary." In *Medieval Gardens*, ed. E. B. MacDougall, 253–78. Washington, D.C.: Dumbarton Oaks, 1986.

Dalton, O. M. "On a Set of Table Knives in the British Museum." *Archaeologia* 60 (1906): 423–30.

Dami, L. *Il giardino italiano*. Milan: Berstetti e Tumminelli, 1924.

Dami, L. "Il giardino italiano nel Quattrocento." *Dedalo* 1 (1920): 368–91.

D'Ancona, M. L. "L'Hortus Conclusus nel Medioevo e nel Rinascimento." *Miniatura* 2 (1989): 121–29.

Deam, L. "Landscape into History: The Miniatures of the *Fleures des Histoires* (Brussels, B.R. ms. 9231–9232)." In *Regions and Landscapes: Treality and Imagination in Late Medieval and Early Modern Europe*, ed. P. Ainsworth and T. Scott, 113–37. Berne: Lang, 2000.

de Garlande, J. *Dictionarius*. In A. Scheler, "Trois traités de lexicographie latine du XIIe et du XIIIe siècle." *Jahrbuch für romanische und englische Literatur* 6 (1865): 142–62.

de Guillaume M. *Le Jugement du roy de Behaigne and Remede de Fortune*. Athens: University of Georgia Press, 1988.

dei Grassi, G. *Art and Architecture in Italy, 1250–1400*. New Haven, CT: Yale University Press, 1993.

de Lespinasse, R. *Les Métiers et corporations de la Ville de Paris. I. XIVe-XVIIIe Siécles; Ordonnances générales, métiers d'alimentation*. Paris: Imprimerie nationale, 1886.

della Vida, G. L. "Pre-Islamic Arabia." In *The Arab Heritage*, ed. Nabih Amin Faris, 25–57. Princeton, NJ: Princeton University Press, 1946.

de Lorris, G., and J. de Meun. *Romance of the Rose*. Princeton, NJ: Princeton University Press, 1971.

Delumeau, J. *Une histoire du paradis. Le jardin des délices* (Paris: Fayard,1992); *History of Paradise: The Garden of Eden in Myth and Tradition*. New York: Continuum, 1995.

de Machaut, G. *Le Jugement du roy de Behaigne and Remede de Fortune*. Athens: University of Georgia Press, 1988.

de Pisan, C. *The Book of the City of Ladies*. New York: Persea, 1982.

de Pisan, C. *La Cité des dames*. Paris: Stock, 1986.

de Troyes, C. *Les Romans de Chrétien de Troyes: Le Chevalier de la Charrete*, vol. 3. Paris: Librairie Honoré Champion, 1965.

Dickie, J. "The Hispano-Arab Garden: Its Philosophy and Function." *Bulletin, School of Oriental and African Studies, University of London* 21 (1968): 237–48.

Dickie, J. "The Hispano-Arab Garden: Notes Towards a Typology." In *The Legacy of Islamic Spain*, ed. S. K. Jayyusi, 1016–35. Leiden: Brill, 1992.

Dickie, J. "The Islamic Garden in Spain." In *The Islamic Garden,* ed. E. B McDougall and R. E. Ettinghausen, 89–105. Washington, D.C.: Dumbarton Oaks, 1981.

Dourveaux, P. *Le livre des simples médecines, traduction française du Liber de simplici medicina dictus Circa instans de Platearius tirée d'un manuscrit du XIIIe siècle (Ms. 3113 de la Bibliothèque Sainte-Geneviève de Paris)*. Paris: Société française d'histoire de la médecine, 1913.

Duby, G. *The Knight, the Lady and the Priest: The Making of Modern Marriage in Medieval France*. Chicago: University of Chicago Press, 1993.

Dufournet, J., and L. Dulac, eds. and trans. *La. Châtelaine de Vergy*. Paris: Lettres Gothiques, 1994.

Dunlop, A. *Painted Palaces: The Rise of Secular Art in Early Renaissance Italy*. University Park: Pennsylvania State University Press, 2009.

Duval, A. "Rosaire." In *Dictionnaire de spiritualité ascétique et mystique*, vol. 13, columns 937–80. Paris: Beauchesne, 1988.

Dyer, C. "The Consumption of Fish in Medieval England." In *Medieval Fish, Fisheries and Fish Ponds in England*, ed. M. Aston, 27–38. Oxford: British Archaeological Reports, 1988.

Dyer, C. "Gardens and Garden Produce in the Later Middle Ages." In *Food in Medieval England: Diet and Nutrition*, ed. C. M. Woolgar, D. Serjeantson, and T. Waldron, 27–40. Oxford: Oxford University Press, 2006.

Dyer, C. "Gardens and Orchards in Medieval England." In *Everyday Life in Medieval England,* ed. C. Dyer, 113–32. London: Hambledon, 2000.

Dyer, C. "Jardins et vergers en Angleterre au Moyen Âge." In *Jardins et vergers en Europe occidentale (VIIIe-XVIIIe siècle)*, 145–64. Auch: Centre culturel de l'abbaye de Flaran, 1989.

Eamon, W. *Science and the Secrets of Nature: Books of Secrets in Medieval and Early Modern Culture*. Princeton, NJ: Princeton University Press, 1994.

Eckbo, G. *Landscape for Living*. New York: Architectural Record with Duell, Sloan, & Pearce, 1950.

Eco, U. *Art and Beauty in the Middle Ages*. New Haven, CT: Yale University Press, 1986.

Einhorn, J. W. *Spiritalis unicornis: Das Einhorn als Bedeutungsträger in Literatur und Kunst des Mittelalters*. Munich: Wilhelm Fink, 1976.

Elias, N. *The Civilizing Process: The Histroy of Manners and State Formation and Civilization*. Oxford: Oxford University Press, 1994.

Ellis-Rees, W. "Gardening in the Age of Humanism: Petrarch's Journal." *Garden History* 23 (1995): 10–28.

Epstein, S. A. "The Medieval Family: A Place of Refuge and Sorrow." In *Portraits of Medieval and Renaissance Living: Essays in Memory of David Herlihy*, ed. S. K. Cohn Jr. and S. A. Epstein, 149–74. Ann Arbor: University of Michigan Press, 1996.

Erlande-Brandenburg, A., P. Y. Le Pogam, and D. Sandron, eds. *Musée national du Moyen Age, Thermes de Cluny: Guide des collections*. Paris: Réunion des musées nationaux, 1993.

Ettinghausen, R. "Introduction." In *The Islamic Garden*, ed. E. B. Macdougall and R. Ettinghausen. Washington, D.C.: Dumbarton Oaks, 1981.

Everson, P. " 'Delightfully Surrounded with Woods and Ponds': Field Evidence for Medieval Gardens in England." In *There by Design: Field Archaeology in Parks and Gardens*, ed. P. Pattison, 32–38. Oxford: British Archaeological Reports, 1998.

Everson, P. "Field Survey and Garden Earthworks." In *Garden Archaeology*, ed. A. Brown and E. Council. *British Archaeology, Research Report* 78 (1991): 6–19.

Everson, P. "Medieval Gardens and Designed Landscapes." In *The Lie of the Land: Aspects of the Archaeology and History of the Designed Landscape in the South West of England*, ed. R. Wilson-North, 24–33. Exeter: Mint Press, 2003.

Everson, P., G. Brown, and D. Stocker. "The Castle Earthworks and Landscape Context." In *Ludgershall Castle, Wiltshire: A Report on the Excavations by Peter Addyman, 1964–1972*, ed. P. Ellis, 97–119. Devizes: Wiltshire Archaeological and Natural History Society Monographs No. 2, 2000.

Everson, P., and T. Williamson. "Gardens and Designed Landscapes." In *The Archaeology of Landscape*, ed. P. Everson and T. Williamson, 139–65. Manchester: Manchester University Press, 1998.

Faral, E., ed. *Les arts poétiques du XIIe et du XIIIe siècle. Recherches et documents sur la technique littéraire du moyen âge*. Paris: Champion, 1924.

Favis, R. S. "The Garden of Love in Fifteenth Century Netherlandish and German Engravings: Some Studies in Secular Iconography in the Late Middle Ages and Early Renaissance." PhD diss., University of Pennsylvania, 1974.

Feller, L., P. Mane, and F. Piponnier, eds. *Le Village médiéval et son environnement. Études offertes à Jean-Marie Pesez*. Paris: Publications de la Sorbonne, 1998.

Ferrante, J. *Woman as Image in Medieval Art*. New York: Columbia University Press, 1975.

Ferrante, J. M., and G. D. Economou, eds. *In Pursuit of Perfection: Courtly Love in Medieval Literature*. Port Washington, NY: Kennikat Press, 1975.

Férre, M. "Les jardins de Louvre d'aprés les vestiges botaniques." *Dossiers d'Archéologie* 110 (1986): 78–82.

Ferry, D., trans. *The Georgics of Virgil*. New York: Farrar, Straus, and Giroux, 2005.

Fisher, C. *Flowers in Medieval Manuscripts*. Toronto: University of Toronto Press, 2004.

Finkenstaedt, T. "Der Garten des Konigs." In *Probleme des Kunstwissenschaft*, vol. 2. Berlin: Walter de Gruyter, 1966.

Fleck, C. A. *The Clement Bible at the Medieval Courts of Naples and Avignon: A Story of Papal Power, Royal Prestige, and Patronage*. Farnham: Ashgate, 2010.

Fleming, J. V. *The Roman de la Rose: A Study in Allegory and Iconography*. Princeton, NJ: Princeton University Press, 1966.

Flint, V. I. J. "The Commentaries of Honorius Augustodunensis on the *Song of Songs*." *Revue Benedictine* 8 (1974): 196–211.

Fontaine, M. M. "La vie autour du château: témoignages littéraires." In *Architecture, Jardin, Paysage: l'environnement du château et de la villa aux XVe et XVIe siècle*, ed. J. Guillaume, 259–93. Paris: Picard, 1999.

Forti, A. "Studi sulla flora della pittura classica veronese." *Madonna Verona* 14 (1933): 57–228.

Fowden, G. "Contextualizing Late Antiquity: The First Millennium." In *The Roman Empire in Context: Historical and Comparative Perspectives*, ed. J. P. Arnason and K. A. Raaflaub, 148–76. Oxford: Wiley-Blackwell, 2011.

Fowler, J. "On Mediaeval Representations of the Months and Seasons." *Archaeologia* 44 (1873): 177–224.

Franz, G., ed. *Geschichte des deutschen Gartenbaus*. Stuttgart: Ulmer, 1984.

Frati, L. "Bibliografia dei manoscritti." In *Pier de Crescenzi. Studi e documenti*, ed. A. Sorbelli, 259–306. Bologna: Società Agraria di Bologna, 1933.

Frauenfelder, R. "Die Symbolik des Gobelins 'Mystischer Garten Mariae' vom Jahre 1480 im Schweizerischen Landesmuseum." *Anzeiger für Schweizerische Altertumskunde* 38 (1936): 133–36.

Freedberg, D. "The Origins and Rise of the Flemish Madonnas in Flower Garlands: Decoration and Devotion." *Münchner Jahrbuch der Bildenden Kunst* 32 (1981): 115–50.

Freeman, M. *Herbs for the Medieval Household*. New York: Metropolitan Museum of Art, 1979.

Freeman, M. *La Chasse à la licorne*. Lausanne: Edita, 1983.

Fridenson, P., L. Niethammer, and L. Passerini. "International Reverberations: Remembering Raphael." *History Workshop Journal* 45 (1998): 246–60.

Friedländer, M. J. *Landscape, Portrait, Still Life: Their Origin and Development*. New York: Schocken, 1963.

Friedman, J. B. "L'iconographie de Vénus et de son miroir à la fin du Moyen Âge." In *L'Érotisme au Moyen Âge. Études présentées au troisième colloque de l'Institut d'Études médiévales*. Quebec: B. Roy, 1977.

Friedman, M. "The Falcon and the Hunt: Symbolic Love Imagery in Medieval and Renaissance Art." In *Poetics of Love in the Middle Ages: Texts and Contexts*, ed. M.
Lazar and J. Lacy Norris, 157–75. Fairfax, VA: George Mason University Press,
1989.

Frontisi-Ducroix, F., and J.-P. Vernant. *Dans l'Œil du Miroir*. Paris: Odile Jacob, 1997.

Fuhrmann, J. "Les différentes sources, caractéristiques et fonctions des jardins monastiques au Moyen Age." In *Vergers et jardins dans l'univers médiéval* [*Senefiance*
28], 111–24. Aix-en-Provence: C.U.E.R.M.A., 1990.

Fulton, R. "Mimetic Devotion, Marian Exegesis, and the Historical Sense of the Song of
Songs." *Viator: Medieval and Renaissance Studies* 27 (1996): 86–116.

Gagniere, S. "Les jardins et la ménagerie du palais des Papes d'après les comptes de
la Chambre apostolique." In *Avignon au Moyen Age, textes et documents*, ed. P.
Amargier et al., 103–9. Paris: Aubanel/Archives du Sud, 1988.

Gall, G. *Leder im europaischen, Kunsthandwerk. Ein Handbuch fu'r Sammler und
Liebhaber*. Braunschweig: Klinkhardt und Biermann, 1965.

Ganim, J. M. *Medievalism and Orientalism: Three Essays on Literature, Architecture
and Cultural Identity*. New York: Palgrave Macmillan, 2008.

Garbari, F. "L'Orto botanico dell'Universita di Pisa." In *Orti botanici, giardini alpine,
arboreta italiani*, ed. F. M. Raimondo, 225–37. Palermo: Grifo, 1992.

Gates, R. J., ed. *The Awntyrs off Arthure at the Terne Wathleyene: A Critical Edition*.
Philadelphia: University of Pennsylvania Press, 1969.

Gaulin, J.-L. "Agronomie antique et élaboration medieval: de Palladius aux Préceptes
cisterciens d'économie rurale." *Médiévales* 26 (1994): 59–83.

Gaulin, J.-L. "Pietro de Crescenzi et l'agronomie en Italie: 12e-14e siècles." PhD diss.,
Université de Paris I, Panthéon-Sorbonne, Paris, 1990.

Gesbert, E. "Les Jardins du Moyen Âge : du XIe au début du XIVe siècle." PhD diss.,
Université de Poitiers, Paris, 2001.

Giamatti, A.B. *Earthly Paradise and the Renaissance Epic*. Princeton, NJ: Princeton
University Press, 1966.

Giannetto, R. F. *Medici Gardens: From Making to Design*. Philadelphia: University of
Pennsylvania Press, 2008.

Gibault, G. "La condition et les salaires des anciens jardiniers." *Journal de la Société
nationale d'Horticulture de France* 20 (1898): 65–82.

Gibault, G. "L'ancienne corporation des maîtres jardiniers de la ville de Paris." *Journal
de la Société nationale d'Horticulture de France* 18 (1896): 153–74.

Gibault, G. "Les anciennes lois relatives au jardinage." *Journal de la Société nationale
d'Horticulture de France* 13 (1912): 824–30.

Gibault, G. "Les couronnes de fleurs et lea chapeaux de roses dans l'Antiquite et au
Moyen Age." *Revue horticole* (1896): 454–58.

Gibault, G. "Les fleurs, les fruits et les légumes dans l'ancien Paris." *Revue horticole*,
n.s., 6 (1906): 65–69.

Gibault, G. "Les origines de la culture forcé." *Journal de la Société nationale
d'Horticulture de France* 20 (1898): 1109–17.

Gilchrist, R. "The Contested Garden: Gender, Space and Metaphor in the English Castle Garden." In *Gender and Archaeology: Contesting the Past*, ed. R. Gilchrist,
109–45. London: Routledge, 1999.

Gillingham, J. "From *Civilitas* to Civility: Codes of Manners in Medieval and Early Modern England." *Transactions of the Royal Historical Society* 12 (2002): 267–89.

Girault, P.-G., ed. *Flore et jardins: Usages, savoirs et représentations du monde végétal au Moyen Âge*. Paris: Léopard d'or, 1997.

Glick, T. F. "Tribal Landscapes of Islamic Spain: History and Archaeology." In *Inventing Medieval Landscapes: Senses of Place in Western Europe*, ed. L. Howe and M. Wolfe, 113–35. Gainesville: University of Florida Press, 2002.

Golombek, L., and D. Wilber. "Gardens and Garden Structures." In *The Timurid Architecture of Iran and Turan*, vol. 1, ed. L. Golombek and D. Wilbur. Princeton, NJ: Princeton University Press, 1988.

Golombek, L., and D. Wilber. *The Timurid Architecture of Iran and Turan*, 2 vols. Princeton, NJ: Princeton University Press, 1988.

Goodall, J. *The English Castle: 1066–1650*. London: Paul Mellon Centre for British Art, 2011.

Goody, J. *The Culture of Flowers*. Cambridge: Cambridge University Press, 1993.

Gothein, M. L. *A History of Garden Art*. London: Thoemmes Continuum, 2003.

Gousset, M.-T. *Eden: le jardin médiéval à travers l'enluminure XIIIe-XVI siècle*. Paris: Albin Michel, 2001.

Gousset, M.-T. *Jardins médiévaux en France*. Rennes: Ouest France, 2003.

Gousset, M.-T. "Le jardin d'Emilie." *Revue de la Bibliothèque nationale* 22 (1986): 7–24.

Grabar, O. *The Formation of Islamic Art*. New Haven, CT: Yale University Press, 1973.

Grant, E., ed. *A Source Book in Medieval Science*. Cambridge, MA: Harard University Press, 1974.

Gratian, "On Marriage (dictum post c 32, 2.2)." In *Medieval Sourcebook*, ed. P. Halsall. NewYork: Fordham University, 1999. http:www.fordham.edu/halsall/source/gratian.html.

Gratias, C. "Le Pavillon d'Anne de Bretagne et les jardins du château de Blois." In *Flore et jardins: Usages, savoirs et représentations du monde végétal au Moyen Âge*, ed. P.-G. Girault. 131–44. Paris: Léopard d'or, 1997.

Grieco, A. "Reflexions sur l'histoire des fruits au Moyen Âge." In *L'Arbre: Histoire naturelle et symbolique de l'arbre, du bois et du fruit au Moyen Âge*, ed. M. Pastoureau, 145–53. Paris: Léopard d'or, 1997.

Greco, G. L., and C. M. Rose. *The Good Wife's Guide: Le Ménagier De Paris: A Medieval Household Book*. Ithaca, NY: Cornell University Press, 2009.

Grieco, A. J., ed. *Le Monde végétal (XIIe-XVIIe siécles): savoirs et usages sociaux*. Saint-Denis: Presses universitaires de Vincennes, 1989.

Griffiths, J., A.S.G. Edwards, and N. Barker, eds. *The Tollemache Book of Secrets: A Descriptive Index and Complete Facsimile*. London: Roxburghe Club, 2001.

Grimal, P. "Les jardins italiens de la Renaissance." In *Jardins et vergers en Europe occidentale (VIIIe-XVIIIe siècles). Jardins et vergers en Europe occidentale (VIIIe-XVIIIe siècle)*, ed. C. Higgonet, 165–73. Auch: Centre culturel de l'abbaye de Flaran, 1989.

Grimal, P. "Preface." In *Jardins du Moyen Âge*. Paris: Léopard d'or, 1995.

Grunebaum, G. E. von. "Aspects of Arabic Urban Literature Mostly in the Ninth and Tenth Centuries." In *Themes in Medieval Arabic Literature*, vol. 4, ed. D. S. Wilson, 280–84. London: Variorum Reprints, 1981.

Guillaume, J., ed. *Architecture, jardin, paysage: l'environnement du château et de la villa aux XVe et XVIe siècle*. Paris: Picard, 1999.

Guillaume, J. "Château, jardin, paysage en France du XVe au XVIIe siècle." *Revue de l'Art* 124 (1999): 13–32.

Guillaume, J. "Le jardin mis en ordre: Jardin et château en France du XVe au XVIIe siècles." In *Architecture, Jardin, Paysage : l'environnement du château et de la villa aux XVe et XVIe siècle*, ed. J. Guillaume, 103–36. Paris: Picard, 1999.

Hadfield, M. *A History of British Gardening*. London: Harmondsworth, 1985.

Hagopian van Buren, A. "La Roulotte de Philippe le Bon." In *Liber Amicorum: Études Historiques Offertes à Pierre Bougard*, 115–22. Arras: Commission départementale d'histoire et d'archéologie du Pas-de-Calais, 1987.

Hagopian van Buren, A. "Reality and Literary Romance in the Park of Hesdin." In *Medieval Gardens*, ed. E. B. MacDougall, 115–34. Washington, D.C.: Dumbarton Oaks, 1986.

Hagopian van Buren, A. "Un jardin d'amour de Philippe le Bon au parc d'Hesdin." *La revue du Louvre et des musées de France* 3 (1985): 185–92.

Hall, D. "The Open Fields of Northamptonshire." *Northamptonshire Record Society* 38 (1995).

Hamilakis, Y. "The Sacred Geography of Hunting: Wild Animals, Social Power and Gender in Early Farming Societies." In *Zooarchaeology in Greece: Recent Advances*, ed. E. Kotjabopoulou et al., 239–47. London: British School at Athens, 2003.

Hamilton, R. W. *Khirbat al Mafjar: An Arabian Mansion in the Jordan Valley*. Oxford: Clarendon Press, 1959.

Hansen, W. *Kalenderminiaturen der Stundenbücher: Mittelalterliches Leben im Jahreslauf*. Munich: Callwey, 1989.

Harris, B. J. *English Aristocratic Women, 1450–1550: Marriage and Family, Property and Careers*. New York: Oxford University Press, 2002.

Harris, J., ed. *The Garden: A Celebration of One Thousand Years of British Gardening*. London: Victoria and Albert Museum, 1979.

Harting, J. E. *The Rabbit*. London: Longman, 1898.

Harvey, J. H. *Early Gardening Catalogues*. London: Phillimore, 1972.

Harvey, J. H. *Early Nurserymen*. London: Phillimore, 1974.

Harvey, J. H. "The First English Garden Book. Mayster Jon Gardener's Treatise and Its Background." *Garden History* 13 (1985): 83–101.

Harvey, J. H. "Garden Plants of around 1525: The Fromond List." *Garden History* 17 (1989): 122–34.

Harvey, J. H. "Gardening in the Age of Chaucer." *Botanical Journal of Scotland* 46 (1994): 564–73.

Harvey, J. H. "Gilliflower and Carnation." *Garden History* 6 (1978): 46–57.

Harvey, J. H. "Henry Daniel: A Scientific Gardener of the 14th Century." *Garden History* 15, no. 2 (1987): 81–93.

Harvey, J. H. *Mediaeval Gardens*. London: Batsford, 1981.

Harvey, J. H. "Medieval Gardens." In *The Oxford Companion to Gardens*, ed. P. Goode and M. Lancaster, 362–67. Oxford: Oxford University Press, 1986.

Harvey, J.H. "Mediaeval Plantsmanship in England: The Culture of Rosemary." *Garden History* 1 (1972): 14–21.

Harvey, J.H. *Restoring Period Gardens*. London: Batsford, 1981.

Harvey, J.H. "The Square Garden of Henry the Poet." *Garden History* 15 (1987): 1–11.

Harvey, J.H. "Vegetables in the Middle Ages." *Garden History* 12 (1984): 89–99.

Harvey, J.H. "Westminster Abbey: The Infirmarer's Garden." *Garden History* 20 (1992): 97–115.

Harvey, P.D.A. *A Medieval Oxfordshire Village: Cuxham, 1240–1400*. Oxford: Oxford University Press, 1965.

Hassall, W. O. "Notes on Medieval Spades." In *The Spade in Northern and Atlantic Europe*, ed. A. Fenton and A. Gailey, 31–34. Belfast: Queen's University of Belfast, 1970.

Haudebourg, M.T. *Les Jardins du Moyen Âge*. Paris: Perrin, 2001.

Heather, P. *Empires and Barbarians: The Fall of Rome and the Birth of Europe*. New York: Oxford University Press, 2010.

Heinz-Mohr, G., and V. Sommer. *Die Rose: Entfaltung eines Symbols*. München: Diederichs, 1988.

Henderson, J. *The Roman Book of Gardening*. London: Routledge, 2004.

Henderson, P. "Clinging to the Past: Medievalism in the English 'Renaissance' Garden." *Renaissance Studies* 25 (2011): 42–69.

Henisch, B.A. *The Medieval Calendar Year*. University Park: Pennsylvania State University Press, 1999.

Henisch, B.A. "Private Pleasures: Painted Gardens on the Manuscript Page." In *Inventing Medieval Landscapes: Senses of Place in Western Europe*, ed. J. Howe and M. Wolfe, 150–70. Gainesville: University of Florida Press, 2002.

Hennebo, D. *Gärten des Mittelalters*, 2nd ed. Munich: Artemis, 1987.

Herlihy, D. "The Carolingian Capitulary, *De Villis*." In *Medieval Culture and Society*. New York: Harper & Row, 1968.

Herring, P. "Cornish Medieval Deer Parks." In *The Lie of the Land: Aspects of the Archaeology and History of the Designed Landscape in the South West of England*, ed. R. Wilson-North, 34–50. Exeter: Mint, 2003.

Herzfeld, E. "Mitteilungen über die Arbeiten der zweiten Kampagne von Samarra." *Der Islam* 5 (1914): 197–203.

Higham, R.A., J. P. Allan, and S. R. Blaylock. "Excavations at Okehampton Castle, Devon, Part Two: The Bailey." *Proceedings of the Devon Archaeological Society* 40 (1982): 19–151.

Higounet, C., ed. *Jardins et vergers en Europe occidentale (VIIIe-XVIIIe siècles)*. Auch: Centre culturel de l'Abbaye de Flaran, 1989.

Higounet, C., ed. "Jardins et vergers en Europe occidentale (VIIIe-XVIIIe siècles)." *Flaran* 9 (1989).

Higounet-Nadal, A. "Les jardins urbains dans la France médiévale." In *Jardins et vergers en Europe occidentale (VIIIe-XVIIIe siècle)*, ed. C. Higounet, 115–14. Auch: Centre culturel de l'Abbaye de Flaran, 1989.

Hirschfled, Y. *The Judean Desert Monasteries in the Byzantine Period*. New Haven, CT: Yale University Press, 1992.

Hobhouse, P. *Plants in Garden History*. London: Pavilion, 1992.

Hodder, I. *The Domestication of Europe*. Oxford: Basil Blackwell, 1990.

Hoeniger, C. "The Illuminated *Tacuinum sanitatis* Manuscripts from Northern Italy, *ca.* 1380–1400: Sources, Patrons, and the Creation of a New Pictorial Genre." In *Visualizing Medieval Medicine and Natural History, 1200–1550*, ed. J. A. Givens, K. Reeds, and A. Touwaide, 51–81. Aldershot: Ashgate, 2006.

Hoogvliet, M. "*Mappae Mundi* and the Medieval Hermeneutics of Cartographical Space." *Regions and Landscapes: Reality and Imagination in Late Medieval and Early Modern Europe*, ed. P. Ainsworth and T. Scott, 25–46. Oxford: Peter Land, 2000.

Hooke, D. "Pre-Conquest Woodland: Its Distribution and Usage." *Agricultural History Review* 37 (1989): 113–29.

Hoppitt, R. "Hunting Suffolk's Parks: Towards a Reliable Chronology of Imparkment." In *The Medieval Park: New Perspectives*, ed. R. Liddiard, 146–64. Windgather: Macclesfield, 2007.

Horn, W., and E. Born. *The Plan of St. Gall: A Study of the Architecture & Economy of, & Life in a Pradigmatic Carolingian Monsatery*, 3 vols. Berkeley: University of California Press, 1979.

Horden, P., and N. Purcell. *The Corrupting Sea: A Study of Mediterranean History*. Oxford: Blackwell, 2000.

Howard, D. *Venice and the East: The Impact of the Islamic World on Venetian Architecture 1100–1500*. New Haven, CT: Yale University Press, 2000.

Howe, J., and M. Wolfe, eds. *Inventing Medieval Landscapes: Senses of Place in Western Europe*. Gainesville: University of Florida Press, 2002.

Howell, M. C. *Women, Production and Patriarchy in Late Medieval Cities*. Chicago: University of Chicago Press, 1986.

Howes, L. L. *Chaucer's Gardens and the Language of Convention*. Gainesville: University of Florida Press, 1997.

Howes, L. L. "Narrative Time and Literary Landscapes in Middle English Poetry." In *Inventing Medieval Landscapes: Senses of Place in Western Europe*, ed. J. Howe and M. Wolfe, 192–207. Gainesville: University of Florida Press, 2002.

Howes, L. L., ed. *Place, Space, and Landscape in Medieval Narrative*. Knoxville: University of Tennessee Press, 2007.

Howes, L. L. " 'The Slow Curve of the Footwalker': Narrative Time and Literary Landscapes in Middle English Poetry." *Soundings: An Interdisciplinary Journal* 83 (2000): 165–81.

Hubert, J. M., trans. *The Romance of "Floire and Blanchefleur": A French Idyllic Poem of the Twelfth Century*. Chapel Hill: University of North Carolina Press, 1966.

Hubert, J. M. "The Romance of Floire and Blanchefleur: A French Idyllic Poem of the Twelfth Century." *University of North Carolina. Studies in the Roman Languages and Literatures* 63 (1966): 13–19.

Huchard, V., and B. Pascale. *Le Jardin médiéval: un musée imaginaire*. Paris: Presses Universitaires de France, 2002.

Hüe, D. "Reliure, clôture, culture: le contenu des jardins." In *Vergers et jardins dans l'univers médiéval [Senefiance 28]*, 155–75. Aix-en-Provence: C.U.E.R.M.A., 1990.

Hunt, T. *Plant Names of Medieval England*. Cambridge: Brewer, 1989.

Hunt, T. "The Song of Songs and Courtly Literature." In *Court and Poet: Selected Proceedings of the Third Congress of the International Courtly Literature Society*, ed. G. S. Burgess, 189–96. Liverpool: Francis Cairns, 1980.

Hunt, T. J. "A Thirteenth-Century Garden at Rimpton." *Proceedings of the Somersetshire Archaeological and Natural History* 104 (1959–60): 91–95.

Hutchison, J. C. *The Master of the Housebook*. New York: Collectors Editions, 1972.

Ibn Luyūn, A. *L'Ile-de-France médiévale*. Paris: Somogy, 2000.

Innes, M., and C. Perry. *Medieval Flowers*. London: Kyle Cathie, 1997.

Isidore of Seville. *Etimologías: Edición bilingue*, vol. 14. Madrid: Editorial Católica, 1982–83.

Isidore of Seville. *The Etymologies of Isidore cf Seville*, ed. S. A. Barney et al. Cambridge: Cambridge University Press, 2006.

Jacquart, D., and C. Thomasset. "Medicine and the Art of Love." In *Sexuality and Medicine in the Middle Ages*, ed. D. Jacquart and C. Thomasset, 87–138. Princeton, NJ: Princeton University Press, 1985.

James, E. C. "Images et faits perdus. Parcs et jardins anciens en Pays de la Loire." *Revue 303* (1991): 32–45.

Janssen, W. "Gartenkultur im Mittelalter." In *Wie viel garten braucht der Mensch?*, ed. G. Bittner and P. L. Weinacht, 59–84. Würtzburg: Würzburger Universitätsvorträge, 1990.

Jashemski, W., and E. B. MacDougall, eds. *Ancient Roman Gardens*. Washington, D.C.: Dumbarton Oaks, 1981.

Jellicoe, J., et al., eds. *Oxford Companion to Gardens*. Oxford: Oxford University Press, 1986.

Jennings, A. *Medieval Gardens*. London: English Heritage, 2004.

Jerome. *Select Letters of Saint Jerome*, ed. and tr. F. Wright. Cambridge, MA: Harvard University Press, 1991.

Jestaz, B. "La villa de Giovanni Rucellai I Quaracchi et ses nouveautes." In *Architecture, Jardin, Paysage: l'environnement du château et de la villa aux XVe et XVIe siècle*, ed. J. Guillaume, 21–28. Paris: Picard, 1999.

Johnson, R. "Historical Returns: Transdisciplinarity, Cultural Studies and History." *European Journal of Cultural Studies* 4 (2001): 261–88.

Johnson, R. "What Is Cultural Studies Anyway?" *Social Text* 16 (1986–87): 38–80, 62.

Jones, P. M. "Herbs and the Medieval Surgeon." In *Health and Healing from the Medieval Garden*, ed. P. Dendle and A. Touwaide, 162–79. Woodbridge: Boydell and Brewer, 2008.

Joret, C. *La Rose dans l'Antiquite et au Moyen Age: Histoire, legends et symbolisme*. Geneve/Paris: Slatkine, 1993.

Joubert, F. *La tapisserie médiévale au Musée de Cluny*, 2nd ed. Paris: Réunion des Musées Nationaux, 1994.

Jourdan, G.-P. "Le sixième sens et la théologie de l'amour, essai d'iconographie sur les tapisseries à sujets amoureux à la fin du Moyen Âge." *Journal des savants* (1996): 137–60.

Kasianitz, R. "Kleinod und Andachtsbild. Zum Bildprogramm des Goldenen Rossls." In *Das goldene Rössl: ein Meisterwerk der Pariser Hofkunst um 1400*, ed. R. Baumstark, 58–88. Munich: Bayerisches Nationalmuseum, 1995.

Kaufmann, A. *Der Gartenbau im Mittelalter und während der Periode der Renaissance: dargestellt in fünf Vorträgen*. Berlin: Grundmann, 1892.

Kazhdan, A., and A. Cutler. "Continuity and Discontinuity in Byzantine History." *Byzantion* 52 (1982): 429–78.

Keevil, G. D. *Medieval Palaces: An Archaeology*. Stroud: Tempus, 2000.

Keevil, G. D., and N. Linford. "Landscape with Gardens: Aerial, Topographical and Geophysical Survey at Hamstead Marshall, Berkshire." In *There by Design: Field Archaeology in Parks and Gardens*, ed. P. Pattison, 13–22. Oxford: British Archaeological Reports, 1998.

Keil, G. "Hortus sanitatis, Gart der Gesundheit, Gaerde der Sunthede." In *Medieval Gardens*, ed. E. B. MacDougall, 55–68. Washington, D.C.: Dumbarton Oaks, 1986.

Keil, I. "The Garden at Glastonbury Abbey: 1333–1334." *Proceedings of the Somersetshire Archaeological and Natural History* 104 (1959–60): 96–100.

Keiser, G. R. "Through a Fourteenth-Century Gardener's Eyes: Henry Daniel's Herbal." *The Chaucer Review* 31 (1996): 58–75.

Kent, S. *Farmers as Hunters: The Implications of Sedentism*. Cambridge: Cambridge University Press, 1989.

Kerridge, E. *The Common Fields of England*. Manchester: Manchester University Press, 1992.

Kessels, L. "The Brussels/Tournai-Partbooks: Structure, Illumination, and Flemish Repertory." *Tijdschrift van de Vereniging voor Nederlandse Muziekgeschiedenis* 37 (1987): 82–110.

Kessler, E. "Le jardin des délices et les fruits du mal." In *Flore et jardins: usages, savoirs et représentations du monde végétal au Moyen Age*, ed. P.-G. Girault, 177–98. Paris: Léopard d'Or, 1997.

Kessler, H. L. *The Illustrated Bibles from Tours*. Princeton, NJ: Princeton University Press, 1977.

Kessler, H. L. *Pictorial Narrative in Antiquity and the Middle Ages* (*Studies in the History of Art*, XVI). Washington, D.C.: National Gallery of Art, 1985.

Kessler, H. L. *Spiritual Seeing: Picturing God's Invisibility in Medieval Art*. Philadelphia: University of Pennsylvania Press, 2000.

Kihm, F. "Du jardin à la table en Allemagne au milieu du XIVe siècle plantes, fleurs et fruits dans le plus ancien livre de cuisine allemand, par François." In *Flore et jardins: usages, savoirs et représentations du monde végétal au Moyen Age*, ed. P.-G. Girault, 75–86. Paris: Léopard d'Or, 1997.

King, C. "The Organization of Social Space in Late Medieval Manor Houses." *Archaeological Journal* 160 (2003): 104–24.

Kirschbaum, E. "Garten." In *Lexikon der christlichen Ikonographie* II, columns 77–81. Rome: Herder, 1990.

Kleindienst, T. "La topographic et l'exploitation des 'Marais de Paris' du XIIe au XVIIe siècle." *Paris et Ile-de-France –Mémoires* 14 (1963): 7–167.

Kluckert, E. *European Garden Design from Classical Antiquity to the Present Day*. Cologne: Konemann, 2000.

Koch, R.A. "Flower Symbolism in the Portinari Altar." *The Art Bulletin* 46 (1964): 70–77.

Koechlin, R. *Les Ivoires Gothiques Français*. Paris: Nobele, 1968.

Kohlhausen, H. *Minnekästchen im Mittelalter*. Berlin: Verlag für Kunstwissenschaft, 1928.

Konig, E. *Franzosische Buchmalerei um 1450: Der Jouvenel-Mater, der Maler des Genfer Boccaccio und die Anfange Jean Fouquets*. Berlin: Gebr. Mann, 1982.

Koniger, M. "Die Profanen Fresken des Palazzo Davanzati in Florenz. Private Repräsentation zur Zeit der Internationalen Gotik." *Mitteilungen des Kunsthistorischen Institute in Florenz* 34 (1990): 245–78.

Krueger, I. "Glasspiel im Mittelalter: Fakten, Funde, und Fragen." *Bonner Jahrbücher des Rheinischen Landesmuseums in Bonn* 190 (1990): 233–320.

Kuhn, A. *Die Illustration des Rosenromans*. Vienna, Leipzig: Tempsky and Freytag, 1912.

Kühn, W. "Grünewalds Isenheimer Altar als Darstellung mittelalterlicher Heilkräuter." *Kosmos* 44 (1948): 327–33.

Kurth, B. "Die Blütezeit der Bildwirker-kunst zu Tournai und der burgundische Hof." *Jahrbuch der kunsthistorischen Sammlungen des allerhöchsten Kaiserhauses zu Wien* 34 (1918): 53–110.

Küster, E. "Belgische Gärten des fünfzehnten Jahrhunderts." *Repertorium für kunstwissenschaft* 41 (1919): 148–58.

Laborde, A. de. *Les manuscrits à peintures de la* Cité de Dieu *de Saint Augustin*. Paris: Société des Bibliophiles Français, 1909.

Laborde, L. *Les Ducs de Bourgogne: Études sur les lettres, les arts et l'industrie pendant le XVe siècle et plus particulièrement dans les Pays-Bas et le duché de Bourgogne*, 3 vols. Paris: Plon, 1849–52.

L'Arbre. Histoire naturelle et symbolique de l'arbre, du bois et du fruit au Moyen Age. Paris: Léopard d'or, 1993.

Lacroix, J. "Les jardins de Boccace ou la fête florentine du récit." In *Vergers et jardins dans l'univers médiéval* [Senefiance 28], 197–213. Aix-en-Provence: C.U.E.R.M.A., 1990.

Lambert, A. "The Ceremonial Use of Flowers." *The Nineteenth Century* 4 (1878): 457–77.

Lambert, A. "The Ceremonial Use of Flowers: A Sequel." *The Nineteenth Century* 7 (1880): 808–27.

Landsberg, S. *The Medieval Garden*. New York: Thames and Hudson, 1995.

Landy, F. "The *Song of Songs* and the Garden of Eden." *Journal of Biblical Literature* 98 (1979): 513–28.

Langlois, E. *Les Manuscrits du Roman de la Rose: description et classement*. Paris, Lille: Tallandier, 1910.

Leach, H. M. "Plant Categories and the Significance of Meaning Changes: The Case of Herbs and Related Terms." *Garden History* 23 (1995): 125–30.

Leber, J.M.C. *Catalogue des livres imprimés, manuscrits, enstampes, dessins et cartes à jouer, composant la bibliothèque de M. C. Leber: avec des notes*. Paris: Techener, 1839.

Leclercq, H. "Fleur de lis." In *Dictionnaire d'archéologie chrétienne et de liturgie* V, columns 1699–708. Paris: Letouzey et Ané, 1923.

Lecoy, F. *La Vie des Peres*. Paris: Société des anciens texts français, 1987.

Lee, A., P. Péporté, and H. Schnitker, eds. *Renaissance? Perceptions of Continuity and Discontinuity in Europe, c.1300–c.1550*. Leiden: Brill, 2010.

Legros, V. "Etude du mobilier métallique des fermes médiévales du 'Belle' à Neuilly-en-Thelle (Oise). Approche technique et fonctionnelle." *Revue archéologique de Picardie* (2001): 1–34.

Lehrs, M. "Der Meister der Berliner Passion." *Jahrbuch der Preußischen Kunstsammlungen* 21 (1900): 135–59.

Le Jardin Médiéval. Colloque a l'Abbaye de Saint-Arnoult-Monastère des arts les 3 et 4 Septembre 1988. Warluis: ADAMA, 1990.

Le Maho, J. "Parcs et courtils, observations sur l'environnement des châteaux de terre et de bois en Pays de Caux aux XIe-XIIe siècles." In *Actes du 105e Congrès national des sociétés savantes, Caen 1980*, 171–81. Paris: Comité des travaux historiques et scientifiques, 1983.

Lemaître, J.-L., and P. de Bonet. *Les Heures De Peyre De Bonetos*. Ussel: Musée du pays d'Ussel, 1987.

Lemoisne, P. A. *Les Xylographies du XIV et du XV siècle au Cabinet des Estampes de la Bibliothèque Nationale*, 2 vols. Paris: G. van Oest, 1927–30.

Leroquais, V. *Le Bréviaire de Philippe le Bon. Bréviaire Parisien du XVe siècle. Étude du texte et des miniatures*. Paris: Rousseau, 1929.

Le Sénécal, J. "Les Occupations des mois dans l'iconographie du moyen âge." *Bulletin de la Société des Antiquaires de Normandie* 35 (1924): 1–218.

Leslie, M. "An English Landscape Garden Before 'the English Landscape Garden'?" *Journal of Garden History* 13 (1993): 3–15.

Leslie, M. "The Hard and the Soft: Interdisciplinarity and Cultural History in Landscape Studies." *Studies in the History of Gardens & Designed Landscapes* 27 (2007): 103–7.

Leslie, M., and T. Raylor. *Culture and Cultivation in Early Modern England: Writing and the Land*. Leicester: Leicester University Press, 1992.

Lesot, S. *Au Temps des jardins médiévaux: Les saisons au Prieuré d'Orsan*. Paris: Editions du Garde-temps, 2000.

Lesueur, P. "Les jardins du Château de Blois et leurs dépendances: Étude architectonique." *Memoires de la Société des sciences et lettres de Loir-et-Cher* 18 (1904): 223–438.

Levi d'Ancona, M. *The Garden of the Renaissance: Botanical Symbolism in Italian Painting*. Florence: L. S. Olschki, 1977.

Levin, W. R., ed. *Images of Love and Death in Late Medieval and Renaissance Art*. Ann Arbor: University of Michigan Press, 1975.

Lewis, C., P. Mitchell-Fox, and C. Dyer. *Village, Hamlet and Field: Changing Medieval Settlements in Central England*. Manchester: Manchester University Press, 1997.

Lewis, M.J.T. "The Origins of the Wheelbarrow." *Technology and Culture* 35 (1994): 453–75.

Lewis, S. "Images of Opening, Penetration, and Closure in the *Roman de la Rose.*" *Word and Image* 8 (1992): 215–42.

Librairie de Bourgogne et quelques acquisitions récentes de la Bibliothèque royale Albert Ier: cinquante miniatures. Bruxelles: Bruxelles Cultura, 1970.

Liddiard, R. *Castles in Context: Power, Symbolism and Landscape, 1066 to 1500.* Macclesfield: Windgather, 2005.

Liddiard, R. "Medieval Designed Landscapes: Problems and Possibilities." In *Medieval Landscapes: Landscape History after Hoskins*, vol. 2, ed. M. Gardiner, S. Rippon, and S. Bollington, 201–14. Macclesfield: Windgather, 2007.

Liddiard, R. *The Medieval Park: New Perspectives.* Macclesfield: Windgather, 2007.

Lieutaghi, P. *Jardin des savoirs, jardin d'histoire, suivi d'un Glossaire des plantes médiévales.* Mane: Alpes de lumière, 1992.

Lightbown, R. W. *Mediaeval European Jewellery with a Catalogue of the Collection in the Victoria and Albert Museum.* London: Victoria and Albert Museum, 1992.

Littlewood, A. "Gardens of the Palaces." In *Byzantine Court Culture from 829 to 1204*, ed. H. Maguire, 13–38. Washington, D.C.: Dumbarton Oaks, 1997.

Littlewood, A. "The Scholarship of Byzantine Gardens." In *Byzantine Garden Culture*, ed. A. Littlewood, H. Maguire, and J. Wolschke-Bulmahn, 13–21. Washington, D.C.: Dumbarton Oaks, 2002.

Littlewood, A., H. Maguire, and J. Wolschke-Bulmahn, eds. *Byzantine Garden Culture.* Washington, D.C.: Dumbarton Oaks, 2002.

Loaiza, K.E. "Sankt Gall." In *Medieval Germany: An Encyclopedia*, ed. J. M. Jeep, 696–97. New York: Garland, 2001.

Lodge, B., ed. *Palladius on Husbondrie.* London: N. Trübner, 1873; reprint, Millwood, NY: Kraus, 1973.

Longnon, J., and R. Cazelles. *Les Très Riches Heures du Duc de Berry, Musée Condé, Chantilly.* London: Thames and Hudson, 1969.

Lorcin, M.-T. "Les '*meschantes herbes des jardins*'." In *Vergers et jardins dons l'univers mediéval*, 237–52. Aix-en-Provence: Université de Provence, 1990.

Lorris, Guillaume de, and J. de Meun. *Le Roman de la Rose.* Paris: Livre de Poche, 1992.

Lorris, Guillaume de, and J. de Meun. *Romance of the Rose.* Princeton, NJ: Princeton University Press, 1971.

Luttikhuizen, G., ed. *Paradise Interpreted: Representations of Biblical Paradise in Judaism and Christianity.* Leiden: Brill, 1999.

Lyna, F. *Le Mortifiement de vaine plaisance de René d'Anjou. Étude du texte et des manuscrits à peintures.* Brussels: Leyde, 1926.

Lyna, F., and C. Van den Bergen-Pantens. *Les Principaux manuscrits à peintures de la Bibliothèque Royale de Bruxelles.* Brussels: Bibliothèque Royale Albert, 1989.

MacDougal, E. B., ed. *Medieval Gardens.* Washington, D.C.: Dumbarton Oaks, 1986.

MacKinney, L. *Medical Illustrations in Medieval Manuscripts.* Berkeley: University of California Press, 1965.

Maguire, H. "Gardens and Parks in Constantinople." *Dumbarton Oaks Papers* 54 (2000): 251–64.

Maguire, H. "Imperial Gardens and the Rhetoric of Renewal." In *New Constantines: The Rhythm of Imperial Renewal in Byzantium, 4th-13th Centuries*, ed. P. Magdalino, 181–98. Aldershot: Variorum, 1994.

Mane, P. "L'iconographie des manuscrits du *Traité d'Agriculture* de Pier' de Crescenzi." *Mélanges de l'Ecole Française de Rome. Moyen Age et Temps modernes* 97 (1985): 727–818.

Manuwald, H., and N. Humphrey. "A Painted Casket in the Victoria and Albert Museum, London." *The Antiquaries Journal* 90 (2010): 235–60.

Marçais, G. "Bustān." In *Encyclopedia of Islam*, vol. 1, 1345–47. Leiden: E. J. Brill, 1960.

Marçais, G. "Les jardins de l'Islâm." In *Mélanges d' histoire et d'archéologie de l'Occident Musulman*, 235. Algiers: Imprimerie officielle, 1957.

Margiotta, M. L. *Il Giardino Sacro: Chiostri E Giardini Della Campania*. Napoli: Electa Napoli, 2000.

Margiotta, M. L., and P. Belfiore. *Giardini storici napoletani*. Naples: Electa Napoli, 2000.

Marien-Dugardin, A. M. "Coffrets à Madone." *Bulletin des musées royaux d'Art et d'Histoire* 24 (1952): 101–10.

Marquand, D. *The End of the West: The Once and Future Europe*. Princeton, NJ: Princeton University Press, 2011.

Martin, H. *Catalogue des manuscrits de la bibliothèque de l'Arsenal*. Paris: Nourit, 1886.

Martin, H., and P. Lauer. *Les Principaux Manuscrits à peintures de la bibliothèque de l'Arsenal à Paris*. Paris: Pour les membres de la Societé française de reproductions de manuscrits à peintures, 1929.

Martin le Franc. *Le Champion des dames*, 5 vols. Paris: Champion, 1999.

Masai, F., and M. Wittek, eds. *Manuscrits datés conservés en Belgique. III, 144–1460. Manuscrits conservés à la Bibliothèque royale Albert Ie, Bruxelles*. Ghent: Éditions scientifiques E. Story-Scientia, 1978.

Masson, G. *Italian Gardens*. London: Thames and Hudson, 1961.

Masson-Voos, C. "Les jardins objets d'attention au Moyen Âge." In *Flore et jardins: Usages, savoirs et représentations du monde végétal au Moyen Âge*, ed. P.-G. Girault, 9–38. Paris: Léopard d'or, 1997.

Matheson, L. M., ed. *Popular and Practical Science of Medieval England*. East Lansing: Michigan State University Press, 1994.

Mathon, C. *L'origine des plantes cultivées: Phytogéographie appliquée*. Paris: Masson, 1981.

Mathon, C.-C. "Des marais aux marchés: Usages et images des plantes dans le Journal d'un bourgeois de Paris 1405–1449." In *Flore et jardins: Usages, savoirs et représentations du monde végétal au Moyen Age*, ed. P.-G.Girault, 87–112. Paris: Léopard d'or, 1997.

Matthew of Vendôme. "Ars versificatoria." In *Les Arts Poétique du XIIe et du XIIIe Siècle*, ed. E. Faral, 106–93. Paris: Campion, 1958.

Matthew of Vendôme. *Les arts poétiques du XIIe et du XIIIe siècle. Recherches et documents sur la technique littéraire du moyen âge*. Paris: Champion, 1924.

Matthies, A. L. "The Medieval Wheelbarrow." *Technology and Culture* 32 (1991): 356–64.

Maury, C. "Un herbier français du XVe siècle: le livre des simples médecines." In *Positions des thèses de l'Ecole des chartes*, 105–8. Paris: Librairie Droz, 1963.

McCann, J. *The Dovecotes of Suffolk*. Ipswich: Suffolk Institute of Archaeology and History, 1998.

McCormick, M. *Origins of the European Economy: Communications and Commerce, A.D. 300–900*. Cambridge: Cambridge University Press, 2001.

McDonagh, B. "Powerhouses of the Wolds Landscape: Manor Houses and Churches in Late Medieval and Early Modern England." In *Medieval Landscapes in Britain: Landscape History after Hoskins*, vol. 2, ed. M. Gardiner and S. Rippon, 185–200. Macclesfield: Windgather Press, 2007.

McLean, T. *Medieval English Gardens*. London: Collins, 1981.

McNeill, T. E. "The View from the Top." In *Melanges d'archeologie medieval. Liber amicorum en hommage à André Matthys*, ed. J. de Meulemeester, 122–27. Liège: Mardaga, 2006.

McNight, G. H., ed. *King Horn, Floriz and Blauncheflur, the Assumption of Our Lady*. London: Oxford University Press, 1962.

McSheffrey, S. "Place, Space, and Situation: Public and Private in the Making of Marriage in Late-Medieval London." *Speculum* 79 (2004): 960–90.

Meiss, M. *French Painting in the Time of Jean de Berry, I, The Late 14th Century and the Patronage of the Duke*. New York: Phaidon, 1967.

Meiss, M. *French Painting in the Time of Jean de Berry, II, The Limbourgs and their Contemporaries*. New York: George Brazillier, 1974.

Meiss, M. *Preface to* Les Très Riches Heures du Duc de Berry. Edited by J. Longnon and R. Cazelles. London: Thames & Hudson, 1989.

Ménard, P. "Jardins et vergers dans la littérature médiévale." In *Jardins et vergers en Europe occidentale (viiie-xviiie siècles)*, 41–69. Auch: Comité départmental de Tourisme du Gers, 1989.

Mercier, F. "La valeur symbolique de l'oeillet dans la peinture du Moyen Âge." *Revue de l'art ancien et modern* 71 (1937): 233–36.

Mérindol, C. de. "De l'emblématique et de la symbolique de l'arbre à la fin du Moyen Âge." In *L'Arbre. Histoire naturelle et symbolique de l'arbre, du bois et du fruit au Moyen Âge*, ed. M. Pastoureau, 105–25. Paris: Le Léopard d'Or, 1993.

Mesqui, J. *Chateaux et enceintes de la France medieval*, vol. 1: Les organs de la defense. Paris: Picard, 1991.

Mesqui, J. *Chateaux et enceintes de la France medieval*, vol. 2: De la défense à la residence. Paris: Picard, 1993.

Metropolitan Museum of Art. *The Secular Spirit: Life and Art at the End of the Middle Ages*. New York: Dutton, 1975.

Mew, K. "The Dynamics of Lordship and Landscape as Revealed in as Domesday Study of the *Nova Foresta*." *Anglo-Norman Studies* 23 (2000): 155–66.

Mew, K. "Through a Glass Darkly: The Dynamic of Landscape and Lordship in the New Forest." *Anglo-Norman Studies* 23 (2001): 155–66.

Meyvaert, P. "The Medieval Monastic Claustrum." *Gesta* 12 (1973): 53–59.

Meyvaert, P. "The Medieval Monastic Garden." In *Medieval Gardens*, ed. E. B. Mac-
    Dougall, 23–53. Washington, D.C.: Dumbarton Oaks, 1986.
Michaud-Fréjaville, F. "Images et réalités du jardin médiéval." In *Jardins du Moyen
    Âge*, 39–62. Paris: Léopard d'or, 1995.
Migne, J. P., ed. *Patrologia Latina Database*. Alexandria, VA: Chadwick-Healey, 1995.
Mileson, S. "The Importance of Parks in Fifteenth-Century Society." In *The Fifteenth
    Century*, ed. L. Clark, 19–37. Woodbridge: Boydell, 2005.
Mileson, S. *Parks in Medieval England*. Oxford: Oxford University Press, 2009.
Mileson, S. "The Sociology of Park Creation in Medieval England." In *The Medieval
    Park: New Perspectives*, ed. R. Liddiard, 11–26. Macclesfield: Windgather, 2007.
Miller, N. "Paradise Regained: Medieval Garden Fountains." In *Medieval Gardens*, ed.
    E. B. MacDougall, 135–53. Washington, D.C.: Dumbarton Oaks, 1986.
Minio, M. "Il quattrocentesco Codice 'Rinio' integralmente rivendicato al medico
    Nicolò Roccabonella." *Atti del Reale Istituto veneto di scienze, lettere ed arti* 111
    (1952–1953): 49–64.
Mitchell, W.J.T. *Landscape and Power*. Chicago: University of Chicago Press, 1994.
Moly Mariotti, F. "Contribution à la connaissance des *'Tacuina sanitatis'* Lombards."
    Arte Lombarda 104 (1993): 32–40.
Moorhouse, S. "Ceramics in the Medieval Gardens." *Garden Archaeology, Council for
    British Archaeology Research Report* 78 (1991): 100–17.
Moorhouse, S. "The Medieval Parks of Yorkshire: Function, Contents and Chronol-
    ogy." In *The Medieval Park: New Perspectives*, ed. R. Liddiard, 99–127. Maccles-
    field: Windgather, 2007.
Monson, C.D.A. *Andreas Capellanus, Scholasticism, and the Courtly Tradition*. Wash-
    ington, D.C.: Catholic University of America Press, 2005.
Morris, P., and D. Sawyer, eds. *A Walk in the Garden: Biblical, Iconographical and
    Literary Images of Eden, Journal for the Study of the Old Testament*, supplement
    series 136. Sheffield: Sheffield Academic Press, 1992.
Mosser, M., and G. Teyssot, eds. *The History of Garden Design: The Western Tradition
    from the Renaissance to the Present*. London: Thames and Hudson, 1991.
Moxey, K.P.F. "Meister E. S. and the Folly of Love." *Simiolus* 2 (1980): 125–48.
Muir, E. *Ritual in Early Modern Europe*. Cambridge: Cambridge University Press, 2005.
Muir, R. *Ancient Trees, Living Landscapes*. Stroud: Tempus, 2005.
Musacchio, J. M. *Art, Marriage, and the Family in the Florentine Renaissance Palace*.
    New Haven, CT: Yale University Press, 2009.
Musper, H. T. *Der Holzschnitt in fünf Jahrhunderten*. Stuttgart: Kohlhammer, 1964.
Naïs, H. "Le *Rustican*. Notes sur la traduction française du traité d'agriculture de Pierre
    de Crescens." *Bibliothèque d'humanisme et de Renaissance* 19 (1957): 103–32.
Nass, M. *Meister E. S. Studien zu Werk und Wirkung*. Frankfurt: Lang, 1994.
Necipoğlu, G. "The Suburban Landscape of Sixteenth-Century Istanbul as a Mirror of
    Classical Ottoman Garden Culture." In *Gardens in the Time of the Great Muslim
    Empires: Theory and Design*, ed. A. Petruccioli, 32–71. Leiden: Brill, 1997.
Neckam, A. *De naturis rerum libri duo*. London: Longman, 1863.
Neckam, A. *De naturis rerum, Libri Duo, CLXVI: De herbis et arboribus et floribus
    horto crescentibus*. Liechtenstein: Kraus Reprint LTD, 1967.

Neckam, A. *Suppletio Defectuum, Book I: Alexander Neckam on Plants, Birds and Animals: A Supplement to the Laus Sapientie Divine edited from Paris, B. N. Lat., Ms 11867*. Florence: SISMEL edizioni del Galluzzo, 1999.

Nichols, S. G., A. Kablitz, and A. Calhoun, eds. *Rethinking the Medieval Senses: Heritage/Fascination/Frames*. Baltimore, MD: Johns Hopkins University Press, 2008.

Nissen, C. *Die Botanische Buchillustration: Ihre Geschichte Und Bibliographie*, 2 vols. and supplement. Stuttgart: Hiersemann, 1951–56.

Nolhac, P. "Pétrarque et son jardin d'après ses notes inédites." *Giornale Storico della Letteratura Italiana* 9 (1887): 404–14.

Northedge, A. "Creswell, Herzfeld, and Samarra." *Muqarnas* 8 (1991): 74–93.

Notz, M. F. "*Hortus conclusus*: Réflexions sur le rôle symbolique de la clôture dans la description romanesque du jardin." In *Mélanges de littérature, du Moyen Âge au XXe siècle, offerts à Mlle. Jeanne Lods*, 459–72. Paris : École normale supérieure de jeunes filles, 1978.

Notz, M. F. "Le verger merveilleux: un mode original de la description?" In *Etudes Jules Horrent*, 317–24. Liège: Presses Universitaires de Liège, 1980.

Nykl, A. R., ed., *Hispano-Arabic Poetry and its Relations with the Old Provencal Troubadors*. Baltimore, MD: Furst, 1946.

O'Keefe, T. "Were there Designed Landscapes in Medieval Ireland?" *Landscapes* 5 (2004): 52–68.

Olivesi, F. *Marguerite en son jardin, le jardin du château de Rouvres dans la seconde moitié du XIVe siècle*, mémoire de maîtrise d'histoire médiévale sous la direction de Mme (M.) Bourin-Derruau. Université de Paris: Panthéon-Sorbonne, 2001.

Olson, G. *Literature as Recreation in the Later Middle Ages*. Ithaca, NY: Cornell University Press, 1982.

Oman, C. *The Great Revolt of 1381*. Oxford: Clarendon Press, 1903.

Oosthuizen, S. M., and C. C. Taylor. "Rediscovery of a Vanished Garden in Bassingbourn, Cambridgeshire, and the Impact of the Lynne family on the Medieval Landscape." *Proceedings of the Cambridge Antiquarian Society* 89 (2000): 59–68.

Opsomer, C. "Sur quelques plantes magiques ou légendaires décrites dans des 'herbiers' du Moyen Ages." *Actes. Congrès de la Fédération des Cercles d'Archéologie et d'Histoire de Belgique* 43 (1975): 491–96.

Opsomer, C., et al. *Le Livre des simples médecines:* Codex Bruxellensis *IV.1024*. Antwerp: De Schutter, 1980.

Opsomer-Halleux, C. "The Medieval Garden and Its Role in Medicine." In *Medieval Gardens*, ed. E. B. MacDougall, 93–113. Washington, D.C.: Dumbarton Oaks, 1986.

Ortega-Tillier, V. "Iconographie du paradis terrestre: Topographie du jardin d'Éden du XVe au XVIIIe siècle." *Polia: Revue de l'art des jardins* 4 (2005): 75–91.

Ovitt, G. *The Restoration of Perfection: Labor and Technology in Medieval Culture*. New Brunswick, NJ: Rutgers University Press, 1987.

Pacht, O. "Early Italian Nature Studies and Early Calendar Landscapes." *Journal of the Warburg and Courtauld Institute* 13 (1950): 13–47.

Padel, O. J. "The Cornish Background of the Tristan Stories." *Cambridge Medieval Studies* 1 (1981): 53–81.

Pastoureau, M. "'Bonum, Mature, Pomum.' Une Histoire Symbolique de la Pomme." In *L'Arbre. Histoire naturelle et symbolique de l'arbre, du bois et du fruit au Moyen Age*, ed. M. Pastoureau, 155–99. Paris: Léopard d'Or, 1993.

Pastoureau, M. "Une fleur pour le roi, jalons pour une histoire de la fleur de lis au Moyen Âge." In *Flore et jardins: Usages, savoirs et représentations du monde végétal au Moyen Âge*, ed. P.-G. Girault, 113–30. Paris: Léopard d'or, 1997.

Paul-Sehl, M. *Recherches en vue d'une reconstitution matérielle du jardin médiéval à l'aide de documents historiques, thèse de troisième cycle en histoire*. Paris: EHESS, 1980.

Paul-Seld, M. "Turf Seats in French Gardens of the Middle Ages." *Garden History* 5 (1985): 3–14.

Pearsall, D., ed. *The Floure and the Leafe*. London: Nelson, 1962.

Pearsall, D., and E. Salter, eds. *Landscapes and Seasons of the Medieval World*. Toronto: University of Toronto Press, 1973.

Pellerin, G. *Outils de jardin*. Paris: Abbeville Press, 1996.

Pestell, T. *Landscapes of Monastic Foundation: The Establishment of Religious Houses in East Anglia c. 650–1200*. Woodbridge: Boydell, 2004.

Petersen, S. E. *The Paradise Garden and the Desert*. Copenhagen: Royal Danish Academy of Fine Arts, School of Architecture, 1995.

Petruccioli, A. "Introduzione." In *Il Giardino Islamico: Architettura, natura, paesaggio*, ed. A. Petruccioli, 7–62. Milan: Electa, 1994.

Petrus de Crescenziis. *Ruralia commoda. Das Wissen des vollkommenen Landwirts um 1300*, 3 vols. Heidelberg: Universitätsverlag C. Winter, 1995–98.

Phipps, W. E. "The Plight of the Song of Songs." In *The Song of Songs*, ed. H. Bloom, 5–23. New York: Chelsea House Publishers, 1988.

Picard, E. "Le château de Germolles et Marguerite de Flandre." *Mémoires de la Société Eduenne* 40 (1912): 147–218.

Picard, E. "Les jardins du château de Rouvres au quatorzième siècle." *Mémoires de la Société Eduenne* 22 (1894): 157–79.

Piehler, P. *The Visionary Landscape*. London: Edward Arnold, 1971.

Piponnier, F. "À la Recherche des Jardins Perdus: Vestiges et Traces Archéologiques des Jardins Médiévaux." *Mélanges de l'Ecole Française de Rome. Moyen Age et Temps Moderns* 106 (1994): 229–38.

Planche, A. "La parure du chef: les chapeaux de fleurs." *Razo* 7 (1987): 133–44.

Platearius, M. *Il Libro Delle Erbe Medicinali: Dal Manoscritto Francese 12322 Della Bibliothèque Nationale De Paris*. Milan: Vallardi, 1990.

Pleij, H. *Dreaming of Cockaigne: Medieval Fantasies of the Perfect Life*. New York: Columbia University Press, 2001.

Pluskowski, A. "The Social Construction of Park Ecosystems: An Interdisciplinary Perspective." In *The Medieval Park: New Perspectives*, ed. R. Liddiard, 63–78. Macclesfield: Windgather Press, 2007.

Polizzi, G. "Le devenir du jardin médiéval? Du verger de la Rose à Cythère." In *Vergers et jardins dans l'univers médiéval* [*Senefiance* 28], 265–88. Aix-en-Provence: C.U.E.R. M.A., 1990.

Pope, A. U., and P. Ackerman. "Garden." In *Survey of Persian Art*, vol. 2, 1432–34. Oxford: Oxford University Press, 1939.

Porcher, J., and Bibliothèque Nationale. *Bibliothèque nationale. Les manuscrits à peintures en France du XIIIe au XVIe siècle.* Paris: Bibliothèque Nationale, 1955.

Postgate, M. R. "Field Systems of East Anglia." In *Studies of Field Systems in the British Isles,* ed. A.H.R. Baker and R. A.Butlin, 281–324. Cambridge: Cambridge University Press, 1973.

Poupeye, C. "Les Jardins clos & leurs rapports avec la sculpture malinoise." *Bulletin du Cercle archéologique littéraire et artistique de Malines* 22 (1912): 51–114.

Prest, J. *The Garden of Eden: The Botanic Garden and the Re-Creation of Paradise.* New Haven, CT: Yale University Press, 1988.

Prevenier, W. *Le prince et le peuple. Images de la société du temps des ducs de Bourgogne, 1384–1530.* Antwerp: Fonds Mercator, 1998.

Price, J. "*Floire et Blancheflor*: The Magic and Mechanics of Love." *Reading Medieval Studies* 8 (1982): 12–33.

Price, L. *The Plan of St. Gall in Brief.* Berkeley: University of California Press, 1982.

Psellos, M. *Chronographia.* Paris: Les Belles Lettres, 1926–28.

Rackham, O. *The History of the Countryside.* London: Dent, 1986.

Rackham, O. *Trees and Woodland in the British Landscape.* London: Dent, 1976.

Rackham, O. *Trees and Woodland in the British Landscape: The Complete History of Britain's Trees, Woods and Hedgerows.* London: Phoenix Press, 2001.

Rahir, E. *La Collection Dutuit: livres et manuscrits.* Paris: Damascène Morgand, 1899.

Randall, L. *Images in the Margins of Gothic Manuscripts.* Berkeley: University of California Press, 1966.

Randsborg, K. *The First Millennium AD in Europe and the Mediterranean: An Archaeological Essay.* Cambridge: Cambridge University Press, 1991.

Rapp-Buri, A. *Der Jungbrunnen in Literatur und bildender Kunst des Mittelalters.* Zurich: Juris-Verlag, 1976.

Rapp-Buri, A., and M. Stucky-Schürer. *Zahm und Wild: kleiner Katalog zur Ausstellung Basler und Strassburger Bildteppiche des 15. Jahrhunderts.* Basel: Historisches Museum Basel, 1990.

Rawcliffe, C. " 'Delectable Sightes and Fragrant Smelles': Gardens and Health in Late Medieval and Early Modern England." *Garden History* 36 (2008): 1–21.

Raynaud, C. "Les relations de l'homme et du jardin au XVe siècle dans les livres religieux, derniers échos du langage iconographique médiéval." In *Vergers et jardins dans l'univers médiéval* [*Senefiance* 28], 289–313. Aix-en-Provence: C.U.E.R. M.A., 1990.

Redford, S. "Just Landscape in Medieval Anatolia." *Studies in the History of Gardens and Designed Landscapes* 20 (2000): 313–24.

Redford, S. *Landscape and the State in Medieval Anatolia: Seljuq Gardens and Pavilions of Alanya, Turkey.* Istanbul: British Archaeological Reports, 2000.

Redford, S. "Rum Seljuk Gardens: Typology and Tradition." *Landscape and the State in Medieval Anatolia: Seljuk Gardens and Pavilions of Alanya, Turkey.* BAR International Series 893 (2000): 91–114.

Redford, S. "Thirteenth-Century Rum Seljuq Palaces and Palace Imagery." *Ars Orientalis* 23 (1993): 219–36.

Reeve, M.M., and M. Thurlby. "King John's Gloriette at Corfe Castle." *Journal of the Society of Architectural Historians* 64 (2005): 168–85.

Reeves, C. *Pleasures and Pastimes in Medieval England*. Stroud: Sutton, 1995.

Reinitzer, H. *Der verschlossene Garten: Der Garten Marias im Mittelalter*. Wolfenbut-tel: Herzog August Bibliothek, 1982.

Renart, J. *The Romance of the Rose or Guillaume de Dole*. Philadelphia: University of Pennsylvania Press, 1993.

Rhodes, J. T., and C. Davidson. "The Garden of Paradise." In *The Iconography of Heaven*, ed. C. Davidson, 69–109. Kalamazzo, MI: Medieval Institute, 1994.

Richardson, A. *The Forest, Park and Palace of Clarendon, c.1200-c.1650: Reconstruct-ing an Actual, Conceptual and Documented Wiltshire Landscape*. Oxford: British Archaeological Reports, 2005.

Richardson, A. "Gender and Space in Medieval Palaces c. 1160–1547: A Study in Ac-cess Analysis and Imagery." *Medieval Archaeology* 47 (2003): 131–65.

Richardson, A. " 'The King's Chief Delights': A Landscape Approach to the Royal Parks of Post-Conquest England." In *The Medieval Park: New Perspectives*, ed. R. Lid-diard, 27–48. Macclesfield: Windgather, 2007.

Ricomini, O.-M. "Les Jardins de la Bible: un regard sur le monde, sur l'homme et sur Dieu." *Polia: Revue de l'art des jardins* 3 (2005): 75–94.

Riley, R. "Flowers, Power and Sex." In *The Meaning of Gardens: Idea, Place, and Ac-tion*, ed. M. Francis and R. T. Hester Jr., 60–75. Cambridge, MA: MIT Press, 1990.

Robb, D. M. "The Iconography of the Annunciation in the 14th and 15th Centuries." *The Art Bulletin* 18 (1936): 480–526.

Roberts, B. K., and S. Wrathmell. "Peoples of Wood and Plain: An Exploration of National and Local Regional Contrasts." In *Landscape: The Richest Historical Record*, ed. D.Hooke, 85–96. London: Society for Landscape Studies, 2000.

Robertson, C. "The Archive, Disciplinarity, and Governing: Cultural Studies and the Writing of History." *Cultural Studies <=> Critical Methodologies* 4 (2004): 450–71.

Robertson, D. W. "The Doctrine of Charity in Mediaeval Literary Gardens: A Topical Approach through Symbolism and Allegory." *Speculum* 26 (1951): 24–49.

Robin, F. *La cour d'Anjou-Provence. La vie artistique sous le règne de René*. Paris: Picard, 1985.

Robinson, C. *Medieval Andalusian Courtly Culture in the Mediterranean: Hadith Bayad Wa Riyad*. London: Routledge, 2006.

Robinson, F. N., ed. *The Works of Geoffrey Chaucer*. London: Oxford University Press, 1957.

Roden, D. "Field Systems of the Chiltern Hills and their Environs." In *Studies of Field Systems in the British Isles*, ed. A.H.R. Baker and R. A.Butlin, 325–74. Cambridge: Cambridge University Press, 1973.

Rose, P. "The Medieval Garden at Tintagel Castle." *Cornish Archaeology* 33 (1994): 170–82.

Rossiter, J. J. "Roman Villas of the Greek East and the Villa in Gregory of Nyssa *Ep. 20*." *Journal of Roman Archaeology* 2 (1989): 101–10.

Rosteau, L. "Herbier et potager d'un bourgeois de Paris." In *Jardins du Moyen Age*, ed. P.-G. Girault, 113–25. Paris: Léopard d'or, 1995.

Ruas, M. P. "The Archaeobotanical Record of Cultivated and Collected Plants of Eco-nomic Importance from Medieval Sites in France." *Review of Palaeobotany and Palynology* 73 (1992): 301–14.

Ruas, M. P. "Les plantes exploitées en France au Moyen Âge d'après les semences archéologiques." In *Plantes et cultures nouvelles en Europe occidentale au Moyen Âge et à l'époque moderne*, 9–35. Auch: Flaran, 1990.

Ruggles, D. F. "From the Heavens and Hells: The Flow of Water to the Fruited Trees and Ablution Fountains in the Great Mosque of Cordoba." In *Rivers of Paradise: Water in Islamic Art and Culture*, ed. S. Blair and J. Bloom, 81–103. New Haven, CT: Yale University Press, 2009.

Ruggles, D. F. *Gardens, Landscape and Vision in the Palaces of Islamic Spain.* University Park: Penn State University Press, 1999.

Ruggles, D. F. *Islamic Gardens and Landscapes.* Philadelphia: University of Pennsylvania Press, 2008.

Ruggles, D. F. "The Mirador in Abbasid and Hispano-Umayyad Garden Typology." *Muqarnas* 7 (1990): 73–82.

Saunders, C. *The Forests of Medieval Romance: Avernus, Broceliande, Arden.* Rochester, NY: D. S. Brewer, 1993.

Schafer, K. H. *Ausgaben der Apostolischen Kammer unter Johann XXII.* Paderborn: Schoningh, 1914–37.

Schimmel, A. "The Celestial Garden in Islam." In *The Islamic Garden*, ed. E. B. McDougall and R. E. Ettinghausen, 11–39. Washington, D.C.: Dumbarton Oaks, 1976.

Schipperges, H. *Des garten der gesundheit. Medizin im Mittelalter.* Munich: Artemis, 1985.

Schmidt, P. "The Multiple Image: The Beginnings of Printmaking, between Old Theories and New Approaches." In *Origins of European Printmaking: Fifteenth-Century Woodcuts and their Public*, ed. P. Parshall and R. Schoch, 37–56. Washington, D.C.: National Gallery of Art, 2005.

Schmidtice, D. *Studien zur dingallegorischen Erbauungsliteratur des Spätmittelalters: Am Beispiel der Gartenallegorie.* Tübingen: Niemeyer, 1982.

Schoeler, G. *Arabische Naturdichtung.* Beirut: Orient-Institut der Deutschen Morgenländischen Gesellschaft, 1974.

Schofield, J. "City of London Gardens, 1500-c. 1620." *Garden History* 27 (1999): 73–88.

Schofield, J. *Medieval London Houses.* New Haven, CT: Yale University Press, 1994.

Schuler, I. *Der Meister der Liebesgärten. Ein Beitrag zur frühholländischen Malerei.* Amsterdam: Van Munster, 1935.

Scully, T. "A Cook's Therapeutic Use of Garden Herbs." In *Health and Healing from the Medieval Garden*, ed. P. Dendle and A. Touwaide, 60–71. Woodbridge: Boydell Press, 2008.

Scully, T. "Les saisons alimentaires du Ménagier de Paris." In *Du manuscrit à la table. Essais sur la cuisine au Moyen Âge et répertoires des manuscrits médiévaux contenant des recettes culinaires*, ed. C. Lambert, 205–13. Paris: Champion-Slatkine, 1992.

Sheail, J. *Rabbits and Their History.* Newton Abbot: David and Charles, 1971.

Sheehan, M. M. "The Formation and Stability of Marriage in Fourteenth-Century England: Evidence of an Ely Register." In *Marriage, Family, and Law in Medieval Europe: Collected Studies*, ed. J. K. Farge, 38–76. Toronto: University of Toronto Press, 1996.

Shephard, P. *Man in the Landscape: A Historic View of the Esthetics of Nature.* College Station: Texas A&M University Press, 1991.

Sherwood, M. "Magical Mechanics and Medieval Fiction." *Studies in Philology* 14 (1947): 567–92.

Siraisi, N. G. *Medieval and Early Renaissance Medicine: An Introduction to Knowledge and Practice*. Chicago: University of Chicago Press, 1990.

Smeyers, M. *L'Art de la miniature flamande. VIIIe aux XVIe siècles*. Tournai: Renaissance du Livre, 1998.

Smith, S. L. *The Power of Women: A Topos in Medieval Art and Literature*. Philadelphia: University of Pennsylvania Press, 1995.

Smith, T. "The Garden Image in Medieval Literature." PhD diss., University of Connecticut, 1967.

Snyder, I. "Jan van Eyck and Adam's Apple." *The Art Bulletin* 58 (1976): 511–15.

Sodigne-Costes, G. "Les simples et les jardins." In *Vergers et jardins dans l'univers médiéval* [*Senefiance* 28], 331–42. Aix-en-Provence: C.U.E.R.M.A., 1990.

Solterer, H. "Letter Writing and Picture Reading: Medieval Textuality and the *Bestiaire d'Amour*." *Word and Image* 5 (1989): 131–47.

Sorbelli, A., ed. *Pier de' Crescenzi (1233–1321): Studi e documenti*. Bologna: Cappelli, 1933.

Speer, O. "Les jardins du paradis: les plantes dans les tableaux des primitifs du paradis musée d'Unterlinden." *Annuaire de la Société d'histoire et d'archéologie de Colmar* 29 (1980–81): 27–47.

Stahl, H. "Eve's Reach: A Note on the Dramatic Elements of the Hildersheim Doors." In *Reading Medieval Images: The Art Historian and the Object*, ed. E. Sears and T. K. Thomas, 162–75. Ann Arbor: University of Michigan Press, 2002.

Stammler, W. "Der allegorische Garten." In *Landschaft und Raum in der Erzählkunst*, ed. A. Ritter, 106–16. Darmstadt: Wissenschaftliche Buchgesellschaft, 1975.

Stamper, P. "Woods and Parks." In *The Countryside of Medieval England*, ed. G. Astill and A. Grant, 128–48. Oxford: Blackwell, 1988.

Stanley, S. *The Enclosed Garden*. Madison: University of Wisconsin Press, 1966.

Stannard, J. "Medieval Gardens and Their Plants." In *Gardens of the Middle Ages*, ed. M. Stokstad and J. Stannard, 37–69. Lawrence: University of Kansas Press, 1983.

Stannard, J. "Alimentary and Medicinal Use of Plants." In *Medieval Gardens*, ed. E .B. MacDougall, 69–91. Washington, D.C.: Dumbarton Oaks, 1986.

Steane, J. *The Archaeology of Medieval England and Wales*. Athens: University of Georgia Press, 1985.

Steane, J. "The Medieval Parks of Northamptonshire." *Northamptonshire Past and Present* 3 (1975): 211–33.

Stetkevych, S. P. *Abū Tammām and the Poetics of the ʿAbbāid Age*. Leiden: E. J. Brill, 1993.

Stocker, D. "The Shadow of the General's Armchair." *Archaeological Journal* 149 (1993): 415–20.

Stocker, D., and M. Stocker. "Sacred Profanity: The Theology of Rabbit Breeding and the Symbolic Landscape of the Warren." *World Archaeology* 28 (1998): 265–72.

Stokstad, M. "The Garden as Art." In *Medieval Gardens*, ed. E. B. MacDougall, 175–86. Washington, D.C.: Dumbarton Oaks, 1986.

Stokstad, M. "Gardens in Medieval Art." In *Gardens of the Middle Ages*, ed. M. Stokstad and J. Stannard, 19–35. Lawrence: University of Kansas Press, 1983.

Stokstad, M., and J. Stannard. *Gardens of the Middle Ages*. Lawrence: University of
  Kansas Press, 1983.

Stones, A. "Illustrating Lancelot and Guinevere." In *Lancelot and Guinevere: A Case-
  book*, ed. L. J. Walters, 125–57. London: Routledge, 1996.

Strabo, W. *Hortulus*. Edited and trans. R. Paen and W. Blunt. Pittsburgh, PA: Hunt
  Botanical Library, 1966.

Stronach, D. "The Garden as a Political Statement: Some Case Studies from the Near
  East in the First Millennium B.C." *Bulletin of the Asia Institute*, n.s., 4 (1990):
  171–80.

Stronach, D. "The Royal Garden at Pasargadae: Evolution and Legacy." In *Archaeologia Iranica et Orientalis: Miscellanea in honorem Louis Vanden Berghe*, vol. 1, ed.
  L. De Meyer and E. Haerinck, 475–502. Gent: Peeters Presse, 1989.

Strong, R. *The Renaissance Garden in England*. London: Thames and Hudson, 1979.

Strubel, A. "L'allégorisation du verger courtois." In *Vergers et jardins dans l'univers
  médiéval* [*Senefiance* 28], 343–58. Aiz-en-Provence: C.U.E.R. M.A., 1990.

Subtelny, M. E. "Agriculture and the Timurid Chahārbāgh: The Evidence from a Medieval Persian Agricultural Manual." In *Gardens in the Time of the Great Muslim
  Empires: Theory and Design*, ed. A. Petruccioli, 110–28. Leiden: Brill, 1997.

Sykes, N. "Animal Bones and Animal Parks." In *The Medieval Park: New Perspectives*,
  ed. R. Liddiard, 49–62. Macclesfield: Windgather, 2007.

Sykes, N. "The Dynamics of Status Symbols: Wildfowl Exploitation in England A.D.
  410–1550." *Archaeological Journal* 161 (2004): 82–105.

Tabbaa, Y. "Control and Abandon: Images of Water in Arabic Poetry and Gardens."
  In *Rivers of Paradise: Water in Islamic Art and Culture*, ed. S. Blair and J. Bloom,
  59–79. New Haven, CT: Yale University Press, 2009.

Tabor, R. "English Bill-Hook Patterns." *Tools and Trades History Society Newsletter*
  11 (1985): 4–17.

Talbot, A.-M. "Byzantine Monastic Horticulture: The Textual Evidence." In *Byzantine
  Garden Culture*, ed. A. R. Littlewood, H. Maguire, and J. Wolschke-Bulmahn,
  36–67. Washington, D.C.: Dumbarton Oaks, 2002.

Talbot, C.H., and E.A. Hammond. *The Medical Practitioners in Medieval England;
  A Biographical Register*. London: Wellcome Historical Medical Library, 1965.

Taylor, C. *The Archaeology of Gardens*. Aylesbury: Shire, 1983.

Taylor, C. "The Archaeology of Gardens and Designed Landscapes." In *"The Remains
  of Distant Times," Archeology and the National Trust*, ed. D. Morgan Evans,
  P. Salway, and D. Thackaray, 59–65. London: Society of Antiquaries of London,
  1996.

Taylor, C. "Bodiam Castle, Sussex." *Medieval Archaeology* 34 (1990): 153–56.

Taylor, C. "Medieval Ornamental Landscapes." *Landscapes* 1, no. 1 (2000): 38–55.

Taylor, C., P. Everson, and R. Wilson-North. "Bodiam Castle, Sussex." *Medieval Archaeology* 34 (1990): 155–57.

Telesko, W. *The Wisdom of Nature: The Healing Powers and Symbolism of Plants and
  Animals in the Middle Ages*. London: Prestel, 2001.

Thacker, C. *The History of Gardens*. Berkeley: University of California Press, 1979.

Thiebaux, M. *The Stag of Love: The Chase in Medieval Literature*. Ithaca, NY: Cornell University Press, 1974.

Thomas, K. *Man and the Natural World: Changing Attitudes in England 1500–1800*. London: Allen Lane, 1983.

Thompson, M.W. "Reclamation of Waste Ground for the Pleasance of Kenilworth Castle, Warwickshire." *Medieval Archaeology* 8 (1964): 222–23.

Thompson, M.W. *The Rise of the Castle*. Cambridge: Cambridge University Press, 1991.

Thorndike, L. *A History of Magic and Experimental Science*, 8 vols. New York: Macmillan, 1923–58.

Thoss, D. *Studien zum Locus Amoenus im Mittelalter*. Vienna: Wilhelm Braumüller, 1972.

Tollemache, C. *The Tollermache Book of Secrets: A Descriptive Index and Complete Facsimile with an Introduction and Transcriptions Together with Catherine Tollemache's Receipts of Pastery, Confectionary & c.* London: Roxburghe Club, 2002.

Tomasi, L.T. "Il giardino dei semplici." In *Storia dell'Universita di Pisa* 1: *1343–1737*, ed. A. Volpi, 363–73. Pisa: Pacini, 1993.

Toni, E. De. "Il libro del simplici di Benedetto Rinio." *Memorie della Pontificia Academia romana dei Nuovi Lincei* 5 (1919): 171–279.

Toni, E. De. "Il libro dei simplici di Benedetto Rinio [part 2]." *Memorie della Pontificia Academia romana dei Nuovi Lincei* 7 (1924): 275–398.

Toni, E. De. "Il libro dei simplici di Benedetto Rinio [part 3]." *Memorie della Pontificia Academia romana dei Nuovi Lincei* 8 (1925): 123–264.

Toubert, R. "Pietro Di Crescenzi." *Dizionario biografico degli italiani* 30 (1984), columns 649–57, http://www.treccani.it/enciclopedia/pietro-de-crescenzi_(Dizionario-Biografico)/.

Touwaide, A. "Bibliographie historique de la botanique: les identifications des plantes medicinales citées dans les traits anciens, après l'adoption du systeme de classification de Linne (1707–1778) [part 1]." *Centre Jean Palerne—Lettre d' Information* 30 (1997–98): 2–22.

Touwaide, A. "Bibliographie historique de la botanique: les identifications des plantes medicinales citées dans les traits anciens, après l'adoption du systeme de classification de Linne (1707–1778) [part 2]." *Centre Jean Palerne—Lettre d' Information* 31 (1998): 2–65.

Touwaide, A. "The Legacy of Classical Antiquity in Byzantium and the West." In *Health and Healing from the Medieval Garden*, ed. Peter Dendle and Alain Touwaide, 26–27. Woodbridge: Boydell Press, 2008.

Touwaide, A. "Medical Plants." *Brill's New Pauly*, vol. 8, ed. H. Cancik and H. Schneider, columns 558–68. Leiden: Brill, 2006.

Turner, D. J. "Bodiam Castle: True Castle or Old Soldier's Dream House?" *England in the 14th Century: Proceedings of the 1985 Harlaxton Symposium*, ed. W. Ormrod. Woodbridge: Brewer, 1986.

Tuve, R. *Seasons and Months: Studies in a Tradition of Middle English Poetry*. Cambridge: Cambridge University Press, 1974.

Ulbert, T. "Ein umaiyadischer Pavillon in Resafa-Rusafat Hisham." *Damaszener Mitteilungen* 7 (1993): 213–31.

Underhill, E. "The Fountain of Life: an Iconographical Study." *Burlington Magazine* 17 (1910): 99–109.

Valéry, M.-F. *Jardins du Moyen âge*. Paris: La Renaissance du Livre, 2001.

Van Buren, A. H. "Reality and Literary Romance in the Park of Hesdin." In *Medieval Gardens*, ed. E. B. MacDougall, 117–34. Washington, D.C.: Dumbarton Oaks, 1986.

Van Buren, A. H. "La Roulotte de Philippe le Bon." In *Liber Amicorum: Études Historiques Offertes à Pierre Bougard*, 115–22. Arras: Mémoires de la Commission Départmentale d'histoire et d'archéologie du Pas-de-Calais, 1987.

Vandenbroeck, P. *Le jardin clos de l'âme. L'imaginaire des religieuses dans les Pays-Bas du Sud, depuis le 13e siècle*. Bruxelles, Ghent: Société Des Expositions, 1994.

Varro, *De rustica*, ed. W. D. Hooper. Cambridge, MA: Harvard Unviversity Press, 1934.

Vesel, Z. "Les traités d'agriculture en Iran." *Studia Iranica* 15 (1986): 99–108.

Vignau-Wilberg, T. "Höfische Minne und Bürgermoral in der Grafik um 1500." In *Wort und Bild in der Niederländischen Kunst und literatur des 16. und 17. Jahrhunderts*, ed. H. Vekeman and H. M. Hofstede, 43–52. Erfstadt: Lukassen Verlag, 1984.

Virgil. *The Georgics of Virgil*, trans. D. Ferry. New York: Farrar, Straus, and Giroux, 2005.

Vogellehner, D. "Garten und Pflanzen im Mittelalter." *Deutsche Agrargeschichte* 6 (1984): 69–98.

Voigts, L. E. "Anglo-Saxon Plant Remedies and the Anglo-Saxons." *Isis* 70 (1979): 250–68.

von Grafenberg, W. *Wigalois: The Knight of Fortune's Wheel*. Lincoln: University of Nebraska Press, 1977.

von Grunebaum, G. E. "Aspects of Arabic Urban Literature Mostly in the Ninth and Tenth Centuries." In *Themes in Medieval Arabic Literature*, vol. 4, 280–84. London: Variorium Reprints, 1981.

von Strassburg, G. *Tristan*. Harmondsworth: Penguin Books, 1960.

Waldheim, H., and E. W. Friedrich. *Die Pilgerfahrt des Hans Von Waltheym in Jahre 1474*. Bern: Stämpfli, 1925.

Walter of Henley. *Boke of Husbandry*. London: Wynkyn de Worde, 1508.

Warner, M. *Alone of All Her Sex*. New York: Vintage, 1983.

Watson, P. *The Garden of Love in Tuscan Art of the Early Renaissance*. Philadelphia: Art Alliance, 1979.

Wells, P. S. *Barbarians to Angels: The Dark Ages Reconsidered*. New York: W. W. Norton, 2008.

Wenzler, C. *Architecture du Jardin*. Cholet: Ouest-France, 2003.

Wescoat, J. L. "Picturing an Early Mughal Garden." *Asian Art* 2 (1989): 59–79.

Wetzel, B., "Der grosse Liebesgarten." In *Als Albrecht Dürers Welt. Festschrift für Fejda Anzelewsky*, ed. B. Brinkmann, H. Krohm, and M. Roth, 123–27. Turnhout: Brepols, 2001.

Whiteley, M. "The Relationship between the Château, Garden and Park, 1300–1450." In *Architecture, Jardin, Paysage: l'environnement du château et de la villa aux XVe et XVIe siècle*, ed. J. Guillaume, 91–102. Paris: Picard, 1999.

Whitney, E. *Paradise Restored: The Mechanical Arts from Anquity through the Thirteenth Century*. Philadelphia: American Philosophical Society, 1990.

Whittick, C. "Dallingridge's Bay and Bodiam Castle Millpond: Elements of a Medieval Landscape." *Sussex Archaeological Collections* 131 (1993): 119–23.

Wilber, D. *Persian Gardens and Garden Pavilions.* Rutland, VT: Tuttle, 1962.

Wilkins, E. *The Rose Garden Game: The Symbolic Background to the European Prayer-Beads.* London: Gollancz, 1969.

Williamson, T. *The Archaeology of Rabbit Warrens.* Princes Risborough: Shire, 2006.

Williamson, T. "Fish, Fur and Feather: Man and Nature in the Post-Medieval Landscape." In *Making English Landscapes,* ed. K. Barker and T. Darvill, 92–117. Bournemouth: Bournemouth University School of Conservation Sciences Occasional Paper 3, 1997.

Williamson, T. *Polite Landscapes: Gardens and Society in Eighteenth-Century England.* Stroud: Sutton, 1995.

Williamson, T. *Rabbits, Warrens and Archaeology.* Stroud: Tempus, 2007.

Williamson, T. *Shaping Medieval Landscapes: Settlement, Society, Environment.* Windgather: Macclesfield, 2003.

Wilson, K. M., and E. M. Makowski. *Wykked Wyves and the Woes of Marriage: Misogamous Literature from Juvenal to Chaucer.* Albany: State University of New York Press, 1990.

Wilson-North, R., ed. *The Lie of the Land: Aspects of the Archaeology and History of the Designed Landscape in the South West of England.* Exeter: Mint Press, 2003.

Winston-Allen, A. *Stories of the Rose: The Making of the Rosary in the Middle Ages.* University Park: Pennsylvania State University Press, 1997.

Wirth, J. "Le Jardin des délices de Jérome Bosch." *Bibliothèque d'humanisme et de Renaissance* 50 (1988): 545–85.

Wittrock, B. "The Meaning of the Axial Age." In *Axial Civilizations and World History,* ed. J. P. Arnason, S. N. Eisenstadt, and B. Wittrock, 51–85. Leiden: Brill, 2005.

Wolffardt, E. "Beitrage zur Pflanzensymbolik: Uber die Pflanzen des Frankfurter Paradiesgartleins." *Zeitschrift für Kunstwissenschaft* 8 (1954): 171–96.

Woodbridge, K. *Princely Gardens: The Origins and Development of the French Formal Style.* London: Thames and Hudson, 1986.

Wright, D.R.E. "Some Medici Gardens of the Florentine Renaissance. . . ." In *The Italian Garden: Art, Design and Culture,* ed. J. D. Hunt, 34–59. Cambridge: Cambridge University Press, 1996.

Zadora-Rio, E. "*Hortus conclusus.* Un jardin medieval au Plessis-Grimoult." In *Mélanges d'archeologie et d'histoire medievale en l'honneur du doyen Michel de Boüard,* 393–404. Geneva: Droz, 1982.

Zadora-Rio, E. "Pour une archéologie des jardins médiévaux." *Monuments historiques* 143 (1986): 4–7.

Zielonka, J. *Europe as Empire: The Nature of the Enlarged European Union.* Oxford: Oxford University Press, 2007.

Zumthor, P. "Narrative and Anti-Narrative: *Le Roman de la Rose.*" *Yale French Studies* 51 (1974): 185–204.

CONTRIBUTORS

Elizabeth Augspach teaches in the department of Spanish and Portuguese languages and literatures at New York University. Born and raised in Buenos Aires, Argentina, she completed her master's degree in English at St. John's University in Queens, New York, and then her PhD in comparative literature with a specialization in medieval studies at the Graduate Center of the City University of New York (CUNY). She has taught courses in English, comparative literature, and Spanish at various CUNY colleges and private universities in the New York area. She is the author of *The Garden as Woman's Space in Twelfth and Thirteenth-Century Literature* (The Edwin Mellen Press, 2004).

Johanna Bauman is the Visual Resources Curator at the Pratt Institute in Brooklyn, New York. Previously she worked at the ARTstor Digital Library and the Bard Graduate Center where she helped to build a digital archive of historic gardens and landscapes. She received her PhD from the University of Virginia and also has a master's in library science from Queens College. She lectures and publishes on the historiography of art history and on medieval garden history, particularly Piero de' Crescenzi's *Liber ruralium commodorum*.

Laura L. Howes is an associate professor of English at the University of Tennessee, Knoxville, where she specializes in Middle English literature and culture. She is the author of *Chaucer's Gardens and the Language of Convention* (University of Florida Press, 1997), editor of *Place, Space, and Landscape in Medieval Narrative* (University of Tennessee Press, 2007), and coeditor (with Marie Borroff) of *Sir Gawain and the Green Knight: A Norton Critical Edition*

(New york: Norton, 2009), as well as the author of several articles. Her current book project, *The Lay of the Land in Medieval Britain*, investigates how Middle English authors conceived of and represented place, space traversed, and landscapes both familiar and strange.

John Dixon Hunt is emeritus professor of the history and theory of landscape at the University of Pennsylvania and the editor of *Studies in the History of Gardens and Designed Landscapes*. He is the author of various books and articles, most recently a book on the gardens of Ian Hamilton Finlay, *Nature Over Again* (Reaktion Books, 2008), as well as *The Afterlife of Gardens* (Reaktion Books, 2004), *The Venetian City Garden* (Birkhävser, 2009), and *A World of Gardens* (Reaktion, 2012). He is currently working on a book about the role of history in contemporary landscape architecture.

Rebecca Krug is an associate professor of English at the University of Minnesota, where she specializes in late medieval English literature and culture. She is the author of *Reading Families: Women's Literate Practice in Late Medieval England* (Cornell University Press, 2002) and of a number of essays, including recent pieces in *The Cambridge Companion to Medieval English Literature* and *The Cambridge Companion to Medieval English Culture*. She is currently writing an essay about lunar gardening in the medieval and modern worlds as well as completing a book about Margery Kempe.

Michael Leslie is a professor of English at Rhodes College. He chaired the Committee of Senior Fellows in Landscape at Dumbarton Oaks and has published on early modern culture and the intersections between literature, art history, history of science and agriculture, and garden history. Founder of the Hartlib Papers Project and coeditor of *Culture and Cultivation in Early Modern England: Writing and the Land* (Leicester University Press, 1992), his most recent publications are editions of two plays by the largely forgotten seventeenth-century playwright Richard Brome, *The New Academy* and *The Weeding of Covent Garden* (HRI Online, 2010).

Robert Liddiard is a senior lecturer in history at the University of East Anglia, where he teaches and conducts research on medieval and landscape history, particularly the history and archaeology of high-status landscapes (secular and ecclesiastical), the vernacular landscape, parks and hunting, and aspects of tenurial geography. He is the author of a series of studies of medieval castles and parkland, including *Anglo-Norman Castles*; *Castles in Context: A Social History of Fortification in England and Wales, 1066–1500* (Boydell, 2002), *The Medieval Park:*

New Perspectives (Windgather, 2007); *Champion: The Making and Unmaking of the English Midland Landscape* (coauthor) (Liverpool University Press, 2013), and most recently *Late Medieval Castles* (forthcoming).

James Schryver is an associate professor of art history at the University of Minnesota, Morris, where he teaches ancient and medieval archaeology and art history. A graduate of Boston University's archaeology department, he earned his masters's and PhD in medieval studies from Cornell University. He is the author of essays on ancient and medieval gardens and garden culture, as well as on issues of identity and material culture in Frankish Cyprus. He has excavated ancient gardens at the supposed site of Horace's Villa in Licenza, the imperial villa on Lake Nemi outside Rome, Villa Adriana, and most recently at Petra, Jordan, as part of the Petra Pool and Garden Project.

Tom Williamson is a professor of history at the University of East Anglia, where he leads the Landscape Group within the school of history. His scholarship addresses all aspects of the English landscape, from later prehistory to the present, including designed landscapes and agriculture. Recent publications include *Rabbits, Warrens and Archaeology* (Tempus, 2007), a second edition of *The Origins of Hertfordshire*, and *Ancient Trees in the Landscape: Norfolk's Arboreal Heritage*. His most recent (coauthored) book is *Champion: The Making and Unmaking of the English Midland Landscape* (Boydell, 2013).

INDEX